COLLINS BOOK OF
BRITISH GARDENS

COLLINS BOOK OF

BRITISH
GARDENS

*A Guide to 200 Gardens
in England, Scotland
and Wales*

GEORGE PLUMPTRE

COLLINS
8 Grafton Street, London W1
1985

William Collins Sons and Co Ltd
London · Glasgow · Sydney · Auckland
Toronto · Johannesburg

First published 1985
© George Plumptre text and photographs 1985

Plumptre, George
   Collins book of British gardens: a guide to
200 gardens in England, Scotland and Wales.
   1. Gardens—Great Britain—Guide-books
   I. Title
   914.1′04858   SB466.G7

ISBN 0 00 216641 0

Maps by Leslie Robinson
Set in Linotron Ehrhardt by Wyvern Typesetting Ltd, Bristol
Made and Printed in Great Britain
by St. Edmundsbury Press Ltd., Bury St. Edmunds

TO MY PARENTS

ACKNOWLEDGEMENTS

My primary thanks must go to the owners who have allowed me to include their gardens in this book, and I would like to thank them and, in many cases, their gardeners, for their help towards my writing of the book and their unfailing helpfulness and hospitality over my visits.

In compiling the list of two hundred gardens to be included in the book I received help from a number of sources; in particular from the National Gardens Scheme, Scotland's Garden Scheme, the National Trust and the National Trust for Scotland. For similar help or other advice I would like to thank John Sales, Rachel Cramshay, Tom Wright, Rosemary Verey, Tony Venison and Hugh Montgomery-Massingberd.

Finally I must thank Robin Baird-Smith and Gill Gibbins at Collins, Vivienne Schuster my agent and, not least, my parents, without whom I would never have been interested in gardens.

CONTENTS

MAPS

ILLUSTRATIONS

INTRODUCTION

A garden is by its very nature ephemeral, a creation constantly in need of maintenance, development and rejuvenation. Nevertheless, despite the enormous rise in expenses of staff and general running costs, the period since the Second World War has seen an unprecedented increase in the number of people interested in gardens and gardening, in knowing about and looking at other people's gardens, and prepared to embark on the open-ended task of making a garden themselves. A clear reflection of this is the number of gardens included in the National Gardens Scheme handbook – in 1981 when I began work on this book the number was about 1250; in 1984 when I finished it had risen to 1700.

Since the Second World War gardens have been noticeably less governed by style and fashion and more by the personalities and ambitions of their creators, and this personal character is one of the most lasting attractions of gardens all over Britain.

Up to the early twentieth century a clear pattern can be traced from medieval and Tudor gardens to the formality of the seventeenth century, strongly influenced by France and Holland, through the landscape revolution of the eighteenth century and the 'Picturesque' romanticism of the early nineteenth century, to the parterres and conservatories of Victorian gardens. By the end of the nineteenth century quantities of new plants from abroad, especially America and south-east Asia, were having an enormous and widespread impact, as were the ideas of William Robinson and Gertrude Jekyll; and these influences have continued through the twentieth century. Leaving aside those with a specialist interest, the modern garden can be seen as a theme on which the number of variations possible is limitless, with the gardener adapting to the relative possibilities and limitations of a site, either developing an existing garden or beginning anew and drawing on one or more styles and influences from the past.

One of the characteristics of this theme is a balance between formality and informality, the former often being achieved in the design, the latter in the planting. Where space allows a more widespread use of shrubs has emerged, in preference to, or in association with, herbaceous or annual plants. And while a distinct hallmark or dominant feature is desirable, so is variety throughout the year, from spring bulbs to autumn colour and later, winter-flowering plants. All these things can be adapted to gardens on any soil and of any size, and people have appreciated that even in the smallest plot the potential is considerable.

A major aim of this book has been to include a wide variety of gardens in terms of their size, position, character and appearance, from all regions of England, Scotland and Wales. Given that the selection for such a book would never be the same from any two people, I hope that it will be of use and interest to both the potential visitor and those who prefer reading about other gardens at home. I was also determined to involve the owners of the gardens as much as possible, for it seems to me that all too often gardens are written about as though they are uninhabited and self-maintaining. Undoubtedly the most rewarding part of my work was visiting the gardens, which I did between the summers of 1981 and 1984. In so doing I was able not only to see and photograph the gardens for myself, but also to talk to the owners and gardeners – very often one and the same – about their interest in gardens, their particular likes and dislikes, their ambitions, aspirations and their problems. I am indebted to them all for their help, kindness and goodwill.

The enormous popularity of gardens open to the public, even if it is for only one or two days a year, proves the mutual enjoyment which opening gives to both owners and visitors. The interest of many smaller gardens for visitors is principally that they can relate them more easily to their own plans than some of the larger, historic settings of the country's stately homes. They also give encouragement by illustrating in many cases the remarkable amount which can be achieved in a short time and without lavish expenditure. For the owners, it is always rewarding to have appreciative visitors; their attitude towards their gardens seems to be a mixture of ambition and affection, summed up by one owner who wrote to me: 'Everything looks beautiful today, and will be even better tomorrow.'

My visits took me to places I had hardly heard of but perhaps a more important discovery was the tenacity of the gardening spirit, the will to create a garden in the most adverse conditions, be it on the side of a mountain, on the north coast of Scotland, next door to an airport or next door to a railway line. Gardens answering all these descriptions can be found in the book. For most gardeners the winter of 1981–2 was the worst in living memory and did untold damage in nearly all parts of the country. But it proved the gardener's confidence in the future, the almost limitless capacity for resilience when quite possibly the fruits of many years' labour had been destroyed. It was this individual aspect of gardening which struck me as enormously important.

Of course the necessity to keep the book to portable proportions has imposed a restriction on extent. In my total of two hundred gardens, a number of the larger, most famous and most written about British gardens, including a number of National Trust grounds, will not be found. This is certainly not due to any lack of appreciation of their qualities, for one realizes more and more how decisive a part they have played in the whole spectrum and history of British gardens. Rather it has been to allow the inclusion of a number of smaller or lesser known gardens which are not documented in the same manner elsewhere. The relatively small number of National Trust properties included is also accounted for by the existence of a comprehensive book by Graham Stuart Thomas, *The Gardens of the National Trust* (Weidenfeld and Nicolson). John Sales, Gardens Advisor to the National Trust, helped me over the selection of those National Trust gardens which are represented here. For other gardens in England and Wales I was advised by many people in the National Gardens Scheme, including all the county organizers. For Scotland I received similar help from the National Trust for Scotland and the Scottish Gardens Scheme.

I hope it will be easy for readers to find their way about the book. The gardens are arranged by regions, and by counties within each region, all alphabetically. There are maps of the regions, and directions are given at the top of each entry for reaching the garden. (*Collins Road Atlas of Britain 1985* pinpoints most of the properties in this book.) Because opening dates change each year, those given are only a guide, and I must stress that visitors should check either in the local press or in any of the following annual guides: *The Guide to Historic Houses, Castles and Gardens, Gardens Open to the Public* (the National Gardens Scheme guide) and Scotland's Gardens Scheme guide. Those gardens open by appointment only would obviously appreciate as much notice as possible when arranging a visit.

George Plumptre

September 1984

ENGLAND AND WALES

EAST ANGLIA

Cambridgeshire
Essex
Norfolk
Suffolk

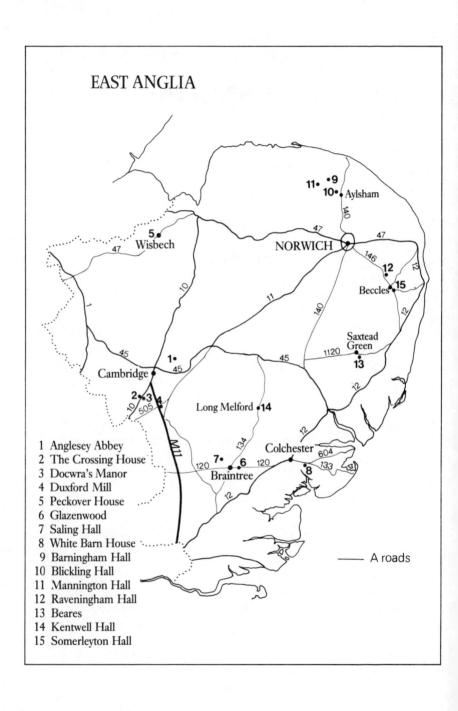

EAST ANGLIA

11• •9
10• Aylsham

NORWICH

5•
Wisbech

12
Beccles 15

Saxtead
Green
13

1•

Cambridge

2•3 4

Long Melford •14

M11

7•
6 Colchester
Braintree 8

1 Anglesey Abbey
2 The Crossing House
3 Docwra's Manor
4 Duxford Mill
5 Peckover House
6 Glazenwood
7 Saling Hall
8 White Barn House
9 Barningham Hall
10 Blickling Hall
11 Mannington Hall
12 Raveningham Hall
13 Beares
14 Kentwell Hall
15 Somerleyton Hall

—— A roads

CAMBRIDGESHIRE

ANGLESEY ABBEY

In Lode, 6 miles north-east of Cambridge on the B1102
Tel. 0223 811 200
The National Trust

Open daily from the end of April to mid-October

Anglesey Abbey's garden, laid out in the 1930s by Huttleston Broughton, 1st Lord Fairhaven, is one of England's few outstanding landscape gardens of the twentieth century. In 1964 Sir Arthur Bryant wrote: 'Our age is not without rich men, yet . . . Huttleston Fairhaven must be almost unique in having created in the middle of the twentieth century a garden which can compare with the great masterpieces of the Georgian era. With patience, single-minded devotion and flawless taste, in an age of war and revolution he has endowed the England of tomorrow with a garden worthy of her past.' Lord Fairhaven endowed and left Anglesey Abbey to the National Trust on his death in 1966.

Anglesey Abbey has a history stretching back for eight hundred years. In 1135 it was founded as an Augustinian priory, which it remained until the Dissolution of the Monasteries in 1535. Thereafter it was owned by a succession of families until 1926 when Huttleston Broughton purchased it. At that time the partly-ruined house was surrounded by the open and uncompromisingly flat fen countryside. The restoration of the house and the collections of art treasures which Lord Fairhaven (he was granted a barony in 1929) brought to it were remarkable achievements, but it was the creation of the garden, extending to about ninety acres in such monotonous surroundings, which revealed a rare and individual talent.

The gardens surround the house on all sides and combine spacious grandeur on a scale rarely seen since the eighteenth century with more intimate enclosures with varying characters. Formal avenues and walks are linked by winding paths through spinneys, and throughout the majestic trees are matched by numerous architectural and other garden ornaments – columns, urns, statues and temples. The gardens suffered terribly from Dutch elm disease and the loss of over four thousand trees has necessitated total replanting in some areas.

Closer to the house are the various smaller, hedge-enclosed gardens, but they are small only in comparison with the other parts of the garden: their scale is often of similar proportions.

To the north of the house the semi-circular Herbaceous Garden, enclosed by beech hedges, contains a straight border two hundred and fifty feet long, and a curved border broken at regular intervals by paved bays with seats flanked by lead tubs containing clipped box. The Herbaceous Garden, like so many others here, is completed by statuary brought to Anglesey Abbey by Lord Fairhaven; a statue of Father Time, reputedly by J. M. Rysbrack (1694–1770) stands on the main lawn.

To one side of the Herbaceous Garden is the narrow, curving Dahlia Garden, again enclosed by beech hedges, where a single long border is filled with forget-me-nots in spring and mixed dahlias in autumn. To the west of the house is the Hyacinth Garden where four thousand blue and white hyacinths are planted each year. The flowerbeds centre on a sundial statue of Time – one of a number in the gardens which came from Stowe – enclosed by yew hedges which form an unusual hexagonal shape. Immediately to the west of the Hyacinth Garden the note of classical simplicity, constantly evoked at Anglesey Abbey, is characterized by a small lawn where a nineteenth-century statue of Narcissus gazes at his reflection in a pool.

Beyond the yew hedge-enclosed lawn immediately to the south of the house is the meandering South Glade, stretching from east to west over hummocky ground. But at the west end the transition from informality to grandeur is emphatically marked by two imposing lead sphinxes who proclaim the Coronation Avenue, a wide sweep of horse chestnuts over half a mile long, planted in 1937 to mark the Coronation of King George VI and Queen Elizabeth. The strength of the avenue's axis is emphasized by two cross-axes; the first about halfway along leads north to the Circular Temple and south to the Apollo Belvedere, with the Pilgrims Lawn, planted with trees and shrubs for autumn colour, behind. Further along the avenue a smaller axis, also of horse chestnuts, crosses at right-angles, leading between enormous urns enclosed by circles of birch trees.

Royal events have occasioned many of the great garden features at

Anglesey Abbey, and in 1953 the Temple Lawns was made out of an eight-acre field to mark the coronation of Queen Elizabeth II. The lawn extends along the north-west side of the gardens and is dominated by the central Circular Temple, formed by ten massive Corinthian columns of Portland stone and enclosed by a clipped yew hedge broken only by one entrance, which is flanked by recumbent lead lions. The centre of the enclosed lawn is dramatized by a marble copy of Bernini's statue of David, made by G. Fossi in 1901, and the overall effect of the temple from different angles is carefully enhanced by the island plantings of trees and shrubs breaking up the grass.

To the east of the house the Arboretum extends from the eastern end of the South Glade to the Quarry Pool in the garden's north-east corner. The quality and interest of the individual trees are heightened by the deliberately spaced planting and the subtle transition to formality as one comes to the two lime avenues leading north to the Quarry Pool.

Formality on the grand scale continues along the garden's northern edge: the Emperors' Walk extends for over a quarter of a mile. This majestic walk was planned in 1953, partly to accommodate the twelve busts of Roman emperors which stand at intervals on marble plinths on one side of the central grass path; on the other side are four enormous eighteenth-century bronze urns. The centre-piece is a large circular bay containing four lead statues of females, backed by copper beeches. A clipped beech hedge forms the eastern boundary of the walk, where the Norway spruces on either side have replaced the original elms. Parallel to the Emperors' Walk to the west is the long narrow path between evergreens called the Warriors' Walk.

Description of the gardens of Anglesey Abbey in part detracts from the logical and satisfying harmony which a progression through the various areas and features reveals – exactly as the creators of the early eighteenth-century landscapes intended. The often massive ornaments counteract the flatness of the terrain with their bold lines while the quantities of trees soften the impressive but sometimes harsh break between the open land and huge fenland sky. In contrast with so many twentieth-century gardens, designed with an intimate air, Anglesey Abbey's gardens impress with their overpowering sense of history and of posterity.

THE CROSSING HOUSE

In Shepreth, 8 miles south-west of Cambridge, ½ mile west of the A10
Tel. 0763 61071

Mr and Mrs Douglas Fuller

Open daily

The Crossing House possesses one of the most unusual signs to be found in any garden: LONDON AND NORTH EASTERN RAIL-WAY. *Beware of the trains. Look both up and down the line before you cross.* The warning gives more than a hint of the garden's origins and character. It forms a small triangle, its two long sides bounded by a road and by the King's Cross to Cambridge railway line, and the Crossing House has always been the home of the keeper of the level-crossing.

Mr and Mrs Fuller moved here in 1959 when he took the job. The garden was non-existent then; there was just a wilderness of railway rubbish and nettles. It was obviously not going to be possible to shut out the trains from the garden – they rattle past ten feet from the house every twenty minutes during the day – and anyway neither Mr or Mrs Fuller minded, having been brought up with trains all their lives. But fast-growing shrubs were planted round the perimeters to help focus the eye on the display of colour which was their first priority. To this end they made a series of raised beds from old railway sleepers; they added variety to the layout and inspired the introduction of small plants.

One of the problems in the early days was the soil; it was thin, in some places non-existent and, like much of Cambridgeshire, it was dry. The raised beds have now been replaced with rock beds – made with a load of Westmorland stone – and these now vary the terrain of the garden even more effectively. The original quick-growing shrubs round the perimeters have largely been replaced with more interesting varieties, climbers and trees, often of fastigiate habit and carefully chosen not to outgrow their welcome. The garden now has over a hundred climbers, including many clematis and climbing roses, trained along the edges of the garden among the standard trees, such as the cut-leaf alder.

Over the years the Fullers have collected plants for all seasons and have specialized in unusual small varieties: alpines, and many herbaceous plants, including some most effective miniature and alpine forms of normally large plants that would otherwise have commandeered the space. Hamamelis provide warm colour in the winter, and early in the

22

year the various spring flowers follow one another – aconites, many varieties of snowdrops and crocuses. The autumn crocuses are also very good and followed by *Nerine schizostylis*. The rock beds support a wealth of alpines with many varieties of sedum, saxifrage, small dianthus, gentians and many others. In other beds alpines are used effectively as ground-cover among shrubs and herbaceous plants.

The smallest part of the garden is the triangle on one side of the house, where the central bed is surrounded by a path of flagstones and camomile, and by smaller rock beds. The main part of the garden is on the other side of the house: a curving lawn effectively gives the illusion of space where a square or rectangle would look like a pocket-handkerchief. To one side a rock bed supports a waterfall into a similarly curving pond, and narrow paths wind between the irregular beds which fill the rest of the space. Contrasting with the miniature size of many of the plants are some which are planted for effect, such as the striking bush honeysuckle, whose red and cream flowers dominate the centre of the garden beside the waterfall.

The Fullers have very effectively used trellis-work round their greenhouses, supporting climbers which act as screens in the summer but can be pruned later in the year. The latest addition has been the border along the far side of the railway track, putting the railway and the trains right into the middle of the garden. Visitors must *not* trespass on the track, even if they look up and down the line. Here, as in parts of the main garden close to the lines, the plants have to be unusually resilient to put up with an annual spraying from the weed-killer train – which sometimes comes without warning – as well as other hazards such as being sprayed with diesel and suffering the blast from passing expresses. Eye-catching form or colour has been another criterion. At one end of the border a purple vine disguises a concrete pillar; among the trees are a variegated acer, two beech and *Acer cappadocica rubra*; and there are variegated cornus, shrub roses, campanulas, foxgloves and sedums along the front.

Considering that it has one of the most unexpected and inhospitable sites for a garden, the Crossing House surprises all its visitors by the enormous variety that can be achieved with small plants. This does not mean only alpines, as many people suspect, and as the garden convincingly proves. British Rail has recently installed automatic level-crossing gates. Although Mr Fuller now works at Shepreth Station, he and his wife will continue to live at the Crossing House. It would be a tragedy if progress on the railways were to endanger a garden which has been made against considerable odds, with such continuous hard work and affection from its creators.

DOCWRA'S MANOR

In Shepreth, 8 miles south-west of Cambridge, ½ mile west of the A10, and 5 miles from the M11 (Junction 11)
Tel. 0763 60235
Mrs John Raven

Open one day a week, the first Sunday in the month from April to October inclusive, and also by appointment

The placid Queen Anne façade of Docwra's Manor, seen from the village green through a wrought iron screen and central gates, belies its exuberant garden. The red-brick façade was added to the originally late sixteenth- or early seventeenth-century farmhouse and in 1919 the farm land was separated from the house by sale. Mrs Raven (a sister of Mrs Michael Stanley, whose garden at Halecat in Cumberland is included in this book) and her late husband, who bought Docwra's Manor in 1954, later managed to buy back some of the land and, more important, the farmyard area and buildings. The shape of much of the garden suggested developing it as a series of separate enclosures formed by the farm buildings, a style encouraged by the flatness of the site and the loss of many of the trees which were originally its main feature. It was a pattern which the Ravens followed with marked success as they steadily built up the garden in stages away from the house.

John Raven, a Fellow of King's College, Cambridge, later wrote *A Botanist's Garden* (Collins, 1971), a book which showed him to be an enthusiastic and knowledgeable botanist and gardener with a refreshingly unorthodox approach. Even though they had a broad plan of distinct enclosures for the garden it was clear from the outset that the plants the Ravens were steadily collecting were going to take precedence over careful design. John Raven disliked removing any plant, and even towards the end of his life, when to many people the garden appeared full to capacity, he could not resist trying new plant combinations or rare varieties. One of the Ravens' particular interests was in grouping plants as a family to reveal the diversity in character of various members of one genus. Parts of the walled garden were given over to this experiment; vegetables were replaced by small shrubs and herbaceous plants, some grouped by botanical family. It was one of the few impositions of order on this remarkable part of the garden, where the Ravens decided to fill the whole area with plants divided by irregularly laid-out paths. In the summer it is a riot of growth and, as is inevitable under such a gloriously liberal regime, many of the family enclaves have been infiltrated by – not unwelcome – aliens.

One exception to the general rule of giving precedence to the plants was one of the first views that the Ravens created to be enjoyed from the back door of the house and, more important, from the kitchen windows during meals. By removing a small section of wall they opened up the area of what was the vegetable garden and replaced it with lawn and a mixed beech hedge (the vegetable garden was banished to a distant part of the ground). Around the lawn plants have steadily been added, but not to the extent of obscuring the view from the house. On the other side of the house is an open lawn with, on its far side, a copper-domed temple given by King's College, a restful scene just holding at bay the melée of flower, foliage and scent in the wild garden and semi-wild garden beyond. Here shrub roses and climbing roses, trained into fruit trees, lilacs and philadelphus, continually compete with many other plants, large and small.

The result in such areas of the garden has been a case of 'survival of the fittest'. Mrs Raven best describes the garden's character as 'in part that of an old country rectory, in another of an overgrown cottage garden'. The 'cottage garden' description, though, potentially detracts from one of the garden's main features, which is its large and varied collection of unusual plants, many of them wild British varieties rarely seen in a garden or small foreign visitors not often seen in England. Where they are not suited to one of the main areas of the garden – the paved garden, or walled herbaceous garden, conifer bed, rock gardens or the blue borders – the smaller varieties can be found a home in a trough or sink. The Ravens made many expeditions to areas around the Mediterranean, returning home with new plants to try out. Unfortunately, the winter of 1981–2 proved too harsh for a number of them, but their quantity and diversity is still of compelling interest. There is not space to list them here, nor m any of the other plants in this splendidly extrovert garden. Though in some parts plants have become overgrown and unalterably intertwined, sometimes at the expense of weaker and more delicate neighbours, the sense of energy in this garden is captivating and in wonderful contrast to the formal serenity of the main façade and village setting. Mi. Raven also looks after a rhododendron and mixed shrub garden at Ardtornish, in the Morveen Peninsular of West Scotland, which is open daily for six months of the year.

DUXFORD MILL

In Duxford, 9 miles south of Cambridge, on the B1379, and off the A505 and
M11 (Junction 10)
Tel. 0223 832 325
Mr and Mrs Robert Lea

Open on Bank Holiday Sunday and Monday in May and August, and the first
Sunday in July, and by appointment for parties of over 25 people

---

The history of Duxford Mill goes back to the Doomsday Book, when it
was recorded: 'One Mill here worth 12s, it is broken but can be
repaired'. There were no thoughts of gardens then. In the nineteenth
century Charles Kingsley was a regular visitor and probably wrote much
of *The Water Babies* during his stays, but the garden one sees today has
only emerged since 1948, made by Mr and Mrs Lea who bought the mill
in 1946 when it was derelict and surrounded by waste land.

Over the years the Leas have planted some five hundred trees, many
as wind-breaks and a number of ornamental varieties too, but the great
feature of the garden are the roses, now numbering some two thousand,
which are planted mainly in three borders. They are of consuming
interest to Mr Lea and he has raised a number himself. To discover the
different plants' flowering times and strengths he used a scheme learnt
from making weather maps when he was in the Royal Air Force: all the
plants were charted for each week of the year with their quantity and
period of flowering scaled between 1/10 and 10/10 coverage of the
plant.

When Mr and Mrs Lea first started the garden one of their main aims
was to make it as labour-saving as possible. Their basic plan called for
long borders, curving along the river, with wide areas of lawn around
them. Amongst the rose borders are various trees and mixed borders,
two of which contain generous asparagus beds.

From the mill, partly weatherboard with a steeply pitched Mansard
roof, and partly brick with a similar tiled Mansard roof, there is an
arresting view down the length of the garden with the main rose border
on one side, the wide lawn and the stream curving through the middle,
to a Regency temple. Originally the burial place of the de Freville family,
this was moved from its original position at Hinxton when threatened by

demolition. Its doorway has Corinthian columns, and inside it is decorated with an allegorical painting by Hamilton Kerr. Looking from the house the perspective beyond the stream is sharpened by pairs of trees – columnar yews and *Robinia pseudoacacia* 'Frisia'. In front of the temple, but planted to either side so as not to obscure it, are a weeping copper beech, shrub roses and a stand of silver birch – *Betula papyrifera*, *B. jacquemontii* and *B. costata* – which are oustanding in the winter.

Sheltering the main rose border are tall Leyland cypresses, but the solid effect of their evergreen foliage is broken by a line of delicate variegated acers, *Acer platanoides* 'Drumondii'. The roses are all floribunda and hybrid tea varieties arranged in descending size from the back, a spectacular display at the height of their flowering period.

A tall weeping willow – some seventy-five feet high and perhaps the highest in the country – stands in the curve of the stream and makes an ideal centre-piece to the combination of lawn and water in this part of the garden. Beyond the far curve of the stream is the most recent rose border which has the interesting addition of a self-watering system, and beyond that a walk leads along the edge of the garden, with a line of *Laburnum vossii* trees behind, to the bridge across the stream. Over the bridge is a large sculpture of two angels, made out of a single block of Portland stone by H. Wiles, the renowned Cambridge sculptor; the angels look towards the house, between mixed shrub and herbaceous borders. The third main rose border curves along this side of the stream, below where it tumbles from the mill.

Beside the mill are a number of interesting trees, including a metasequoia, a seedling from a tree at Arley Castle in Worcestershire, home of Mr Lea's uncle, which was itself one of the original seedlings sent to Britain from the Arnold Arboretum, USA in 1948. The trees lead to the top of the garden where the Leas plan to make a spring water garden with a series of small streams and pools. They have already planted many *Primula denticulata* and there are more young metasequoias behind. For the rose enthusiast Duxford Mill is especially interesting, but this new feature will undoubtedly give the garden a far wider appeal.

PECKOVER HOUSE

In the centre of Wisbech, north of the River Nene

Tel. 0263 733 471

The National Trust

Open five afternoons a week from April to October inclusive

Peckover is one of a series of Georgian houses on the North Brink of the River Nene; the plain brick façade gives little idea of the richness of its interior or of the garden which lies behind the house. It was owned by the eccentric Quaker dynasty of Peckover for a hundred and fifty years, but most of the planting has been done since the property was given to the National Trust in 1943 by the last member of the family, the Hon. Alexandrina Peckover. In particular the garden has been restored and developed since 1968 when the present gardener came to Peckover, and who maintains the garden with part-time help today. It has always had an atmosphere of secrecy about it, sometimes reinforced by its division into three main areas.

Some old trees survive around the lawn immediately behind the house, but the ginkgo at the far end and the tulip tree have recently been replaced by young specimens; a sad loss amongst these older trees was a large fern-leaf beech, but again a new one has been planted near the summerhouse. One of the most attractive trees at Peckover is on this lawn, *Sophora japonica*, planted in 1968. The Wilderness Walk leads through shrubberies round the lawn's east perimeter; at the far end, behind the ginkgo, is a marble statue set in an alcove in the brick wall. All round the garden, in fact, and enclosing the central area, the eighteenth-century walls shelter plants and add character.

On the opposite west side of the lawn from the Wilderness Walk is an area of informal beds, with a wall beyond, filled with flowering shrubs, including many philadelphus, and small ground-cover plants – a number of different hostas, alchemillas and vincas. In one corner is a typically Victorian summerhouse with rustic wooden pillars. Along the path are three metal rose arches, and on the lawn at the north end is the 'Bandstand', an arbour with a circular domed canopy draped with honeysuckle and roses.

The main borders at Peckover lie between brick walls and are divided

28

into compartments each containing a variety of plants of one colour, which mirror each other on either side of the path. Roses and clematis are trained on the walls and also mix together up delicate metal pillars along the path; the whole effect in the summer is most picturesque. At the north end of the path is the Orangery; the three huge orange trees, moved here from Hagbeach Hall, are reputed to be over three hundred years old. Now plumbago and a large collection of fuchsias add to the display of plants. At the south end is the second Victorian summer-house, placed beyond a lily pool flanked with clipped yew hedges and surrounded by hydrangeas, peonies and lilies.

A path leads from beside the summerhouse between striking plants of the variegated *Cornus alba* 'Elegantissima' further west to the third main area: more informal lawn and trees as a counterpart to the lawn in front of the house. This area used to be the kitchen garden, from which a nursery border continues. Among the trees on this lawn are a large beech dominating one corner, a medlar, a black mulberry and a quince, and at the far end is an eye-catching hedge of golden privet. Next to the Orangery, against the back wall of this garden, is the Fern House.

This addition and the recent borders – as well as a mixed border there are others containing mostly low Victorian plants, and plants for autumn effect – mark the improvements which the National Trust has achieved without disturbing Peckover's peaceful atmosphere. This is one of the less-frequented National Trust properties and many of the visitors who come primarily to see the house are pleasantly surprised by the garden they discover.

ESSEX

GLAZENWOOD

Near Bradwell, 4 miles east of Braintree, ½ mile south of the A12
Tel. 0376 83172
Mr and Mrs D. A. H. Baer

Open on Friday from early April to mid-July and on selected Sundays in spring
and summer, and by appointment

The long two-storey house of Glazenwood was built in 1803 and almost
from its beginning was a home of horticulture. By 1805 Samuel Curtis,
who published a number of now rare and valuable botanical books, was
already planting quantities of fruit trees and shrubs in the garden,
though he did not actually buy the property until 1819. His garden was
soon to be opened to the 'Nobility and Gentry' for an annual subscrip-
tion of two guineas, and his magazine included coloured illustrations of
its plants painted by the daughters in his family of thirteen children. The
only survivors of Curtis's planting are a few old pear trees in the
Woodland Garden and the two magnolias, *M. grandiflora* and *M.
denudata*, trained against the south wall of the house. Mr and Mrs Baer's
predecessor cut them to the ground, but the trees have since recovered
to a healthy size; they shelter hebes and have some interesting company
on the house-wall – *Bignonia radicans*, variegated jasmine, climbing
roses and clematis. The very unusual semi-circular avenue of limes
planted to the east of the house is now thought to be original Curtis
planting too.

Glazenwood was sold on Curtis's death in 1860, though by then he
was no longer domiciled there. Between 1876 and 1934 the property
was regularly rented out by its new owners. One of the tenants was an
Irish racehorse-owning family, and the limes provided a shaded trotting
ring. From 1900 until 1963 the area to the west of the house was covered
in hot-houses for peaches, complete with underground stoves and hot
pipes. The Cunard liners were supplied from here until refrigerated

transport and foreign competition threatened the business. A decision to produce tomatoes instead was too late, and the business folded. For many years Glazenwood and its garden became almost derelict; the ginkgo planted by Curtis had grown into the house from one side and out through the roof before the arrival of Mr and Mrs Baer in 1964 set extensive restoration in train.

Once this was complete they turned their attention to the garden. To the south of the house old rose beds were replaced with a croquet lawn. The hot-houses and underground pipes were swept away and in their place came the large West Lawn. Only the peach packing-house was retained to become the summerhouse for the swimming pool. In fact the summerhouse is really the hub of the garden, which now extends into the surrounding woodland to the south-east of the house where the few Curtis pear trees are to be found. The layout is informal, a series of paths leading round the borders planted mainly with shrubs against a background of yew and hornbeam hedges. Cornuses and viburnums are outstanding, especially in the long border stretching along the edge of the main lawn, where there are also philadelphus, magnolias and laburnum. The Woodland Garden contains roses, viburnums and cornus, as well as azaleas, kalmias, camellias and parrotias, among a number of mature trees and more recent additions. Hydrangeas both here and along the bottom of the garden make a fine feature in late summer. There are a number of eucalyptus in the garden – a line of them borders the main area of garden to the east – and a more surprising find still are the three eucryphias.

However, perhaps the most striking feature throughout the garden are the roses. Climbers such as 'Wedding Day' and 'Kiftsgate' are trained into trees and highlight the woodland on two sides of the main lawn. The tennis court next to the swimming pool is completely screened with the pink climber 'New Dawn'. Along two sides of the court the main rose border is filled with old-fashioned shrub roses, while along its other long side the border planting is mixed with many hibiscus, especially prominent in late summer. One of the Baers' most recent additions to the garden is the 'twig garden' on the north side of the West Lawn. Here they have planted a variety of cornuses, all of which have striking winter barks.

There is a far greater variety of plants in the main garden than it is possible to mention here, and throughout Mr and Mrs Baer have achieved with the help of one full-time gardener and other part-time help a standard of restoration it would have been hard to imagine twenty years ago. They have saved, and improved upon, the legacy of an important figure in the history of English gardens and botany.

SALING HALL

In Great Saling, 6 miles north-west of Braintree, off the A120
Tel. 0371 850 243
Mr and Mrs Hugh Johnson

Open 3 afternoons a week from mid-April to mid-October and closed in
August; by appointment for parties

Saling Hall is a fine red-brick seventeenth-century manorhouse with
gabled ends on the main entrance front. It is better known as the home
of Hugh Johnson and, as one would expect from the author of the
International Book of Trees, and *The Principles of Gardening*, he has made a
striking garden, extending it to an area of about twelve acres and
planting an extensive collection of rare and unusual trees.

Although still immature this main area of garden is already of
considerable interest which can only increase as the trees mature. There
are deciduous and coniferous varieties, some indigenous to Britain and
many from various foreign parts, but too numerous to list. They are all
planted informally in an uneven area of mown grass broken by the water
of the pond, 'the Red Sea' towards the far end, and by the Japanese
Garden beneath a bank closer to the house.

The old Walled Garden, dated 1698, is a complete contrast, enclosed
and traditional in its layout. A central herringbone brick path leads
between mixed borders to a pair of Irish yews; on both sides the borders
are backed by columnar junipers with apple trees beyond. Box hedges
enclose these borders and provide a contrast of orderliness with the
mixture of shrubs and herbaceous plants with which the borders are
filled. One striking tree that has been added to the garden is the *Robinia*
'Frisia' in one corner.

The peaceful atmosphere of the Walled Garden and the old Rose
Glade near the house is especially noticeable when compared with the
main area, where a feeling of growth and continual change is very
strong. A more formal Long Walk leads to the Water Garden on one side
of this area, but one senses that both the areas of water and a number of
shrubs are intended to enhance the garden's outstanding feature,
trees. To the specialist the garden's interest is compelling, but even the
less knowledgeable visitor will find plenty of rewarding features here.

WHITE BARN HOUSE (The Beth Chatto Gardens)

Near Elmstead Market, 5 miles east of Colchester on the A133
Tel. 020 622 2007

Mrs Beth Chatto

Open Monday to Saturday from March to October inclusive except Bank
Holidays and Monday to Friday from November to February inclusive except
for two weeks over Christmas and New Year

Neither house nor garden existed in 1960 on the then distinctly
unencouraging site in a county not known for its gardens and plagued by
droughts: a south-west-facing slope of arid gravel sloped down to a
wilderness along a boggy ditch in continually waterlogged clay; on the
far side of this a north-east-facing slope led up to a few boundary oaks.

The work involved in clearing the site before any sort of garden could
be planned was considerable. A split-level single-storey house was built
on the south-west-facing slope, after which the garden's different areas
were steadily evolved. Undoubtedly much of the garden's interest
derives from its total contrasts: the Mediterranean Garden on the
south-west-facing slope below and around the house; and the damp,
sometimes saturated Water Garden along the valley below. In these
different areas Mrs Chatto has built up enormous collections of plants.
Her interests have expanded beyond her own four acres of garden to the
highly successful commercial nursery which she runs on an adjacent
site. Here the quantity of plants should satisfy any customer, and they
include some varieties that might baffle even the most knowledgeable.

The steps and terraces of the house have been incorporated into the
Mediterranean Garden; with the raised beds they help retain the
precious soil. Though this may be arid, especially during the summer
months, the variety and quantity of plants at times is luxuriant. Particularly striking are the *Genista aetnensis*, *Cytisus battandieri*, cistuses,
buddleias, salvias, euphorbias, saxifrages and many other small plants,
all clinging to their thin and stony base. The columnar *Chamaecyparis
lawsoniana* 'Ellwoodii' that dominates the terrace greatly adds to the
character of this area.

The contrast as one descends to the Water Garden is immediate. The
bog and ditch have been formed into a series of ponds, around which

primulas, *Osmunda regalis*, gunnera – of prehistoric monster proportions – and other damp-loving plants thrive. One of the main features of the Water Garden is the use of shades of foliage to provide the luxuriant atmosphere, rather than colour of flowers. The growth of some of the trees, such as the taxodiums and the paulownia, is hard to credit, given that none of them is over twenty-five years old. On the bank farthest from the house a series of paths wind along the edges of the ponds, or higher up into the woodland area. Beneath the oaks and other trees here are many of the best spring flowers – erythroniums, meconopsis, primroses, trilliums and hellebores.

It is the constant attention and knowledge lavished on each of the numerous plants that has made this garden such a success, enabling every one to have as hospitable site for its particular needs as possible. The garden is still expanding; there is a recent Mediterranean border beside the entrance drive, a sort of 'proof of the pudding' to those visitors to the nursery too busy to visit the gardens, and there are large new island beds on the slope towards the nursery. It is unlikely that such a skilful and questing plantswoman as Mrs Chatto would ever be satisfied, but her achievement at White Barn House would stand as a monument to most gardeners.

NORFOLK

BARNINGHAM HALL

Near Matlaske north-west of Aylsham between the A140 and the B1149
Tel. 026 377 250
Sir Charles and Lady Mott-Radclyffe
Open on one or two Sundays in the year and by appointment for parties

Barningham Hall is an example of Humphry Repton's architecture as opposed to his landscape design, on which his reputation was built; in 1807 he added an east wing to the already fine seventeenth-century house on the instructions of the present owner's great-great-grandfather, John Thruston Mott.

As well as altering the appearance of the house, Repton transformed its surroundings. Where the park sloped down to the woods on one side of the house he made the lake, a focal point of many of the views to be enjoyed in these gardens. Of his other additions much survives, particularly the trees in the park and red-brick Walled Garden with original éspalier apple trees still growing; the walls here are in especially good condition. In recent years the gardens have been simplified in an attempt to cope with the problems of maintenance, but Sir Charles Mott-Radclyffe has planted a large quantity of young trees as replacements in the park, especially in the long mixed avenue crossing it from the main entrance front of the house.

Despite some reductions the impressive herbaceous border on the south of the house has been retained, in summer the main feature of the gardens. This leads to an enormous hornbeam hedge with yew buttresses, whose size suggests that they were part of an original seventeenth-century garden. The hedge screens a lawn dominated by a series of Irish yews which may be of similar age to the hedge and buttresses; a small

Rose Garden shelters beneath the hornbeam hedge. The planting round the lawn is kept to a simple mixture of trees and shrubs. The view of the lake from the main lawn below the herbaceous border is particularly impressive.

Barningham displays that clear and satisfying balance between house, gardens and park which will always be the hallmark of a landscape designer of Repton's ability. It is a balance that can survive against considerable odds and in the hands of its present gardeners will provide continuing interest and attraction for years to come.

BLICKLING HALL

1½ miles north-west of Aylsham on the B1354

Tel. 0263 733 471

The National Trust

Open five days a week from April to October inclusive

Later eighteenth- and early nineteenth-century additions have not detracted from Blickling's appearance and reputation as one of the most exquisite Jacobean houses in England.

Robert Lyminge redesigned the house between 1619 and 1625 for Sir Henry Hobart, Lord Chief Justice to James I. Fresh from his work at Hatfield House for Robert Cecil, 1st Earl of Salisbury, Lyminge was limited in his plans for Blickling by Sir William Dagworth's existing fourteenth-century house and the rectangular moat enclosing it. As a result a relatively old-fashioned building emerged round two courtyards rather than the more typical Elizabethan and Jacobean E- or H-shaped houses. Lyminge counteracted the narrowness of the south façade facing the road by giving it superb proportions and decoration. The corner towers surmounted by lead cupolas and the three curving gables – both features which appear at Hatfield – produce a memorable impression. The tall central bell-tower, which replaced Lyminge's original, and the open arcades linking the main block with the wings were added to the south front by John Adey Repton – Humphry's son – in about 1830. Otherwise the south front is unchanged, as is the east front, whose five gables and corner towers face the main gardens.

Immediately beneath this façade is the old moat, which has probably been dry since the seventeenth century but which continues beneath the north front. The planting in the moat has been done by the National Trust and contains a variety of climbers, wall plants and flowering shrubs: hydrangeas, clematis, camellias, old roses and some more unusual varieties, such as *Trachelospermum jasminoides variegatum*, which take advantage of the sheltered position.

The large rectangular parterre beyond the moat on the east front was laid out in 1872 for Lady Constance Talbot, wife of the 8th Marquess of Lothian. He had inherited Blickling in 1850 from his aunt, Lady Suffield, daughter of the 2nd Earl of Buckinghamshire. The 1st Earl had been Sir John Hobart, 5th Baronet, who became the 1st Lord Hobart in 1728 and the 1st Earl of Buckinghamshire in 1746. The work on the parterre was carried out by W. E. Nesfield and Matthew Digby Wyatt, both well-known Victorian architects. Despite the difference of two hundred and fifty years between their creations there is outstanding harmony between this garden and the warm red-brick façade of the house. Nesbitt laid out an elaborate parterre on levelled ground enclosed by retaining walls; terraces, steps and balustrades were designed by Wyatt. The central fountain was one of a number of ornaments which the 1st Earl of Buckinghamshire bought when Oxnead Hall, the nearby seat of the Paston family was demolished in 1731. In the 1930s the parterre was greatly simplified by the 11th Marquess of Lothian, with advice from Mrs Norah Lindsay, and her designs survive today. The flowerbeds are confined to four bold squares with domes of clipped yew on the corners, and herbaceous plants which fill them are graded in height to give a domed effect. Beyond these square beds, divided by wide lawns, are blocks of clipped yew, shaped rather like grand pianos, which were part of the original parterre, as was the long herbaceous border on its south side beneath the retaining wall. On the terrace above this are Japanese cherries and cornus, hydrangeas and shrub roses.

Wyatt's central flight of steps on the far side of the parterre lead up to the main vista in the gardens: a gentle hill through the middle of the Woodland Garden to a Doric Temple at the far end. The temple was recorded by a visitor to Blickling in 1741, and was probably built for the 1st Earl of Buckinghamshire by Matthew Brettingham, better known for his work at Holkham Hall. Also dating from the eighteenth century, but later – about 1790 – is the fine Orangery hidden away on the south side of the Woodland Garden. Architecturally it is outstanding; possibly it was designed by Humphry Repton. Although Repton did not provide a Red Book for Blickling he did supply plants for the 2nd Earl of Buckinghamshire and Lady Suffield, whose family he also worked for at nearby Gunton Hall. Inside the Orangery is a statue of Hercules by Nicholas Stone, Inigo Jones's famous master-mason; like the fountain it too came from Oxnead Hall.

The Woodland Garden was probably originally seventeenth-century, and may have been designed by Lyminge who was paid in 1628 'in pte of his covenant for ye Garden'. Part of the native woodland was replanted in the seventeenth century with oak, beech, sycamore and yew. The original design would have been in the form of a Wilderness, a popular element in seventeenth-century gardening of which a similar example has recently been reconstructed at Ham House. The Woodland Garden at Blickling is enclosed on three sides by raised terraces and, on either side of its wide central path, is divided by a series of avenues and paths – parallel, at right-angles and diagonal. The three main avenues were planted with Turkey oaks, limes and beeches in the late nineteenth century and there are many fine standard trees and rhododendrons throughout the woodland; a variety of shrubs and ornamental trees line the main central vista. One small clearing existed in the 1790s when it was called Lady Buckinghamshire's Garden. Enclosed by beech hedges and containing a small summerhouse, it is now called the Secret Garden. It really is an unexpected corner, a model of simplicity, with lawns surrounding a small sundial (dated 1697) most rewarding in the early morning or evening when the beech hedges are dappled by the sunlight slanting through the trees all around.

The trees and lawns sloping to the park and lake on the north front match the eighteenth-century character of the façade. Though the building remains in close harmony with Lyminge's work – in particular the corner towers which flank this and all the other façades – it was extensively remodelled by William Ivory in about 1779. Both William Ivory and his father Thomas were employed by the 2nd Earl of Buckinghamshire to make alterations to Blickling. This sunken lawn replaced a formal square pond, and although there is no conclusive evidence it is likely that either Humphry Repton or his son John Adey made the mile-long lake and laid out the park. Trees are certainly the main feature on the north front including an enormous Turkey oak beyond the lawn, and Oriental planes on the higher ground between it and the bottom of the Woodland Garden. More recent additions are the small-leafed limes backing the Oriental planes, and the London planes near the lake. A wide gravel walk leads from the north-east corner of the house to a flight of steps up to a garden seat. In an inventory of 1793 this raised area was called a 'Prospect View', something which, also known as a belvoir, was positioned to give views away from the gardens to the park.

The west front of the house was also considerably altered by Thomas and William Ivory. Originally it looked on to a typically late seventeenth-early eighteenth-century pattern of three avenues in the form of a *patte d'oie*, recorded on a plan of 1729 and a drawing slightly earlier by Edmund Prideaux. The formality of this was naturalized in the prevailing late eighteenth- or early nineteenth-century fashion, again probably by Humphry Repton or his son. Now the main feature of the North Garden is the collection around the nineteenth-century pool enclosed by yews.

The 11th Marquess of Lothian who, as described, reshaped the East Garden in the 1930s, was one of the leading statesmen of the inter-war period; during his career he held the posts of Secretary to the Prime Minister, Lloyd George, between 1916 and 1921, Under-Secretary of State for India, and, at the outbreak of the Second World War, Ambassador to Washington, where he died in 1940. Acutely aware of the dangers that threatened the survival of country houses, and without children, Lord Lothian bequeathed Blickling with its estate of 4,500 acres to the National Trust. Its acquisition was possibly the most important milestone, up till then, in the Trust's career as a country house owner, and it has remained one of their most treasured – as well as most important – properties ever since.

MANNINGTON HALL

2 miles north of Saxthorpe off the B1149, 18 miles north of Norwich
Tel. 026 387 284
The Hon. Robin and Mrs Walpole

Open on Wednesday, Thursday and Friday from June to August inclusive, and on Sunday from May to September inclusive

The originally fifteenth-century house at Mannington was bought with its estate in about 1740 by Horatio Walpole, younger brother of the famous statesman and Prime Minister who was later created 1st Lord Walpole of Wolterton. However it was not purchased to become a home; it was occupied as a farmhouse for the rest of the eighteenth and first half of the nineteenth century. Not until 1864 did a member of the family live at Mannington, when another Horatio Walpole, 4th Earl of Orford (of the second creation) moved to the house from his eighteenth-century mansion at Wolterton. The move was prompted by the Earl's enthusiasm for 'antique' and Gothic architecture, to which Mannington was certainly closer than Wolterton. His nephew continued to live at Mannington between 1895 and 1905 when he returned to Wolterton, which he had had restored. In 1969 Robin Walpole took over Mannington; as well as some restoration to the house he has made considerable additions to the gardens. Due to a link with Peter Beales' Roses, the well-known nursery and rose-grower, roses have become the main feature of this picturesque and partly old-established garden.

The 4th Earl of Orford made certain alterations to the house, but retained most of its medieval appearance, its old moat and the drawbridge on the west side by which the courtyard and front door are reached. He introduced the temple which now stands at the south end of the stretch of lawn called 'the island', lying between the moat and the lake. Inside the temple is a statue of 'Architecture' who holds the plan of a Palladian house in her hand. More in line with his own interest are the series of 'ruined' follies which he erected across the road to the south-west of the main gardens around the genuine ruin of a Saxon chapel. The 4th Earl's leaning towards the Gothick was shared by many of his contemporaries, but his antipathy towards women, his other dominant trait, was nothing short of misogyny. One of his two equally uncomplimentary (Latin) inscriptions either side of the front door reads: 'A tiger is worse than a snake, a demon than a tiger, a woman than a demon and nothing is worse than a woman.'

Other than the 4th Earl's architectural additions, the frame of the lake, some of the trees and shrubs and the old buildings, most of the garden's appearance today has been conceived by Robin and Laurel Walpole. Between the drawbridge and the house is a sheltered Walled Garden whose old walls were battlemented in the nineteenth century; this would probably have been the original fifteenth- and sixteenth-century garden. Clematis, honeysuckle and wisteria are trained on the walls, and the borders beneath them contain herbaceous plants and roses. A silver weeping pear is one of the attractive small trees here.

Also within the moat, to the south of the house, is the Rose Garden. This was begun in 1969 around the lawn beside the moat; now there is a pattern of beds down each side and around the three busts at its far end. Perhaps the most attractive view at Mannington is across the Rose Garden and moat to the temple and lake beyond the 'island' lawn. The Scented Garden to one side of the Rose Garden was planted in 1980. Enclosed by hedges, its pattern of beds – modelled on the design of the dining-room ceiling – contain a variety of scented plants, including many herbs. It is a charmingly intimate part of the gardens.

At the south end of the lake behind the 4th Earl's temple, is a recently made lawn. The main feature of the large 'island' lawn in front of the temple is the series of island beds planted in the late 1960s and early 1970s. As well as flowering cherries and a variety of shrubs, roses are the outstanding plants. Beyond the drive to the west of this lawn is an area known as the Horses' Graves: family horses were buried here during the nineteenth century, and their graves are now surrounded by rhododendrons and, in the spring, by snowdrops, crocuses and tulips. Robin Walpole planted the Lime Avenue along the drive in 1975, leading to the fine entrance gates. He has also added a number of young trees, such as Japanese red cedar and a fastigiate beech, in the Chapel Garden, and cleared parts of the old Shrubbery Garden beyond the 'ruins'.

In the North Walled Garden he has created an extensive Rose Garden, divided up into areas with old-fashioned roses from different periods, planted in appropriate historical patterns. It is an adventurous project and one which reflects the energy that has played such a large part in the substantial improvements at Mannington since 1969.

RAVENINGHAM HALL

14 miles south-east of Norwich, east of the A146, between Lodden and Beccles
Tel. 0508 46322

Sir Nicholas Bacon, Bt

Open on selected Sundays between May and August and by appointment

---

Sir Nicholas Bacon only inherited Raveningham Hall in 1982 on the death of his father, Sir Edmund, and gives all the credit for the garden's creation to his mother, Priscilla, Lady Bacon, who now lives in a smaller house close by. On first impression Raveningham has the appearance of a traditional country house garden extending to four acres, set securely in surrounding parkland and built up round old-established features, such as the red-brick Walled Garden and the Long Terrace across the south front. Closer inspection reveals that Lady Bacon brought a number of interesting and unusual plants to the garden which make it a little out of the ordinary and enliven its atmosphere of rural tranquillity.

The fine red-brick house was built and the park laid out at the end of the eighteenth century. The park's outstanding feature is the wide Lime

Avenue to the south of the house, but in both park and garden there are a number of mature copper beeches of a particularly good strain, with leaves of an unusually dark purple. The house was added to at the end of the nineteenth century and again, far more extensively, by Sir Nicholas's grandfather – another Sir Nicholas – at the beginning of this century. When Sir Edmund and Lady Bacon inherited Raveningham in 1947 they removed Sir Nicholas's additions, returning the house to a more manageable size and its original Georgian proportions.

With characteristic ingenuity Lady Bacon retained part of the walls of what had been Sir Nicholas's sitting room, on the south-east corner, and made a little Courtyard Garden where a selection of plants benefit from the sheltered position – the autumn-flowering *Clematis rehderana, Pieris forestii, Hebe hulkeana, Fremontodendron californicum* and a variegated jasmine. Immediately to the east of the courtyard is a small formal Rose Garden, enclosed by brick walls and yew hedges and recently planted with a mixture of floribunda roses. Pride of place among the plants here must go to the *Trachelospermum jasminoides* 'Variegatum' trained against the south-facing wall, a most beautiful but unusual and tender climber with strongly scented white flowers, also *Buddleia tibetica.* Towering behind the Rose Garden to the east is a copper beech and a holly whose deep green leaves are highlighted in summer by the white flowers of a 'Kiftsgate' rose.

The Long Terrace which stretches from one side of the garden to the other, gives the garden a formal axis round which the other areas are planned. At the east end there is a thatched summer house; at the west end a yew arch and hedge behind enclose a white bench. Immediately in front of the house a low brick wall divides the terrace from the large lawn which extends to the southern edge of the garden. Central steps divide the wall and on either side is a narrow border of silver- and grey-leafed plants mixing with irises, white, pink and blue lavender, shrub roses and small euphorbias. Euphorbias are a striking feature throughout the garden and in the Walled Garden to the north-west of the house Lady Bacon grows a number of varieties which she sells to Pulbrook and Gould, the well-known London florists, for flower arranging.

The main lawn is bounded to the east by a border of shrub roses and a long yew hedge behind which is one of Raveningham's two areas of shrubberies, one each side of the lawn. Here, among other trees and shrubs are a striking liquidambar, an ancient Judas tree, a number of magnolias and in the borders beneath there are dense coverings of low plants, such as small geraniums, which minimize weeding. The shrubbery to the west is equally rich, with *Davidia involucrata,* the 'Pocket-handkerchief Tree', a ginkgo, a variety of sorbus and viburnums and, trained into the yew trees behind, 'Wedding Day' and 'Rambling Rector' and 'Brenda Colvin' roses. An open glade to the north of this shrubbery is planted with one of Lady Bacon's special prides, a collection of over thirty varieties of snowdrops. Not only have the shrubberies been planted with special attention to the grouping of plants, but also to retain and enhance the many vistas, such as the one south-west from the terrace past the west shrubbery to the flint and stone tower of the parish church in the park.

To the north of the main terrace path, close to the yew arch and bench at its west end, is a mixed border which exemplifies the variety Lady Bacon has brought to Raveningham and includes a number of unexpected visitors to this often exposed and cold part of Norfolk: *Eucalyptus niphophila*, which is susceptible to frost damage, *Osmanthus delavayi*, a free-standing *Magnolia grandiflora*, a variegated tulip tree and young variegated ginkgo, and a colourful display of lilies.

Lady Bacon has not limited her planting to the main areas of the garden: the walls of outhouses to the north of the house support more unusual climbers such as the rare Spanish clematis grown over a large white Judas tree, an azara – there is another on the south-facing wall behind the main terrace and a *Wattakaka sinensis*, at least fifteen years old.

From the mixed border a path leads north through an informal area of trees and shrubs to the Walled Garden and Raveningham's largest border, twenty feet deep and stretching right along the south-facing outside wall of the kitchen garden; it is filled with a mixture of shrubs and herbaceous plants with fruit trees trained on the wall behind. The Walled Garden itself is planted with the quantities of plants for sale, either as cut flowers or for growing. They will be a reminder to visitors of Raveningham's many charms.

SUFFOLK

BEARES

In Saxtead, off the A1120 between Saxtead Green and Dennington
Tel. 0728 723 232
Mr and Mrs S. A. Notcutt

Open by appointment from April to mid-November

Since the early 1960s Mr Notcutt, a member of the well-known horticultural family, has transformed and expanded an originally derelict area round an old Suffolk farmhouse into a plantsman's garden full of interest and variety despite the difficult boulder clay. As he lightheartedly says, 'Statues, pots and pans and ironmongery are not tolerated.' Throughout the garden the plants are clearly labelled by Mrs Notcutt with meticulous care, a labour much appreciated by visitors.

Planted in a modern, informal style, the garden has expanded from the house to fill the present area of well over two acres. The farmhouse and buildings probably date from the seventeenth century, as do the ponds and ditches. The original horse pond, south-east of the house, has been rendered into a small moat encircling an island with banks planted with a great variety of shrubs and perennials, such as *Euphorbia griffithii* 'Fireglow', Dunwich rose, a weeping pear, a Nozomi rose and pampas grass. Aster 'Lady in Blue' surprises visitors because it is never affected by mildew in this site. To the north of the pond is a magnificent *Xanthina* 'Canarybird' rose, the first herald of spring.

This is an all-year garden, however; for example an outstanding bank of winter-flowering heathers can be seen from both the house and the road. The south front of the house looks on to a terrace and provides shelter for many tender plants including *Fremontodendron*, 'Californian Glory', *Ceanothus impressus*, *Carpentaria californica*, *Campsis radicans* and *Abutilon megapotanicum* 'Kentish Bell'.

To the west of the lawn is an old orchard underplanted with bulbs and groundcover and interspersed with roses, fuchsias and other shrubs. Among the trees are *Paulownia imperialis*, *Malus* 'Golden Hornet' and a number of dwarf conifers. West again of this area a small glade displays an 'Albertine' rose trained over an old apple tree; *Parrotia persica* and *Fraxinus oxycarpus* provide autumn colour here. There is much autumn interest elsewhere in the garden, like the celastrus, covering an apple tree, which has spread spectacularly in fifteen years. Cotoneaster are plentiful throughout the garden and those with autumn colour are retained. Among autumnal display plants are the blue flowers of *Ceratostigma plumbagunoides*, and the shrubs of *Photinia villosa*, *Rhus cotinus* 'Laciniata', and *Cotinus Americanas*. One of the most prominent trees in the garden is *Catalpa bignonoides* 'Aurea' displayed against a background of *Picea omorika*, the Serbian spruce. Nearby *Picea pungens* 'Koster' might surprise a number of visitors, thriving as it does on the sticky alkaline soil.

The garden originally ended with a ditch marked by *Acer grosseri* 'Hersii', but soon after they began planning the Notcutts decided to extend the garden along the boundary between the two adjacent fields into an area called The Drift. Inspired by Westonbirt, this is now the garden's outstanding feature, tempting visitors to walk to the far end where there is a seat. The Drift stretches to the north-west, therefore one side benefits from south-westerly sun, while the other is largely in shade. This difference, however, has meant that the walk could be planted with two contrasting groups of groundcover opposite each other. In places the wide grass path is flanked by sheltering conifers, a background for flowering trees and shrubs, and plants for autumn foliage, including *Acer cappadocicum*, *amelanchier*, *liriodendron*, *Prunus sargentii* and many rowans. Many of the plants here, such as *Hibiscus suriacus* varieties, thrive despite exposure to cold east and north winds.

This is certainly not a garden where plants are regimented; rather they are allowed healthy freedom, as shown by *Clematis montana* 'Rubens' which, having covered an old tree stump near the fish pond has spread into an adjacent apple tree. A number of genera has received special attention in the garden, notably the tree peonies, penstemons and fuchsias as they succeed one another through the summer. Numerous different geraniums are used as groundcover, as are poly-gonums and the Christmas Rose and seem to be immune from the attentions of visiting rabbits.

KENTWELL HALL

In Long Melford on the A134
Tel. 0787 310 207
Mr and Mrs Patrick Phillips

Open three days a week from Easter to mid-July, five days a week from mid-July
to the end of September inclusive

Kentwell is particularly interesting because of the considerable restoration Patrick Phillips has undertaken on house and garden since he bought the property in 1971. Both unquestionably merited such attention.

The deep red-brick Tudor house was always completely enclosed by a moat, as it is today; later moats were added to enclose the East Garden and the main Walled Garden to the north, so that the whole was set romantically on an island. The original moat is older than the house, possibly thirteenth-century, and the oldest part of the house, the Moat House, forms the present west wing. It was built in the fifteenth century by John Clopton, a prominent Lancastrian whose family lived at Kentwell from the late fourteenth century until 1661, when Sissilia D'Arcy, the last surviving descendant, died. Further additions had been made to the house throughout the sixteenth century to give it its present typically Tudor 'E'-plan and attractive towers and cupolas surmounting the wings. Virtually no additions were made to the exterior thereafter, but after a serious fire in 1826 Robert Hart Logan, the then owner, employed Thomas Hopper to restore the interiors, maintaining their Tudor appearance.

It is likely that there were gardens in Tudor times, but it was not until the late seventeenth century that details of work are recorded. Sir Thomas Robinson, a wealthy lawyer, was living at Kentwell then and he built the square brick dovecot, which remains as built with nearly six hundred nesting boxes and a working potence. It is likely that he also made the moat enclosing the Walled Garden to the north of the house, today notable for the éspalier fruit trees – plums, pears and apples – some of which are estimated to be three hundred years old, and were therefore planted by Sir Thomas. Recently some forty different varieties of apple have been recorded, including many extremely old and now unusual English varieties. Sir Thomas came to an unlucky death in 1683, jumping from the window of his London chambers during a fire. His greatest contribution to Kentwell was probably the Lime Avenue which he had planted in 1678 flanking the drive for three-quarters of a mile. The avenue was very nearly lost when Richard Moore, a spendthrift successor in the late eighteenth century sold the trees to Mr Clementi, a piano-maker. Fortunately only five were cut down before Richard's mother bought the rest back. Richard divorced his wife, Sidney Arabella, for 'unlawful familiarity, criminal intercourse and adulturous conversation' with a steward at Kentwell. He ended his days in a debtors' prison but not before he had made a number of alterations to Kentwell and atoned by planting the five Cedars of Lebanon that give the Cedar Lawn to the east of the house its name.

The Bence family owned Kentwell between 1838 and 1937 and Sir Connop and Lady Guthrie, their tenants from 1928 to 1936 made substantial alterations to the gardens. Little of their work was discernible when Patrick Phillips bought Kentwell, but he and his wife Judith are restoring parts. In the Guthries' time the stretch of moat to the north Walled Garden had been separated from the moat around the house and drained to become a Sunken Garden. An herbaceous border stretched along beneath the wall, with shrub roses and trees opposite and, at the end nearest the house, a large Rockery. The trees that were planted behind the roses have now grown far beyond their originally intended size, but the planting in the Sunken Garden has disappeared.

Lady Guthrie also laid out borders – mainly herbaceous – in the Walled Garden. The areas around the fruit trees there are now mainly lawn to help reduce labour but a welcome piece of work in the current restoration of the Vinery at the far end from the house. There is a pattern of rosebeds on the side of the Walled Garden closest to the house; an interesting feature in the walls are the narrow Gothic arched doorways, added in the nineteenth century. A section of moat along the back of the Walled Garden survives, as does another stretch to its west now recently cleared. On the far western edge of the garden is the Yew Walk, a marvellous tunnel of dark green foliage whose age is difficult to estimate. When Mr and Mrs Phillips set about restoring it the yew was so overgrown that the pathway in between had been completely obscured where the two sides of yew had grown together.

Lady Guthrie also planted the yew hedge stretching from the back bridge over the moat on the north-west corner of the house; one of Kentwell's most attractive features is the octagonal summerhouse built out from the wall by the bridge into the moat. To the west of the house, opposite the old Moat House, are four acers and the Yew Lawn; these latter trees, planted by Lady Guthrie, have recently had to be drastically pruned. Little of her planting in the Shrubbery next to the Yew Lawn survives except the daffodils and snowdrops in spring, but it is being replanted.

The restoration of a house and garden the size of Kentwell is an ambitious and brave undertaking. The house has clearly recovered itself and the brick wall and bridge in front of it are attractively swathed in climbing roses. Restoration work in the gardens must be a continuing process, but the worth of what has already been achieved makes one eager to return.

SOMERLEYTON HALL

5 miles north-west of Lowestoft off the B1074
Tel. 0502 730 224
The Lord and Lady Somerleyton

Daily except Saturday from end May to end September; also Thursday, Sunday and Bank Holiday Mondays in April and May

---

Somerleyton Hall is intriguing as a legacy of the wealth of early Victorian industrial magnates, a piece of social as well as architectural history which today, without some of the more extravagant features of its original gardens, still conveys the solid self-confidence, punctuated by occasional flights of fancy, of the nineteenth century.

The estate was bought in 1843 by Sir Morton Peto, a renowned Victorian entrepreneur who had built up a fortune in the construction of railways. He was also the main contractor for the building of the new Houses of Parliament, and because of this the architect he employed to transform the existing late sixteenth-, early seventeenth-century house at Somerleyton was John Thomas. Thomas was a relatively little-known protégé of Sir Charles Barry, the architect of the Houses of Parliament, whose reputation rests largely on his work as a sculptor, particularly his stonework and statuary for the Houses of Parliament. At Thomas's hand Somerleyton metamorphosed: red brick dressed with ornate stonework; a French Renaissance-style arcade and suitably elaborate porch; an Italianate campanile; and, over the stables, a clocktower housing a timepiece made by Vullimy – Royal clockmaker for many

48

years – as a model for the proposed clock of the Houses of Parliament but rejected as too expensive; it was quickly snapped up by Peto and removed to Somerleyton. This was the house made as Peto wanted – fashionable and a fitting reflection of the wealth and status he had achieved.

Predictably Peto employed one of the most fashionable garden designers of the day, W. A. Nesfield, to lay out an intricate parterre to the west of the house and to design the Maze to the north-east. He asked Joseph Paxton, with whom he was well acquainted, to make the Walled Garden to the north of the house. Paxton shared his interest in railways, and Peto was the first person to guarantee £50,000 towards the Great Exhibition of 1851 for which Paxton built the Crystal Palace. At Somerleyton Paxton also built the Camellia Houses along the south of the Walled Garden and the range of Greenhouses, with their distinctive 'ridge-and-furrow' roofs – a design which he developed. Because of his close association with Peto it is possible that Paxton collaborated in making the key element of these gardens, normally attributed solely to Thomas, the Winter Garden.

The Winter Garden, immediately to the north of the house was described as 'a crystal building in the Renaissance style with a mosque dome'. It must have been an incredible sight at night, the central fountain, exotic plants and ornate stonework and arches illuminated by a host of gas jets. It was possibly Peto's last financial fling for by 1861 – only ten years after the Hall was finished – he was spectacularly in debt to the tune of £4 million, and in 1863 Somerleyton was sold privately to Sir Francis Crossley Bt, three years before Peto finally went bankrupt, on a scale to which he had become accustomed in everything he did.

Sir Francis was another whose fortune, like Peto's, was derived from the boom expansion of early Victorian industry. With his two brothers he had inherited their father's carpet factory in Halifax. The brothers had the foresight to buy the patent of the first steam-driven mechanical carpet loom, a machine which was to make them the largest carpet manufacturers in the world. Sir Francis's grandson became the 1st Lord Somerleyton and grandfather to the present Lord Somerleyton.

Sadly the Winter Garden proved totally impractical and unmanageable for Peto's successors and it was demolished between 1914 and 1915. Now only two colonnaded corridors remain. Its site is now filled by a Sunken Garden with flowerbeds beneath the low retaining walls on the various levels. It is partly enclosed by the Conservatory and the surviving colonnades, whose pattern is continued by arches of clipped yew joining the brick wall which divides the West Garden from the North Lawn.

The demolition of the Winter Garden was the only major alteration to the grounds until the beginning of the Second World War when the patterns of the parterre were filled in with grass. The parterre has subsequently been replanted with a less intricate pattern of rosebeds surrounded by lawn and supplemented by domes of clipped golden and green yew as laid down in Nesfield's original design, and by various garden ornaments. Leading away from the south-west corner of the parterre is a feature that pre-dates Peto, the Lime Avenue, estimated to be two hundred and fifty years old.

In contrast to the architectural and formal atmosphere of the Parterre and Sunken Garden, the North Lawn stretching away from the house and Sunken Garden is a spacious area of trees with large island beds of rhododendrons, azaleas and various other shrubs. Among the trees are cedars, wellingtonias and monkey-puzzles planted in the nineteenth century, a fine *Eucalyptus gunnei* grown from seed brought back from New Zealand by the 1st Lord Somerleyton in 1920, and a *Metasequoia glyptostroboides* planted by Lord and Lady Somerleyton in 1963. A recent architectural addition to the North Lawn is the Pavilion, built and used during the filming of a television programme. Perhaps the outstanding tree here is a *Pinus radiata*, the Monterey pine, normally found thriving in milder areas than the east coast of England.

Paxton's Camellia Houses are still here, immediately to the north of the North Lawn on either side of the wrought-iron gates and colossal portico at the entrance to the Walled Garden, and his glass houses now contain a wonderful collection and display of exotic plants. Though most of the Walled Garden has been grassed over, there are fine herbaceous borders down the central path from the gates to the glasshouses; the groups of sweet peas trained over wooden frameworks are most effective in these borders, which are generally well-planned.

To the east of the Walled Garden is a long pergola draped with climbing roses, clematis, vines and wisteria, mauve, white and pink. Behind this is Nesfield's Maze, now the outstanding surviving feature of Peto's gardens. The path winds through an intricate pattern of yew hedges for four hundred yards – if no mistakes are made along the way – and emerges into the central clearing where there is a Pagoda on a raised mount. Visitors returning towards the house pass the only formal area of the North Lawn, the Private Garden, or M'Lady's Garden, a quiet enclosure surrounded by hedges and containing statues and flowerbeds.

Despite the considerable size of the gardens at Somerleyton the visitor is immediately struck by their extremely high standard of maintenance and the skill with which twentieth-century gardeners both preserve and renew their predecessors' work.

THE HEART OF ENGLAND

Bedfordshire
Gloucestershire
Hertfordshire
Northamptonshire
Warwickshire

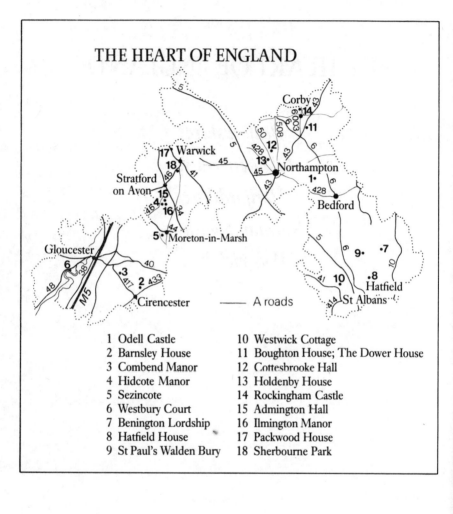

THE HEART OF ENGLAND

1 Odell Castle
2 Barnsley House
3 Combend Manor
4 Hidcote Manor
5 Sezincote
6 Westbury Court
7 Benington Lordship
8 Hatfield House
9 St Paul's Walden Bury
10 Westwick Cottage
11 Boughton House; The Dower House
12 Cottesbrooke Hall
13 Holdenby House
14 Rockingham Castle
15 Admington Hall
16 Ilmington Manor
17 Packwood House
18 Sherbourne Park

BEDFORDSHIRE

ODELL CASTLE

10 miles north-west of Bedford, between the A6 and the A428
Tel. 0234 720 240
The Lord and Lady Luke

Open two Sundays during summer

The garden which one enjoys today at Odell Castle is the achievement
of Lord Luke. In 1962 the present house was built using materials from
a Georgian building on the same site, on ground sloping south down to
the River Ouse. The Georgian house had been in ruins since the 1930s
and the garden had suffered corresponding neglect over the thirty years
until Lord Luke began work.

Trees are one of the main beauties of this garden with various mature
specimens providing much of the atmosphere. Lord Luke's plan has
been to plant new trees as an inner ring to older ones, both as
companions and for continuity as old trees are taken out. A splendid
example of this may be seen on the east side of the wide, sloping lawn in
front of the house, where beech and chestnuts have younger trees in
front of them among which the pink-flowered chestnuts are specially
striking.

The walls of the house and terracing have been imaginatively used to
support and enhance the planting of smaller varieties. Along the terrace
on the west side of the house are floribunda roses beneath a row of
mixed cherries, including two *Prunus subhirtella* 'Autumnalis' whose
white flowers appear between November and March. An indigofera
against the house is another striking addition. A further high terrace wall
supports a number of climbers and wall plants trained up from the
herbaceous border below. Outstanding are the two *Clematis montana*

53

'Elizabeth' which together give a marvellous, thick display of pink flowers. Close by on the same wall is a *Cytisus battandieri*, with its scent of pineapple. Along the north edge of the lawn on this side of the house is another narrow border beneath the sheltering canopies of beech and chestnut marking the garden's road-side boundary.

A wooden arbour covered by climbing roses on this lawn encloses a small pond. Beyond it are a cedar, a wellingtonia and a *Parrotia persica* and, in place of the old vegetable garden, a variety of trees and shrubs including viburnums, cornus, small evergreens and lilacs. An apple walk, though, has been retained from this part and now the lawns on either side are planted with ginkgo, catalpa and a golden Lawson Cypress.

From here one looks back over slightly terraced grass to the main terrace in front of the house. Near a fine old sycamore there are a Judas tree and a mulberry – both twenty years old – buddleias and rose beds, with shrub roses planted informally closer to the house. An old mill beside the river can be seen from here through a specially made cutting in the trees and it is along the river that Lord Luke's most recent work is taking shape, a Water Garden which will be visible from the house and terrace. It is a fine example of the sympathetic approach, accentuating natural features with selective planting, which has restored this garden to its former beauty.

GLOUCESTERSHIRE

BARNSLEY HOUSE

In Barnsley, 4 miles north-east of Cirencester on the A433
Tel. 028 574 281
Mrs David Verey

Open Wednesday all year, on the first Sunday in May, June and July, and by
appointment

In the twenty years before David Verey's death in 1984, the Vereys
achieved a widely held and well deserved reputation for their garden at
Barnsley House; it is a remarkable achievement in such a space of time.
It is no surprise to discover that between them David and Rosemary
Verey possessed four most valuable qualifications for garden-making;
he was an architect and architectural historian, and she is a plantswoman
and garden historian, and one can see that all their talents have been
continually brought into play in this garden. It is the product not only of
two keen and critical minds, but also of the widely diverse and long
established tradition of English garden-making.

When they moved to Barnsley House in 1951 the Vereys inherited
much that encouraged the making of a garden. The house was originally
built in 1697 of Cotswold stone. By the middle of the eighteenth century
it had become the village rectory; at that time the garden to the south and
east of the house was enclosed by stone walls, with a wonderful Gothic
summerhouse, built in 1770, facing diagonally across the garden
towards the house from the north-western end of the wall. In 1830
considerable alterations were made by the Rev. Adolphus Musgrave,
who gave the house its present Tudor-Gothic appearance with a gabled
third storey and, on one end, a small colonnaded verandah with a
castellated roof, in front of which Mrs Verey's Knot Garden has its
place. His successor, Canon Howman, planted the now mature trees

which stand as shelter round the drive to the west of the house. Yew hedges and box were also added near the Walled Garden in the nineteenth century.

It was not until after the upbringing of their children, Mrs Verey says – a period of cricket, croquet and ponies – that she could really turn her attention to creating a garden. There is no aspect of garden history or design in which she is not interested, and Barnsley reflects the wide spectrum from which she has drawn inspiration. A good garden needs a firm structure and yet one hankers after the more random cottage-garden style of planting. Mrs Verey has the ability to adapt historical precept to her own ideas and aspirations with originality. Thus she has overcome one of the great dilemmas of modern gardens, how to achieve a balance between formality and informality. At Barnsley the one is rendered by carefully-sited architectural features and many vistas, the other in the border planting.

It is difficult to divide the garden into areas because in a sense its closely linked elements flow into one another round three sides of the house. There is a development from the old trees on the entrance side to the open lawn with the Wilderness at the far end, on the west of the house, and again to the south-east, where the Vereys have made the greatest changes and additions to the garden. The Wilderness has been planted since 1962 with a wide variety of trees including twelve different types of Sorbus, flowering cherries and malus, a *Paulownia tomentosa*, metasequoias and a ginkgo, a tulip tree, a catalpa, a wellingtonia and a cedar; they provide a backdrop to the lawn throughout the year.

The shape of the Walled Garden to the south and east to the house was largely determined by two strong axes, one made by the paved path flanked by pairs of clipped, columnar Irish yews (planted by Mr Verey's parents in 1948) which leads from the house to a wrought-iron gate in the stone wall, the other going at right-angles and stretching the full length of the garden. In 1964 the Gothic summerhouse was joined by the perfect companion, a Classical temple, also made in 1770. A gift from Fairford Park it was re-erected at Barnsley stone by stone on the east side, facing across the garden to the south-west. Now, with a paved terrace and lily pool in front, it makes a marvellous focal point from the west of the garden where a fountain made by the sculptor Simon Verity forms a balanced contrast. On one side of the wide grass path leading to the fountain is a deep border filled mainly with various shrubs and trees; along the other side stretches an avenue of limes, leading straight into one of Barnsley's most distinctive features, the Laburnum Walk. In June it is an unforgettable sight to look west along the limes to the golden tunnel of laburnum, underplanted with purple *Allium aflatunense*. The fountain itself is fun: jets of water from frogs' mouths splash against a stone table carved with two rams. The sound of the water accompanies the visitor along the wide border; at one point a gap in the yew hedge behind reveals the exquisite and perfectly-sited form of another Simon Verity work, a hunting lady who stands modestly amongst the shrubs on the far side of the main lawn. Strolling eastwards towards the pillars of the temple one may admire the main flower borders around the paved path and yews dividing a smaller lawn on the south side of the house; from spring till autumn there is something out in them, though June and July are their best times. On one side of the paved path is Mrs Verey's Herb Garden.

There is much else – the Vegetable Garden, planned as a decorative potager; the rugosa rose hedge; the strawberry vine on the colonnaded verandah; the huge *Rosa longicuspis* which almost smothers the wall by the kitchen door and behind the Herb Garden; and the two weeping cherries. Everywhere the symmetry of the Vereys' garden planning has been complemented by attention to detail in its execution, so that within Barnsley's four acres there is a feast for any visitor at any time of year.

COMBEND MANOR

Near Elkstone, 7 miles north of Cirencester off the A417
Tel. 028 582 331
Mr and Mrs Noel Gibbs

Open on selected Sundays in summer

Although relatively little known at present the garden at Combend Manor will be of increasing interest in years to come. Part of the garden was designed by Gertrude Jekyll in 1929 and although most of the plantings in the borders she designed have disappeared, her original drawings survive. Mr and Mrs Gibbs are embarking on a major plan of restoration with the help of Tim Rees, a young garden designer. It will not be possible to restore her work in its entirety but when complete the garden will once again demonstrate a striking contrast between small enclosed areas of detailed planting and views to the open wooded Cotswold hills all around.

A number of mature trees, many of them dating from the nineteenth century, give the garden a sense of establishment, particularly on the lawn to the south-west of the house. As well as a weeping ash, a beech, a Deodar cedar, a large dome of clipped yew and an old mulberry tree, a pair of slender Scots pines are perfectly positioned to frame the best view from the garden to the countryside beyond. On the slope below the lawn, reached by a small bridge over what was possibly the ha-ha, flowering trees have become densely overgrown; cherries and laburnums have survived. One of the laburnums, left in situ after it had been blown down, has adapted quite happily and continues to flower in a virtually horizontal position. Once cleared, most of this slope will become a Heather Garden, and the tops of the tall beeches at its foot will be clipped and trained into a lower hedge.

The neighbouring part of the garden slopes southwards directly away from the house. A swimming pool used to occupy the lower lawn but this has now been removed and replaced by a sloping lawn bordered by a pair of autumnal shrubberies designed to carry the eye on down the slope and out towards the wooded vista. From this enclosure, a stone path passes under a very pretty arch, probably designed by Sidney Barnsley, and dated 1925 with the initials A.L. The arch leads to what was certainly Miss Jekyll's main vista in the garden: the gravel path stretching down the south-facing slope to a wrought-iron gate at the bottom, with impressively deep and long borders on either side. Both of these borders have been completely replanted, the western one in a faithful restoration of the 1929 plans. In July and August this herbaceous border is a most dramatic sight and although perhaps fractionally vulgar to the modern taste, its graduated colour change from whites and silver, through yellows and blues to a climax of purples and oranges and then symmetrically back to the whites and yellows shows Miss Jekyll's skill at creating a vivacious centrepiece to the garden.

It is perhaps slightly surprising that the area of greatest character in the garden is not directly below the house, but to the south-east beyond this main path which continues in a line with the arch to make a very strong cross axis to the main thrust of the garden which is down the slope. Immediately one enters this part of the garden the path, of grass, acquires small rectangular enclosures on either side surrounded by yew hedges; the pattern is continued on a slightly smaller scale beyond the main path crossing until the Kitchen Garden, sheltered by stone walls, is reached.

Above the yew enclosures the existing Rose Garden will be removed, but the apple orchard and éspalier apple trees on either side of the path will stay. Below the yew enclosures to the south is one of the most attractive areas of the garden, showing considerable Gertrude Jekyll influence. Steps lead down to a terrace, with a croquet lawn, surrounded by low stone walls; in the far corner is a very pretty small garden house. On the top side of the terrace is an herbaceous border backed by a yew hedge.

The note of formality found on the terrace disappears immediately one takes the flight of steps to the sloping lawn and the pond, originally a monastic carp pond. The simple view across the lawn past a sycamore and young silver weeping pear contrasts with tsugas and cypresses, and a large juniper near the edge of the pond; these are going to be thinned. Many of the trees here, planted by Mr Gibbs' father, are of considerable beauty and interest, such as the *Pinus wallichiana* close to the pond. To the right of the lawn above the pond is a hedge of Portuguese laurel planned by Gertrude Jekyll, and a little Water Garden which has already been restored and planted with Inverewe primulas, kingcups and gunnera.

Below the pond the main Water Garden continues along a stream whose banks have been planted with hostas, lysichitums and, in contrast, a delicate miniature acer. Very striking on either side of the stream are two large domes of clipped holly, which one suspects were positioned by Miss Jekyll to lead the eye further down to the old orchard, now planted with a selection of interesting trees, in particular a stand of eight metasequoias and a weeping purple beech. As one reaches the bottom of the garden at this point there is a spectacular view out to the hills to be enjoyed.

Away from the main area of the garden on the south-facing-slope is the courtyard, surrounded on three sides by the house, one of the old monastery buildings and a tithe barn. There are rose beds on the small terrace at the back, kolkwitzia, magnolia and other wall plants trained against the buildings, and along the top of the low wall in the middle of the courtyard will be a narrow border of grey- and silver-leafed plants. Close by the 'shady border' is one of the first main areas that will be restored: a concentration of lavender will form the basis of this part of the garden.

It is a very exciting thought that an old-established garden with an enviable position and the particularly interesting connexion with Gertrude Jekyll is going to be restored, and that visits to the Gibbs over the next few years will reveal the steady progression of the work.

HIDCOTE MANOR

4 miles north-east of Chipping Camden, 1 mile east of the A46 and the B4081
Tel. 0386 77333
The National Trust

Open daily except Tuesday and Friday from April to October inclusive

Hidcote Manor and its inspired creator, Lawrence Johnston, are distinguished members of a select company of gardens made by one person in a single lifetime. When he bought Hidcote in 1907 there was no vestige of a garden round the manor house and the site, though rural and secluded, was on a windswept hilltop on the north-eastern outposts of the Cotswolds, not exactly promising. When he died in 1958, having given Hidcote to the National Trust in 1948 and moved to his second home in the South of France, Johnston had created a garden of ten acres whose architectural and horticultural harmony and variety demonstrates for many people the best qualities of twentieth-century gardens. Its component features are as widely copied as they are admired, but its atmosphere, instilled by a shy man of fastidious taste and deep gardening knowledge, could never be reproduced.

One of Hidcote's most important balances is between the intimacy of the various enclosed areas and the theatrical beckoning of the three main vistas; one across the spacious Theatre Lawn, the other two narrower but no less impressive, from the Circle along the Red Borders to the Stilt Garden beyond, and from one of the pavilions which divide the Red Borders and Stilt Garden along the Long Walk.

Throughout the garden hedges provide both the orderliness of overall architecture and the basis for secrecy and surprises, enclosing, dividing and yet joining through narrow openings aligned along axes, and concentrating the eye along views. Perhaps it was the influence of France, where Lawrence Johnston spent his youth, which inspired him to use hedges as the framework of his garden: as well as providing shelter the different plants used – yew, box, beech and copper beech, holly and hornbeam – match the variety of planting in the areas they enclose.

The manor house of Cotswold stone has never played a prominent part in the design at Hidcote and its influence has always been subtly underplayed. Instead, the gardens which spread out from its walls seem to gather their own momentum and take pride of place while the house stands modestly aside. Closest to it on the south is the Old Garden, dominated by an aged Cedar of Lebanon, one of the few existing features when Lawrence Johnston came to Hidcote, and divided by a series of borders whose summer flowers are of soft pinks, mauves and white with silver foliage plants.

From the central borders of the Old Garden one of Hidcote's main axes extends west through The Circle to the Red Borders and up steps to the Stilt Garden. The contrast between the exuberant colours of the spreading plants in the Red Borders, the exquisite, architectural formality of the twin gazebos and restrained clipped hornbeams of the Stilt Garden beyond, encompasses more than a measure of the genius at work at Hidcote. Parallel to and north of this axis is the Theatre Lawn, a study in chaste simplicity, where the wide lawn enclosed by yew hedges leads to a single stately beech on its raised dais.

The Circle which is the prelude to the Red Borders is also the launching point of another axis, to the south. The variety in the hedges runs riot round the small Fuchsia Garden – green and variegated holly, yew, box and copper beech. Beyond, on the same axis, is the Bathing Pool Garden, its circular pool enclosed by yew hedges broken on the far side by a pedimented doorway of yew leading to a circular lawn.

The interest of the Red Borders and the vista of which they are part are such that the surprise of an unexpected and unannounced view, through the left gazebo along the Long Walk sloping down to the stream and up the other side, could not be more complete. No detail seemed to escape Johnston; both the vista through the Red Borders and Stilt Garden and the Long Walk end in pairs of wrought-iron gates, a boundary and an invitation to the spectacular views beyond.

Grandeur at Hidcote, like everything, is never overdone. Along the Long Walk from the gazebo steps one is tempted to branch off west into the Pillar Garden, where columns of English yew tower above borders of 'Hidcote' lavender and a rich variety of peonies, or east into Mrs Winthrop's Garden, named after Johnston's mother. Here the colour theme is blue and yellow, highlighted by the soft greens of the enclosing beech, lime and hornbeam hedges. At the Long Walk's lowest point the Stream Garden beckons to either side, its waters lined with lush, damp-loving plants.

No doubt Johnston sensed that Hidcote would not be complete without a Woodland Garden, so he planted the large area to the east of the Long Walk, beyond the stream, with trees and shrubs notable for autumn colour and berries, and called it Westonbirt. And on the very far, north side of the garden from here the nostalgic call for an old-fashioned kitchen garden is answered, but with a characteristically individual note, in the central double borders filled with old French roses backed by Irish yews.

Lawrence Johnston was always an avid plant-collector and went on a number of expeditions himself in search of unusual varieties. His garden will always be an outstanding plant collection but it is a mark of his modesty that only one or two of the numerous outstanding plants he raised are named after him – most are named after his garden. He would no doubt have been equally reticent had he known that the influence of his garden is probably as great as any other created in the twentieth century.

SEZINCOTE

1½ miles south-west of Moreton-in-Marsh off the A44 between Moreton and Evesham

Tel. 0386 700 444

Mr and Mrs David Peake

Open on Bank Holidays and Thursday and Friday throughout the year except December

Sezincote has a unique architectural style and the gardens that surround it manage both to be in harmony with that style and to blend the house into its unlikely English surroundings, so far removed from its Indian inspiration.

In 1795 Colonel John Cockerell returned from Bengal, where he had made a fortune in the East India Company, and bought the estate of Sezincote from the 3rd Earl of Guildford, son of the Prime Minister, Lord North. Cockerell died three years later and left Sezincote to his younger brother, Charles. He it was who employed their third brother, Samuel Pepys Cockerell – so named because their grandfather was a nephew of the famous diarist – as architect for the new house.

S. P. Cockerell was himself surveyor to the East India Company and had considerable knowledge of Indian architecture; also he called on Thomas Daniell, the artist who specialized in paintings of India, for advice. Cockerell's chief inspiration for the feature and general appearance of his house was the architecture of Akbar, Moghul Emperor from 1556 to 1605. By blending Muslim and Hindu styles Akbar had hoped to bring some harmony to the divided areas of his empire. At Sezincote the pillars and horizontal beam over the front door are Hindu, the *chattris* (the small minarets on the four corners of the house), the 'peacock-tail' arches over some of the windows and the great dome surmounting the roof are all Muslim. The whole effect is enhanced by the deep golden stone of which the house is built; it came from Bourton-on-the-Hill, but may have been artificially stained.

Humphry Repton was consulted over layout of the grounds but though it is likely that he designed the park with its lake at the bottom, the precise extent of his work is not known; he did not produce one of his famous Red Books for Sezincote. Much of the original design of the gardens was inspired, and probably to a large extent designed, by Daniell. He certainly designed the bridge that carries the drive over the stream. It is supported by pillars and the water flows through a series of channels between stepping-stones; the balustrades along the top are surmounted by Brahmin bulls. He also designed the Temple to Surya at the top of the stream's valley called the Thornery. Surya was the Hindu sun god; there are Brahmin bulls either side of his little Temple.

In 1884 the Cockerell family sold Sezincote to James Dugdale and when Sir Cyril Kleinwort, Mrs Peake's father, bought it from Mr Dugdale's daughter-in-law in 1944, both house and garden needed considerable restoration. The work in the garden was largely done by Lady Kleinwort with advice from Graham Thomas. Perhaps her outstanding contribution was the South Garden, based on a traditional Moghul 'Paradise Garden'. Formal canals on either side of an octagonal fountain are flanked by columnar Irish yews, substitutes for the cypresses that would have been used in India. On the far bank from the house cornus, yews and willows grow beneath the contrasting canopy of a copper beech. The surroundings almost demanded such a garden, for as well as the south front of the house – perhaps the best façade – the exquisite Orangery curves around the west side of the garden. In contrast to the house, the Orangery is built of clear silvery-white stone, and in its shape and decoration it is a rare, possibly unrivalled, piece of garden architecture. The stonework has recently been restored for the second time since 1955.

In front of the house the park slopes away in an archetypal eighteenth-century manner. The largest area of the gardens is to the north, stretching down the course of the stream. On the lawn here a variety of flowering trees and shrubs have been planted beneath the mature trees, including another huge copper beech: viburnum, cornus, magnolia, malus and *Kerria japonica*. Towards the Thornery are more maples and, trained into a large yew on the bank behind the pool and temple, are a 'Kiftsgate' and a 'Paul's Himalayan Musk' rose – unusually large even for these two ebullient characters. Around the pool are trees and shrubs planted largely for foliage contrast, as they are throughout the Thornery as it descends to the bridge. Many of the maples are of outstanding size, but there are smaller and more delicate specimens, such as the weeping white mulberry and the gleditsia, while groups of hostas and damp-loving plants spread along the banks of the stream.

Below the bridge the stream descends in a series of pools surrounded by plants which spread out to the paths and lawns sloping down either side. The uppermost, the Snake Pool, has a central column around which is twined a three-headed serpent; particularly striking on the island are the yellow *Primula florindae*. Primulus, in company with hydrangeas, also surround parts of the Rock Pool. Above this, on the edge of the park, are four Cedars of Lebanon which could have been planted by Repton; another outstanding tree is the weeping hornbeam, *Carpinus betulus* 'Pendula', said to be the largest in England.

On either side of the stream conifers mix with flowering shrubs: various hydrangeas and fine *Cornus kousa*; the purple form of the Smoke Bush, *Cotinus coggygria*; maples and cercidiphyllums, flowering trees, including mangolias and cherries; and trees such as ash planted particularly for autumn colour. It is a considerable and diverse collection, a fitting garden for such an unforgettable house.

John Betjeman was a visitor to Sezincote when Colonel and Mrs Arthur Dugdale lived there, and in *Summoned by Bells* he paid tribute:

> Down the drive,
> Under the early yellow leaves of oaks;
> One lodge is Tudor, one in Indian style
> The Bridge, the waterfall, the Temple Pool –
> And there they burst upon us, the onion domes,
> *Chajjahs* and *chattris* made of amber stone:
> 'Home of the Oaks,' exotic Sezincote:
> Stately and strange it stood, the Nabob's house,
> Indian without and coolest Greek within,
> Looking from Gloucestershire to Oxfordshire;
> And, by supremest landscape-gardener's art,
> The Lake below the eastward slope of grass
> Was made to seem a mighty river-reach
> Curving along to Chipping Norton's hills.

WESTBURY COURT

9 miles south west of Gloucester on the A48
Tel. 0684 292 919 and 427
The National Trust

Open Easter Monday and weekends from April to October inclusive, and from
Wednesday to Sunday inclusive and Bank Holidays from May to September
inclusive

Tucked away south-west of Gloucester, Westbury Court is a unique
gem of garden history. That it survived the Landscape Movement of the
eighteenth century at all is remarkable and since its acquisition by the
National Trust in 1967 its story has been a triumph of restoration.
Today it is the unrivalled example of a seventeeth-century Dutch-style
water garden.

The garden was originally laid out between 1696 and 1705 by
Maynard Colchester, a man apparently content to devote his money and
energy to his garden rather than to improvements for his sixteenth-
century house. Everything about his garden clearly reflected the strong
Dutch influence in architecture and gardening, widespread at the time.
The main features were the long canal with an unusually tall summerhouse or pavilion at one end, and a rectangular parterre beyond filled
with bulbs, flowering trees and shrubs. At the other end of the canal
from the pavilion was an ironwork *clairvoyée*, another typically Dutch
feature, despite its French name, which was used along the edges of
gardens to give an illusion of size.

Westbury was inherited in 1715 by a nephew, another Maynard
Colchester. Although the dating is not absolutely clear he added the T-
shaped canal, parallel to the long canal, with a statue of Neptune astride
a dolphin in its centre, the gazebo in the corner of the garden beyond
here and a second *clairvoyée* in the wall opposite the end of his canal.
Because, by the mid-eighteenth century, it was unlikely that he would
have continued with a formal style of gardening, it seems that he did all
this before building a new Palladian house in place of the old between
1745 and 1748.

These two generations of creativity were followed by many of neglect
(although, ironically, this played a large part in Westbury Court's

65

survival as it did at Melbourne Hall in Derbyshire). In 1805 the Palladian house was partly destroyed by fire and subsequently demolished, and the family moved to their other estate at Micheldean, to some extent keeping up the garden at Westbury. They moved back in 1895 and built a third house. This, joined on to the pavilion at the end of the long canal, almost totally obscured the pavilion's elegant features. In 1960, when house No. 3 was demolished by a property speculator, the pavilion was nearly destroyed completely. Thereafter Westbury's sorry fortunes at last improved, particularly when it became clear that the National Trust had raised enough money to take on and restore the garden.

It was a daunting task and one unlikely to have been achieved with any credibility had not Maynard Colchester's personal accounts book for 1696 to 1708 survived. Not only did these give extensive details of the work done, they also confirmed the accuracy of most of the view of Westbury by the early eighteenth-century engraver, Kip, and were particularly useful for the restoration of the pavilion and the replanting.

Now the pavilion, once again raised up on its four-pillared loggia, the tall sash windows restored and surmounted by pediment, sloping roof and cupola, is reflected in the dredged and rebuilt long canal. The T-shaped canal underwent similar treatment; the ground between them has been kept to grass, with the yew hedges, and the yew and holly topiary replanted as they were in Maynard I's day. The Myrobalan plums which were also here have been restored, but the large parterre described in the accounts books and shown by Kip has been moved to beyond the T-shaped canal: a Dutch-style 'cut' parterre as opposed to the more usual French-style *broderie* pattern. Around it the clipped evergreens and flowering fruit trees form a quincunx pattern. The small Walled Garden beside the gazebo has been replanted with plants grown in England before 1700, and with roses.

Compared with the hundreds of gardens which disappeared without surviving even two hundred years Westbury Court is lucky; but it deserves to be. Such an exquisite survivor from the seventeenth century does not exist anywhere else in Britain and possibly not in Europe.

HERTFORDSHIRE

BENINGTON LORDSHIP

In Benington, 5 miles east of Stevenage
Tel. 043 885 668
Mr and Mrs C. H. A. Bott

Open on Easter Monday and May Bank Holidays, and on Wednesday and
Sunday afternoons from May to July inclusive

Both the house and garden at Benington Lordship contain considerable
character. The house was originally built at the beginning of the
eighteenth century on the far older site of a Norman castle, of which the
ruined keep remains in the garden and the old inner moat forms the
boundary on one side. The old castle provided the inspiration for
George Proctor's addition in the 1830s of a mock-Norman flint
gatehouse and a partly 'ruined' curtain wall along the edge of the moat, a
clear example of the fashion for the picturesque that was widespread at
the beginning of the nineteenth century. Most of the garden dates from
the Edwardian era and was begun around 1906 by Mr Bott's grandparents. It is these areas which Mr and Mrs Bott, who inherited in 1973,
have restored and, in places, replanted.

The 'Norman' gatehouse and wall, with one side of the Georgian
house, form a courtyard dominated by a large *Magnolia soulangiana*, but
also notable for the *Fremontodendron californicum* trained against one
wall. The genuinely ruined keep to the south of this area is now a Winter
Garden, with evergreens and winter-flowering plants. The Botts have
removed some of the beds from the Rose Garden in front of the south-
facing Georgian façade in order to simplify the pattern, and they have
also re-planted most of the roses. There are also many climbers against
the house wall: *Solanum crispum*, *Carpentaria californica*, honeysuckle
and roses.

67

Benington's west front has an Edwardian addition and verandah, and commands the best view of the gardens, across the wide lawn sloping down to the two lakes which originally formed part of the old moat. Beyond, in the park, is an ancient oak avenue. Along a narrow terrace leading from the south-west corner of the house are three Irish yews; a gravel path follows the line of the old carriage drive to a beech walk, carpeted with snowdrops in early spring, with the church at the end of it. The planting is kept simple all round the lakes except at their north-west end where the Edwardian Rockery stretches up the slope to a screen of tall cypresses. The size and antiquity of the Rockery gives it great character. Many of the plants have been replaced and there are now primulas, primroses, daphnes and viburnum. It is best seen from the far side of the lakes, so that the view extends through a cutting to the small enclosure of Shylock's Garden higher up: yew hedges enclosing a little lawn with a central lead statue of Shylock and on beyond this secluded area to a flight of stone steps leading back towards the house.

A path leads north from Shylock's Garden to the wrought-iron gates of the Walled Garden. Just before the Walled Garden it crosses the most unexpected axis of the gardens – the outstanding double herbaceous border that stretches down the slope between the Walled Garden, and the shrubs that border Shylock's Garden and the Rockery. Especially when viewed from the bottom, the slope of this border is particularly effective; its depth and length make it Benington's outstanding feature in midsummer. At the bottom to the north is the orchard, a more restrained area of apple blossom and daffodils bordered by a yew hedge below the Walled Garden. Although this is mainly given over to vegetables, the old borders have been partly restored along the central path with mixed shrub and flowers, and a small plant sales area developed at the end. Looking up the herbaceous border along the outside of the Walled Garden, one sees that the perspective is continued east above the brick wall by pleached limes.

The herbaceous border and the Rose Garden are planned to give the garden a peak during the midsummer. Mrs Bott is philosophical about late summer: frequently severe drying-out in the soil, particularly in August, combines with school holidays and the harvest to eradicate work on the garden until autumn. It is encouraging to find people who accept the problems of their garden and the need for it to fit in with other demands. In 1977 Mr Billot became gardener and since then much has been achieved.

HATFIELD HOUSE

In Hatfield
Tel. (Hatfield) 60227
The Marquess of Salisbury

Open: West Gardens, daily except Monday; East Gardens, Monday only, from
the end of March to the beginning of October

Hatfield has always had gardens appropriate to the architecture of
Robert Cecil's memorable Jacobean house and to the remaining wing of
the old episcopal Palace of Hatfield built in 1497, but there can have
been few times when they have achieved such a rich array of planting as
in recent years since the present Marchioness of Salisbury, wife of
Robert, the 6th Marquess, has restored and replanted the different
areas. Always sensitive to and inspired by the garden's Elizabethan and
Jacobean origins, Lady Salisbury has retained their structure and layout
but added a new dimension with her planting.

Robert Cecil, 1st Earl of Salisbury, acquired Hatfield from James I in
exchange for his palace at Theobolds. He built his new house at
Hatfield between 1607 and 1611, incorporating the existing gardens
round the Old Palace and at the same time laying out more gardens to
the east of the new building. The East Garden forms a series of
descending formal gardens originally laid out for Cecil by Thomas
Chaundler beneath the terrace along the East front. The terrace is
supported by a high brick retaining wall, surmounted by a stone
balustrade and four seventeenth-century stone figures. Eighteenth-
century landscaping considerably altered the aspect here but restoration
by the 2nd Marquess in the mid-nineteenth century and now by Lady
Salisbury has reinstated an impressive degree of formality.

From the terrace flights of balustraded steps lead down to right and
left to the main Rose Parterre. In the central wall beneath the steps a
three-tiered fountain forms the lower centrepiece of the view as one
looks back to the house from the far end of the parterre's long central
lawn; eight yews have recently been planted along the lawn to be clipped
into bollards which will reinforce the stately air. On either side four pairs
of hedge-enclosed beds overflow with old-fashioned roses, but also
have room for a mixture of other flowers so characteristic of Lady

Salisbury's work at Hatfield. To north and south of the beds double avenues of tall, slender standard evergreen oaks, their heads clipped into domes, form axes without dividing the beds from the long mixed borders beneath the boundary walls on either side of the parterre.

The lawn terrace immediately to the east of the Rose Parterre has recently been planted with a cross-avenue of mixed old varieties of fruit trees. Beyond, on a further lower level, is the East Garden's second main feature, the yew-hedged labyrinth, which as much as any other part of the garden is reminiscent of the style of Hatfield's origins.

Elizabeth I was held at the old Palace of Hatfield as a child and it was there she learned that she had become Queen of England. The palace originally had four wings surrounding an open courtyard. Between 1980 and 1981 Lady Salisbury replanned the courtyard as a Knot Garden devoted to plants grown in England in the fifteenth, sixteenth and seventeenth century; many are plants introduced by John Tradescant the Elder, who was Robert Cecil's gardener. Patterned brick paths surround beds filled with a haphazard arrangement of plants, as they would have been in Elizabethan times. The steep grass banks which surround the new Knot Garden are enclosed by a wooden, diamond-patterned trellis fence.

The site of the other main area of garden round the old palace is now the Upper West Garden. The beds here have all been replanted by Lady Salisbury and surround a central circular pool lined with lavender hedges. Like those in the Knot Garden, the beds are filled with a rich variety, spring flowers leading into the summer display of roses, herbaceous and a host of other plants. The large square is enclosed by yew hedges with circular bastions on each corner and entrances on all four sides. Outside the hedges are broad strips of lawn and pleached lime walks, which complete this garden's satisfying composition.

Scented plants were very important to the Elizabethans and beyond the pleached lime walk which forms the west boundary of the Upper West Garden, Lady Salisbury has laid out and planted an enchanting Scented Garden. The centrepiece is a Herb Garden filled with every imaginable herb and divided by a double border. Stone slabs alternate with camomile along the paths and the herbs, which spill out from the beds, are partly contained by hedges of sweet briar. Small formal gardens on either side of the Herb Garden, simply divided by cross-paths, contain stone urns filled with scented geraniums and a circular enclosure or box. Paths from both the Scented Garden and the Upper West Garden lead south into the Wilderness, thirteen acres of open woodland where one wanders among magnificent mature trees, a variety of smaller trees and shrubs, and luxuriant plantings of daffodils.

The manner in which Lady Salisbury's gardens hark back to Hatfield's distinguished early days and harmoniously complement the architecture of the house and old palace is inspired, a mood further encouraged by survivors from those heady days such as the medlar tree in the East Garden, planted by John Tradescant, and the mulberry tree in the Upper West Garden, one of four planted by James I.

ST PAUL'S WALDEN BURY

½ mile north of Whitwell and 5 miles south of Hitchin on the B6515
Tel. 043 887 218
The Hon. Lady Bowes Lyon, and Mr and Mrs Simon Bowes Lyon

Open on selected days in summer, and by appointment for parties

Probably created by Edward Gilbert between 1725 and 1730, St Paul's is a rare and remarkable survivor of the seventeenth-century-inspired style of formal gardens whose death-knell was sounded by William Kent and the eighteenth-century Landscape Movement. As with its contemporaries – Melbourne Hall in Derbyshire and Bramham Park in Yorkshire – St Paul's survival was partly due to neglect in the nineteenth century. The property passed to the Earls of Strathmore when Edward Gilbert's granddaughter, Mary Eleanor Bowes, married the 9th Earl in 1767. The present north front of the house, with its octagonal wings, was completed then.

Few of the events of Mary Eleanor Bowes' celebrated and scandalous affair with and marriage to Andrew Robinson Stoney took place at St Paul's. However her dog Tirsi is buried beneath an extravagant poem in the yew roundabout where, supposedly, Stoney fought a duel for her honour and later seduced her. In 1778 Mary Eleanor erected to the south of the house the statue, possibly by John Cheere, of Charity with three children (a copy of which stands in the Rhododendron Walk at the Royal Lodge, Windsor). St Paul's passed to the family of Mary Eleanor's first husband; their name became Bowes Lyon. Through most of the nineteenth century they did not live permanently at St Paul's, dividing their time between here and Glamis Castle, their historic Scottish home (whose gardens are described in a later chapter of this book). A number of conifers were added to the woodland during this period but in other respects the gardens were left largely untouched.

The 14th Earl, when still Lord Glamis, did live at St Paul's; he made various additions to the house and around 1910 he replaced the original avenue of elms, stretching away to the east of the house, with the present limes. St Paul's is best known during his time as the childhood home of Queen Elizabeth the Queen Mother, his youngest daughter. It was her younger brother, David Bowes Lyon (later Sir David and president of the Royal Horticultural Society), who substantially restored the formal garden.

Edward Gilbert laid out his gardens to the north of the house, where the ground slopes down into a dip and away again up the far side. The site was well suited to formality. The sloping ground increased the perspective along the series of allées he laid out. From the lawn in front of the house three allées radiate into the woodland, originally oak, beech and hornbeam. The widest central one stretches for 600 yards to a statue of Hercules and a horse chestnut avenue. The statue has been attributed to Jan van Nost, as have the two pairs of wrestling gladiators on the sides of the lawn. The north-west allée leads to a statue of Diana, a fairly recent acquisition, while the north-east is aligned with distant church tower. This, the alignment of an axis of the garden with a feature of the surrounding countryside, added a distinctly eighteenth-century flavour to the generally older style of the gardens.

Two further main allées stretch across the garden. One lies along the bottom of the dip with, at its western end, a temple brought from Copped Hall in Essex; at the other end the allée leads to one of the garden's most beautiful views, across the lake to a temple with a portico façade. The temple was built by Sir William Chambers and came from Danson Park in Kent. The other cross-allée stretches between the statue of Diana and a statue of Venus and Adonis, by Scheemakers, brought to St Paul's in 1964. The statues of Diana and Hercules are linked by yet another allée forming the north-west boundary of the formal garden; from the open glade round Hercules the vista continues to the east, and the octagonal red-brick gazebo built in 1735 on the north-east corner. The winding, informal paths throughout the wood are mostly eighteenth-century.

In many ways Edward Gilbert's garden was old-fashioned, especially when the strict and simple formality of its vistas was compared with the work of men like Addison, Switzer and Bridgeman. Their kind of formality had clear sympathies with the more natural style that would emerge supreme by the mid-eighteenth century. Because of its rarity the style of St Paul's is of enormous interest today. Not only is it a real garden as opposed to the far larger landscapes of the later eighteenth and early nineteenth century, but it is a garden whose very conception is far removed from those of the nineteenth and, more especially, the twentieth century, where the importance of plants often dominates. The simple harmony between the allées, hedges, statues, temples and trees, the supremacy of design over content, is visually immensely satisfying.

When David Bowes Lyon came to live at St Paul's in 1932 the gardens had begun to decline. He replanted the hedges along the allées, mainly replacing the old hornbeam with beech. Along the eastern edge he replaced the old beech avenue which led up the hill past Venus and Adonis to the octagonal gazebo with limes. The gazebo was restored by Geoffrey Jellicoe after it had been severely damaged by a land mine during the Second World War. In the western part of the gardens a large clearing between the statues of Diana and Venus and Adonis had become overgrown, and with the help of Geoffrey Jellicoe this area was cleared and restored. Part of Edward Gilbert's original design, the open glade is a wonderful surprise feature along the allée between the two statues. The rotunda on a mound at the top and the copy of the famous Greek statue of a discus thrower – always known at St Paul's as 'The Running Footman' – were also original to the garden. The pond was made formal, and steps and sphinx (also from Copped Hall) were added during the garden restoration.

As well as restoring the old formal garden Sir David began planting extensively in the western part of the Woodland Garden. At the same time he started a shrub and herbaceous garden to the west of the house with seventeenth-century barns as a picturesque background. Both in the woodland and this part of the garden his work has been more than complemented by the extensive planting which Simon Bowes-Lyon has carried on since 1961.

Even in these areas of most recent planting, to the west of the house, the formality of the original pattern is evident in one formal allée which stretches away to the focus of a statue of Cain and Abel fighting. Despite its age of two hundred and fifty years and the continual changes which perforce have taken place, the garden retains many of its original characteristics: harmony with the surrounding countryside and the importance of features outside the garden such as the church tower, the central importance of the house as a focus for many of the garden's views and allées, and the balance of concealment followed by surprise discovery which continues to delight visitors. At the same time it is the relationship between old and new which is one of the outstanding features at St Paul's.

WESTWICK COTTAGE

In Leverstock Green, off the A414 between Hemel Hempstead and St Albans
Tel. 0442 52129
Mrs Donald Macqueen

Open one Sunday per year, and by appointment

In 1946 Mrs Macqueen and her late husband bought a pair of derelict cottages that were on the verge of being condemned and in the middle of two acres of wilderness and rubbish. Now the restored cottages stand in similarly transformed surroundings; a garden for all seasons combining plants of specialist interest with a traditional cottage-garden appearance. It shows clearly the success to be enjoyed by planning a garden in close harmony with its house, particularly if the house is the centrepiece, as it is here. Once the debris had been cleared and the ground turfed, the siting of borders, trees and shrubs was all done by Mrs Macqueen from the cottage windows. There has been steady development ever since: as Mrs Macqueen remarks, what started as a three-year plan is still in progress.

The specialist interest in the garden is plants for flower-arranging, at which Mrs Macqueen is a widely known expert. Flowers for cutting were an important requirement in the early stages, added to which have been numerous foliage plants, vital both to Mrs Macqueen's arrangements and the garden. An eye for plant combinations – balance of colour and texture – is a prerequisite for arranging and this talent has been carried over into the garden. Where space is limited the smallest details can assume paramount importance, and simplicity often produces the most successful effect.

A profusion of plants in a well planned setting is always especially striking in a relatively small garden. The main border here starts at the windows of the house and runs alongside the lawn to the far side of the garden. Mainly a summer border with a mixture of herbaceous plants, careful additions to it now provide interest earlier in the year, particularly 'Crown Imperial' lilies. Further variety is given by selected shrubs and small trees at the back: standard wistaria, an amelanchier and a eucalyptus. The main shrub border runs along the far side of the lawn from the cottage, a strong but not uniform boundary to the garden. The narrow border along the front of the cottage has mixed spring bulbs followed by a display of lilies.

There is no reason why gardens of this size cannot contain views full of interest. Looking across the lawn from the herbaceous border the far part of the garden is dominated in the spring by the pink and white blossom of *Prunus* 'Kanzan' and *P.* 'Ukon', set off by colour in the surviving part of an old orchard which Mrs Macqueen retained, dominated by a huge old pear tree. The blending of features and plants for different seasons is continuous; beneath the shade of the cherries are two small rock gardens whose dampness supports primulas and primroses, with hostas and euphorbias for foliage. Beyond the cherries *Acer* 'Brilliantissimum' catches the eye at the back of a mixed spring border – azaleas, heathers, lilies and hellebores. This side of the cottage supports a fine Banksian rose, complemented by a border of shrub roses in front. In another corner of the garden Mrs Macqueen has started a woodland garden. Because of the scale the plants are of especial interest – already there are unusual double primroses and erythroniums.

It is hard to believe that Westwick Cottage was once derelict wasteland. It is one of a number of outstanding small gardens in Leverstock Green which are open to the public together. They provide varied interest, and welcome respite from the rush of traffic on the M1 in the distance.

NORTHAMPTONSHIRE

BOUGHTON HOUSE; THE DOWER HOUSE

Between Weekley and Geddington on the A43, 3 miles north of Kettering
Tel. 0536 82279
The Duke and Duchess of Buccleuch; Sir David and Lady Scott
Boughton House: Open regularly from August to October inclusive
The Dower House: Open two Sundays in the year and by appointment

Between 1683 and 1749 the 1st and 2nd Dukes of Montagu transformed the surroundings of Boughton House. Before he started work on the gardens the 1st Duke, who had been Charles II's Ambassador Extraordinary to France, added the French-inspired north wing now dominating the main approach. His gardens were similarly French-inspired, as was usual at that time, but with some Dutch influence deriving from his gardener, van der Meulen. Van der Meulen laid out a great parterre, decorated with numerous ornaments, he made ponds, fountains and a cascade. The 2nd Duke removed the parterre and added a large lake, the Broad Water, to the west of the house. His passion for avenues earned him the nickname 'John the Planter'. Though his ambition of an avenue straight from Boughton to London, seventy-seven miles away, was never realized, he did pretty well. The Broad Walk, a double and in parts sevenfold avenue of limes stretching westward to beyond the main Stamford – Kettering road is one of two avenues surviving as spectacular evidence of his work. Those that were of elm have disappeared, though over two miles have recently been replanted with limes.

The present Duke, besides restoring the Broad Water in 1976 – an exciting excavation of thousands of tons of silt – and replanting trees in the park, celebrated their Silver Wedding anniversary in 1978 by restoring for the Duchess the Fish Court pond in the old sixteenth-century part of the house, round which she has made a charming White Garden. Irises, hostas and foxgloves surround the pool, and in the borders along the walls are a mixture of plants, with climbing roses, clematis and jasmine on the walls. Against a south-facing wall of the Stable forecourt the Duchess has also made a blue and yellow border: many different delphiniums are among the mixed herbaceous plants.

Clipped yew hedges lead from the north side of the house to the west front, kept suitably simple and dominated by the superb view across the lawn to the Broad Water and lime avenue. To the south of the house the Lily Pond is one of the few surviving features from the 1st Duke of Montagu's work; it is now sheltered all round by mature trees. Boughton exemplifies the ideal balanced harmony between the parkland setting and the smaller, more intimate corners of its garden.

Nothing could smack less of grandeur than the garden of the Dower House – in fact an east wing of Boughton House – made by Sir David Scott, initially with his first wife, and since 1970 with his second wife, Valerie Finnis.

In 1947 the garden left by Sir David's parents consisted of a small area of traditional flower garden in front – to the south – of the house, and a separate vegetable garden. Sir David wanted to make a shrub garden, but ground available for expansion was scarce. In the end he annexed a square beyond the vegetable garden, making the whole area two acres. The new ground had been part of Boughton's deer park, but since 1907, when the deer had been fenced out, it had declined into an overgrown wilderness. Steadily the land was tamed again – with no help, although both Sir David and his wife were over sixty – and planting began in a random fashion round the paths winding into the undergrowth. Conditions were not exactly advantageous, with an alkaline and heavy clay soil and a north-facing slope, but the Scotts were not daunted; in a few years a wide variety of trees and shrubs had become established and the quality of the garden was beginning to emerge.

Sir David's first wife died in 1965, and in 1970 he married Valerie Finnis whose arrival heralded a number of additions to the garden. Her particular interest was in smaller plants. During thirty years at Waterperry, near Oxford, she had already built up a good collection and many of these plants were moved to the Dower House. A series of raised beds, which now total about two hundred yards, were made round the vegetable garden with old railway sleepers. The Scotts' different styles have led to a degree of segregation – superficial only – with the area of shrubs and trees above the vegetable garden becoming known as David's garden. This now contains over fifty island beds and a countless variety of trees and shrubs – flowering, ornamental, and evergreen – for all times of the year. Each bed is named; a recent addition has been 'The Ninety-fifth Birthday Bed', made to celebrate Sir David's birthday in 1982. In the two hundred yards of raised beds around the vegetable garden, parts of which are made up with imported acid soil, there are numerous rare plants. The area in front of the house is still mainly a flower garden; now it includes a number of old stone troughs, and has a more diverse character and appearance.

The combination of two such rare gardeners, the variety and quality in the garden and the production-line proportions of their own propagating will ensure the continuation of this 'home for plants'. The fact that most of it was never planned but evolved naturally is part of its charm. The very evident knowledge and affection which has been lavished upon it over many years always ensure a pleasurable visit.

COTTESBROOKE HALL

10 miles north of Northampton between the A50 and the A508
Tel. 060 124 732

The Hon. Lady Macdonald-Buchanan

Open two or three Sundays in the year

In a county blessed with many fine houses Cottesbrooke has few peers, but somehow it has enjoyed a far less celebrated reputation than many of its neighbours. Built by Sir John Langham Bt in the first decade of the eighteenth century, the house shows interesting similarities of design with Easton Neston near Towcester, which Hawksmoor completed in 1702. The central block of seven bays, linked to arcaded wings enclosing the original south entrance courtyard and surmounted by a flat roof and balustrade, is given great elevation by the Corinthian pilasters. The central axis of Cottesbrooke is aligned with the spire of Brixworth Church, three miles away; Easton Neston is aligned with that of Green's Norton at a similar distance. But an immediate difference between them – and one which also makes Cottesbrooke unusual in a county where local stone has always been the predominant building material – is the deep red brick with which the house is built, highlighting the effect of the stone pilasters. The house was slightly changed at the end of the eighteenth century by the 4th Baronet, who employed Robert Mitchell as his architect. Alterations included the additions of bows to the east and west fronts to accommodate designs for the dining- and drawing-rooms, and Mitchell also built the entrance gates, lodges and the original outstanding bridge over the lake in the large park. The gardens, which were added in the nineteenth century, and have been given especial character by Lady Macdonald-Buchanan, nonetheless blend in with the prevailing eighteenth-century atmosphere.

The main gardens are a series of walks and different areas to the south and west of the house. A number of alterations were made in the early twentieth century but much of the planting has been done by Lady Macdonald-Buchanan since she and her late husband, Sir Reginald, bought Cottesbrooke in 1937. The entrance is now on the north front and the courtyard to the south is planned formally, with clipped yew and four lead figures which Lady Macdonald-Buchanan's father, Lord Woolavington, bought from Stowe when it became a school in 1923. Beyond the courtyard the park stretches to the lake and Mitchell's bridge, of which a replica was made elsewhere in the park when the lodges were moved and the drive approached from a different angle. On the lawn to the east of the courtyard is one of Cottesbrooke's finest trees, a very large tulip tree; to the west the lawn leads to an area of trees and shrubs including rhododendrons and various conifers, ilex, beech, a silver weeping pear, a metasequoia and a *Davidia involucrata*. Beyond here is an unexpected Paved Garden, which Lady Macdonald-Buchanan has planted with small borders of mixed summer flowers – stocks, geraniums, small roses and penstemons – and which gives a lovely view over the park.

Through wrought-iron gates on the west side of the courtyard is an inviting walk mainly enclosed by yew hedges. Along one side stand four more stone figures, also from Stowe, among whom are Socrates and Homer; at the far end is a white seat. Opposite the statues part of the walk is bordered by a brick wall broken by an impressive pair of wrought-iron gates set between brick piers surmounted by eagles. An herbaceous border marches with the wall and turns at right-angles round its corner to become west-facing. The visitor is constantly aware of the garden's well-conceived unity, and subtle links of views or features such as the Paved Garden and this herbaceous border continuing from one area into another. Two terracotta urns stand in front of the herbaceous border and opposite them a pleached lime walk leads to another statue; beyond that the eighteeth-century lodges can be glimpsed on the edge of the park.

The wall mentioned above is part of the Walled Garden where the borders round the circular pool used to be filled with roses but these have been replaced with a variety of trees and shrubs including a number of magnolias and, among some conifers, a cryptomeria. One old-established architectural feature here is the brick pergola in one corner. On either side of the gates leading out south to the Yew Walk are borders of strikingly red geraniums.

There is a smaller pond sunk immediately beneath the west side of the house; mixed borders escort a paved path towards the park; roses, peonies, agapanthus, phlox, alchemilla and spiky yuccas, shaded in one place by an old acacia tree. The whole area of the borders is exceptionally planned – a brick wall along one side, on the other old and evocative Cedars of Lebanon on the lawn, and one of the garden's two weeping beeches among the trees at the far end.

Separated from the main gardens is the Wild Garden on part of the stream flowing through the park. It is planted simply with ornamental trees; especially good are the various acers and cherries. Along the stream are bamboo and gunnera. Beyond the small brick bridge the garden continues to a line of old hornbeams hanging over the water. In the early summer, when the leaves are fresh and the cherry blossom is out, this is a place of quiet, natural beauty.

With their parkland setting and superb house as a centrepiece, the Cottesbrooke gardens have a number of inherited advantages, but it is an indication of the quality of planning that they have developed an individual character and interest, in harmony with but not dominated by their surroundings.

HOLDENBY HOUSE

In Holdenby 7 miles north-west of Northampton off the A50
Tel. 0604 770 786

James Lowther Esq.

Open on Sunday and Bank Holiday Mondays from April to September inclusive, on Thursday in July and August, and by appointment for parties

---

When the Parliamentarian Captain Adam Baynes demolished most of Sir Christopher Hatton's great palace at Holdenby, the stone was sufficient to build a whole street of Northampton.

Hatton, who had been Elizabeth I's Lord Chancellor, had built his house round two enormous courtyards; in its day it was supposed to be the largest house in England. After Hatton's death the house was ceded to the Crown in lieu of his debts, and remained in Royal ownership until the Civil War. In 1647 Charles I was imprisoned at Holdenby but the house reverted to the Crown after the Restoration. Only one range from one of the courtyards had been left by Baynes, and this survives, with some later alterations. In the eighteenth century it had belonged to the 1st Duke of Marlborough; through female descendants it passed to Colonel John Lowther, grandfather of the present owner. The most intriguing remains of the old Elizabethan house are the two arches, dated 1583, now standing in a field to the east; they were originally the entrance arches to the base court leading to the two main courtyards.

The skeleton of Sir Christopher Hatton's gardens, which extended over twenty acres, remains under grass; the plateau, flanked by two raised terraces which he levelled in order to make them, is still visible. In the area closest to the house some smaller gardens have recently been extensively restored, with a stress on their old Elizabethan character. In 1980 Rosemary Verey designed the small, intimate Elizabethan Garden below the west side of the house, now the most enchanting corner of the gardens. Enclosed by yew hedges and by the brick and stone walls of the Kitchen Garden and stables, it contains only plants that were available in 1580 and, characteristic of an Elizabethan garden, many herbs. Opposite the narrow entrance in the yew hedge is a seat enclosed by a yew arch. The central sundial is surrounded by four different thymes, and a simple pattern of four inner and four outer beds. The plants are mainly for foliage effect. The four inner beds have santolina and variegated hollies on the corners and hedges of southernwood along the back. The main area of each of these inner beds is filled with one contemporary blue flower – for instance, cornflower and love-in-the-mist. Along the front are box plants that will form low hedges, and the small alpine strawberry, a delightful ground-cover. The outer beds contain white antirrhinums, taller artichokes and acanthus as well as lavender.

Behind the south yew hedge of this garden the terrace along the front of the house ends most effectively in a curved wall with 'Kiftsgate' and 'Wedding Day' climbing roses trained over it. The walk divides the Elizabethan Garden from the 'Too Too' fragrant border and Croquet Lawn in front of the house. The fragrant border was originally part of a nineteenth-century garden and is named after Lady Annaly's dog which is buried there (Colonel John Lowther married the elder daughter of the 3rd Lord Annaly). Rosemary Verey replanned this border in 1981, concentrating on scented plants, mixing shrubs, herbaceous and herbs: smaller sage, pineapple sage and other herbs cover the ground beneath hybrid musk roses, lilacs and philadelphus. The Croquet Lawn has a shrub border on its east side.

To the east the gravelled walk continues past an iris border below the house walls, with *Magnolia grandiflora*, *M. soulangiana* and wisteria trained against the stonework, to the gardens on the far side of the house. Along a wall built out from the east side is the silver border; this wall behind marks the line of the old palace. Below here yew hedges enclose a lawn with central rosebeds, a fish pond and statue. At the far end here wrought-iron gates lead through a yew hedge to the Elizabethan arches. Although detached from the gardens these are not forgotten; their style is echoed by the seventeenth-century arch over the gateway into the courtyard of the house.

At the bottom of the south-facing slope in front of the house is the lake, one of a line of three ornamental ponds made for the old Elizabethan gardens. The lake has recently been cleared, and willows, rhododendrons and azaleas have been planted round its banks, restoration begun which allows visitors to enjoy an attractive view across the water and up the slope to the house, with its lofty chimneys. Facing north away from the gardens the entrance front provides one of the best views at Holdenby, particularly in the spring – down the sycamore drive thick with daffodils. It has a timeless quality that only serves to underline Holdenby's history.

ROCKINGHAM CASTLE

2 miles north of Corby on the A6003
Tel. 0536 770 326

Commander and Mrs Michael Saunders Watson

Open on Sundays and selected weekdays from Easter to September inclusive

William the Conqueror built Rockingham Castle to command the northern valley of the River Welland. Rockingham was visited regularly by the Norman and Plantagenet Kings – Henry I may have made the first garden at the castle when he ordered a vineyard to be planted in 1100. By the sixteenth century, however, the importance of Rockingham to the monarchy had declined, and the castle was leased to one Edward Watson in 1530. He converted the castle into a house, and it is from this date that the first gardens appeared on their present sites. In 1619 his grandson Sir Lewis Watson purchased the freehold, and the family was established.

Rockingham suffered badly during the Civil War; it was stormed by the Roundheads who occupied the Castle and later demolished the curtain walls and keep. Lewis Watson, 1st Lord Rockingham, returning after the War, used the rubble firstly to fill in the ditch which encircled the north wall of the castle, and the remainder to create a series of terraces, culminating in the landscaped mound on the site of the old keep. Dividing the terraces from the steep drop to the Welland Valley is a feature which may have survived from Edward Watson's garden. The hedges of the Yew Walk are now over four hundred years old: it is called the Elephant Walk as, over the years, the yew has been clipped into great domes resembling elephants. Behind the mound is a circular Rose Garden enclosed by a yew hedge laid out to conform to the design of the Norman keep on which it stands. The date of origin of this garden is not known; it was probably created by Richard Watson in the early nineteenth century.

Beneath the west terrace is the garden in the ravine. Called The Grove in the eighteenth century, it was made into a typical Victorian shrubbery by Richard and Lavinia Watson in the first half of the nineteenth. They also made the last major alterations to the castle, employing Salvin to build the Flag Tower. *Bleak House* may seem a far cry from Rockingham, but Charles Dickens was one of their guests and he was supposed to have seen the ghost of Lady Dedlock in the Elephant Walk; so the garden is mentioned in the book.

The large terrace to the north-west of the house, bounded by the range of building containing the Flag Tower, by the Elephant Walk and the curving outer wall on its far side, has a lawn with perimeter paths whose simplicity intensifies the views beyond. Passing the Elephant Walk, the south boundary of the terrace, one comes to the first main area of flower gardens, the Cross Garden. It was formally laid out by the Rev. Wentworth Watson at the beginning of this century, replacing a Victorian garden of similar but more detailed design. The lawns are divided by paths with clipped hedges of lavender and domes of evergreens; the beds of roses containing floribunda 'Peuneille Poulson'.

On the castle side of the Cross Garden the remains of the old moat are now a Rock Garden, and a path along this side between standard roses leads below The Mount. This too may have been part of Edward Watson's garden: such things were popular features in Tudor times.

Now it is planted with a variety of trees and shrubs, and a later pergola on the far, south, end. Below the pergola another path leads eastwards at right angles, to the circular Rose Garden; the beds are filled with a variety of hybrid teas and surrounded by lawn. Beneath the south-facing wall round part of this lawn is an herbaceous border and a small Herb Garden; climbing rose, *Magnolia grandiflora, Cytisus battandieri* and *Campsis radicans*, the 'Trumpet Vine', are trained on the wall. The Rose Garden looks out to the south on to the Tilting Ground, a lawn planted with a variety of flowering and ornamental trees and shrubs. The Lime Walk leading south along one side of this marks the line of the old castle ramparts. Rockingham is one of the few remaining sites where the full extent of the Normans can be viewed without interruption by later building.

By 1965 the Victorian ravine shrubbery had become hopelessly overgrown. With advice from Kew Gardens, Commander Sir Michael Culme-Seymour (who had inherited from the Reverend Wentworth Watson in 1925) cleared and replanted the area with two hundred species of trees and shrubs. A few of the interesting plants were retained from the nineteenth-century planting – such as the Sikkim spruce, *Picea spinulosa* – but the majority today like the ginkgo and the very fine 'Tree of Heaven', *Ailanthus altissima*, blending beneath the canopy of mature beech and chestnut, were planted by Sir Michael. Woodland informality is a well-conceived contrast to the gardens close to the castle; the path, known as 'Lady Faith Walk', after Sir Michael's wife, leads up the opposite side of the ravine, where vistas of the castle and the Welland Valley open up between the trees before descending to the two ponds, and back up the steep slope to the Elephant Walk. Contrast and yet accord, an embodiment of Rockingham's turbulent history.

WARWICKSHIRE

ADMINGTON HALL

In Admington, 6½ miles south of Stratford-on-Avon between the A34 and the
A46
Tel. 0789 87279
Mr and Mrs J. P. Wilkerson

Open one or two Sundays per year, and by appointment

Admington Hall is shown on the Sheldon Tapestries in the Victoria and
Albert Museum, dated 1590, and the three-gabled north front of the
house could date from then. The more memorable side of the house,
however, faces south; an exceptional Georgian façade was added in the
eighteenth century and this sets the tone for most of the grounds.
Colonel and Mrs Horton bought Admington in 1936 and did much to
build up the garden, as have the Wilkersons who moved here in 1970.

Of immediate interest along the drive past the east side of the house
are the twelve clipped yew trees. They are obviously of considerable age
and represent the twelve Apostles: eleven stand inside the entrance
gateway and the twelfth, Judas, stands outside alone. Beyond the drive,
to the east of the house is the brick walled garden of about one acre: low
box hedges round the vegetable patches impose some old-fashioned
formality, and the old range of stables provide a perfect backdrop to the
north. Along the south wall are Mrs Wilkerson's 'cottage borders'. Her
description is absolutely right for in summer these borders are a mass of
floribunda roses, lupins, delphiniums, lilies and aquilegias, with rambling roses trained along wires behind. The path between them, leading
to an old sundial is perfectly aligned with the Georgian south façade of
the house. The other feature of note in the Walled Garden is the
climbing geranium in the greenhouse, reputed to be over sixty years old;
it gives a spectacular mass of vermilion flowers in summer.

On the South Lawn are two Cedars of Lebanon so positioned as to frame the house to perfection yet without detracting from the view, which Mrs Wilkerson has recently improved enormously by removing the fence which divided the lawn from the paddock to the south and replacing it with a small ha-ha. Replacing the long border on top of a raised wall, she has planted pinks and rock roses, so the only vertical feature here will be the new Cedar of Lebanon planted to mark the three-quarter-century in 1975 and to carry on eventually from the other two. Originally along the east side of the lawn there were double herbaceous borders but one has now been removed to cut down on labour and the other modified to mixed shrubs and herbaceous, an informal mixture probably more suited to this position. Behind the herbaceous plants are 'Nevada' and 'Penelope' roses and viburnum, with larger lilacs and philadelphus behind them and finally flowering trees in the long grass at the back. One of the most attractive features along this border are the groups of sweet peas trained up pea-sticks.

On the west side of the lawn is the Water Garden, originally made by the Hortons and added to by the Wilkersons. From the main pond at one end, almost enveloped by beeches and hostas, the stream flows past a large weeping willow and eventually to a chestnut walk at the bottom of the garden, full of daffodils in spring. Along its course the stream is host to a variety of aquatic plants: primulas, lysitichums, hostas, gunnera and *Caltha polypetala*, as well as a number of dwarf acers. Through the beeches round the main pond a Woodland Walk extends west out of the garden, in which the Wilkersons have replanted extensively with a large variety of trees to replace the elms killed by disease.

After the open lawn, the majestic trees and busy Water Garden, the small enclosure beneath the west side of the house is perfectly secluded. In the narrow border below the wall tulips are followed by peonies, overhung by climbing roses and clematis, including 'Hagley Hybrid' trained on the stonework. Opposite is a yew hedge with a chestnut walk behind. Every garden which possibly can should have such a contemplative corner; in fact the whole garden at Admington has a great many of the features and characteristics so important to an informal country house garden of this style. Without any pretence at being grand, it subtly enhances the qualities of the house while quietly stating its own presence.

ILMINGTON MANOR

In Ilmington, 8 miles south of Stratford-on-Avon between the A34 and A46
Tel. 060 882 230

Dennis Flower Esq.

Open three or four Sundays during the year

Ilmington Manor was restored from a nearly-derelict state by the previous occupant to Mr Flower's parents and it is since they came here in 1919 that the present garden has been created out of the remnants of an old orchard and little else.

It is a typical early twentieth-century garden, given shape by the many yew hedges which form both the boundaries and the enclosures within them. The borders and general layout of the garden are its outstanding features; without a quantity of unusual plants, they are typical of a period when balanced construction was as important as contents.

The gabled stone manor house was built in 1600; the tithe barn of the same period adjoining one end forms the second side of an entrance court. The garden's framework is largely built up round three main axes, two leading away from the house, and one stretching right across the centre of the garden. Opposite the south-facing entrance front a step leads up from the courtyard between low balustraded walls to a path with herbaceous borders on either side and clipped yew columns at the far end. The south lawn beyond, with two old walnut trees, is enclosed with yew hedges. On the west front is the Rose Garden – formality in miniature. It too is enclosed by clipped yew hedges, and the narrow paved path leads uphill from the house between rows of lemon-scented thyme, lavender and standard roses to a stone sundial. Behind the standards are beds of roses, including 'Iceberg' and 'Red Devil', and one pink rose which was one of the originals planted by Mr Flower's parents, and whose name they have never discovered. Beyond the sundial the path continues out of the Rose Garden between yew topiary.

On the north side of the Rose Garden, and facing across the garden, is the summerhouse, focal point for the third and largest axis from the stone seat on the far south side. It is an outstanding vista from the seat between the long Double Rose Border, across the large lawn which dominates the centre of the garden and between the yew hedges of the

87

Rose Garden to the two pillars and tiled octagonal roof of the summer-house, put up in 1924. The double Rose Border was originally herbaceous, but was replaced in the 1960s. It is a spectacular sight in June – 'Arthur Bell', 'Felicia', 'Frühlingsgold', 'Cerise Bouquet', 'Marguerite Hilling' and 'Charles de Mills' to name but some – and the same varieties are planted symmetrically opposite each other on either side of the central path which leads from the steps up from the central lawn, past the garden's second sundial to the stone seat.

The old orchard to the west of the rose borders and central lawn makes for informal contrast, with daffodils and crocuses in the long grass, as does the Dutch Garden west of the Rose Garden so called because it was originally planted with tulips. Today it is more akin to an English cottage garden than a Dutch Garden, for the tulips have been replaced with a carefree mixture of summer flowers: dianthus, small roses and tricolor violas around standard honeysuckle, the only staid notes being the surrounding yew hedges and pattern of paths, to the central statue of two children.

The Flower family have achieved the most important of harmonies, that between house and garden.

PACKWOOD HOUSE

2 miles east of Hockley Heath, off the A34 and 11 miles south-east of Birmingham
Tel. 056 432 024
The National Trust

Open on Wednesday, Sunday and Bank Holiday Mondays from April to September inclusive, and at weekends in October

---

The history of Packwood, as with a number of Britain's old-established gardens, was for many years bound up with legend, and although part of the legend has now been disproved this in no way detracts from the extraordinary and overpowering effect of the rows of huge, clipped trees which fill the famous Yew Garden.

The main area of garden lies immediately to the south of the house, whose roofscape of steep gables and towering brick chimney stacks proclaim its sixteenth-century origins. The timber-framed building was rendered over and subsequently altered and added to, in particular by John Fetherston during the seventeenth century (whose family had lived at, or near, Packwood since the fifteenth century). John Fetherston was in the past credited with originally laying-out not only the brick-walled courtyard called the South Garden, immediately in front of the house and the raised terrace, but also the Yew Garden beyond.

The Yew Garden is said to represent the Sermon on the Mount. The quantity of clipped yews represent The Multitude, divided by a central path. At the far southern end a raised path running from east to west across the garden is flanked by twelve yews, larger than those of The Multitude, known as the Twelve Apostles. In the centre, where the two paths cross, are four enormous trees – the Four Evangelists. Beyond, at the climax of the garden, a spiral path leads between clipped box hedges to the raised Mount, surmounted by a single tree called The Master, or the Pinnacle of the Temple.

While it is likely that the single tree on the Mount and those flanking the raised path immediately beneath it were part of John Fetherston's original plans for the garden, it is now certain that the trees forming The Multitude were not planted until the mid-nineteenth century, when they replaced an existing orchard. But despite this the Yew Garden presents a wonderfully imposing and unique spectacle. So evocative are the ranks of yew columns that the Sermon story is easy to believe.

Although the full extent of John Fetherston's work in the garden is not certain, it is probable that he enclosed the brick-walled South Garden and raised the terrace between it and the Yew Garden; of the four gazebos at each corner of the South Garden, that in the north-east corner is Carolean. We are fortunate in that a plan of 1756 clearly shows the extent of the garden at this time, with the courtyard enclosed and the raised terrace divided in the centre by the flight of elliptical stone steps up to the fine pair of eighteenth-century wrought-iron gates, which now open onto the Yew Garden. Also shown are the thirty arched recesses along the south-facing wall of the terrace, which were 'bee boles' for beehives.

During the eighteenth century the main approach to the house was from the west, where the drive followed a causeway across the lake; parts of a mixed avenue survive today in the park. The most interesting feature on this west side is a plunge bath, built in 1680 and surrounded by a yew hedge, which has always been called the 'Roman Bath'.

From the mid-nineteenth century the Fetherston family leased Packwood until they sold it in 1869. From then on both house and garden went into serious decline until 1905, when the property was bought by Alfred Ash. It was his son, Graham Baron Ash, who presented the property to the National Trust in 1941. Until that time father and son lovingly restored and improved Packwood and it is thanks to them that it survives as it is today.

Graham Baron Ash removed the remnants of the old orchard and in its place completed the planting of yews which now form The Multitude. The raised terrace, which had become virtually smothered with ivy, was cleared and today's herbaceous borders were planted along either side of the paved path. His most important addition was the rectangular Sunk Garden which fills most of the east half of the South Garden. Here narrow borders retained by low brick walls and filled not only with herbaceous plants but also smaller herbs, pinks and pansies, descend to a central lily pond.

The herbaceous borders which Graham Baron Ash planted on either side of the central path leading from the house to the raised terrace were removed during the Second World War to save labour, but beneath the south-facing wall of the South Garden and on one side of the East (entrance) Courtyard, two impressive herbaceous borders have been retained.

As well as bringing the colour of his borders and Sunk Garden to enhance the warm brickwork of the South Garden, Graham Baron Ash restored, and where necessary rebuilt, the four gazebos at each corner – two of them forming the east and west focus of the raised terrace – which are such a special feature of Packwood. In 1935 he added the wrought-iron gates in the west wall of the courtyard to mark the Silver Jubilee of King George V.

Today at Packwood one enjoys the harmony between its charming seventeenth-century features, the improvements and additions by Graham Baron Ash and the later work of the National Trust. And no attempt to distinguish legend from fact is necessary to appreciate the rare beauty of the Yew Garden, whose monolithic trees encourage an appropriate atmosphere of mystery.

SHERBOURNE PARK

3 miles south of Warwick off the A49
Tel. 0926 624 255
Mr Charles and the Hon. Mrs Smith-Ryland

Open on selected Sundays in summer, and by appointment

The garden at Sherbourne Park, planned by Mrs Smith-Ryland since 1960, is a fine demonstration of the art of utilizing what you cannot change. Two features – the attractive house built in 1730 and the spire of the parish church built in 1863 by Sir Gilbert Scott – dictate the axes, with some mature trees as markers.

The east, entrance front of the house is dominated by the view across the ha-ha at the end of the large lawn to the park, in particular to a stand of oak trees. Mrs Smith-Ryland has added a selection of ornamental trees to two old acacias on the north side of the lawn which, when mature, will make a very effective screen; they include *Acer* 'Brilliantissimum', a fastigiate hornbeam and *Betula jacquemontii*. The east façade, with narrow borders in front and climbing roses and clematis trained on the brickwork, is flanked by two low curving walls with statues of a shepherd and shepherdess in front; a small gateway in the south wall leads to the main garden.

The church spire is immediately visible beyond the garden's west boundary wall, as it remains from almost every point on this side of the house. Opposite the house is the Croquet Lawn flanked by large shrub borders which lead the eye down the lime avenue, through the park and over the River Avon. Along its west edge, backed by the swimming-pool wall is a mixed border of pink and mauve: shrub roses, dianthus, campanula, honeysuckle at the house end, and a *Clematis jackmanii* at the far end. The swimming-pool, so often little more than an eyesore in the middle of a garden, has been successfully merged into the rest with *Solanum jasminoides album*, *Cytisus battandieri* and *Romneya coulteri* on the walls, large tubs filled with a mixture of flowers, and the old tiled changing-house at one end, whose roof has all but disappeared beneath a white rambling rose, *Lonicera tragophylla* and a *Campis bignonia*.

From here the garden makes clear deference to the influence of the church; two lawns separated by a wide border of large shrubs and trees stretch in its direction. At the bottom an old yew tree has recently been decorated with Paul's Himalayan Musk rose. Immediately below the swimming-pool one lawn has been planted with an avenue of sorbus leading to a small, formal box parterre totally different from anything else in the garden. Within the low hedges are miniature shrub roses, standard wisteria and honeysuckle, and low grey-leafed plants. The view back to the house and to a screen of mixed trees and shrubs along the north edge of the garden is made most attractive by a copper beech and holm oak.

Directly beneath the churchyard wall is a small White Garden enclosed by yew hedges. Around the central sundial are four columnar junipers with roses, white potentilla, lilies and philadelphus; some of the plants, such as *Carpentaria californica*, *Abutilon vitifolium album* and hebes, suffered badly in the winter of 1981–2 but have now quite recovered and the little garden is a charming variation on a popular theme. Its demure air contrasts strongly with the arboretum, planted with various trees, that surrounds a lake made in 1976 on the south side of the churchyard wall. From the White Garden the other lawn leads back in the direction of the house. Curving rows of silver weeping pears were planted here to mark the Smith-Rylands' Silver Wedding in 1977. The trees, aligned with the steps to the north through the middle of the central tree and shrub border, focus on a sculpture and narrow the prospect south to the park. They also could be seen to mark the twenty-fifth birthday of this garden, designed to provide interest and yet to reduce maintenance and which will steadily improve with maturity.

LONDON
AND THE SOUTH EAST

Kent
London
Surrey
Sussex

LONDON AND THE SOUTH EAST

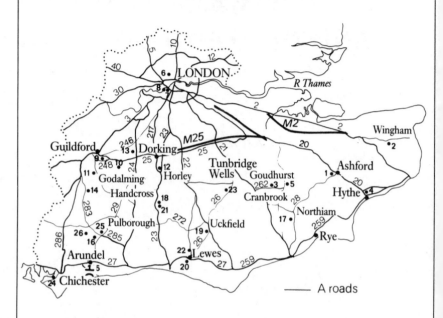

1 Godinton Park
2 Goodnestone Park
3 Ladham House
4 Sandling Park
5 Sissinghurst Castle
6 46 Canonbury Square, N1
7 Strawberry House, W4
8 Walpole House, W4
9 Chilworth Manor
10 Coverwood Cottage and Lakes
11 Hascombe Court
12 The Moorings
13 Polesden Lacey

14 Vann
15 Berri Court
16 Coates Manor
17 Great Dixter
18 The High Beeches
19 Horsted Place
20 Nightingales
21 Nymans
22 Offham House
23 Penns in the Rocks
24 Rymans
25 South Corner House
26 The Upper Lodge

KENT

GODINTON PARK

Off the A20, 1½ miles west of Ashford at Potter's Corner
Tel. 0233 20773
Alan Wyndham Green, Esq.

Open Easter and Sundays from June to September inclusive and by appointment for parties

A sweep of medieval parkland, with ancient oaks and some of the oldest chestnuts in England, endows Godinton with an air of history and romance, which is enhanced by the red-brick gabled house, its form reflected in the gables and battlements of yew round about. The picture tells of Jacobean and Edwardian days, and more ancient times still.

In the eighteenth century Sam Driver, a follower of 'Capability' Brown who also worked at nearby Goodnestone Park, made some alterations to the park; the long poplar avenue away from the house was planted in the nineteenth century. The gardens were laid out at the beginning of this century by Sir Reginald Blomfield, an adherent of formal design, and further alterations were made between the wars by Mr Wyndham Green's grandmother, the Hon. Mrs Bruce Ward. During the Second World War the house was requisitioned by the army; at its end Mr Wyndham Green cleared out the chickens, who had added the garden to their own domain; relaid the lawns, which had been ploughed up; and brought out the statues, which had been safely hidden in the cellar. Since then he has restored and replanted the gardens extensively, retaining their Edwardian character.

· Blomfield's plan for Godinton was a series of varied but interlinking areas on three sides of the house, enclosed by the long, boundary yew hedge which is now such a feature; the hedge was continued to enclose the entrance courtyard on the north side as well. Beside the court, at the northern end of the garden's main axis he laid out a small topiary plat of box and yew round a statue of Pan.

To the south of this topiary garden are the main lawn, the herbaceous borders and the formal pool. An opening in the yew hedge beyond the pool forms a linking prospect or belvoir from the gardens to the park. Blomfield's other main work was to the west of the house where he made alterations to the walled Kitchen Garden to include a converted oast house, and created the Italian Garden, with a loggia, next to it.

Today Blomfield's layout still dominates the gardens and much of the planting adopts his generally formal style. Mr Wyndham Green replanted the Rose Garden immediately to the south of the house, adding smaller foliage plants beneath the floribundas, and renewed many of the plants in the herbaceous borders, where annuals help with the summer display. The long border beneath the outside wall of the the Kitchen Garden has again been replanted, with a stress on foliage and texture in the shrubs and trees.

One of Mr Wyndham Green's most effective additions is the mixed avenue of whitebeams, *Sorbus aria* and flowering cherries along the path which leads to the belvoir. To one side he has partly surrounded the formal pool with weeping willows and a beech hedge; in summer these and the large clumps of water lilies are a fine sight. Blomfield's retention of the Wild Garden was perhaps surprising but it was a most fortunate plan, as today it is the prime glory of Godinton in spring, with its great variety of bulbs beneath the trees; in the autumn there are cyclamen here.

Maintenance of Godinton's twelve acres is often a taxing problem; it takes the three gardeners a month to clip the hedges. But the hard work that is gardening's other name is totally belied by the garden's nostalgic charm and its harmony with house and park.

The formality of the Sunken Garden at Chenies Manor House, Buckinghamshire is a recently laid out reminder of the house's Tudor origins.

Jenkyn Place, Hampshire; the wrought-iron gates provide a suitable introduction to the spaciously proportioned herbaceous borders beyond.

Survivor from a Victorian hey-day, the conservatory at Somerleyton Hall, Suffolk.

Undisturbed tranquillity at The Mill House, Oxfordshire, the house reflected in the water which gives it its name.

The Jacobean gatehouse at The Manor House, Cranborne, Dorset provides an ideal backing for climbers and is integral to the character of this old-established garden.

Camellias in the woodland garden at Englefield House, Berkshire, and a view down the path to the open parkland beyond.

Water lilies, primulas and a host of other acquatic plants adorn the pond at Brook Cottage, Oxfordshire.

The raised terrace at Harington Hall, Lincolnshire, along which Tennyson's love Rose Baring walked, the inspiration for his poem 'Maud'.

Minterne, Dorset; the eighteenth-century balustraded bridge across the stream which divides the Woodland Garden to the left, notable for its old-established rhododendron collection, from the park, stretching away to the right.

One of the four bridges across the stream at Pennyholme which is the backbone of this remote Yorkshire garden.

The Manor House, Whalton, Northumberland; a border of white tulips leads to a pillared summerhouse possibly designed by either Robert Lorimer or Edwin Lutyens, both of whom worked on the house.

The Sunken Garden at Acorn Bank, Cumbria. The stone steps lead to the main area of informal orchard surrounded by borders beneath enclosing stone walls.

Looking past a decorated lead tub at St Anne's Manor, Nottinghamshire, a garden whose variety is reflected in this view.

Springtime at Nymans, Sussex; magnolias and daffodils surround the memorial urn to Oliver Messel.

GOODNESTONE PARK

South of the B2046 between the A2 and Wingham
Tel. 0304 840 218 and 840 107
The Lord and Lady FitzWalter

Open on Monday, Wednesday, Thursday and some Sundays from April to June inclusive, and by appointment

To many visitors Goodnestone possesses a peculiarly English air of romantic beauty. There is a nostalgic quality in the harmony between the old house and its surrounding trees and lawns, and the predominance of evocative, traditional plants of soft colour and heady scent.

In the eighteenth century the open parkland came almost to the walls of the red-brick Queen Anne house; the older trees near the terraced lawns with their wide central stone steps – cedars, many holm oaks (also found by the stable yard), some gnarled sweet chestnuts and Scots pines – are survivors from this time. Stone dressings and an imposing portico were later Georgian additions to the house, and in the 1830s a sunken brick wall was built to the east of the house to divide the garden from the park. The sloping lawns were levelled and terraced at that time. The next period of major activity came after the First World War at the hand of Lord FitzWalter's aunt, Emily FitzWalter, wife of the 20th Lord FitzWalter. Beyond the lawns to the west of the house, on the edge of the wood behind the long carriage drive and avenue of horse chestnuts, she laid out a rockery with huge boulders of York stone and built a pool with flint buttresses for aquatic plants. Nearby she planted the now tall *Magnolia hypoleuca* (*obovata*) and rhododendrons in what is the only small patch of acidic soil in the gardens as well as a still thriving *Nothofagus* 'Fusca', at the time a most unusual tree. Other outstanding plants she brought to Goodnestone include *Abelia triflora*, which hangs over one of the gates into the Walled Garden, and cut-leaf alder, *Alnus glutinosa* 'Imperialis' and *Garrya elliptica* near the house.

Goodnestone was requisitioned by the army during the Second World War; neglect during those years and a serious fire that gutted the top two floors of the house in 1959 were two major problems that Lord and Lady FitzWalter faced after they had moved into the house in the

1950s. Since the 1960s, however, Lady FitzWalter has revived the garden with plantings that have retained its old-fashioned character. New borders contain many effective plant associations; on the lower terrace to the east of the house tall cypresses and pittosporum form an evergreen shelter round *Daphne odora*, with auriculas in the spring and regale lilies later. Above the retaining wall of this terrace are two enormous 'Nevada' roses framing the eastward view of the park from the house in line with fastigiate yews flanking the stone steps. In front of evergreen laurels which mark the boundary between the garden and the woods around the carriage drive more daphnes have been planted with *Magnolia stellata*, *Osmanthus delavayi* and reticulata irises beneath. The rockery and pool gardens had become completely overgrown; after clearing them Lady FitzWalter has planted *Eucryphia* 'Nymansay', *Cornus kousa* and *C. kousa* 'Rubra', *Nyssa sylvatica* and more magnolias. The rockery now contains dwarf acers, and round the pond are arums and primulas, especially the yellow *P. florindae*.

The eighteenth-century Walled Garden at Goodnestone fulfils the ideal of an old-fashioned English garden. Filled with flowers, fruit and vegetables, it is hidden away beyond venerable Cedars of Lebanon, now stripped of their tops and many limbs by gales and snow damage. Entrance to this secret place is gained through a gate set in an unusual flint arch; a profusion of summer flowers and climbers frames an unexpected view out between brick piers to the grey tower of the village church. Old-fashioned roses, outstanding throughout the gardens, here spill out of borders where they mix with clematis trained over wooden arbours, pinks and small grey-leafed plants. On the mellow brick walls climbing roses and clematis compete for space with a white jasmine and more unusual *Jasminum stephanense*, *Solanum jasminoides*, *S. crispum* and *Cytisus battandieri*. The far wall, beneath the church tower, is covered with a huge wisteria; from this section of the garden the central path leads between borders of peonies, hydrangeas, and more roses. To one side a grass path leads down to a decorative wrought-iron seat beneath a wooden arbour, again hung with roses. There is a remarkable free-standing *Magnolia grandiflora*, an *Ilex aquifolium* 'Ferox argentea' and, in a secluded corner, a pink border beneath another of the walls. Behind the yew hedge which backs the Rose Garden to the west a path leads between arches in the brick walls. The gables and tall chimneys of the seventeenth-century Dower House, glimpsed behind the eastern wall, complete the picture. Sheltered by the walls and the woods around the carriage drive the garden in the summer is a medley of soft colours and intoxicating scent.

Visitors to Goodnestone unfailingly get lost in its surrounding maze

of small lanes, the charm in being 'off the beaten track'. The maintenance of more than ten acres is an extremely demanding task, one
tackled by Lord and Lady FitzWalter and John Wellard, their gardener,
and some part-time help for the past twenty years. In describing their
achievements the author can hardly fail to be a little biased: Goodnestone is his parents' home and the garden he was brought up in. Not
only to the family but to many visitors, it bears witness to the care and
affection that have been lavished upon it.

LADHAM HOUSE

Near Goudhurst off the A262
Tel. 0580 211 203
Betty, Lady Jessel

Open on selected Sundays through summer and by appointment

Sir George Jessel, a noted botanist, bought Ladham House about a
century ago. The Heather Garden to the east of the house was laid out
by W. Golding, the Edwardian designer, but most of the large collection
of interesting and unusual trees and shrubs were planted by Lady
Jessel's late husband, another Sir George, who inherited in 1930. There
is sharp contrast between the formal gardens to the south of the house,
and the informal areas beyond the lawn to the north and east, but
throughout there is the stamp of plantsmanship and a high standard of
maintenance.

The main feature of the formal areas is the Double Border, planted by
the present owner, that leads away from the front door of the house.
Flower and foliage are given equal importance, with a stress on grey,
pink, white and yellow; shrub roses and peonies blend with cistus,
potentilla and artemesia. A pair of *Magnolia watsonii*, both over thirty
feet high, stand either side of the stone seat at the border's far end. On
one side of this area is the walled Rose Garden; its formal pattern and
planting have recently been changed, but not the many outstanding wall
plants, including ceanothus, clematis, abutilons, *Azara serrata* and
Carpentaria californica.

The plants of the much larger informal garden, sheltered by a belt of
trees and thriving in the partly-acid loamy soil, have reached a fine

maturity. As well as more recent and exotic additions, there are some impressive standard trees on the large lawn in front of the house, especially beeches, green and copper, limes and oaks. A yew walk leads to a statue of a man and dog, but beyond this any hint of formality recedes completely among the plantings of flowering trees and shrubs. Their variety ensures not only an unusual display through the spring and early summer months, but outstanding autumn colour. Around the far side of the lawn from the house are a number of island beds filled with massed rhododendrons, and *Viburnum plicatum* 'Mariesii', enkianthus and berberis. Towards the Heather Garden one finds more variety: *Styrax japonica*; *Halesia monticola*, larger and more striking than the better-known 'Snowdrop Tree' (*H. carolina*); *Embothrium coccineum*, whose bright red flowers are always spectacular – many maples and, among the flowering shubs, *Cornus florida rubra*, *C. kousa* and eucryphias.

The Bog Garden is a mass of hostas, irises and *Osmunda regalis*, the Royal Fern. All around the dense bank of larger trees, including a very large *Metasequoia glyptostroboides* planted in 1950, malus, cercidiphyllum, *Liquidambar styraciflua* and *Perrotia persica*. From the Bog Garden semi-woodland extends up the side of the garden with paths winding between banks of rhododendrons and azaleas and, in one glade, beneath beech and copper beech and a very large embothrium. One of the outstanding trees in the garden is the *Magnolia campbellii* 'Betty Jessel', which was bought as a seedling from Darjeeling and gained both an Award of Merit and a First Class Certificate from the Royal Horticultural Society. Its flowers are deep red as opposed to the more normal pink of *M. campbellii* and appear towards the end of April.

Lady Jessel says that her main problem in the garden is rabbits, on whom she wages war with the aid of three semi-wild cats and, occasionally, a man with a ferret. Neither this nor any other problem is apparent to the visitor; Ladham is a place of order and attraction that any gardener would wish to emulate.

SANDLING PARK

North-west of Hythe; entrance of the A20
Tel. 0303 66516
Major A. E. Hardy

Open each Sunday in May and the first Sunday in June

Three generations of the Hardy family have tended the garden at Sandling Park since its purchase in 1897 by Major Hardy's father. Many outstanding trees and ponticum rhododendrons dating from the mid-nineteenth century form the basis of the collections, protected by a perimeter of ponticums: a Monterey pine, *Pinus radiata*, a Douglas fir, *Pseudotsuga meziesii* and a Sitka spruce, *Picea sitchensis*, as well as cedars and a very large tulip tree.

The original Georgian house, built for the Deedes family, was bombed in 1942 and after the Second World War Major Hardy built a much smaller replacement on the same site above the lawns which slope down to the main area of the thirty-acre garden. Made on a south- and south-west-facing bank, the garden takes on a colourful appearance at many times of the year. Horticultural interest is spiced from time to time by an occasional oddity, such as the pile of cannon balls cast at the Hardy family's foundry in Yorkshire for the siege of Sebastopol, surmounted by one enormous specimen for which a large enough gun was never found.

Variety is the keynote at Sandling; any of the paths leading into the Woodland Garden will discover something different. The shade provided by the tall beech and oak is ideal for the various plants thriving in the greensand soil, but perhaps the outstanding feature is the enormous banks of rhododendrons and azaleas spread throughout the garden. The collection has been built up steadily since the beginning of the century; the first coloured hybrid, the pink *Rh.* 'Cynthia', was planted in 1900. There are quantities of specie and hybrid plants with their multitude of colours – Major Hardy has raised a number of hybrids himself – and new additions are constantly being made, both by him and his son Alan, who is equally knowledgeable and involved in the garden.

Amongst the rhododendrons and azaleas many other families are well represented, especially magnolias and camellias, many of which are long established and an impressive size. As well as these larger plants the series of small streams and ditches flowing down the slope provides ideal sites for many aquatic species, like the Bog Arum and lysichitums. Different candelabra primulas are particularly good, not only along the streams, but in great splashes of colour round many of the paths. Spring and early-summer here are often breathtaking; daffodils and later bluebells maintain an atmosphere of natural woodland but most spectacular of all is the Maytime carpet of Lily of the Valley.

Among the mature trees there are few to rival the giant alder, *Alnus glutinosa*, which stands over eighty feet high near the middle of the garden, the largest recorded specimen in Europe. Of very different habit is the weeping beech, *Fagus sylvatica* 'Pendula', on the edge of the Woodland Garden by the lawn at the top of the garden. Nearby is the other outstanding beech at Sandling, a cut-leaf beech, *Fagus sylvatica heterophylla*. Also at the top of the lawn, at one side of the house, is the yew-enclosed Rose Garden, ranged along one of the walls of the large walled Kitchen Garden behind.

Such a varied and well established collection, in particular of rhododendrons and azaleas, is rare, and it is exciting to think that the Hardys seem determined to continue expansion.

SISSINGHURST CASTLE

2 miles north-east of Cranbrook, 1 mile east of Sissinghurst village on A262
Tel. 0580 712 850

The National Trust

Open daily except Monday from April until mid-October

The gardens at Sissinghurst have become a legend since they were created by Harold Nicolson and Vita Sackville-West during the 1930s. Of course, it is not only the qualities of the gardens but the controversial and flamboyant careers of their creators which draw people to Sissinghurst; but it is Sissinghurst's instant ability to strike a chord, its intensely nostalgic and romantic mood, the satisfying clearly defined lines of its design balanced by the irrepressible planting, which account for such world-wide fame.

To two minds like those of Harold Nicolson and Vita Sackville-West, both compelled by English history, the potential of Sissinghurst when they bought it in 1930 was immediately evident, despite its delapidated state. For Vita Sackville-West, whose romantic interest in her family and their home at Knole was a life-long obsession, the surviving parts of the Tudor manor at Sissinghurst were irresistible. These remains – the long Main Wing and the Tower to the east, the cottage on the south side of the garden, the Priest's House in the north-east corner and the moat forming a dog-leg around the north-west corner – provided the initial framework for the garden plans.

There is no doubt that it was a creation of rare brilliance, this combination of Harold Nicolson's designs of vistas and walks and Vita Sackville-West's planting. The different parts of the gardens were developed with their own character and appearance, so that the overall effect has been seen as a series of rooms and corridors, similar in concept to Hidcote. Small enclosed areas of busy planting, in the White Garden, the Rose Garden and the Cottage Garden, contrast with the architectural coolness of the courtyard between the Main Wing and the Tower and the pastoral simplicity of the Orchard, which was left filling the large space in the centre of the garden.

The courtyard is dominated by columnar yews echoing the elevation of the Tower, and along the north wall the purple border matches the deep hue of the brickwork. Through the Tower is the Tower Lawn; from here the White Garden beckons from the north and the Rose Garden from the south. The White Garden is planted in front of the Priest's House and its pattern of box-edged beds filled with grey and white plants around a central arched canopy, designed by Harold Nicolson, is one of Sissinghurst's most admired features. The quality of plants here is matched in the Rose Garden, filled with an unrivalled collection of old-fashioned and shrub roses. Harold Nicolson's hand is again evident in its Yew Rondel, the name deriving from the circular floors of the oast-house towers which are such a feature of the Wealden countryside. From the Rondel is one of the garden's most rewarding vistas, back across the Tower Lawn to the White Garden. On the other, south, side the path between yew hedges leads out into the Lime Walk extending east to the Nuttery and, in the south-east corner, the Herb Garden.

There has been a moat at Sissinghurst for five hundred years. The Moat Walk, parallel to the Nuttery, runs along the old wall of this section of the moat, now dry, and leads to the surviving stretch of water. The Moat curves round two sides of the Orchard, whose open informality was a fundamental part of the plan for Sissinghurst: by keeping the central area unobtrusive the diversity of the gardens was thrown into relief. It was Vita Sackville-West's idea to train climbing roses into the old apple trees and to plant a rich variety of spring bulbs as well as autumn crocuses throughout the unmown grass.

The western boundary of the Orchard is a yew hedge, behind which runs the Yew Walk, a narrow path between hedges designed by Harold Nicolson. The Yew Walk's effective 'off-alignment' – it leads from the top of the Rose Garden to the top of the White Garden, the right-angle path into which is a marvellous surprise – is typical of the intricacy of design which plays such a vital part at Sissinghurst.

When Vita Sackville-West died in 1962 she left Sissinghurst to her son Nigel and in 1967 he made it over to the National Trust. The National Trust has at times been criticized for making alterations but these have always been by necessity and, however much of a pilgrimage it may be for garden-lovers, Sissinghurst – like any garden where the planting is so fundamental – could never be preserved as a museum. And despite alterations in its appearance it will never lose the influence of the partnership who created it.

It is just possible that in the future gardens such as Sissinghurst and Hidcote will become unfashionable, but at the moment their popularity, both to visitors and as models and inspiration, is at its zenith.

LONDON

46 CANONBURY SQUARE

London N1

Tel. 01 226 8147

Miss Peggy Carter

Open one or two Sundays in spring and summer, and by appointment

This small London garden lies behind two end of terrace Georgian houses built in 1805, the earliest of the many fine terrace houses in Canonbury Square.

The brick wall that originally divided the two gardens has been partly retained round a small terrace enclosed by vines. The main garden combines trees, shrubs and smaller plants on a carefully planned series of levels and has a small fishpool on one of them.

For such a comparatively small garden there are a surprising quantity of trees, including a large ash in one corner, and *Prunus subhirtella*, *Malus* 'Lemoinei' and *Amalanchier canadensis*. A flagged terrace leads from the house to the lawn flanked by flower borders; particularly good here are the lilies. Although roses don't generally thrive in this garden, notable exceptions are 'Fantin Latour', 'Whitewings' and 'The Garland'. Among the various climbers around the perimeters of the garden the most striking is *Hydrangea petiolaris*.

The lawn ends in a raised bed where a small classical statue of Hebe is attended by two lions; it gives a natural focal point seen from the house. A group of three figures – The Walkers by Arthur Mackenzie – is well sited on a small brick terrace under the *Prunus subhirtella*.

Miss Carter's careful siting of her many plants overcomes the limitations of the garden's size. Each plant and feature is placed to reveal its best points but she has nonetheless created a complete garden, a balanced combination of effects.

STRAWBERRY HOUSE

Chiswick Mall, London W4

Tel. 01 994 3052

Beryl, Countess of Rothes

Open on one Sunday in mid-April and one Sunday in June

The attractive Georgian house overlooks Chiswick Mall and the River Thames but gives little idea of the garden that lies behind. This originally formed part of Chiswick Gardens which pre-dated those at Kew, but the present outstanding layout – one-third of an acre – dates from shortly after the First World War.

The potentially commonplace rectangular shape of the garden is given great variety by the different features and the quantity of plants, which effectively avoid any feeling of uniformity. The paved courtyard beside the house provides an impressive welcome: large camellias, an outstanding feature of the garden, on both sides, and a *Hydrangea petiolaris* trained on one wall. From the courtyard steps lead up between imposing gate-piers to the central lawn and the main vista of the garden, across a circular pond with a statue of the Goose Girl, along the brick path and through the pergola to a small statue at the far end, a natural focal point from the courtyard, giving an illusion of distance. It is only close to the statue that one realizes it stands between two compost boxes.

The pergola is the largest single feature in the garden. Trained over it are wisteria, climbing roses and clematis, as well as *Abutilon megapotamicum* on one of the pillars, and there are many ground-cover plants roundabout. A number of large trees provide both height to the general appearance of the garden, and a canopy to shade some of the smaller plants beneath. They include magnolias, an old mulberry, cherries, and two old pear trees.

The garden is effectively designed with axes on both sides of the main, central one. To the east of the central lawn and borders a seat is backed by a gorgeous bank of camellias. The size of many of the plants shows that they must be of considerable age, possibly planted soon after the garden was planned. Looking north from the seat one sees two smaller ponds, separated by a sunken bed of irises and candelabra primulas. One pond has a single jet fountain, the other has a statue of a minstrel boy with pan pipes; these also are surrounded by irises and other damp-loving plants.

Under the mulberry tree on the north-west of the garden it has been possible to grow a camellia, mahonia, stephandra and ceanothus, with a groundcover of woodruffe, ivy and wild strawberries.

Apart from the camellias the main summer feature are the raised mixed flower borders of the central lawn; tree peonies have been planted behind them. Throughout summer clematis and climbing roses provide a continuous display along the walls that enclose the whole garden, although the yellow flowers of the tall *Fremontodendron californicum* on the east side are the real highlight. Despite the fact that most of the garden is dry and shady it has been possible to grow a large variety of shrubs by adding peat and leaf-mould. Together with the features described, such plantings make this a town garden with unusual depth of content and interest.

WALPOLE HOUSE

Chiswick Mall, London W4
Tel. 01 994 2297
Mr and Mrs J. H. Benson

Open on two Sundays in summer

Walpole House, with its imposing façades of red brick, is mainly Queen Anne but made round an originally medieval building. It occupies a similarly enviable Thames-side position to its neighbour, Strawberry House, though its garden is considerably larger. Lawns and mature trees, a central path flanked by stone pedestals, all successfully disguise the urban surroundings and promote an atmosphere of almost rural peace only just disturbed by the hum of traffic along the Great West Road and jets flying overhead en route to Heathrow Airport.

Outstanding among the mature trees are the two fastigiate poplars which have attained spectacular height in contrast to the spreading mulberry tree close by the house; there is also a tulip tree, a eucalyptus, and acers at the back of the garden. Much of the present garden was planned by Mr Benson's grandmother, in particular the area of paving stones in front of the house, and the steps up to the lawn.

Shrub roses border the east side of the lawn but the main area of planting is on the west side, beyond metal arbours on which climbing roses are trained. A large pond is surrounded by densely planted irises, many of which are also planted in groups of a single colour on little islands in the pond. Beneath a wall on one side of the pond is a deep border of herbaceous plants.

The garden is at its best in summer after a fine display of spring bulbs, but whatever the season the greatest attraction is to find a mature garden, larger than the usual rectangle, right in the middle of London.

SURREY

CHILWORTH MANOR

In Chilworth, 3½ miles south-east of Guildford off the A248
Tel. 0483 61414
Lady Heald

Open on selected days in summer, and by appointment

A long history, punctuated by the strong influences of successive characters is a valuable and instantly recognizable quality in a garden. Chilworth Manor gardens have this air of establishment and have moreover survived periods of neglect to provide a framework for modern additions.

The oldest parts of the manor house, in particular the south front facing entrance drive, date from the seventeenth century and were built by Vincent Randyll, a gunpowder maker and the oldest parts of the garden, other than the monastic stew ponds to the south-west, date from his time at Chilworth. It is possible that John Evelyn, the diarist, visited here – his family were also gunpowder makers in this part of Surrey.

In all, the gardens descend from the north in seven levels. It is difficult completely to distinguish between the seventeenth-century parts of the garden, and those added later by Chilworth's best known and most colourful occupant, Sarah, Duchess of Marlborough, who owned the property between 1721 and 1744. The present enclosed garden to the north of the house is called the Duchess's Garden, and she built the present north front of the house, with its rather eccentric imbalance between pilasters and windows. A map of 1728 showing a number of Chilworth's present outstanding features is invaluable. It shows three gardens to the north of the house, an enclosed central Flower Garden opposite the north front, with a Kitchen Garden to the east and an

109

orchard on the other side. The latter two have gone but the Duchess's Garden survives in its original layout – three terraces and surrounding walls, including the huge retaining wall along the west side which, because of the slope of the ground, rises to twenty-five feet at the end closest to the house. It represents a great success in overcoming the considerable challenge of its construction at that time. The clairvoyée in the wall at the top of the Duchess's Garden would seem to date from the seventeenth century, as possibly do the huge Irish yews on the terraces in front.

The present three levels of the Duchess's Garden are lawn, but above each of the three ascending retaining walls are the original terraces. On these, old apple trees produce a sea of blossom in the spring; daffodils and aubretia are followed in the summer by roses and other plants training over the stonework. One of the flights of steps is flanked by huge senecio.

Outside the enormous west wall of the Duchess's Garden is a mixed border, much of which is being re-planted. Behind its blend of shrubs and herbaceous plants some of the old climbing roses reach to the top of the wall. On the next level down the seventeenth- and eighteenth-century parts of the house meet at a small paved courtyard. Climbers on the walls here include roses, ceanothus and vines; peaceful seats among the tubs of plants look over the lawn to the sloping parkland. Lower down again in the largest part of the garden that slopes past the west side of the house a silver and white border is planned; below this is the area round the old ponds, where a Rockery was added in the nineteenth century. Much of this area of trees and shrubs is being restored to open up plantings of rhododendrons and azaleas, primulas and other damp-loving plants round the water. There are many outstanding mature trees here, too, including oaks, a Californian redwood, a *Magnolia grandiflora* and *Choisya ternata*, the Mexican orange. Two other fine trees are the tulip tree and catalpa planted by Lady Heald, the latter planted in 1952 to mark the accession of The Queen.

Ten acres is a large area for any one gardener with occasional help, but at the moment considerable work is being done to restore the borders and some of the more overgrown areas on the edges of the garden, work that can only enhance even further Chilworth's historical features and associations that are so much a part of its peaceful atmosphere.

COVERWOOD COTTAGE AND LAKES

Peaslake Road, Ewhurst, 7 miles south-west of Dorking off the A25
Tel. 0306 731 103
C. G. Metson Esq.

Open two Sundays in May

Coverwood Gardens were originally laid out in 1909 for M. Stephens, an ink magnate, in an imposing position on a long, wooded, south-facing ridge. The gardens are owned by Mr Metson, who bought the estate in 1957. The cottage has its own smaller garden of about one and a half acres, designed and planted by Mr Metson and his late wife in 1978, and paths lead from here past Mr Metson's farm to the ten acres of the Bog and Water Garden beyond.

The cottage garden extends in a south-easterly direction along a slope, backed to the north by tall trees. These include good specimens of *Cedrus atlantica* (blue cedar), *Aesculus indica* (Indian chestnut) and a tall *Liriodendrun tulipifera* (tulip tree), an ideal backdrop. A long mixed border stretches along the top of the garden to a set of wrought-iron gates at the far end. On the slope below is a small Arboretum whose varied trees include *Prunus subhirtella* 'Autumnalis', *Cornus florida*, *Malus* 'Golden Hornet', *Laburnum voissii*, *Ginkgo biloba* and a number of *Crataegus*. Closer to the cottage, to its east, a small lawn is flanked on the upper side by a retaining wall which supports a border of shrubs, including a mixture of floribunda roses and daphnes, and on the lower side by roses trained against a wooden pergola. Below the cottage the steep slope has been banked up to allow room for a wide terrace border; the slope is bounded on its lower side by a clipped holly hedge.

The cottage garden has already achieved considerable maturity, and has many interesting plants, but in a sense it is primarily a prelude for the Bog and Water Garden, the main path to which leads along a huge beech hedge stretching down the slope from the cottage. This garden was originally laid out in 1910 by the construction of four lakes of varying sizes descending from springs. Views across the water, and the woodland nature of the area, give the garden a natural charm which is enhanced by the quantities of plants, particularly rhododendrons and azaleas, which have been added.

The lakes extend from south-east to north-west, each with its own character and surroundings; beyond, to the south, paths lead through an azalea wood into the Woodland Garden which extends round to an area of springs at the top, east end. The Woodland Garden has a great variety of interesting trees: *Sequoiadendron giganteum*, *Stewartia gemmata*, *Davidia involucrata*, *Oxydendron arboreum*, and many others. The perpetual dampness of this area is shown by the stand of *Taxodium distichums* on the east side of the upper lake. This lake, with its water lilies, has the most striking surroundings – a long arbour with stone columns curving along its north-west side and opposite the huge form of an old rhododendron in front of two towering wellingtonias. Mature trees are a notable feature around the waterside, and the second lake is overhung by a deep purple copper beech. Down the line of lakes the planting gets steadily thinner, blending in with the natural woodland, to the lowest and largest lake, at the far end of which spurs of woodland curve in from either side.

The combination of greensand soil and damp conditions ensures that as well as the rhododendrons and azaleas a variety of other ericaceous plants thrive. On either side of the paths winding through the woodland area, banks of larger rhododendrons and azaleas are highlighted by a great variety of hostas, lily-of-the-valley and trilliums. Lysichitums, both white and yellow, and *Gunnera manicata*, are outstanding among the damp-loving plants along the various streams, in many places blending their luxurious leaves with candelabra primulas.

Where a gale recently damaged the trees in one part of the woodland the open ground has now been replanted with a variety of young trees, which have added considerable interest to the area; they include sorbus, sweet chestnuts, nothofagus, prunus and various varieties of oak. Their youthful shapes contrast with a stand of towering beech and Scots pines to one side, but this balance of large and small trees and other plants is a strong characteristic of the Water and Woodland Gardens.

HASCOMBE COURT

3½ miles south-east of Godalming off the B2130
Tel. 0486 32254
Mr and Mrs M. E. Pinto

Open on selected days in summer

In its heyday Hascombe Court must have been one of the outstanding house and garden combinations of the early twentieth century. The site in itself is commanding – steeply sloping ground to the east with spectacular views across wooded hills, as there are from the end of the lawn on the south front. But a decade or so of steady decline showed how vulnerable gardens are to neglect, particularly when the anticipated garden labour is no longer available. At one stage Hascombe was in danger of being left in the hands of property developers who wanted to divide it into three separate units. Since they came to Hascombe in 1979, however, the Pintos have embarked on extensive and adventurous restoration exciting to see and they have undoubtedly saved one of Surrey's finest gardens.

The house, designed by Coleridge, a student of Lutyens, in 1906 is one of his outstanding large country houses, built of brick and timber with a steeply sloping tiled roof – all materials typical of Lutyens' style. While the main entrance and courtyard on the north front are impressive, almost forbidding, the front extending towards the lawns is more relaxed. It has two bays, from one of which Coleridge built a Pergola extending to the west. On the east side he made a brick Loggia, the roof of which formed a balustraded balcony for the first-floor windows.

A huge north–south axis was laid out in the garden with double herbaceous borders over a hundred yards long extending from the north entrance courtyard, and another pair of borders of similar proportions stretching either side of the lawn to the south. The planting of these borders was planned by Gertrude Jekyll, as was the planting of the terraces below the east front. Then in the 1920s Sir John Jarvis 1st Bt, planned considerable extensions to the gardens, mainly to the east and to the north and south borders. He was assisted by Percy Cane whose plan, drawn up in 1925, still exists.

Cane's most impressive addition was the Japanese Garden on the steep slope below the east front. This garden, with its huge boulders of imported rock, was constructed by workers from Jarrow on Tyneside whom Jarvis brought down to Hascombe during the Depression, part of an idea known as 'The Surrey Scheme' by which Jarvis and others found temporary jobs for five thousand unemployed.

Between the wars there were twelve gardeners, one of whom spent two months in the early summer exclusively watering the banks of rhododendrons that stretched along the hill to the south of the Japanese Garden. Such a regime, and a large garden with much detailed planting, was bound to be susceptible to post-war conditions. Mr and Mrs Jacobs, who bought Hascombe in 1950, continued the standard for some years but after the death of Mr Jacobs the gardens declined until the Pintos began their restoration.

The double borders to the north of the house are in the process of restoration; they now lead to a summerhouse. Behind the yew hedge on the west side is the large walled Kitchen Garden. The yew hedge along the east side is backed by an avenue of flowering cherries planned by Cane, and beyond these are two small hedge-enclosed gardens: a Paved Garden with a formal central pool, acers and shrub roses; and a formal Rose Garden. Formality ends with the wide glade stretching from here east to a distant terrace on the ridge of the hill. This is a Woodland Garden planned by Jarvis on the same scale as the herbaceous borders but contrastingly informal. Along the glade are many cedars, and on either side conifers, birches, acers, flowering cherries and more unusual trees, such as a eucryphia. All these have now attained considerable size, especially the acers.

From the hilltop terrace the views are spectacular, and Brenda's Walk, named after one of Sir John Jarvis's daughters, leads back to the east front. Formality returns to the two terraces here, designed by Cane; the lower one is balustraded with acers at either end and a central pool and lion's head fountain set in the retaining wall. Below the terraces the tumbling levels of the Japanese Garden have been considerably restored, rock plant shaded by old Japanese maples replacing the weeds and moss that had obscured many of the rocks. The Japanese summerhouse at the bottom is also restored.

The herbaceous borders to the south of the house, always called the Colour Borders, are now grassed over and lawn stretches unbroken to a far terrace. East of this lawn paths lead into woodland filled with magnolias, camellias, rhododendrons and azaleas. Originally these trees were all planted along different levels as a series of walks, an orderliness now partly restored by clearing. Even so, the semi-wild state of the now enormous plants is wonderfully picturesque – fifteen-foot camellias,

white and red intertwined, and unruly rhododendrons romping downhill through the trees. There are unusual trees in all the various
woodland parts of the gardens, including embothrium, eucalyptus,
nothofagus and *Cryptomeria japonica* 'Spiralis'; the acers throughout are
outstanding.

Not all the original features of Hascombe's twenty acres can be
restored, but Jekyll's Lavender Walk, pergola and her southern herbaceous border, have been; the results so far are impressive, and a just
reward for a garden which, with its house, is supremely representative of
a period and its style.

THE MOORINGS

In Russells Crescent, Horley near the town centre, between the A23 and the
B2036
Tel. 02934 5371
Dr and Mrs C. J. F. L. Williamson

Open on the last weekend of June, and by appointment

On first impression the surroundings of The Moorings do not appear
greatly encouraging for the creation of a garden: in the middle of a town,
four hundred yards from the railway station and less than a thousand
yards from the terminal buildings of Gatwick Airport. The ground is flat
and much of the soil undrainable clay. But Dr Williamson is as
philosophical about the problems as he is about the creation of his one-
acre garden which he describes as a 'non-specialist general practition-
er's garden'. It is a totally modern garden, far removed from idyllic rural
surroundings, and its degree of maintenance is dictated by a demanding
and time-consuming career. Nevertheless, over the last twenty years Dr
Williamson has built it up to be full of interesting plants within an
atmosphere of enclosed peace that defies jets, trains and urban life.

Dr Williamson has avoided the temptation to overcompensate for
these setbacks by filling his garden to the point of obscuring layout and
individual plants. The terrace along the main garden front is highlighted
by a selection of interesting plants trained against the house, in
particular a *Magnolia lennei*, a *Carpentaria californica*, and a palm,
Trachycarpus fortunei. The large lawn instils a feeling of space before the

main area of planting which begins with the Rose Garden on its far side: modern and old-fashioned shrub roses are surrounded by ramblers trained on wooden trellis-work; 'Constance Spry' is one of the most striking varieties. Beyond the Rose Garden paths lead into different areas of the garden, and despite the small size there is much variety. The path along one side of the garden leads to a pool surrounded by hostas and other water-loving plants backed by some trees from the old apple orchard. A golden catalpa is one of the striking trees that Dr Williamson has planted in this part: there is also a paulownia, a tulip tree and a beautiful variegated poplar. They all help to break the line of vision and set up an impression of depth and space. At the far end away from the house is a small vegetable garden.

The main grass path beyond the Rose Garden down the centre of the garden is Dr Williamson's most successful creation. The path is secluded by mixed borders of overhanging trees, of shrubs and herbaceous plants – conifers, both prostrate and columnar, acers and lilacs, some rhododendrons, peonies, shrub roses, and a variety of herbaceous, including eremurus and phlox. One problem in small gardens is that plants very often get too large, so many of the trees at The Moorings were chosen with care to grow upwards rather than outwards, but in the borders this is not so much of a problem and a slightly overgrown appearance, especially among the larger trees and shrubs, only serves to enhance the air of enclosure. Elsewhere in the garden are a large weeping willow, nothofagus, several robinias and a silver weeping pear; and hardy hybrid rhododendrons interplanted with *Hydrangea sargentiana* beneath mature oaks form an effective boundary to the garden. Between this boundary and the main border is the garden's second, smaller lawn displaying more standard trees: a ginkgo, a fastigiate blue cedar, a davidia, a eucalyptus and a weeping elm.

Much of Dr Williamson's success derives from his sensitivity in choosing and arranging his plants, and not a little from a wry sense of humour, retained despite the failure of many plants to cope with the soil conditions. 'At the end of the garden,' he remarked, 'is the only rising ground, some three to four feet high, where I grow my rock plants and contemplate the view.' The words belie a great enthusiasm for his plot, and a view well worth seeing.

POLESDEN LACEY

3 miles north-west of Dorking, off the A246
Tel. (Bookham) 58203
The National Trust

Open daily all year

Polesden Lacey was one of the last outposts of Edwardian country house life. Today that is still the main characteristic of the eminently comfortable house and its gardens, large parts of which were either planned for display or for produce. The Hon. Mrs Ronnie Greville, whose husband, son of the 2nd Lord Greville, had bought Polesden Lacey in 1906, kept up the gardens and continued to entertain lavishly after Captain Greville's death in 1908 until the Second World War. Since they took on the property in 1942, the National Trust have retained most of Polesden's Edwardian additions without allowing them unduly to dominate older parts of the grounds.

Polesden Lacey is blessed with a superb setting on the south-west-facing slope of the North Downs; some of the planting dates from the eighteenth century but mainly from the early nineteenth century, when the present house was built. The first house at Polesden was built in 1632 and it was this house that the playwright, Richard Brinsley Sheridan, bought in 1796. His great contribution to Polesden Lacey is the Long Walk which he extended from an earlier terrace dated 1761. Now it stretches east along the valley for over a quarter of a mile, from tall columns surmounted by lions to a Doric portico at the far end. The old house disappeared when Sheridan's son sold the property to Joseph Bonsor in 1819 and he it was who built the present Regency villa, designed by Thomas Cubitt, between 1821 and 1823. After the house, the grounds: between 1824 and 1825 Bonsor planted over twenty thousand trees, and gave Polesden Lacey its setting both round the house and in the parkland – particularly in the Mole valley to the south. He also built the Walled Gardens and many of the cottages.

When the Grevilles bought Polesden Lacey, Bonsor's house was nearly a century old, and his trees – beeches that thrived in the well-drained chalk soil, limes and others – were mature. Captain Greville's lavish plans, drawings of which hang in the house, were not implemen-

117

ted but significant alterations were made to the gardens, particularly round the house and the Walled Gardens. Most of these alterations were planned by Mrs Greville and carried out by an impressive team of gardeners, thirty-eight before the First World War and still fourteen in 1938. The household regime appears to have been strict, with notices forbidding staff to walk on the lawns; a first offence incurred a fine of 2s 6d, the second apparently brought dismissal. Most of her alterations remain, as does the extensive collection of statuary and sculptures she brought to the gardens. The flower gardens continue to reflect the lavish scale of Edwardian leisured life and only some areas of garden produce such as the glasshouses which used between thirty and forty tons of coke a year during the 1930s, have been discontinued.

The colonnaded south front covered, like the other fronts, with wall plants including: ceanothus, euonymus, escallonia, *Clematis armandii* 'Snowdrift' and *Eccremocarpus scaber*, looks out over lawns sloping to the park and valley. One of Mrs Greville's additions was the box-edged borders close to the house for annuals – between fifteen hundred and two thousand are still raised every year. Beyond the lawn to the west of the house is a small enclosure where Mrs Greville is buried. Her tomb is bordered by four eighteenth-century French statues of The Seasons, and the hallowed ground is enclosed on three sides by yew hedges. Entry to the Walled Gardens is through a pair of wrought-iron gates, matched by a similar pair at the far end of the central path, and immediately the Rose Garden, laid out for Mrs Greville, assumes its dominant role within the brick walls. Rose borders beneath them and four large areas of roses divided by paths covered by the National Trust, in typical Edwardian style, by wooden pergolas contain nearly two and a half thousand rose plants. Climbers are trained on the walls and along the pergolas that meet at the central fourteenth-century Venetian well-head. The varieties are mostly those grown in the Edwardian era, their colours softer than many modern varieties; but although Mrs Greville had all the beds dug out to eighteen inches in 1938 and filled with loam, some do not thrive in the shallow soil. Beyond the Rose Garden the central path continues, crossed at one point by a deep peony border; to one side are smaller lavender and iris gardens enclosed by yew hedges. At the west end of the path is an herbaceous border and outside the West Gates the Winter Garden and unique thatched bridge over the estate road, sunk deep enough in 1861 for the estate traffic to be invisible from the gardens, something Mrs Greville no doubt approved.

Along the outside of the lower, south wall is the Long Herbaceous Border, much enhanced by early flowering shrubs trained against the brick. Originally the border was one of a pair along the path, but even without its partner the proportions are impressive. It is clear, though, that some of the plants struggle against the wind, poor soil and watering difficulties. In the south-west corner of the Croquet Lawn below the Long Herbaceous border is an impressive statue of Diana, goddess of hunting, and beyond her the Rock Garden, built of vast boulders of Westmorland stone.

1923 saw what was perhaps the zenith of Mrs Greville's career at Polesden Lacey, when the Duke and Duchess of York (later King George VI and Queen Elizabeth) spent part of their honeymoon here. Golf appears to have been the order of the day; still, during their stay they each planted a blue spruce, *Picea pungens* 'Glauca', on the western side of the great sloping lawn below the south front. These are now among a collection of 'Royal' trees including more blue spruces – one planted by King Alfonso XIII of Spain in 1920 and the other by King Fuad of Egypt in 1929; not surprisingly, as doyen of his age, King Edward VII had planted two trees – a black mulberry in 1907 and a copper beech in 1909. As well as these illustrious standards a great many other trees were planted at Polesden Lacey in Greville times, including many of the cedars around the house and other conifers.

Polesden Lacey's thirty acres are now maintained by a staff of five men, headed by Mr Hall. Maintained and renewed, like the beech avenue along the drive, where young trees were planted outside the old ones before the latter were felled, the preservation of these older features ensures the continuance of a wonderful setting for Polesden Lacey's particular glories.

VANN

Near Chiddingfold, 6 miles south of Godalming off the A283
Tel. 0428 793 413
Mr and Mrs M. B. Caroe

Open for selected weeks from April to July inclusive, and by appointment

---

The gardens at Vann were mainly laid out by the present owner's grandparents, Mr and Mrs W. D. Caroe, with the added interest of help and advice from their friend and neighbour, Gertrude Jekyll. The gardens Caroe planned were typical of the early twentieth-century – a series of rather formal features round the house leading to more 'natural' areas further off by the stream and pond; so when Gertrude Jekyll was consulted in 1911 much of the work was complete, but her influence on parts of the lower Water Garden is still evident. Since then much of the garden has been replanted by the Caroes' parents and themselves.

The original sixteenth-century house was altered in the early seventeenth century, added to again in 1695 and yet again in the 1730s. Caroe's own alterations increased the size of the house considerably and all these changes and additions account for the heterogeneous mixture of brick, tile and timber styles which lends a particular charm to Vann. Caroe incorporated the outbuildings and old barn into the house in 1907, forming a small courtyard round the eponymous Old Garden. It has a distinct cottage-garden appearance within the walls and the hornbeam hedges, added in 1963. Mixing around clipped yews moored amongst old roses are peonies, hardy fuchsias and small campanulas; close to the barn is a border of blue and yellow, with grey foliage plants. Behind the silver weeping pear the hornbeam hedge has been trained into an arch; the central brick path leads out to the road through a small gate beneath another arch, of clipped yew. This corner makes an attractive and intimate introduction to the rest of the garden.

One of the main features on the other, east, side of the house is the Pergola. Its piers of Bargate stone and the wooden beams above have roses, clematis and other climbers trained over them; below are mixed borders with many bulbs and plants of striking foliage: hostas, ferns and geraniums as well as hellebores and iris. Along with the Pergola the outstanding formal feature at Vann is the Yew Walk, leading up to the north-east corner of the garden. Yew hedges enclose paths to either side of narrow rosebeds with a sunken stream along the middle; marsh marigolds, primulas, ferns, cowslips and primroses thrive in the perpetually damp ground, and aubretia spreads all over the stream's retaining stone walls. At the far, north, end a bronze winged angel attended by standard wisterias stands beneath a large red-leafed acer: there were two acers but the garden suffers from honey-fungus, which killed the other.

The pond immediately south of the Yew Walk, into which the stream flows, is surrounded by oaks and aquatic plants, and the Water Garden stretches along the course of the small stream as it flows out again south, with the path crossing back and forth. Native oaks and birches offset the more exotic acers and flowering cherries, and in the unmown grass around are numerous varieties of wild and naturalized flowers: snowdrops, bluebells, celandines, erythroniums, fritillarias, daffodils, irises and lilies. In the spring this blend of flowers beneath the blossom clearly reveals the restrained hand of Gertrude Jekyll, for whom such plant associations were constantly absorbing. Today some of the earlier strictness in planting has gone.

Mrs W. D. Caroe kept the furthest area of the Water Garden purely white – any intruders such as purple fritillarias or foxgloves were rigorously removed. Now they mix freely, but it is her influence that accounts for the profusion of snowdrops, white irises and lilies.

Blending easily into the surrounding woodland and countryside, Vann is a garden full of natural charms that suit the multifarious styles of the house. The Caroes are replanning part of the area beyond the orchard to the north of the house. The style of garden allows labour-saving methods of maintenance and they manage with the minimum of part-time help, but this does not detract from their achievement in keeping nearly five acres to their present standard.

SUSSEX

BERRI COURT

In Yapton, 5 miles south-west of Arundel, off the A224
Tel. 0243 551 663
Mr and Mrs J. C. Turner

Open on selected days in summer

Since they came to Berri Court in 1970 the Turners have largely re-
planned the garden of just over two acres into eleven small gardens
linked together on all sides of the attractive and originally Queen Anne
house. Visitors will not be surprised to learn that Mr Turner runs a
commercial nursery, because plantsmanship is an immediately
recognizable quality at Berri Court: throughout the gardens one of the
main attractions is the way areas in a traditional style blend with more
modern features and plants.

The undulating ground on either side of the drive which approaches
from the south lends itself to the flowing style of island beds and lawns in
this area to the south and west of the house. The style extends right
round to the south-east of the house where it ends in front of the high
south-facing flint wall of the Walled Garden with a border of many
interesting and tender plants, including a Chilean berberis, a small bush
myrtle and the larger *Myrtus luma*. In one corner of the border is *Cornus
controversa* 'Variegata'. The Turners took out a number of mature trees
in parts of the garden, to open up space but retained the Scots pines
along the drive and one huge *Cupressus macrocarpa*, of which a whole row
was taken out on the roadside. The macrocarpa dates from around 1890
and stands near the bottom of the small formal garden below the terrace
along the south front of the house. This is kept simple with lawn and a
central pool. On one side is a small Dutch summerhouse; on another in
summer is a border of white tulips backed by low clipped box, which sets

off nicely Berri Court's white exterior. Across the drive from the formal garden are two small beds of old-fashioned roses. As well as looking for quality in the many individual plants, the Turners have laid out the garden with a careful eye, to provide enticing views along the paths between borders. This is most true of the area round the grass tennis court on the west side of the house. Very sensibly the nets round the court are removable in order not to detract from the view. Behind the court is a long deep border filled with mixed trees and shrubs, well planned with the tall trees at the back. At the back also are eucryphias, and outstanding eucalyptus. Many of the garden's large collection of rhododendrons and azaleas, both specie and hybrids, are contained in this border. Other eucalyptus – there are over ten different varieties – have been planted with large shrub roses in the area of long grass to the north of the house and have attained a spectacular size in a very short time.

Below the tennis court, many of the island beds have more rhododendrons and azaleas; in one is the early-flowering variety *Rh.* 'Christmas Cheer', whose pink flowers, fading to white, are such an encouraging sight in winter when spring is still a long way off. Around a large beech tree, bamboo has been planted effectively as low groundcover, indeed all the island beds are noteworthy for their use of groundcover; at the bottom of the garden, groups of small Solomon's Seal are closely planted near a stand of snake-bark maples and eucalyptuses, and in other borders hostas and *Trillium grandiflora* fill the spaces between larger shrubs. The most charming groundcover plant of all in the garden is *Cornus canadensis*, the 'Creeping Dogwood', with its tiny, white star flowers.

Wrought-iron gates open from the east side of the house on to the Walled Garden, a simple plan of borders round a large lawn. There are many old-fashioned climbing roses on the walls, and against the house a wisteria and *Actinidia kolomikta*. Among the large trees here are an enormous prunus and *Magnolia delavayi*, but there is also a variety of shrubs and smaller plants. Through a small gate on the north side of the garden is the miniature Rose Garden, planted with small shrub roses.

Some of the tender plants in the garden have already been mentioned, but there are also an *Acacia dealbata* and an azara trained on the walls of the house. It is a garden where the year-round interest of plants is carefully balanced with an awareness of the effect of their position and appearance, a point well illustrated by the two laburnum trees spreading over the old part of the house; they can be seen and appreciated immediately one enters the gate. Berri Court is certainly a garden that deserves to be better known.

COATES MANOR

Near Fittleworth off the B2138
Tel. 079 882 356
Mrs G. H. Thorp

Open on selected days in May and July, and by appointment

Everything about the garden at Coates Manor denotes the care and thoughtfulness with which it was planned. Since 1960, when the Thorps came to live at the small Elizabethan manor house, Mrs Thorp has sought to grow a garden in keeping with its character, at the same time as accepting certain limitations – a need to keep maintenance to a minimum, long dry spells in summer and occasional sharp, late frosts. When they came to Coates Manor both garden and house were in a state of disrepair, but patient work has brought results. Like so many people, Mrs Thorp was not an experienced gardener when she started but has steadily overcome this by a combination of enthusiastic gleaning of ideas and knowledge from a variety of sources and the undoubted application of a discerning eye and mind.

It is the association of trees and shrubs and their foliages that is the garden's outstanding feature. Prior experience as a flower arranger in particular taught Mrs Thorp the value of foliage and foliage combinations. The garden is thus never a blaze of colour but everywhere the juxtapositions and general layout are constantly striking and, especially with her judicious use of evergreen plants, Mrs Thorp has achieved a garden with much year-round interest.

The subtle foliage blends are immediately apparent in the border round the lawn in front of the south-east facing entrance to the house, principally purple, gold and grey: the brilliant *Gleditsia triacanthos* 'Sunburst' is underplanted with purple and green sage, with *Elaeagnus pungens* 'Maculata' and a closely-clipped bay tree. A copper beech stands to the west beyond the gate from the gleditsia, and beneath a sorbus is *Cornus nuttallii*. The late frosts have discouraged the growing of acers, with their limitless variety of foliage, but this has certainly not proved an obvious setback to Mrs Thorp, for there are plenty of ideal alternatives of which the cornus family is one. In front of the entrance is a small paved terrace with white hebes to either side, and white agapanthus underplanted with white campanulas across the terrace.

The walnut tree that replaced an old apple tree on the front lawn was a typically thoughtful piece of planting, for walnuts were thought to have been introduced into England in 1590, the year the house was built.

A long brick wall, covered with many interesting climbers, stretches to the north-east, away from the corner of the house, dividing this area in front from the main garden to the north-west. From the front an open archway, covered in variegated ivy, frames a *Liquidambar styraciflua* 'Worplesden' perfectly positioned on the lawn to the north-west. From the main garden side the archway is equally highlighted, by a clipped copper beech hedge with standard wisteria on one side; and in the corner to the right of the archway the umbrella-like canopy of *Prunus* 'Tsubama', raised by Captain Collingwood Ingram, is complemented by the spreading evergreen *Juniperis media* 'Pfitzeriana Aurea' beneath.

Opposite the house a small enclosed path leads off the lawn to the north-west to the simple grouping of an old vase with a blue spruce, a ginkgo, camellias and hostas. The lawn on this side of the house was originally a tennis court. Now one of the main borders has been extended into the grass; in fact Mrs Thorp has created an effective tunnel with the path of lawn curving between the headland of this border, reaching out to the sundial, and another border below. Some of the best combinations in the garden are of blue and yellow, and one of the best in this border is a 'Mount Etna Broom' and golden catalpa with a blue spruce and blue agapanthus below. Here are also a number of cornus, including *C. kousa chinensis* and *C. mas variegata* and one of the few acers, *A. griseum*. Close by is a birch; its white bark is even more striking than that of the cinnamon coloured acer, a cross between *B. jacquemontii* and *B. papyrifera* and its form similar to the latter variety.

The long hedge of Lawson cypress along the north-west boundary of the garden is broken at one point by a low brick wall revealing a view out to fields and the town of Petworth. The greater surprise, however, is the small Walled Garden in front of the south-west corner of the house, hidden from sight from the main lawn. This is a corner for quiet enjoyment on a warm summer evening, though it can be seen from the house. This garden has been given year-round floral interest. On the walls are clematis 'Perle d'Azur', variegated jasmine, honeysuckles, ceanothus, a purple vine and climbing hydrangea. As well as choisya and philadelphus in the borders, there are penstemmons, sage, violas and alliums; and a cleodendrum bears witness to its sheltered position.

The many combinations of plants throughout the garden hold ideas for visitors, and within the area of only one acre Mrs Thorp has unquestionably succeeded in providing an appropriate setting for a small, unassuming manor house, which was her original aim.

GREAT DIXTER

½ mile north of Northiam and 8 miles north-west of Rye off the A28
Tel. 0797 43107
The Lloyd family

Open daily (not Monday except Bank Holidays) from April to mid-October inclusive

Great Dixter's reputation as one of the outstanding gardens of the twentieth century is firmly established, due to the creative flair of four people. The old manor house was bought in 1910 by Nathaniel Lloyd. With the help of his friend, Edwin Lutyens, he embarked on the restoration of the house and design of the garden; their work was carried on after Lloyd's death by his wife and later by their son Christopher Lloyd, whose influence has been most striking in recent years.

The oldest part of Great Dixter was built between 1450 and 1464; the hand of Lutyens in restoring the house and farm buildings is easily discernible and is integral to the setting of the garden. His designs of steps, walls and archways there link the various areas and levels together with great ingenuity. Still, his plans did not always meet with approval, and in many places where Lutyens suggested brick walls Nathaniel Lloyd preferred to use yew hedges which, with the yew topiary, now give Great Dixter so much of its character. Nathaniel Lloyd also designed the Sunken Garden, with the restored farm buildings on two sides.

One of Mrs Lloyd's main influences on the garden were the areas of meadow grass planted with wild flowers, among which are many other naturalized varieties. But perhaps the decisive influence has been Christopher Lloyd's enormous knowledge as a plantsman, developed partly through his work at Great Dixter. It is refreshing to meet someone who revels in labour-intensive gardening, and the detail of his planting certainly evinces no illusions about the effort needed to gain the desired results in a garden of this nature.

The architectural appearance of the yew hedges, topiary and walls, together with the enormously varied planting link all the different areas – the old Vegetable Garden, the Sunken Garden, the Walled Garden, the main lawn with topiary, the Rose Garden, the orchard and the Long Border, they lie all around the house, a central presence of brick, timber and deep, tiled roof whose style and colour are caught up by the barn, the oast and other farm buildings. The two brick arches, one leading from the Sunken Garden to the small Walled Garden, and from the Walled Garden to the lawn below, are outstanding examples of Lutyens' work. In many areas, however, it is Christopher Lloyd's more recent planting that really sets off the older framework made by his father and Lutyens' to best advantage. This is particularly evident in the Sunken Garden, where the climbers and wall plants include abutilons, clematis, vine and *Schisandra grandiflora fubrifolia*; and in the borders round the paths and the ornamental pool containing olearia, skimmias, hydrangeas, ferns and bamboos.

On the west side of the large lawn to the south of the house, now dominated by Nathaniel Lloyd's yew topiary, is the Rose Garden: small, intimate, divided by stone paths and containing a well chosen collection of old-fashioned and old hybrid tea roses, with a loggia converted out of an old cowshed. Clematis are the ideal accompaniment to the roses. The Orchard beyond the Rose Garden is an area of the meadow planting developed so successfully by Mrs Lloyd: naturalized crocus, narcissi, fritillarias, anemones, wild orchids and autumn crocus. Their random appearance among the long grass here, as well as in a small sunken area between the house and Vegetable Garden and in the lawns leading to the front door, contrasts with more closely planted parts such as the Long Border, planned for almost year-round interest.

The Long Border, stretching away from the house to the east, is perhaps Christopher Lloyd's outstanding achievement. Essentially a mixed herbaceous and shrub border, its appearance has been evolved over many years, with constant attention to the balance of individual plants and colourful associations within the overall picture. Despite its size of over two hundred feet long and fifteen feet wide there are no open spaces; the levels of the border descend from small trees and tall shrubs at the back, through lower shrubs and herbaceous plants to the smaller herbaceous and perennials, many of which spread out on to the flagstone path.

The old Vegetable Garden above the Long Border to the north has been partly developed as a supply area for the adjoining nursery. The yew hedges and topiary, a dominant feature in this part of the garden, reinforce the formality of this series of small enclosures, many of the paths hedged in by box, yet there is no real conflict of style between the work of Nathaniel Lloyd and Lutyens and their successors. This is perhaps the outstanding overall characteristic of Great Dixter, that the different works of the strong characters who have influenced its development are so harmoniously reconciled within the framework of the old buildings.

THE HIGH BEECHES

1 mile east of Handcross on the B2110
Tel. 0444 400 589
The Hon. Edward and Mrs Boscawen

Open on Bank Holiday Monday in spring, one Sunday in autumn and all year by
appointment for parties

The High Beeches is a legacy of one of England's foremost gardening
families, the Loders, and in particular of Colonel Loder who began
gardening there in 1906 and continued until his death in 1966. Less well
known than the Loders' other two gardens in Sussex – Wakehurst Place,
now leased by the National Trust to the Royal Botanic Garden, Kew,
and Leonardslee, still owned by the Loder family – the quality of the
High Beeches' individual plants and the manner in which they enhance
the natural woodland setting, make it a woodland garden *par excellence*.

Sir Robert Loder bought the High Beeches in 1849 and considerably
expanded both the existing house and garden. His children shared his
interest in plants and two of his sons, Edmund and Gerald, began their
own gardens at Leonardslee and Wakehurst Place respectively. The
High Beeches was inherited by Sir Robert's second son, Wilfred, who
died in 1902. His widow lived in the house until she died in 1943 and left
it to their son, Colonel Loder, who had by his early twenties shown a
keen interest in and knowledge of gardening.

Colonel Loder did not look to the existing formal gardens laid out
round the house by his grandfather, but instead turned his attention to
the site of about twenty-five acres some distance to the south of the
house beyond a large meadow on a south-facing slope. The slope was
well wooded and dropped to a stream valley, with smaller streams fed by
numerous natural springs dividing the slope at intervals. The naturally
varied contours of the site needed no alteration but by judiciously
thinning the mature trees Colonel Loder opened up vistas and allowed
space for the addition of more colourful and unusual specimens, taking
the fullest advantage of the terrain to display the wonderful variety of
individual plants to their best advantage.

Throughout the High Beeches trees and shrubs, either individually
or in groups, are used architecturally so that the garden has as much
strength in its design and framework as in its contents. One of the most

striking characteristics here is that there is no overcrowding: the plants have been built up around a series of open glades and vistas whose spaciousness only enhances their effect, the numerous shades of colour, both of flower and foliage. Colonel Loder was acquisitive and highly selective, and knowing many of the other leading gardeners and garden-owners of his day he had access to plants of the highest quality from many species. As well as spring and early summer flowering plants he concentrated on autumn colour, so that today the garden is arguably at its most impressive during those months.

Colonel Loder was unmarried, thus on his death there were no children to inherit his garden. It was on the point of being acquired by timber merchants when Mr and Mrs Boscawen, who knew the garden and recognized its unique qualities, stepped in. The original house had been burnt out after it was hit by an aeroplane in 1942 and they built a smaller new one, designed by Claud Phillimore, facing south across the large meadow to the garden in the valley.

Approaching from the two fish ponds on the western edge of the meadow the first view into the garden is down the ghyll of a small stream, fed from the ponds by a waterfall and kept open, save for the broad trunks of mature beeches, to allow the eye to carry into different areas of the garden beyond. To the west is Forrest's Bridge, named after the famous plant-hunter, George Forrest, and surrounded by various rhododendrons, many of which he introduced from the Himalayas and China. Just beyond the bridge is one of his most renowned introductions, the brilliant red *Rhododendron griersonianum*.

One might expect in a Loder garden an area dominated by the famous 'Loderi' hybrid rhododendrons, and the Loderi Walk lies beyond Forrest's Bridge, near the garden's western edge. In contrast to these more closely-planted areas is the Glade, which stretches through the bottom of the garden: mature deciduous trees blend with various evergreens outstanding of which is the *Picea breweriana* 'Brewer's Weeping Spruce' on the rising ground to the south. Beyond this is the largest of the many nothofagus which Colonel Loder introduced to the garden, *Nothofagus dombeyi*. Close to the Glade is a circular pond; its edges are planted with primulas, many varieties of which are outstanding throughout the garden, gunnera and other damp-loving plants. A path leads east from the pond over the new bridge and past one of the garden's largest and most impressive trees, a fern-leaf beech, to one of the oldest areas of planting around an oak seat. Here three plants close to each other illustrate High Beeches' depth and quality of contents: *Cornus kousa*, raised from seed collected by Ernest Wilson and planted in 1914; a superb *Davidia involucrata*, the 'Pocket-handkerchief Tree', perhaps Wilson's most famous introduction to Britain; and finally the rarest of the trio, *Tetracentron sinense*, particularly remarkable for its foliage and catkins.

The stress on autumn foliage is evident throughout the garden. The Boscawens have undertaken to grow national collections of pieris and stewartia, the latter with particularly good autumn colour. As well as a great variety of acers there are parrotias and liquidambars and, among late-flowering trees, eucryphias. One of the best autumn trees is a specimen of *Nyssa sylvatica*, now over fifty feet tall, whose leaves turn bright red. But even visiting the garden at this late time of the year, one passes the Magnolia Garden, close to the path out into the meadow, dominated by a huge tree of *M. sargentiana robusta*, which, together with the equally large specimen of *M. veitchii* above the house, is the largest of many magnolias here. While the quality of Colonel Loder's original planting and landscaping are very evident, the manner in which they have been subsequently maintained and developed by Mr and Mrs Boscawen deserves equal praise.

HORSTED PLACE

1 mile south of Uckfield on the A26
Tel. 082 575 315
Lady Rupert Nevill

Open at Easter, and three days a week from May to September inclusive

---

Horsted has an enviable site, with views to the South Downs, but is ideally protected from the north and north-east by a belt of beech trees. The gardens of Horsted Place, designed by Dawkes and built in 1851 by George Myers who carried out much of Pugin's work, were redesigned in the 1960s by Sir Geoffrey Jellicoe in keeping with their Victorian origins. The part-formality of some of Jellicoe's layout is balanced today by Lady Rupert's love of blending flowers, of filling her borders to overflowing and in particular of filling the garden with scent to create 'a delicious pot-pourri of scent for all the seasons'.

Within Jellicoe's design for the area round the main lawn to the east of the house, the sense of movement given by the iron baskets of roses and pansies 'floating' across the lawn was inspired by the work of the modern

Brazilian landscape designer, Roberto Burle Marx, yet based on Humphry Repton's plans for the gardens of the Brighton Pavilion. There are also rose-covered arches to lead the eye; their profusion of flowers in June is cleverly highlighted by the foliage of weeping silver pear, purple acer and other striking plants in the border at the lawn's eastern end. Along the south side of the lawn are the cool green leaves of Jellicoe's pleached limes, with 'windows' cut to give views over the parkland. The paved terrace round the south and east sides of the house demonstrates perfectly Lady Rupert's pot-pourri planning and avoidance of open spaces: rose and cistuses mix with junipers, pinks, campanulas and other plants beneath two large magnolias trained on the walls.

There is a strong air of secrecy in the garden – a number of paths lead off from the far, east end of the main lawn to 'unknown' destinations. An apple tunnel curves to a metal rotunda from the garden of an old house in Richmond. It is set among lavender and rosemary and hung with the clusters of small climbing roses and montana clematis, a perfect example of how much more a garden gives when abundant scent is added to visual effect. Another path leads through a small gate in a hornbeam hedge, bending between high lilacs, rhododendrons, azaleas and camellias to the Round Garden, hidden and shaded by huge beech and sycamore. The circular lawn is surrounded by thick shrubberies with occasional highlights of colour – philadelphus and, later in the year, hydrangeas – amongst the varying green shades of numerous hostas, some with luxuriantly large leaves, and clipped box. The Round Garden proves afresh the simple beauty of green – in such an enclosed woodland setting other colour is almost superfluous.

The trees and shrubs along the path leading from the south-east side of the garden to the old Orchard and Walled Garden jostle to overhang the path. It is an over-fussy visitor who minds having to hold aside a branch of scented azalea or hydrangea, or to lift the branch of a magnolia prodigal with white flowers. Only the eucryphias, with their slightly fastigiate habit, do not interfere with one's progress to the far end where immediate reward is a view back across the fields and lime hedge to the Gothick house. The somewhat intoxicating effect of proximity to the plants and their scent and colour is at its strongest along the curving embrace to the laburnum passage, beneath the benison of 'Golden Rain'. Near one end of this passage is a huge copper beech, perhaps the most striking tree at Horsted; but there are also some limes of a similar age, and younger trees, including a liquidambar and a tulip tree, all with particularly attractive foliage.

Horsted is a garden with many personal associations for Lady Rupert and her late husband, Lord Rupert, to whom it meant so much. It is a garden created for enjoyment and relaxation and its appeal is immediate. The blends of colour and scent may seem unstudied and sometimes near-riotous but they prove irresistible, conjuring in the memory perpetual summer.

NIGHTINGALES

In The Avenue, Kingston, 2½ miles south-west of Lewes off the A27
Tel. 07916 5673
Mr and Mrs Geoffrey Hudson

Open on two Sundays in summer, and by appointment

Nightingales is an outstanding example of what can be done with a very small area in a short time. The garden totals half an acre, and other than the old trees at the bottom nothing was planted before 1977. Since then the Hudsons have succeeded in collecting a host of different plants, and at the same time working round a pattern so that from many angles the garden seems larger than it is.

Few visitors would believe that half an acre could contain a shrub rose garden, a pond garden, three herbaceous borders, tender shrubs and climbers, standard trees, a paved terrace and large selection of terracotta pots with plants from the Mediterranean.

By keeping a central area open with lawn and surrounding it with different features, Mr Hudson has imposed form and ensured that there is something of interest throughout the year. Successful plant associations are particularly important in a small garden such as this: not only do they provide overall harmony but striking combinations, such as the large white clematis 'Marie Boisselot' trained into the bright blue Ceanothus, 'Southmead', become outstanding features.

The two standard trees on the lawn, a *Cotoneaster cornubia* and a *Betula papyrifera* with striking white bark, show that even in restricted space single trees planted for effect can certainly be accommodated. Both are under-planted with cyclamen. The other main trees are *Prunus sargentii*, *P. serrula*, *P. Tai Haku*, *Eucalyptus gunnii*, *Robinia* 'Frisia' and the old Bramley apple and rowan. A tiny pond containing a golden carox is surrounded by candelabra primulas, hellebores, angelica and shrub roses: 'Frühlingsgold', 'Nevada', *moyesii*, 'Canary Bird' and *rubrifolia*.

There are many geranium species including the native Lancastriense, and in the herbaceous border along one side of the lawn is a varied crowd of plants large and small. Tender plants are a *Carpentaria Californica*, a callistemon from Australia, *Salvia neurepia*, yuccas, plentiful cistuses, crinum and agapanthus. The York stone terrace is surrounded by a brick wall on which grow a vine, *Campsis radicans* and *Jasminum polyanthum* and *J. revolutum*. A flagstone path edged with lavender and pinks passes through an arch, at the base of which is *Romneya coulteri*, to a fuchsia border.

Even in half an acre such a concentration of plants, many of them challenging to grow, requires much work, and from their healthy state and immaculate appearance one would certainly not believe that Mr Hudson is only able to garden at weekends. His main problem is a lack of space to test all his ideas, but the garden is expanding into the area behind the house, which will soon be totally surrounded. Gardeners with larger or smaller space at their disposal will find much here to intrigue and delight them.

NYMANS

At Handcross, off A23/M23
Tel. 0444 400 321
The National Trust

Open daily except Monday and Friday from April to October inclusive

---

Since Ludwig Messel acquired Nymans in 1890 the garden has been steadily built up by three generations of his family to become one of the most acclaimed in England. Ludwig Messel's son Leonard bequeathed the property to the National Trust on his death in 1953 since when his daughter, Anne, Countess of Rosse, has been the garden's director.

Ludwig Messel began work on the gardens straight away. The Pinetum, curving in a horse-shoe round a daffodil meadow, was planted in the 1890s and now the ranks of spire-like conifers form a dense belt of varying shades of green; their gloomy atmosphere was lightened by Leonard's extensive clearing and replanting with rhododendrons, eucryphias and other more decorative varieties. Ludwig also planted the Lime Avenue along the garden's east boundary, leading from the Pinetum meadow to a balustraded prospect commanding views to the

Weald and South Downs. At the same time he developed the orchards and Walled Garden, divided by the now-famous Summer Borders.

The Sunken Garden with its architecture and formal beds, the Heather Garden and the Japanese Garden were all Ludwig's work, so that by the time of his death in 1916 Nymans had both the foundations for future generations to work upon, and also an extensive collection of plants. He had been helped by various members of his family: his architect brother Alfred designed the temple in the Pinetum; his daughter Muriel worked with William Robinson on the design of the Summer Borders centred on the four towers of yew topiary topped with huge crowns and the Italian fountain; and most of all his son Leonard, who inherited Nymans and cared for it for nearly forty years thereafter.

Among Leonard Messel's additions, as well as further quantities of plants to rival those collected by his father, were the stone Italian loggia and Byzantine urn in the Sunken Garden to the south-east of the house. Leonard became an enthusiastic sponsor of plant-collecting trips and many of the more unusual plants at Nymans, both specie and hybrid, of which he raised a great number himself, originate from seed collected in Asia, South America and Australasia.

It is the variety and yet fluid unity of Nymans' different parts, the changes of mood they inspire combined with the exceptional collections of rare plants, which make it such a complete garden. Even the loss of the house, almost completely destroyed by fire in 1947 and now a gaunt shell save for one occupied wing, has not detracted from the garden's appearance; in fact the house has become even more part of the garden, its ruined walls and empty windows romantically clad with climbers.

Since Lady Rosse's and the National Trust's management of the gardens there have been further replanting and new additions, so that today the number and variety of plants defy enumeration. Parts of the garden retain a distinctly period appearance, particularly the Heather Garden and Rock Garden towards the south corner of the gardens, and the Pergola beyond them built of huge stone pillars in the 1890s and now covered by old wisterias; these were originally specially imported from Japan as tiny seedlings.

Among the more recent additions is the Rose Garden to the north-west of the Walled Garden, planted with old-fashioned roses by Lady Rosse in the 1960s. The Walled Garden itself is a medley of colour and scent which steadily builds up from the spring bulbs and early flowering trees to the climax of the Summer Borders in full flower. Nymens epitomizes those many outstanding twentieth-century gardens created with new and previously unobtainable plants but made into something essentially English.

OFFHAM HOUSE

In Offham, 2 miles north of Lewes on the A275
Tel. 07916 4824

Mr and Mrs H. S. Taylor and Mr and Mrs H. N. A. Goodman

Open one or two Sundays in summer

Offham House beneath the South Downs is an example of the limitless permutations possible within English architecture at its best. At first sight from the drive the house has a late seventeenth-century façade of typical proportions: two storeys and an attic with dormer windows, seven bays of which the central three project; but Offham is completed to perfection in an unusual manner by a facing of knapped flint, accentuated by the white surrounds to the windows and the white stone dressing of the projections. The garden front has two bays, the flintwork alternates with brick and the roof is of tiles rather than slate, and strongly hipped. The gardens round the house have been partly simplified for ease of maintenance but, linked by wide areas of lawn they still have abundant interest, particularly the various borders and hedges.

As admirable complement to the proportions of the entrance façade, the garden to the front is a simple rectangular lawn with a circular pool and a fountain, and one of the two statues at Offham by Sir Charles Wheeler. Around the lawn are some of the interesting trees – many planted by previous owners of Offham – including sorbus, a copper beech and a silver weeping pear.

The main garden is a series of terraces on sloping ground below a large lawn. Two flights of stone steps lead from the main lawn, which has clearly been levelled at one stage, perhaps for a tennis court or croquet lawn. One flight, covered by clematis over a wooden arbour, gives a marvellous long perspective downhill, between rose borders to a sundial surmounted by Atlas, to a double herbaceous border and fountain at the bottom. The bank along the bottom edge of the lawn here is planted with mixed spring bulbs and wild flowers; below the bank a grass path leads to an old marble seat, an outstanding piece of allegorical art. The scrollwork of Leda and the Swan is dated 1676, contemporary with the house. There are many fine views from the main lawn, the effect of which are heightened by the various hedges, especially by the high box hedge behind this seat.

The other main axis of the garden is at right-angles with the rose borders and herbaceous borders. A great peony border, a hundred yards long is the garden's most spectacular feature, the same ten-foot-high box hedge behind off-setting the deep colours of these flowers and the more delicate aquilegias planted amongst them. On the other side of the border's path are beds of sweet williams with roses trained along fencing. The profusion of all these plants in mid-summer within the formal layout is all the more striking.

There is much else of interest at Offham besides the various borders. There are smaller combinations, like the *Ceanothus* 'Italian Skies' underplanted with miniature pinks either side of the other flight of steps from the main lawn, this one overhung by a rose arbour. In contrast to the spaciousness elsewhere the Lily Pond, with its pretty fountain and statue, is almost enclosed, surrounded by lilacs, cherries and shrub roses as well as an old ceanothus and *Cornus macrophylla*. At the far end of the garden is an informally planted Arboretum with many weeping trees: maples, ash, lime, beech, birches and stands of copper beech. An old orchard has a number of Judas trees planted among the apples and cherries, and there is a walled vegetable garden, immaculately planted and maintained.

Somehow, it is no surprise to hear that Trollope was a visitor here. There is an ordered vitality about the place that would have suited him and yet is individual. Offham House accomplishes enchantment, and deserves to be better known.

PENNS IN THE ROCKS

Near Groombridge, 7 miles south-west of Tunbridge Wells off the A26
Tel. 08927 6244
The Lord and Lady Gibson

Open two or three days during summer

Dramatic surroundings of ancient rocks and steep, closely wooded hillsides seem an exercise in the Romantic amid the generally domestic landscape of the Kent and Sussex borders. Huge outcrops of Tunbridge Wells sandstone to the south of the house, originally called Rocks Farm dominate the site. Indeed the rocks – reckoned to be about five thousand years old – pre-date any sort of house; as Christopher Hussey observed, in *Country Life*, they may even have been the site of Mesolithic huntsmen's dwellings. The house belonged to Guglielma Springett from Ringmer, wife of William Penn, the celebrated Quaker after whom Pennsylvania was named; she bought the farm as part of her dowry and during the time of their successors, between 1672 and 1762, the present name emerged.

The mood of the place appealed to the imagination of the poet Dorothy Wellesley, also an enthusiastic gardener, who moved here in 1925. Parts of her garden survive and her memory is kept alive by the Temple of Friendship she built at the top of the slope opposite the south front of the house. It is dedicated to her fellow writers including W. B. Yeats, Walter de la Mare and Vita Sackville-West; their names are inscribed on stone slabs along with an ode to poets by the Elizabethan Thomas Nash, a tablet with some lines from W. B. Yeats and a matching tablet of some of Dorothy Wellesley's own poetry.

The Gibsons bought Penns in the Rocks in 1956, since when they have made considerable alterations. They moved the entrance from the east front, which is part of the early nineteenth-century additions to the house, to the neat Georgian façade of the south front, added by William Penn's grandson, also William, in 1737. In many of their alterations to the gardens they were advised by Lanning Roper, and now there is variety all round the house – a Walled Garden beyond the courtyard on the east, the Rocks and Woodland Garden to the south and, beyond the West Lawn, the park sloping to the lake.

The rectangular Walled Garden is planned on a strong north–south axis between pairs of wrought-iron gates. In Dorothy Wellesley's time the plan was more detailed and labour-intensive, with geometric flowerbeds in the lawn, and flowering cherries with beds of irises beneath flanking the central path. Now the main borders are round the walls, an informal mixture of flowers, roses, herbaceous and some shrubs and climbers, including in one corner a huge wisteria. The cherries have been replaced with pears underplanted with alternate beds of single pink rugosa roses and santolinas and rue, edged with box; and the lawns are broken only by a variety of standard trees. The axis continues through the north gates to an informally planted mixed orchard, and through the south gates into an avenue of flowering crab apples extending to a semi-circular stone seat before a curving yew hedge.

To the east of the avenue is a rectangular swimming pool typical of the inter-war period, with a pavilion backing the Walled Garden and at the other end a seat, designed by Lutyens, with flanked clipped bay trees in

Versailles tubs on either side. West of the avenue are informal plantings of various flowering fruit trees, shrub roses, philadelphus and lilacs along the valley of a small stream leading to the Lily Pond with a fountain of a boy riding a dolphin. A well-positioned limestone urn amongst these shrubs, placed with a long straight vista back to the house, and the simple wooden gate at the top of the garden (based on one at Pusey House, Oxfordshire) which is both an appropriate and attractive boundary with the fields, say much for the Gibsons' attention to detail.

The view out from the south front – or back from the Temple of Friendship – gives possibly the most long-lasting image of Penns in the Rocks, particularly in spring and early summer, when the glade is filled with daffodils and Lent lilies, then the scented yellow *Rhododendron luteum*. But the Gibsons have created another view, past the huge cedar on the West Lawn, that is a piece of pure eighteenth-century landscape. At the bottom of the park lies a lake made since the 1960s and, on its far side, glimpsed among trees, is an Ionic temple rescued from Finchley Manor in north London.

The combination of aesthetic and natural appeal has always been finely balanced at Penns in the Rocks – ancient boulders with Georgian façade, natural woodland with more ordered planting – and this lake and temple are clearly signs of the continuing tradition.

RYMANS

Near Apuldram, 1½ miles south-west of Chichester off the A27 and the A286
Tel. 0243 783 147
The Hon. Claud and Mrs Phillimore

Open on occasional days in summer

Isolated on the flat, exposed stretch of land between Chichester and the sea, Rymans by 1950 still retained much of its medieval layout, so that one can well understand why the architect Claud Phillimore and his wife .
Anne felt drawn to the place. The compact and ancient building is intriguing, and the derelict garden proved an irresistible challenge to which they brought to bear the combined forces of his architectural knowledge and experience and her background of a childhood and upbringing at Tresco Abbey in the Isles of Scilly. The result is a garden

full of charm yet thoroughly in keeping with the dignified house it surrounds.

William Ryman, a merchant and lawyer, acquired an older Hall-house here in about 1400. He is believed to have supplied the Ventnor stone of which the bell-tower for Chichester Cathedral was made, some of which conveniently found its way to his house to become the addition to the original building of a three-storeyed tower and small wing which was his office. Between the seventeenth and twentieth centuries neglect set in; the property was let to farmers by owners who lived elsewhere. Improvements and discreet additions were belatedly made by the antique dealer who bought Rymans in 1910 and created attractive walled enclosures on the south side of the house. Here the present Iris Garden replaced an old barn: the Rose Garden is on the site of the old calf yard and its nearby byre became a gardener's cottage. Rather further from the house, to the north-east, a potting shed and new stables were formed from the old stables and piggeries. A later owner in the 1930s added a brick-walled garden, enclosing an acre of ground to the north, but when the Phillimores took over, these areas and much surrounding ground were again in an overgrown and neglected condition.

The south front of the old dwelling overlooks a small oblong Garden Court enclosed by stone and rubble walls, divided by cross-paths lined with lavender hedges, with a stone-edged pool in one corner. In contrast to this restrained simplicity of design many of the climbers trained on the walls of the house and open portico, or loggia – clematis, *Solanum crispum* and *Vitis coignetiae* – grow unchecked. A small flight of steps leads south from the house to the Rose Garden, an unrestrained mixture of old-fashioned roses, tulips: other flowers and shrubs have been planted round lawns and along flagged paths beneath crab apples and flowering cherries, some of which are host to climbing roses and honeysuckle. At the far end two small statues guard the entrance to the Iris Garden: beds surrounding an octagonal pool with an old stone seat on the far side – an invitation to stop and look back at the house.

Small gateways, and a sense of expectancy as to what lies beyond them, are an important part of pleasure at Rymans. The old Orchard on the west side is completely hidden from the rest of the garden until entered by the narrow doorway beside the tower. Hedges of yew and escallonia at either end shelter the trees, dominated by an old holm oak. There are cyclamen and daffodils beneath the old apples and two *Magnolia grandiflora* trained on the walls of the house. Northwards, beyond the escallonia hedge is a rectangular lawn and beyond the lawn, partly hidden by a hedge of rambling roses, is the Duckery, a secluded cul de sac with mixed shrubs round a pool, and an avenue of flowering malus leading to a small summerhouse.

To the east of the Duckery is the Walled Garden which the Phillimores have successfully linked to other parts of the garden by a series of strong axes. One of these stretches from the Duckery to the main ride of the woodland through arches in the east and west walls. Wrought iron gates are set in the north and south walls. The north gates give on to the two hundred yard long avenue of *Populus robusta*: from the end of this contrasting views to Apuldram Church, close by on one side, to the distant tower of Chichester Cathedral on the other can be enjoyed. Beyond the south gate designed by Mrs Phillimore is a stone statue, aligned to be visible from the front door of the house centrally between the piers and urns of the main courtyard entrance. The plots of vegetables and grass in the Walled Garden are divided by mown grass paths with flower borders filled at different times with daffodils, polyanthus, peonies and herbaceous. One of the simplest combinations is the forget-me-nots beneath tulips leading to the south.

The Phillimores have planted many interesting trees in the woodland, and the rides through here continue as natural progressions from the paths closer to the house. Part of the woodland is Coronation Copse, planted in 1953. With the necessary shelter assured, Rymans benefits from mildness deriving from proximity to the sea and throughout the garden many plants bear witness as much to this as to Mrs Phillimore's interest in tender plants. In the Walled Garden is an enormous *Ceanothus arboreum* 'Trewithen Blue', and in front of the house, among the trees by the entrance court, is a very large *Hoheria sexastylis*, besides specimens of *Hoheria lyalli*. Abutilons, azara, callistemon, *Trachycarpus fortunei* and *Myrtus luma* and many others lend a wild, exotic air to Rymans' venerable seclusion.

SOUTH CORNER HOUSE

In Duncton, 3½ miles south-west of Petworth on the A285
Tel. 0798 42143
Major and Mrs Shane Blewitt

Open two days in mid to late summer, and by appointment

The one-acre site at South Corner House has many advantages which
Major Blewitt has made full use of in his planning. The ground is
undulating and slopes away to the east, and beyond the road running
along the west side of the garden are the rising beech woods of the South
Downs.

The garden was probably landscaped in the 1920s but other than the
tall Irish yews by the roadside wall all the planning has been done by
Major Blewitt. Trained on the house are the pink climbing rose 'Mme
Gregoire Staechlin' between a wisteria and winter-flowering clematis
and, in a sheltered corner, *Carpentaria californica*. Vigorous types of
abutilons also thrive in protected spots round the house. A note of
formality is given to the old terrace by the lavender and by the small
Walled Garden below, leading to a thick arch of clematis at the end.

Major Blewitt's herbaceous border proves decisively that there is
plenty of room for a large feature in a small garden. The border curves
along the roadside wall from a silver weeping pear at the top, thirty yards
long and eight feet deep. The size of the border has allowed Major
Blewitt a sufficient variety of plants to ensure flowering for as long as
possible through the summer, with particular attention to colour groupings and plant combinations, but it is still a traditional border, with no
shrubs or non-herbaceous plants.

In the lower garden to the south are four shrub borders with old apple
and cherry trees around, one with a clematis trained into it and another a
'Mermaid' rose. In the shrubberies are cornus, 'Blanc Double de
Coubert' and 'Buff Beauty' roses, a cut-leaf elder, and *Fatsia japonica*;
the more unusual variegated fatsia is elsewhere in the garden. The
formality of the miniature circular Rose Garden contrasts well with the
shrubberies and with the Bank at the far end of the garden, being
covered in shrub roses such as the single 'Golden Wings': hebes, hostas
and *Rosa moyesii* mix happily together beneath a large snake-bark acer. It

is close to here that the ground slopes away most markedly, past an island of peonies and plants with variegated leaf beneath a cherry and a standard robinia. Other trees in this part of the garden include sorbus and a tulip tree. Beyond the gate is a damp area which Major Blewitt would dearly love to make into a Water Garden and woodland with spring bulbs and moisture-loving plants.

Two small greenhouses are filled with numerous varieties of geraniums, and many rare and interesting plants, the fruits of Major Blewitt's propagation. Partly because of its small size the garden does have an air of intimacy built round trees that shield some areas from immediate view. Whatever the climatic and soil conditions, gardens always respond to attention and enthusiasm. South Corner House is no exception and it is hard to credit that Major Blewitt is but a weekend gardener, such are the results he achieves.

THE UPPER LODGE

In Stopham, 1 mile west of Pulborough off the A283
Tel. 079 882 532

J. W. Harrington Esq.

Open on selected Sundays in April and May, and by appointment

---

The Upper Lodge has the busy appearance of any very small cottage garden, with quantities of plants on every side, but it is a cottage garden with a difference. Far from having mainly traditional summer flowers, it is filled for the most part with acid-loving and often unusual plants. Mr Harrington was head gardener at a larger house in Stopham village, and started his own garden properly only on his retirement in 1970. It is immediately obvious that this is a plantsman's garden and the layout is also carefully planned to avoid overcrowding or imbalance.

Some of the most interesting and tender plants are trained on the walls of the house. Two of the garden's many ceanothuses are here, *C. arboreum* 'Trewithen Blue' and 'Cascade', as well as *Ribes speciosum, Fremontodendron californicum* and, on one corner, *Azara microphylla*. An outstanding plant of *Viburnum burkwoodii* is trained against the wall facing a small lawn; osmanthus and daphnes grow opposite and azaleas, heathers and pittosporum at one end of the lawn. There is not room to separate different parts of the garden with any real amount of space, so a screen of low éspalier apples cleverly divides a shrub border in front of the house from the vegetable garden behind. In this border are some of the daphnes and pieris, both of which are well represented.

Rhododendrons abound, including a really large plant of *Rh*. 'Cynthia'. Behind the house, where the garden rises in a series of terraces, the rhododendrons are most effective, with the largest plants at the top. There are also many camellias, including a strikingly-placed plant of *C*. 'Donation' at the end of the path along the first terrace. Camellias and rhododendrons together surround one of the two laburnum trees, both of which are of considerable size but which add invaluable height, as does an *Acer pensylvanicum*. Many smaller plants are used simply but to great effect, like the lily-of-the-valley which edge the path leading to 'Donation' on the first terrace. Between the terraces and the house, azaleas in pots, ceanothus 'Pudget's Blue' and a climbing hydrangea trained on the small shed, and *Garrya elliptica* on the house deal admirably with the problem of how to make a backyard belong in the garden.

This is mainly a spring and early summer garden, with a peak of colour in mid-May. Cherries have been carefully chosen not to outgrow their positions, a number of fastigiate varieties among them. In front of the house drum-head primulas surround a *Magnolia stellata* – the perfect variety for a small garden such as this. Polyanthus are everywhere, planted among shrubs or grouped in borders, with many other spring bulbs – crocuses, daffodils and snowdrops.

Mr Harrington has a larger variety of plants than many much bigger gardens, and he lavishes constant expert attention and affection on them. Many visitors will be surprised at how so many plants, including a number of trees and shrubs, fit so easily into a small area. They will also be surprised at how long they linger in a small garden; for anyone seeking ideas Upper Lodge will be of consuming interest.

THE NORTH OF ENGLAND

Cumbria
Durham
Lancashire
Northumberland

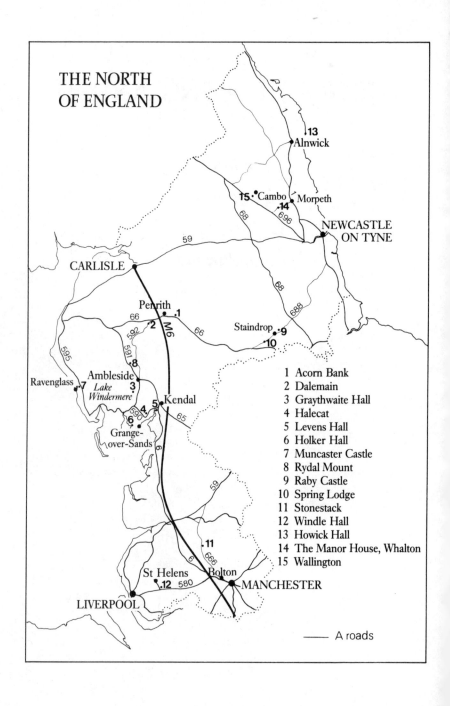

THE NORTH
OF ENGLAND

13 Alnwick

15 Cambo **14** Morpeth

NEWCASTLE
ON TYNE

59

CARLISLE

Penrith **1**
66
2
M6
592
591
66 Staindrop **9**
10

595

8

Ravenglass **7**
Ambleside **3**
*Lake
Windermere*
Kendal
4 **5**
599
6
65
Grange-
over-Sands

9

59

11

St Helens Bolton
12 580
LIVERPOOL
666
6
MANCHESTER

1 Acorn Bank
2 Dalemain
3 Graythwaite Hall
4 Halecat
5 Levens Hall
6 Holker Hall
7 Muncaster Castle
8 Rydal Mount
9 Raby Castle
10 Spring Lodge
11 Stonestack
12 Windle Hall
13 Howick Hall
14 The Manor House, Whalton
15 Wallington

68

696

68

688

——— A roads

CUMBRIA

ACORN BANK

North of Temple Sowerby, 6 miles east of Penrith off the A66
Tel. 0966 33883
The National Trust

Open daily from April to October inclusive

Acorn Bank is one of the smallest and least-known of the National Trust gardens, but its size and reputation are totally disproportionate to its charm and fascination. A long history is tinged with the romance of the Knights Templars who first settled here and occupied the site from the early twelfth century; it is from them that the nearby village of Temple Sowerby takes its name. They were followed by the Knights Hospitallers, who remained from 1312 until 1543 when the Dissolution of the Monasteries extended to religious houses and the property was granted to Thomas Dalston. His family remained for over two centuries. The gardens were enclosed with walls during the seventeenth century and it is probable that in the eighteenth William Dalston added many features to them, including the ha-ha bordering with the park.

After Acorn Bank had passed from the Dalstons to the Boazman family, it was bought in 1930 by Dorothy Una Ratcliffe (Mrs McGrigor Phillips), poet, author, botanist and traveller who had a nostalgic fascination in the old house. She restored the name of Temple Sowerby Manor, and planted 30,000 daffodils of 65 varieties as well as establishing the area of wild flowers on the bank planted with oaks. In 1950 she gave the property to the National Trust who reverted to the name of Acorn Bank. The house is now let to the Sue Ryder Foundation.

The garden lies to one side of the house and is divided into two rectangles by another wall which was originally heated; hostas now grow along this central wall. In the larger, upper area the pattern is one of traditional semi-formality. The National Trust has undertaken a considerable amount of restoration and re-planned the borders beneath the walls around the central orchard in this area. The orchard itself is divided by a path backed by clipped yew hedges and an avenue of *Prunus cerasus* 'Rhexii' – a thoughtful choice, as this variety has been established in England since the sixteenth century. It is also one of the parents of the Morello cherry, a number of which are trained on one of the walls with Leopard and Martagon lilies in front of them.

The borders are mixed and various: hybrid tea roses beneath the Georgian Clockhouse, and shrub roses opposite. The deepest border is beneath the top wall of the garden, a traditional mixed border, with herbaceous and other plants. The original idea to alternate fruit trees and roses on the walls behind failed and now, though there are climbing roses on the wall at the far end, the stress is on clematis, one of which is *Clematis chrysocoma*; the garden already has the beginning of an interesting collection.

At the far end of the yew walk are one of a number of very pretty pairs of gates around the garden, which combine with the brickwork to offset the flowers perfectly. This pair are hung with the large flowers of *Clematis jackmanii* 'Superba' on either side, as well as *Weigela florida* 'Variegata'. There is a small Sunken Garden beside the house with a circular pool and cherub-and-dolphin fountain. Rock plants trail over the low walls and steps, and in the wall behind are the garden's most striking pair of gates, which Mrs McGrigor Phillips is said to have brought back from Verona (it is likely that she also brought back many of the other ornaments in the garden, including the pair of bronze Medici vases in front of the house). On the wall beside the gates is an unknown variety of *Clematis montana*.

The smaller part of the Walled Garden originally contained fruit trees and vegetables. The National Trust have made it into a Herb Garden filled with nearly 250 different plants. Three damsons were retained from the old fruit trees, and at one end of the Herb Garden is a vinery badly in need of repair. The quantity of herbs and the imaginative design make the Herb Garden an outstanding feature at Acorn Bank; it also strikes an historical note, for the original gardens of the Knights Templars and Hospitallers would have grown large quantities of herbs.

The acorn bank itself lies beyond the house, and the top wall of the garden slopes down to the Crowdundle Beck with glimpses of the Pennines in the distance beyond the meadows. It is a natural and wild area compared with the rest of the garden, just as Mrs McGrigor Phillips planned it; wild flowers and daffodils carpet the bank beneath the oaks, to which younger replacements have been added.

Acorn Bank is worth visiting at any season – in the spring, when the wild garden above the stream is at its best and the orchard in the Walled Garden is filled with daffodils, narcissi and blossom; in the summer, when the borders are filled with colour; or in winter when its affinity with the lonely and remote countryside of this strangely undiscovered area is perhaps strongest. The atmosphere is always one of seclusion rarely disturbed over centuries. If it is one of the smallest it is also one of the brightest National Trust gems.

DALEMAIN

3 miles south of Penrith and the M6 (Junction 40), on the A592
Tel. 085 36223
Mr and Mrs Bryce McCosh

Open daily except Friday and Saturday from Easter to mid-October

Dalemain has a long history, stretching back to the reign of Henry II when the original building, a fortified Pêle tower, was recorded. One can still see the strategic advantages of the position, on raised ground north-west of where the Dacre Beck joins the Eamont river two miles east of Ullswater. After the addition of a medieval hall Dalemain was considerably expanded during the sixteenth century; the outstanding south-facing façade, built of local pink ashlar stone, was added in the early eighteenth century.

The garden has evolved with the house, and the combination of long establishment and traditional planting gives it a warm, old-fashioned atmosphere. Certain areas, such as the Knot Garden to the west of the house, were originally Elizabethan, but most of the present layout was the work of the Hasell family after Sir Edward Hasell bought Dalemain in 1679; Mrs McCosh was born Sylvia Hasell. Sir Edward further enclosed the Walled Garden on the sloping ground to the west of the Knot Garden and laid out the long terrace along the south side of the house, with its impressive buttressed retaining wall. He decorated the terrace – the sundial was made for him by Richard Whitehead of Kirkby Stephen in 1688 – and planted an unusual Grecian silver fir, *Abies cephalonica*, at the furthest end, now an imposing feature.

From the terrace one looks out south and south-west over the park laid out by Sir Edward's son, another Edward, after he had completed his additions to the house. At one point he dammed the Eamont to form a small lake, and to the south-east of the house an ancient hump-backed bridge spans the Dacre Beck which carried the coachroad as it traversed the parkland. During the nineteenth century the planting in the garden was steadily expanded, reaching a peak towards the end of the century with a head gardener, William Stuart, renowned for his camellias, and in more recent years Mrs McCosh has made sensitive additions and alterations.

The terrace remains largely unaltered and leads along the house against which is a deep herbaceous border. Roses such as 'Albertine', Easleas 'Golden Rambler', and 'Blairii II' have been planted between stone urns which decorate the deep ha-ha wall above the eighteenth-century Low Garden. Most impressive is the huge *Clematis montana* 'Rubra' trained against the wall of what was originally the Pêle tower. The terrace leads to a high bank dividing the garden into its two main areas: above, to the north, is the area of enclosed Walled Garden and below the only remaining part of the Low Garden, known as the Wild Garden, extensively planted by Mrs McCosh's mother in the 1930s and added to regularly.

The Knot Garden retains its sixteenth-century pattern and now the box-enclosed beds are filled with low plants, mainly herbs, such as lemon-scented balm, variegated mint, pineapple mint, golden marjoram and *Viola cornutica*, both mauve and white forms. In spring tall tulips make a striking contrast to the carpet of varying foliage. Immediately to the west is a mixed shrub border and beyond here the main area of the Walled Garden slopes gently upwards, enclosed by the seventeenth-century walls on its north and west sides, and by the tall yews and copper beech which overhang the bank to the south. Below the north boundary a deep border stretches right to the top west wall, filled mainly with old-fashioned roses; among the best of these are 'Fantin-Latour', 'Boule de Neige', 'Shropshire Lass' and the damask roses 'Isphehan' and 'Marie Louise'. Throughout Dalemain planting is not regulated, and at intervals in this border between roses are herbaceous plants and other shrubs such as the large tree peonies and kolkwitzia, the Beauty Bush. Most striking are blue Himalayan poppies, a great feature of the garden which came originally from Mr and Mrs McCosh's other garden at Huntfield set among the hills on the borders of Peebles and Lanark in southern Scotland.

The path along this shrub rose border ends at the Georgian alcove-summer house set in the top wall, paired by the older gazebo which also looks towards the house from the opposite, south, corner of the wall.

The view from here is one of the most satisfying in the whole garden, across the lawn which fills most of the slope and is dotted with old, gnarled apple trees to the eccentric mêlée of rooftops beyond. It is cleverly accentuated by borders curving round from north and south at the top of the lawn to fastigiate yews and cherries. The lawn is broken halfway down the slope by a low flight of steps, on either side of which are weeping cherries and clipped box. The little mixed border of peonies, tulips and meconopsis to one side is matched by one on the other which is a mass of lily-of-the-valley and agapanthus.

At the steep flight of stone steps leading from the upper enclosed garden to the Low Garden, the mood changes subtly but without losing any of its warmth. Here the ground is thickly planted with bulbs, originally brought by the sackload in the 1930s; earliest and most spectacular are the aconites, which also fill another small wood in the garden called the Grove. In the Low Garden flowering and ornamental trees have been added to older standards, notably the 'Dawyck' beech, the ornamental maples and the avenue of mixed cherries curving to the far south-west side where the Dacre Beck flows by. Among the tall, unmown grass and wild flowers, Martagon lilies, Solomon's Seal and various hostas follow the spring bulbs. The view back to the south-west front of the house is as rewarding as any at Dalemain, the buttressed terrace wall a reminder of its defensive origins amid peaceful tranquillity.

GRAYTHWAITE HALL

4 miles north of Newby Bridge on the west side of Lake Windermere
Tel. 0448 31333

M. C. R. Sandys, Esq.

Open daily from April to May inclusive

The gardens at Graythwaite were laid out between 1889 and 1895 by Thomas Mawson. It was his first important commission and set him on a career in which he enjoyed the largest international practice of any landscape-designer of his period, though he spent much of his life in Windermere. Mawson was employed by Colonel T. M. Sandys, whose family had lived at Graythwaite since the early sixteenth century. The house had been extensively altered earlier in the nineteenth century, but it was set in a hollow closely surrounded by dense plantings of mature trees and shrubs which allowed no views out. Mawson was commissioned to landscape the surrounding six acres and later explained in writing his original aims: 'The design of these grounds, which is entirely new, is arranged so as to obtain as much of the picturesque as possible.'

Garden design at the end of the nineteenth century was at its most eclectic, borrowing freely from the styles of numerous periods and alternating freely between formality and informality, something clearly reflected in Mawson's work at Graythwaite. It is hard to visualize the quantity of earth-moving and excavation involved in the creation of a landscape such as Graythwaite's.

Huge numbers of trees were removed, particularly from the rise immediately to the east of the house. The high ground to the west, beyond the small stream which flows from north to south, was also extensively cleared to open up vistas and to allow for more selective planting of mixed conifers and deciduous specimens. Mawson certainly landscaped the stream, introducing a series of bends and cascades and building a small arched bridge of local stone. Now it divides the open lawn to the south of the house from the Woodland Garden to the west.

Mawson further improved the setting and outlook of the imposing house by creating a series of terraces round the south- and west-facing fronts. To the south he altered the lie of the land so that the large open lawn sloped with undulations down from the highest point in the south-east to the garden's lowest corner in the south-west. In the course of the work cowsheds, barns and a smithy were removed and in their place appeared judiciously sited Scots pines and Douglas firs, cypress, thuja and beech. To the east of the house the stables, which occupied a raised, level area, were removed and re-sited to make way for a formal, enclosed Dutch Garden.

Major Sandys, who came to Graythwaite in 1963 but who had been gardening there for some years previously, has steadily built upon the foundations laid by Mawson and considerably expanded the range of planting, especially rhododendrons, but has recently handed over the administration of Graythwaite to his son, Myles. Graythwaite, like most gardens in the Lake District, is eminently suited to the cultivation of rhododendrons: proximity to the west coast ensures both high rainfall and a certain degree of mildness from the passing Gulf Stream. Along Graythwaite's stream and on the slope to the west of it rhododendrons and azaleas are closely planted, among them many first-class specie and hybrid plants – *Rhododendron hemslayanum*, with slightly scented white flowers, *R. litiense* with delicate yellow flowers and, among the hybrids, 'Butterfly', whose primrose-yellow flowers are flecked with crimson.

Mawson's terraces round the house, and the series of impressive flights of stone steps leading down to the lawn remain unaltered, and although the pattern of beds in the Rose Garden has been changed it, too, retains its original formality. The quality of Mawson's landscaping is clearly revealed in the view south from the terraces: across the wide lawn sloping down from the battlemented yew hedge and high ground to the south-east to the superb beeches which pre-date Mawson, and to the pond formed by the stream in the south-west corner of the garden.

The Dutch Garden is also unchanged. The little space is enclosed by dense, closely clipped yew hedges; on the south and west sides the entrances are through most attractive pairs of wrought-iron gates, each flanked by stone statues of cherubs. The beds are edged with low box hedging; and in spring they are appropriately planted with strident red tulips followed by summer annuals. Most of the garden's character is, however, given by the two rows of domed yew topiary, the top half golden, the bottom half dark green. The paths and steps ascending to the gates of the Dutch Garden are lined with various flowering shrubs and small trees, making a mêlée of scent, flower and leaf: lilacs, acers, mahonias, *Magnolia sieboldii*, one of the few fragrant varieties, an unusual autumn-flowering hybrid viburnum, *V. x bodnantese*, whose rose-tinted flowers are strongly scented, and a selection of dwarf rhododendrons, such as *R. orbiculare*.

If Graythwaite's greatest debt is to its late Victorian creator, the Sandys family have perpetuated and built upon his work in a confident and sympathetic manner. The vantage point which affords the best views of the gardens, the summerhouse on a small south-west facing promontory close to the Dutch Garden, was not the work of Mawson but a later addition by the Sandys. From here one looks across the complete picture of terraces, lawn, stream and woodland, a view which conclusively demonstrates the quality of both landscape and plants.

HALECAT

In Witherslack, 10 miles south-west of Kendal off the A590
Tel. 044 852 229
Mr and Mrs M. C. Stanley

Open two Sundays a year and by appointment

Halecat's position on only a slight hill allows it a wonderful view to the south-east to Arnside Knott in the distance, a view greatly enhanced by the garden in its foreground. The garden terracing effectively moulds it into the larger surroundings, and the bronze of much of the garden foliage offsets and relieves the grey tones of the countryside. Mr and Mrs Stanley returned to Witherslack after the Second World War and began work on the borders that are such a feature here. There is also a small nursery garden.

The garden descends in levels, from a paved terrace round two sides of the house which is effectively continued along one side of the garden beside an herbaceous border and above the sunken lawn in front of the house. A third terrace, with a summerhouse and double mixed border, is reached by turning right between two obelisks with a sloping lawn and border. The double border is filled with old-fashioned roses and tall delphiniums, and at two points comes out into headlands with old-fashioned roses trained along ironwork. With a beech hedge on one side and a grey stone wall on the other, this lower terrace is warm and sheltered when in full-summer flower.

The garden is at its best in June and July, when the tumbling cream-coloured mass of *Cytisus praecox*, the 'Warminster Broom', and ceanothus lead the eye along the side terrace by the house, through the gates into the garden and towards the distant view. The narrow borders around two sides of the main lawn are planned to give a succession of colour: daffodils backed by philadelphus and an undulating hedge of potentilla. Another retaining hedge, at the bottom of the border, is a clever blend of purple prunus and whitebeams, best seen when the azaleas have finished flowering.

In the summer the blend of roses, shrubs and perennials fills the garden with exuberant colour and scent. The walls of the house are covered by the yellow flowers of a Banksian rose and 'Madame Gregoire Staechlin', with tree peonies in the border below. From the top terrace the herbaceous borders stretch away, one to the left on the same level, another under the south-facing wall and the double border leading to the summerhouse. The whole garden shows clearly how effective planting for both foliage and flowers can be, especially when set against an outstanding view.

LEVENS HALL

5 miles south of Kendal off the A6, and north-west of the M6 (Junction 36) Tel. 0448 60321

O. R. Bagot, Esq.

Gardens open daily from Easter to September inclusive

It is extremely unlikely that when Guillaume Beaumont laid out the gardens at Levens between 1690 and 1720 he envisaged his neat pattern of yew and box mushrooming into the huge topiary specimens of today. Despite some replacement, probably during the nineteenth century, the original garden is unique in age and appearance; today the yew and box have long outgrown their original pattern and seem to be a random array of shapes and sizes. And while the garden is completely seventeenth-century in its conception, it was laid out with an adjoining park – now separated from it by the A6 – whose style, despite an overall formality typical of the seventeenth century, shows some of the earliest leanings towards the landscape ideal which took over in eighteenth-century England, led by William Kent and others.

Beaumont, who was trained in France by André le Nôtre before coming to England, laid out the garden and park at Levens for Colonel James Grahme. The yew and box were originally part of a parterre, the spirit of which is retained today by the box-edged beds filling the garden between narrow paths. As well as the parterre Beaumont planted The Rondel enclosed by beech hedges with four allées leading off on opposite sides. Time has made this the other great feature of the garden, for the beech hedges are as truly enormous and impressive as the topiary, their cool, light-green leaves the perfect foil for the sombre, dark yew. Beaumont's training has left its mark also in the planning of the mixed avenue, aligned with one of the beech allées and stretching straight out into the more informally planted parkland and indeed in his avenue of oak, elsewhere in the main park.

Beaumont so impressed Colonel Grahme's daughter, Catherine – who became the Countess of Suffolk and Berkshire – that after his death she insisted on maintaining the intricate parterre despite, one feels sure, constant suggestions from her eighteenth-century contemporaries to remove such an out-of-date feature. Later neglect meant that in the nineteenth century nine miles of low box hedging had to be re-planted and it was probably at this time that replacements were made among the topiary specimens. The present owner's parents took enormous interest in the gardens: while Mrs Bagot was an expert plantswoman, her husband successfully fought a battle to save Beaumont's avenue in the park from destruction by a motorway.

Behind the battlemented yew hedge along one side of the garden is the old orchard; herbaceous borders lead from this to one of the beech allées and into the Rondel. On the opposite side of the Rondel another allée leads to more herbaceous borders beyond which are the ha-ha (one of the earliest in England) and the old avenue of mixed trees in the nearby parkland. Leading out of the Rondel, at right-angles to those already mentioned, are the other two allées. One leads towards the house, aligned with the cedar on the lawn of the Topiary Garden, the other to the far end of the garden.

One of the main areas of planting by the parents of Hal Bagot (the present owner) is the long border beneath the wall along the far side of the Topiary Garden from the house; it goes past the orchard to the far end of the garden. With climbers and old fruit trees on the walls, this border contains many shrubs, including cornus and philadelphus; at one point there are massed irises on the other side of the path. And away from the main area of the garden, on the opposite side of the house from the Topiary Garden is a small Secret Garden, enclosed by yew hedges and overflowing with lilacs, shrub roses, peonies, hydrangeas and hostas.

Today the Topiary Garden contains a number of intriguing characters among the clipped yew. Largest of them is the 'Umbrella Tree', which certainly pre-dates the seventeenth-century garden. On one side is 'The Howard Lion', which records the garden's connection with the Howard family, and nearby is a huge dome of yew known as 'The Judge's Wig'. Beneath the yew and box formal beds are filled with wallflowers and forget-me-nots in the spring, followed by summer bedding plants; where the topiary forms an 'L' on one side, the beds contain roses. In this part of the garden are an early nineteenth-century ginkgo and a recent metasequoia, and the wall-climbers include wisteria, *Garrya elliptica* and *Actinidia kolomikta*.

Much of this garden is very labour-intensive – not only the summer bedding but more especially the hedge-clipping. Until 1936 it was all done with hand-clippers and took four men six weeks, and even now, when electric clippers are used, it takes two men six weeks. Visitors should appreciate this when admiring the topiary and hedges whose immaculate and healthy appearance completely belie their age, and also the fact that the whole garden represents a significant chapter in English gardening history.

HOLKER HALL

½ mile north of Cark off the B5278 from Haverthwaite and 4 miles south-west of Grange-over-Sands

Tel. 044 853 328

Hugh Cavendish, Esq.

Open daily except Saturday from Easter Sunday to October inclusive

---

Parts of Holker date from the sixteenth century but the largest and most imposing section of the house dates from 1873, rebuilt by the 7th Duke of Devonshire after an extensive fire in 1871. Holker has been the home of the Dukes of Devonshire at various times but the last Duke to live there was the ninth; Hugh Cavendish is a cousin of the present Duke.

The superb park, stretching away from the house on three sides and covering two hundred acres, was laid out in the eighteenth century; the gardens, which cover twenty acres, are the work of more recent generations of the Cavendish family – their variety of plants tells of continuous work by keen and expert gardeners over many decades. Both Hugh Cavendish's grandmother and mother have left their mark at Holker, and he and his wife Grania have recently transformed parts of the smaller formal gardens on the south side of the house while maintaining and improving the informal woodland which covers the sloping ground to the north and west.

Holker's low-lying position very close to the west coast gives it the luxury in this part of the country of an unusually mild climate, with abundant rain and a rich loamy soil. This combination not only encourages rapid and energetic growth in most plants but enables some to achieve spectacular size. Today the flowering trees and shrubs, and others with brilliant foliage, bring the garden to peaks in spring, in early summer and again in autumn. However, when the borders are in full flower and the Woodland Garden has assumed a heavy, full-leafed richness, the mid-summer weeks can be just as rewarding.

The formal areas of the garden are traditional both in appearance and planting. The oldest part lies below the paved terrace on the south side of the main, Victorian, block of the house. The thick, dark yew hedges which line the cross-paths dividing the garden into four, and the sentry like columns of Irish yew guarding flights of steps on the upper and lower sides, lend an air of long-established solemnity. The deep borders are filled with herbaceous plants except on the far side from the house, where peonies mix with shrub roses. In these two south borders a colourful prelude to the summer flowers is provided by distinctive domes of the dwarf Japanese rhododendron, *Rhododendron yakushimanum*.

Three years ago Mr and Mrs Cavendish re-designed the area immediately to the west. Here the south and west sides are bounded by tall clipped hornbeam hedges; along the south side, marble busts are set in hedge alcoves. There are four large flowerbeds, each centred on a silver weeping pear. In 1983 they similarly re-planned the third formal area, in front of the south side of Holker's older wing. A beech hedge stretches along the south side of this new area and the symmetry of large borders is softened by the variety of the planting: rhododendrons and azaleas in the borders closest to the hedge, and mixed shrubs and herbaceous plants closer to the house. Throughout this garden wrought-iron pillars and arbours will soon be swathed with clematis, honeysuckle and climbing roses.

The contrast between these areas and the Woodland Garden is immediately apparent: though rhododendrons and azaleas are a major feature of the latter, its general character opens out into wide glades and grass slopes beneath mature standard trees – oak, beech, ilex and many conifers – and a collection of younger trees and shrubs whose origins range through most areas of the temperate world. One approaches to see huge, old rhododendrons surrounding a pool and fountain which throws a jet of water high into the air; other notes of formality are retained: the flight of stone steps leading steeply up from the pool and fountain to a statue of Neptune, and the Victorian Rose Garden, north-west of a large open lawn. In spring and early summer the glades and slopes are covered with daffodils, bluebells and other bulbs and wild flowers. A number of species are grouped together for effect, such as the stand of cercidiphyllums, whose autumn colouring is among the best of any trees, and there is a stand of the delicate, variegated *Acer platinoides* 'Drummondii'. Elsewhere catholic mixtures of plants offset each other's qualities. Towards the north-west corner are eucryphias, massive pieris and, in a group of rhododendrons, one of the most striking hybrids to be found anywhere, 'Hawk', with its pure yellow flowers.

The northern edge of the Woodland Garden is bounded by a wall which protects many tender shrubs such as the *Carpentaria californica*. Along the wall are two of the garden's best magnolias, *M. campbellii*, and one of its best offsprings. *M. veitchii*; a pair of the much smaller and more delicate magnolia 'Leonard Messel' flank the doorway in the wall. The combination of early summer flowering and autumn foliage is best illustrated close to this doorway by one group which includes some of the most attractive trees in the garden: *Stranvaesia davidiana*, *Oxydendrum arboreum* and *Cornus controversa*. All these three have attained prodigious size, made more noticeable by a group close by of the smaller shrubs, *Enkianthus campanulatus* and *E. cernuus rubens*.

Partly because of its size, but also because of its balanced variety, Holker is never the same on two visits, always offering new surprises and pleasures.

MUNCASTER CASTLE

West of Ravenglass off the A595
Tel. 065 77203
Mrs P. Gordon-Pennington-Ramsden

Open daily (except Monday) from Easter to September inclusive

---

John Ruskin called the view from the front door of Muncaster Castle 'the gateway to paradise'. The pink granite castle, partly thirteenth-century and built on the site of a Roman fort, commands the whole valley of Eskdale stretching away below to the highest Cumbrian hills in the far distance. To this superb setting Sir John Ramsden added one of the finest, and now one of the best established, collections of rhododendrons and azaleas in the country.

Sir John financed, among others, two expeditions by the plant-collector Kingdon Ward in the 1920s; thus many of the plants at Muncaster, raised from seeds sent back by Kingdon Ward from the Himalayas, are not found in other gardens. Sir John had already built up a considerable collection at Bulstrode in Buckinghamshire when he inherited the Castle from the last Lord Muncaster in 1917. Now he was able to plan a garden on a far larger scale than Bulstrode with the help of Mr John Millais. The mildness of Muncaster's position, right on the Cumbrian coast, the protection of existing woodland to which Sir John added, and the sloping ground all provided an ideal site for his plants, especially many of the large-leafed rhododendrons.

Much of the planting is along the considerable main drive from the lodge gates. On either side banks of rhododendrons and azaleas are sheltered by mature beech and many conifers, including sequoias and Douglas firs. Among the other trees are nothofagus, of which the garden contains eight different varieties, and eucryphias, many of which are over 30 feet tall; *Nothofagus procera* and *Eucryphia cordifolia* are particularly good specimens of these two families.

To the visitor walking along the drive the progression of banks of azalea, in particular the scented yellow luteum, in front of rhododendrons seem endless. The scale of the planting is impressive and in the true tradition of the select group of large gardens built up with plants from the various collecting expeditions. Groups of candelabra primulas in the many damp areas on either side provide an almost welcome diminution in plant-size.

The woodland stretches away behind the drive on one side and continues round the hill to where many of the rhododendrons raised by Sir John are planted. Originally the seedlings were set out in regimental rows to be moved later on. In the areas where they were not moved the plants have grown up to form dense and natural rhododendron woodland, the leaves and trusses of flowers forming a canopy. Towards the top of the garden are some of Sir John's outstanding specie rhododendrons. Best of these are the large-leafed varieties, especially the collection of *R. sinogrande*. Sir John also raised the Muncaster hybrid rhododendrons, including *Rh.* 'Joan Ramsden' and *Rh.* 'Muncaster Mist', many of which are in this woodland garden. The other outstanding plant here is *Pieris Formosa var. forrestii*.

These areas are all some distance from the castle, which looks out in the opposite direction across Eskdale. Here the gardens are even more spectacular. Below the wide terrace to one side is a steep valley called the Ghyll, filled with rhododendrons, azaleas and other ornamental trees and shrubs, such as purple and green maples.

The dramatic character of Muncaster is completed by the long grass terrace which stretches beyond the Ghyll round the side of the hill beyond. Made at the end of the eighteenth century, it is comparable with those at Duncombe Park, Rievaulx and Polesden Lacey. They were all designed to capitalize on a view and so was this: the whole way along the

Muncaster terrace one looks over the box hedge with yew battlements at intervals to the valley beyond. The remoteness of Muncaster's position makes such a feature even more unexpected, as is the whole rich experience that the castle and gardens provide.

RYDAL MOUNT

In Grasmere, off the A591 between Grasmere and Ambleside

Tel. 096 633 002

Mrs Mary Henderson

Open daily except Tuesday from November to February inclusive

---

The poet William Wordsworth lived at Rydal Mount from 1813 until his death in 1850, during which time he planned and planted most of the four-and-a-half acre garden around the small house. For Wordsworth himself, and the rest of his family, it seems to have been a favourite home. Its setting is typical of much of the Lake District; perched on a hill, looking to the lakes of Windermere in the distance to the south, the Rydal Water closer at the bottom of a hill to the west, and all around the lakeland hills. It was a fit setting to illustrate Wordsworth's ideal that a garden should be in harmony with the surrounding countryside, with 'lawn and trees carefully planted so as not to obscure the view'. The garden remains virtually as he planned it and has been maintained with especial care since Mary Henderson, who is the poet's great-great-granddaughter, bought the house.

The layout of the terraces and planting of most of the large trees is Wordsworth's work, though much of the planting, particularly the rhododendrons, was done after his time. To the south, in front of the house, the smaller area of garden leads to The Mount, a raised circle used in the ninth century as a look-out and for beacon fires to raise the alarm at the approach of border raiders. Most of the garden is to the west, where the ground slopes away with a steeper slope rising behind to the north. Along here Wordsworth enhanced the upper 'sloping' terrace, probably made by eighteenth-century owners. In between the stones of the steps leading to the terrace from the house he recorded that 'yellow flowering poppies and wild geraniums' grew. At the far end of the terrace he built a quaint rustic summerhouse of wood and local stone. Here he came to compose his poetry, or to walk to the small terrace beyond looking out over Rydal Water. Stretching along the slope lower down Wordsworth made Isabella's Terrace, named after Isabella Fenwick, who became a close friend of the family. This slope and the terrace now have a particular charm, with purple acers, a large, spreading cut-leaf beech and ferns growing in the shade beneath the low retaining wall. The ground below the summerhouse falls away steeply and in spring is a mass of bluebells. A series of small streams provide the setting for a Water Garden; below that is a raised croquet lawn shaded by large sycamores and a copper beech.

The continual glimpses through trees of the fells, and occasionally of Rydal Water, make one of the great attractions of the garden. From the croquet lawn a sloping lawn made by Wordsworth leads back to the house. He surrounded the lawn with flowering shrubs but now there is a herbaceous border along one side and a number of large rhododendrons. Colour in the garden is at its height when these and the old-fashioned azaleas are in flower, but in a garden of such informality and close association with its surroundings colour is not of primary importance; that is more the mood of the place, and the character given to it by its former illustrious tenant.

DURHAM

RABY CASTLE

1 mile north of Staindrop on the A688
Tel. 0833 60202
The Lord Barnard

Open Wednesday and Sunday from Easter to June inclusive, and daily except
Saturdays from July to September inclusive

The imposing medieval castle, mainly built in the fourteenth century, is
set in gently rising parkland, landscaped in the mid-eighteenth century,
when the moat was drained and the High and Low Ponds constructed.
The detachment of the garden proper, although there are lawns and
shrubs within the enceinte, is similar to many Scottish gardens.

Set within a ha-ha on a south-facing slope looking across the park to
the castle, the large walled garden at Raby was made in the latter part of
the eighteenth century by the 2nd Earl of Darlington. The surrounding
brick wall, formerly heated for the propagation of fruit, is outstanding,
but the more striking feature of the garden's original framework is its
enormous, bulging yew hedges, over two hundred years old and thought
by some to have been planted in the days of the first owners of the castle,
which enclose the central section of the garden, leading down to the
arched south entrance gate in the bottom wall. This was constructed in
1894, and the fine wrought-iron gate (with monogram CB for Christopher, the first Baron Barnard) was brought up from the family church at
Shipbourne, in Kent.

The central parts of the garden have been redesigned, leaving the
East Garden, which used to be cultivated as a market garden, and part of
the West Garden, to be altered in due course. The present Lord
Barnard's mother, the Dowager Lady Barnard, devoted much of her

time to the garden, in particular to the various borders. The largest border which she made stretches along the north wall of the East Garden, replacing a long line of greenhouses which would be difficult to maintain today. The area was grassed over, when the market gardening came to an end, and only a tulip tree and a *Prunus purpurea* were retained. In July the border presents a striking bank of colour, mostly interesting old varieties of blue and yellow – *Buddleia alternifolia* from China and *Echinops ritro* among the blue, and, of particular interest among the yellow, *Asphodel lutea*, *Baptisia tinctoria*, *Inula helenium*, *Macleya cordata* from China, *Verbascum thapsus* and *Veratrum album*.

Most of the garden's new designs and planting are in the central section. A rustic summerhouse with brick pillars stands between mixed herbaceous and shrub borders against the top wall. In front of it is a formal Rose Garden round a central square with standard Albertine rose. Below, young yew hedges form four enclosures, each with a standard maple of different variegated foliage. The central section between the yew hedges stretches to the south gateway in the lower wall. Different features descend the slope: an herbaceous border along the top; in front, a low stone wall covered with grey leaved and rock plants; and below, a pattern of rose beds leading to a large circular pool adorned with urns and a central statue. The third section formerly had an old Victorian conservatory which has now gone, and in its place is a small conservatory with a pergola on either side, and two large raised beds, filled with colourful and scented plants. In front of the conservatory is a lawn, edged with a border of shrub roses, and a hedge of old briar roses. A beech hedge divides the lawn from the informal Heather Garden below. This is a recent addition, which is filled with many varieties, interplanted with low conifers, especially junipers.

Although much of the garden is new, possibly the most interesting single feature is one of the oldest, for in a specially built Fig House, on the outside of the south wall of the garden, is the Raby fig tree, a White Ischia, brought to Raby in 1786 by William Harry, Lord Barnard, heir to the Earl of Darlington. It fills the house, which is sixty feet long, eight feet wide and twelve feet high, and fruits annually. Also growing, and still fruiting, in the West Garden is the Raby red currant, which is well over a hundred years old. The carnation named Raby Castle may be seen in the border near the north entrance to the garden.

With its framework of old walls and hedges, Raby is a good example of a garden recently re-planned to cope with the problems of maintenance, and at the same time providing visitors with much of interest. It will be satisfying to watch the new areas mature within the old surroundings.

SPRING LODGE

North of the A66 in Barnard Castle, opposite Bowes Museum
Tel. 0833 38110
Colonel W. I. Watson

Open one Sunday in May and one Sunday in July

When Spring Lodge was originally built for Colonel Watson's family by Bonomi in 1825 it stood secluded, with its own open ground on all sides. In the 1870s, however, the Bowes Museum was completed, towering to the north, much to the indignation of the Watson family.

In fact the garden at Spring Lodge is and always has been virtually dictated by the weather, which is often uncompromisingly bad, with heavy frosts and snowfalls each winter and persistent gales racing down the Tees valley from the west. Colonel Watson with his late wife, and his mother before them, cleared some areas of the gloomy Victorian yews and hollies while leaving others as very necessary shelter.

As a result the combination of the older, Victorian parts of the garden, particularly the sheltered Walled Garden to the east of the house, with the more recent, carefully blended additions gives Spring Lodge an established and peacefully traditional appearance.

The entrance front faces west, and round the drive which comes in from the north-west is a selection of trees which illustrates the balance of old and new: mature beech and a tall columnar cypress with a young malus in front. On the wall by the entrance gates a group of plants are thriving despite the hostile conditions: *Cytisus battandieri* is a most unexpected discovery, *Actinidia kolomikta*, *Magnolia soulangiana* and *M. sieboldii*; Colonel Watson grew the latter from seed.

A victim of the regular hazards faced in the garden was the large old Cedar of Lebanon which stood on the circular forecourt lawn to the west of the house; it was blown down in a gale some years ago and crashed into the house; a silver weeping birch has taken its place. Beyond to the west, is a winding border, protected by tall yews behind, a colourful mixture mainly of shrubs including *luteum* azaleas, *Enkianthus campanulatus* and *Pieris forestii*. As well as a variety of lilies the blue Himalayan poppies are particularly striking, as is *Abutilon vitifolium*, whose survival is a border-line case because of the weather.

The main, south front of the house overlooks a terrace and lawn to a small park stretching eastwards. Notable trees in the park are the oaks and a copper beech. Along its west edge is a wide grass path along which Colonel Watson and his wife planted a variety of standard rhododendrons; mainly hybrids, they include 'Countess of Athlone', 'Earl of Athlone', 'Moser's Maroon' and two of the best Exbury hybrids, 'Carita' and 'Albatross'.

Returning towards the house one passes *Prunus serrula* 'Tibetica' with copper-red, peeling bark. From here the view across the south lawn is dominated by the huge domes of clipped yew at the far, eastern end. These are now kept closely clipped into shape, as is a delightful piece of Victoriana immediately behind to the east – a weeping beech which has been clipped into a dome and hollowed out inside to make a summerhouse. Colonel Watson has recently incorporated the meadow to the east into the garden; it is dominated by an enormous elm and he has added daffodils and a variety of acers, planted singly.

In the Kitchen Garden to the north of the beech summerhouse the regular beds are all still enclosed by low clipped box hedging; somewhat less regular is the expansive 'Bobby James' climbing rose, which has smothered an old plum tree. Beyond the west boundary wall of the Kitchen Garden is the most sheltered square in the garden, protected by walls on its east and north sides, by dense clipped yew to the south and by the house to the west. Herbaceous borders stretch along the east and south sides, again enclosed by box hedging, in which peonies and phlox are striking features. The long central rectangle of rosebeds has lost the box hedging; the beds are filled with a mixture of shrub roses such as 'Piccadilly', 'King's Ransom' and 'Gay Gordons'. Along the north wall is a narrow border; the peaches and nectarines behind testify to the unusual degree of warmth.

Slightly detached from the rest of the garden by farm buildings is a narrow strip along the road where Colonel Watson has planted climbing roses to drape over the wall and a *Buddleia davidii* for the butterflies. At the west end of this area are two enormous old cherries and from here one returns to the west front of the house. It too is covered by climbers on either side of the front door, *Clematis macropetala* and *C.* 'Comtesse de Bouchard', both of which have luxuriously large flowers. They are a graphic illustration of the degree to which the old Victorian trees fend off the worst onslaughts of the weather, thus enabling younger plants to establish themselves.

LANCASHIRE

STONESTACK

In Turton, 4½ miles north of Bolton via the A666 leading to the B6391.
Tel. 0204 852 460

Mr and Mrs F. Smith

Open two days in May and two days in August

Mr and Mrs Smith built Stonestack in 1959 in a third of an acre. Since then they have steadily acquired more land and the garden now totals two acres, its varied character and appearance reflecting this periodic expansion.

The house faces west and the garden curves round from the south-east, with the road beyond to the north of the house. A firm framework of paths, steps and hedges gives the garden unity while simultaneously overcoming the problem of uneven terrain – a problem, that is, until tackled in this way and thereafter responsible for much of the garden's character. Where the ground slopes steeply on the west side Mr Smith has constructed ingenious ramped paths of the plentiful local stone. He has also put in a series of small drainage systems, very necessary as the fields above the house to the north and north-east drain into the garden.

The garden's rich quantity of plants is immediately obvious in the entrance drive, flanked by borders of mainly mixed shrubs: *Daphne mezereum*, dwarf rhododendrons, hypericums and pieris. The lawn to the south-east of the house has a border of shrub roses; the bank of mixed rhododendrons and azaleas behind forms the boundary along the road. The border immediately in front of the house, which continues round to the west front, is one of a number in the garden which Mr and Mrs Smith bed out in the summer. This one is filled with standard fuchsias trained against frames.

The lawn on the west front slopes gradually to the ramped paths. The layout on the north side of the lawn clearly shows the careful and effective planning which Mr and Mrs Smith have put into all parts of the garden. A pond, which they made, is backed by an herbaceous border on the north side and extending west to end in a bed bedded out in spring with polyanthus and in summer by a brilliant mixture of abutilon and standard fuchsias. Along the north side of the herbaceous border a clipped holly hedge makes a most effective background.

From the ramped paths a terrace extends south; cherries mixed with maples along the top overhang a lower terrace bed filled with hebes, berberis, spirea, hydrangeas and juliana. On the bottom terrace is a heather bed, and the ramped paths here curve down the slope to the bowl-like lowest part of the garden, an oval lawn simply planted with sorbus, beech and willows. The path continues round the far west side with a shrub border and protective cypress hedge behind.

Not all the water flowing into the garden has been drained away underground, and on the north side of this lowest part of the garden a small stream flows through the Bog Garden, closely planted with hostas, irises, gunnera, primulas and dwarf rhododendrons, including the striking red 'Elizabeth'. Immediately beside the Bog Garden Mr and Mrs Smith's practical approach led to the creation of a Rock Garden: the steep grass slope had proved a continual problem for mowing and so it gave way to alpines and other small plants.

On the western edge of the garden is a small, sunken Rose Garden, entrance to which is gained through a delicate set of wrought-iron gates, one of a number of similar sets in the garden. A flagged terrace and steps lead down to the pattern of beds with standard roses in their centres and a mixture of shrub roses, including 'Tip Top', 'Picasso' and 'Trumpeter'. Among the plants sheltering against the walls here are *Eucryphia nymanensis* and *Phygelius capensis*, both fairly tender and so unexpected discoveries.

From the Rose Garden a path leads east along the edge of the garden. To the north is the constant view of fields dropping away to the west, while on the other side is a border bedded out with spectacular pelargoniums, again trained against frames to achieve maximum height.

The combination of Mrs Smith's skills as a plantswoman and Mr Smith's training and work as a surveyor and architect has left its mark through this busy, colourful and smoothly planned garden. Although many areas are demanding both in terms of time and the necessary support system of greenhouses and potting-sheds, Mr and Mrs Smith maintain Stonestack on their own to immaculate standards of order and colour.

WINDLE HALL

5 miles west of Junction 23 on the M6 and north of the East Lancs Road (A580)
via the bridge from St Helens (south side)
Tel. 0744 23534
The Lady Pilkington

Open two Sundays in July and September and by appointment

Windle Hall, home of the Pilkington family since the early nineteenth
century, has become something of an oasis amid the industrial and
urban conglomerates of Merseyside and St Helens. In high summer in
the main Walled Garden to the north of the house, when the many
hundreds of roses – the outstanding feature of the garden – are in
bloom, it is hard to imagine that the centre of St Helens is but two miles
away.

Both Lady Pilkington and her late husband have been enthusiastic
rose-growers all their lives, indeed they first met at a rose show. Since
she came to Windle in 1961 Lady Pilkington steadily developed the site,
most of which was an old kitchen garden. It is a garden unashamedly
dominated by brilliant summer colour, perhaps an old-fashioned idea
today. Nonetheless one should not allow the overall effect to obscure the
quality of this rose collection, which includes some fifteen hundred
plants of over fifty varieties.

The narrow west front of the house looks over an open lawn, a simple
aspect in contrast with the profusion of flowers in the Walled Garden to
the north and north-east. The far side of the lawn is bounded by a stone
balustrade broken by steps to a lower lawn and pool with a Copenhagen
mermaid figure poised on a rock in its centre. Beyond here a belt of
woodland, filled with bluebells in spring, stretches right round the west
and north boundaries of the garden. In the west woodland Lady
Pilkington has placed a delicately made rotunda with a wrought-iron
dome, surrounded by a variety of young trees, as a memorial garden to
Lord Pilkington.

The north-west part of the garden is a large lawn with the high beech
trees of the sheltering woodland beyond. In the 1960s Lord and Lady
Pilkington commissioned an interesting addition to the gardens from
Henshall and Son – the limestone Rockery round a small stream, and

the tufa rock Grotto. From the Rockery a border of the old-fashioned luteum azaleas stretches beneath the west side of the tall wall separating the main garden on its other side, in early summer a heady scented mass of brilliant yellow.

Immediately below the north front of the house is a sunken Rose Garden, a pattern of beds filled with various hybrid tea shrubs. Not surprisingly, among the quantity of plants which sets the standard for the other beds and borders of roses in the larger walled area, one finds 'Sir Harry Pilkington', named much earlier after Lady Pilkington's husband.

Steps up from this sunken garden lead to a path between luxurious herbaceous borders along the west side of the Walled Garden. These are backed on one side by the boundary wall and on the other by fruit trees, and their depth and length allows for a most impressive array of herbaceous plants, carefully arranged in descending height from front to back.

On the far, north side of the Walled Garden the path is covered by a pergola swathed with roses, laburnum and clematis. Between here and the house is the main lawn, divided by a mêlée of rose borders, hedges and poles supporting climbers along the main path. Acers and fruit trees spread their varying shades of colour; another herbaceous border extends beneath the east boundary wall to the greenhouses. Between here and the house is a small formal garden, a pattern of small herbaceous borders, rose borders, clipped box and yew, and a central lily pool.

From the slightly raised position in this corner of the gardens one can look out across the seemingly endless ranks of roses, summer annuals and herbaceous plants, a spectacular display in summer and a fitting tribute to the enthusiasm and expertise of Lady Pilkington and her late husband.

NORTHUMBERLAND

HOWICK HALL

Near Howick, 6 miles north-east of Alnwick off the B1339
Tel. 066 577 221

Howick Trustees Ltd

Open daily from April to October inclusive

Mention of the wild and lonely Northumbrian coast conjures up a picture both remote and imposing; Seaton Delaval, Vanbrugh's huge and brooding masterpiece; Holy Island and Lindisfarne Castle, and Alnwick Castle, the seemingly impenetrable border fortress. In such surroundings the garden at Howick forms an oasis where rare and often exotic plants thrive in an unexpected micro-climate of sheltered warmth.

Howick is the seat of the Grey family; their strong political tradition stretches back to Lord Grey, whose Whig government passed the Reform Bill in 1832. Lady Mary Howick, daughter of the 5th Earl Grey, argues that when the Tories were in power all through the Napoleonic Wars, Whig politicians retired to their country seats, and that the plantings of large trees at Howick date from this time. In 1930 Lady Mary's father 'discovered' four acres of acid soil where a patch of whinstone outcrops from the surrounding limestone. This enabled him to start the Woodland Garden, the existence of which was also made possible by Howick's sheltered coastal climate. Until then the gardens at Howick had consisted of terraces round the imposing but not unwelcoming eighteenth-century house, with its symmetrical wings linked by low colonnades.

The terraces, descending to the stream valley, are best in summer, with borders of agapanthus, roses and herbaceous. Central steps lead to a small pond surrounded by yew hedges and shrub roses. Below the corner of the balustraded top terrace is an unusual Muncaster variety of *Clematis montana*. To one side of the terraces is a meadow where daffodils and autumn crocuses appear in profusion. Behind the house is a long glade which has recently been altered and now contains plants with outstanding foliage, but it is the Woodland Garden, away from the house, that is the area of greatest interest and beauty.

The garden covers an area above a steep bank down to a fast-flowing stream and the mature woodland continues all around. It soon became clear to Lord Grey that as well as rhododendrons and azaleas, some of which had been grown from seed collected on Asian expeditions in the 1920s and the 1930s, more tender trees and shrubs could be grown here. Throughout the Woodland Garden flowering trees, shrubs and smaller plants are mixed around paths and glades. Rhododendrons and azaleas provide much of the garden's framework: old-fashioned azaleas, in particular the scented yellow luteum variety, grown in banks along many of the paths, in one place combining with blazing pieris, in another overhung by the exquisite flowers of *Magnolia wilsonii*. In another small glade this magnolia's white blooms hang like Chinese lanterns over bluebells, primulas and blue meconopsis. The most spectacular magnolias at Howick are the two *M. campbellii*, both between forty and fifty feet tall; another, smaller, variety is *M. salicifolia*. Many of the eucryphias that thrive here were among Lord Grey's early plantings, as were the acers – especially *Acer griseum* – and the cercidiphyllums, whose autumn colour follows the eucryphia flowers. With so many evergreen plants, foliage is of major importance throughout the year. Two plants of different sizes but equally striking appearance in this respect are hostas and pittosporums. In contrast, and confirming beyond doubt the mildness of Horwick's climate is *Embothrium lanceolatum*; its flower-clusters actually touch each other along the branches, so well does it thrive, giving an impression of a scarlet mass.

From the Woodland Garden a meadow leads back to the terraces, a gentle transition to these more formal areas of the garden and a wonderful sight at different times of the year: daffodils are followed by a thin sprinkling of mixed tulips in its long grass, then by the white and mauve colchicums in autumn. Around the meadow are a copper beech, a golden oak and a superb *Davidia involucrata*. Years in a political wilderness may have seen the start of Howick's gardens, but the knowledge and enthusiasm with which they are maintained provide the visitor with one of Northumberland's more memorable sights.

THE MANOR HOUSE

In Whalton on the B6524, south-west of Morpeth
Tel. 067 075 205
Mr and Mrs T. R. P. S. Norton

Open by appointment only

The long, irregular, wisteria-covered façade of the Manor House, and the narrow formality of its front rosebeds and lawn blandly disguise from any village passer-by the beauty that lies behind. In fact it is difficult to recognize the Manor as one house or to guess at the ample size of its courtyards, gardens and stables for one house and three adjacent cottages have been joined together. Sir Robert Lorimer, the noted Scottish architect, worked on part of the house but it is the imprint of Sir Edwin Lutyens which is far more apparent in both the house and the garden.

The fact that Lutyens worked here may easily have stemmed from his connection with Blagdon Hall, the nearby home of the Ridley family. Whatever the reason, his work was extensive. As well as unifying a good deal of the rear exterior, he designed most of the interiors, including some outstanding rooms. Although some of his garden features – a pergola, a sunken rose garden and a long yew hedge – have gone, enough remain as part of the present design to enhance the enormous charm of this mixture of warm colour and attractive architecture.

Large arched white doors from the front of the house form the perfect entrance to a courtyard effectively linking house and garden. The courtyard walls are covered in the pink flowers of *Clematis montana rubens* which, on first impression, seems to be everywhere. Two short pergolas have been placed along the top of the far stone wall; an herbaceous border and a border of shrub roses form a right-angle in front of another. At the top of the garden a classical summerhouse with stone columns stands beside a white border containing mixed tulips in early summer. The wall behind this, surmounted with stone pinnacles, is swathed with the everpresent clematis, and at its other end stands a second summerhouse, in total contrast to its companion – a sloping tiled roof, wooden columns and small latticed windows.

After the war Mr Norton's mother made many additions to the

garden including the corner laburnum orchard beyond the old walled Kitchen Garden: from a narrow arch in the yew hedge one enters to be surrounded by its golden racemes. Its hidden glory is in keeping with the 'surprise' nature of the Manor House and its garden, and the deceptive skill with which such attractions have been laid out.

WALLINGTON

12 miles west of Morpeth, near Cambo on the B6342, and off the A696
Tel. 067 074 274
The National Trust

Open all year

Sir Walter Caverley Blackett, who lived at Wallington between 1728 and 1777, was very much a man of his times. During Daniel Garrett's alterations and additions to his house, built in 1688, Sir Walter planned new gardens, extensions and alterations and continued to do so on and off for the rest of his life as he responded to changing styles. There are semi-formal woods with avenues, ponds and paths – probably the work of Mr Joyce in 1737, in the style of Bridgeman, though their origins were seventeenth-century; and there is a folly, erected later on a distant hill – eighteenth-century landscaping at its most flamboyant.

The basis of Sir Walter's plans survive in the two woods to east and west of the house, with subsequent alterations by his Trevelyan descendants. The planting of these two woods – the former with its China Pond and Garden Pond, the latter with Boat House, Middle and Top Ponds – were the first steps in Sir Walter's gardening ambitions, probably what he referred to in his notes for 1737 when he recorded: 'New gardens made'.

With their planting complete, the next major task was to make the Walled Garden, incorporating the Garden Pond and the slope above. The top Portico Wall and central south-facing Portico House, designed by Garrett probably in about 1740 and blessed with one of the most striking façades of any gardener's cottage of its time, are all that remain today. The China Pond was adorned in 1752 with what the Duchess of Northumberland called 'a very expensive Chinese building'.

It was not long after this that Sir Walter's attention was caught by the original screen wall and central entrance arch to Wallington's courtyard. These he removed and replaced with the present coachhouse, the cupola joining the two wings of the stable court being re-erected on a rise to the north-east of the house. In 1755 the Wansbeck valley to the south of the house was deemed due for alteration: once dammed and broadened to more suitable proportions, Sir Walter threw across a three-arched balustraded bridge, designed by James Paine.

One of Sir Walter's last additions was the present Walled Garden and its pavilion, called the Owl House, laid out between 1760 and 1769 in the dell to the east of the large Garden Pond and earlier Walled Garden. The only mildly surprising fact about Sir Walter's projects was that he did not induce 'Capability' Brown, the master of eighteenth-century landscape born and brought up in nearby Kirkharle, to leave his own mark on them – but he did re-plan an area around Rothley Lake at the far end of the estate in 1765.

The most important of Sir Walter's gardening successors was Sir George Otto Trevelyan, who inherited Wallington in 1886. Over the intervening years most of the East and West Woods had reverted to natural woodland and most of Sir George's attention was focused on the Walled Garden, which he re-fashioned considerably. It was probably to give full rein to his ideas for this that he removed the flowerbeds his father, Sir Charles Edward Trevelyan, had laid out in the west lawn. One oddity Sir George brought to Wallington was a stone from the Giant's Causeway, purchased when he was First Secretary for Ireland between 1882 and 1884; it now stands close to the house on the east lawn. He also built the conservatory in 1908, made the rectangular yew enclosure lower down in the Walled Warden, and put up the fine wrought-iron gates between the stone piers in its south wall.

Since they acquired Wallington from Sir Charles Philip Trevelyan in 1941 the National Trust have concentrated on restoring and replanting the later Walled Garden to bring it to its present appearance; work began on this in 1960. Its entrance is through the Neptune Gate to the terrace along the raised, north side of the garden. *Cytisus battandieri* in the border to the left benefits from the sheltered position; many other plants in this mixed border are also of soft colours – yellow, mauve and blue. The terrace wall is surmounted by a series of eighteenth-century lead figures, and below them the main area of the Walled Garden stretches down from the fountain pool and curving steps made by Mary, Lady Trevelyan in 1938.

A brick path, flanked by herbaceous borders of blue and yellow, slopes from the terrace beneath arches hung with honeysuckle to a circular paved yew enclosure containing a terracotta urn brought back from Italy by Sir George. The large conservatory is now filled with a display of slightly tender plants: heliotrope, passion flower, bougainvillea, *Cassia corymbosa* and *Abutilon pictum*; their scent and colour combine with the sound from the marble-walled fountain erected by Sir George in 1910. Outside again, a long mixed border of shrubs stretches along the far wall, and another yew enclosure is now filled with a collection of ornamental trees. From the Stream Garden, made when the stream was raised out of a sunken culvert, the display of climbing roses and clematis on the brick wall below the terrace can be seen on the way back up to the fountain pool.

The National Trust have planted some rhododendrons and azaleas in the East Wood, but otherwise both this and the West Wood have largely been left in their natural woodland state. The West Wood, though, was given a grand vista in 1970, an avenue of broad-leafed limes leading from the south terrace in front of the house to a large eighteenth-century urn of Portland stone, the pair to which stands opposite on the East Lawn. Simplicity of lawns and terracing is maintained round the house to west, east and south, in which direction lie the ha-ha and the park. This simplicity, and the walk through the East Wood, serve to heighten the effect of the planting in the Walled Garden, now Wallington's main area of horticultural interest. Historical interest, in its development and in the personalities involved, is present every step of the way.

NORTH WALES AND THE WEST MIDLANDS

Cheshire
Clywd
Gwynedd
North Powys
Shropshire
Staffordshire

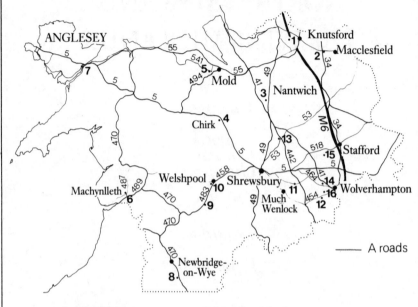

NORTH WALES AND THE WEST MIDLANDS

ANGLESEY

Knutsford
Macclesfield
Mold
Nantwich
Chirk
Stafford
Welshpool
Shrewsbury
Wolverhampton
Machynlleth
Much
Wenlock
Newbridge-
on-Wye

—— A roads

1 Arley Hall	9 Maenllwyd Isaf
2 Capesthorne	10 Powis Castle
3 Cholmondeley Castle	11 Benthall Hall
4 Chirk Castle	12 The Dairy House
5 Gwysaney Hall	13 Hodnet Hall
6 Brynhydryd	14 Swallow Hayes
7 Plas Newydd	15 Little Onn Hall
8 Llysdinam	16 Wightwick Manor

CHESHIRE

ARLEY HALL

6 miles west of Knutsford, 5 miles from the M6 (Junctions 19 and 20) and the
M56 (Junctions 9 and 10)
Tel. 056 585 284
The Hon. M. L. W. Flower

Open Tuesday to Sunday from Easter to October inclusive

The Tithe Barn at Arley is contemporary to the earliest of a series of
homes that have existed on the site since the mid-fifteenth century. The
present house dates from the nineteenth century and was the work of
Rowland Egerton-Warburton, who inherited Arley from his great-
uncle in 1813 and lived there until his own death in 1891. His interests
and talents were varied and considerable and included architecture. He
employed a local architect, George Latham, for his new house, which
was to be built in a romantic, Jacobean style, but took most of the
decisions himself. Possibly that is why the work continued intermittently
for thirty years.

The gardens, totalling eight acres, were made between 1830 and
1860; the only eighteenth-century feature Egerton-Warburton retained
were the surrounding brick walls but virtually all of that framework and
many of his garden's outstanding features survive today, thanks largely
to considerable restoration by the present owner's parents, Viscount and
Viscountess Ashbrook. For fifteen years after the Second World War
they continued to run the kitchen gardens as market gardens, but in
1960 they decided to end this, to restore the rest of the gardens and to
open them to the public as a way of helping costs.

Egerton-Warburton planned the gardens with his wife Mary and a
map they made, dated 1846, survives as clear evidence of the similarities

179

between the original unity and variety of the different enclosures and the gardens in their present form. Within the preserved brick walls surrounding parts of the garden and the park in front of the house they planned axes of different gardens, all joined smoothly together with vistas or through gateways. It was very much a precursor of the 'enclosure' or 'room' style of gardening, developed at Sissinghurst and Hidcote, which has become so popular in the twentieth century.

One of the most remarkable features were the herbaceous borders. These appear on the plan of 1846 and are probably among the oldest and most impressive in England. Double borders stretch for ninety yards between the grass terrace called the Furlong Walk, which divides the gardens from the park, and the Alcove Summerhouse. A brick wall runs behind one side and a tall yew hedge behind the other. Clipped buttresses of yew are also used to divide the borders into sections, with particular associations of blue and yellow plants with grey-leafed and other foliage plants. Many of the plants today are the same as those that appeared in a watercolour of the borders painted by George Elgood in 1889 which appeared in *Some English Gardens* by Gertrude Jekyll, published in 1904. Wrought-iron gates framed by honeysuckle lead from the herbaceous borders into the Walled Garden. This was originally the kitchen garden but is now much simplified, a wide lawn with a central pool surrounded by four fastigiate beech, and floribunda roses. Many of the climbers trained on the walls are tender and benefit from their warm, sheltered position.

The other great feature of the Arley gardens, unique in this country, is the avenue of cylindrically clipped ilex, which does not appear in the 1846 plan but which was planted shortly afterwards. Possibly the idea came from Italy, as Rowland and Mary Egerton-Warburton travelled extensively on the continent. Wonderful in their own right, the trees are also a good example of the planning that went into the garden. Aligned with the wrought-iron gates into the kitchen garden on the far side of the herbaceous borders, the avenue leads to a downward flight of steps flanked by imposing stone vases to where philadelphus and other shrubs surround a circular lawn with a stone sundial. From here one may look out across the ha-ha to the park.

Some of the enclosed areas of the gardens are small and intimate, like the Fish Garden beside the Ilex Avenue, its sunken pool surrounded by dwarf conifers. Beyond here is The Rootree, whose name alone is intriguing. It was originally made by Mary Egerton-Warburton as a rockery but became very overgrown. After clearance in the 1960s it was replanted with small rhododendrons and azaleas, primulas, lysichitums, the Osmunda fern and other water-loving plants around its pond. Above

The Rootree along one side of the gardens is The Rough, where standard trees and shrubs – stewartia, acers, magnolias, liquidambar and azaleas – are planted in the rough-mown grass; there are spectacular 'Giganticum' lilies. Lady Ashbrook made two other small, peaceful gardens, the Herb Garden and the Scented Garden, in 1969 and 1977 respectively. She also improved the Flag Garden, made by Antoinette Egerton-Warburton in 1900, in a corner by the Tithe Barn, with pink floribunda roses, lavender and various climbers for the walls. Throughout, the gardens at Arley are maintained to a high standard and a visit is always rewarding.

CAPESTHORNE

5 miles west of Macclesfield on the A34
Tel. 0625 861 221

Lieutenant-Colonel Sir Walter Bromley-Davenport

Open on Sunday from April, on Wednesday and Saturday from May, on Tuesday and Thursday from July, all to September inclusive; and on Good Friday and Bank Holiday afternoons

---

Capesthorne has been the home of the Bromley-Davenport family and their ancestors since Domesday times. The oldest parts of it were built in 1722 by the architects Francis Smith of Warwick and his brother William Smith of Wergs in Staffordshire and the surrounding parkland, lakes and bridges were laid out for that house. Alterations by Blore and Salvin in the nineteenth century gave the house its present Jacobean appearance and brought it to its impressive size. The main garden, which lies between the house and the lake to one side, was probably laid out at the same time but, along with other areas, they have been recently re-planned by Russell Smith, largely to enable three full-time gardeners to maintain an area tended by eight before the Second World War.

The imposing effect of the entrance courtyard is softened by climbing roses trained along the wall on either side of the entrance gates, and by roses and honeysuckle trained up the pillars of the stone colonnade along the central block of the house. In striking contrast to the grand scale of the house and most of the gardens is the little enclosed garden beside the Georgian chapel, between the house and the main garden leading to the lake. Clipped yews, hostas and climbing roses against the brick chapel walls all somehow lend a cloistered air.

The large area of the main gardens was originally divided into four squares with extensive flower beds and borders; along the edge of the lake was a fuchsia hedge and a border filled with brightly-coloured annuals. Now the area has been greatly simplified into two large lawns divided by a central double herbaceous border stretching down to the lake and backed on either side by large *Acer brilliantissimum* and fastigiate apples. At the top a pair of fine Italian wrought-iron gates from Wootton Hall in Derbyshire are set between piers in a brick wall. Stretching away beneath the wall on either side of the gates are long borders of mixed shrubs and herbaceous plants. Round the corner a large rose bed has been planted.

A long terrace stretches along the opposite side of the house from the entrance, leading to a group of trees which have all been given to Lady Bromley-Davenport over the years as Christmas presents. Beneath one side of the terrace the supporting wall is covered in climbing roses. An intimate sunken courtyard garden beside the house contrasts with the open lawn beyond the terrace, partly broken up by avenues and groups of trees planted by Russell Smith. A group of young poplars stand close to some older ilex, and on opposite sides of the lawn are a hawthorn avenue and a path flanked by limes on one side and maples on the other.

Both here and in the main area of garden towards the lake one can see very clearly what has been achieved to break up the large open areas of the garden while keeping the workload to a minimum.

CHOLMONDELEY CASTLE

6 miles west of Nantwich, between the A41 and the A49
Tel. 082 922 202

The Marquess of Cholmondeley

Open on Sunday and Bank Holidays from Easter to September inclusive

Cholmondeleys have lived at Cholmondeley since the twelfth century. The present hill-top house was designed by the 4th Earl and built in 1801, a romantic 'gothick' castle overlooking the valley. The Earl was created 1st Marquess in 1815; in 1817 he commissioned Sir Robert

Smirke, a professional architect, to add extra towers, and since then the castle has remained unchanged.

Even the castle's dramatic setting, with its huge park dropping away to the south and east, extending to about forty acres, could not disguise the fact that when the present Marquess and Marchioness came here in 1950 the gardens, then mostly planted with dense laurels, bamboo and rhododendrons, were generally in need of rejuvenation. Many of the outstanding trees on the slopes, such as the two Cedars of Lebanon, the oaks, ilex, swamp cypress and wellingtonia, were probably planted shortly after the castle was built, and parts of the existing gardens, such as the terrace on the south and east fronts and the Temple Garden below the long slope to the south of the castle, were also already laid out. The present large and varied selection of plants, however, and considerable restoration and re-designing have been their own work.

In the late 1950s Lord and Lady Cholmondeley were advised by Mr McKenna, a noted expert on Snowdonia, on restoring the rockery and waterfall in the Temple Garden, and at the same time they set about clearing the area above the rockery, along the stream which flows into the Temple Garden from the west. In the 1960s they were helped by James Russell, the garden designer, with the re-designing of many areas and extensive new planting of mainly flowering and ornamental trees and shrubs.

There are two temples in the Temple Garden – one of stone with four pillars which stands on an island and originally came from the old house, the other a circular rotunda with a wrought-iron dome which Lord and Lady Cholmondeley added. The Temple Garden stream flows between clumps of huge gunnera as well as other waterside plants until it eventually flows over the waterfall into the lake. Here again is a profusion of plants, but it is the Temple Garden's composition – the balance of the two buildings, the rockery, the lake and the surrounding trees, shrubs and other plants which make this the most picturesque part of the Cholmondeley gardens.

Each of the different areas in the garden has its own character and appearance. Below the slope of the south-west of the castle is The Glade, informally planted mainly with trees and shrubs – acers, rhododendrons and azaleas – but also with many smaller plants: Himalayan blue poppies, hostas and early cyclamen. Among the many magnolias are *M. lennei, M. denudata, M. wilsonii*; and two striking individual plants are *Davidia involucrata* and *Cornus florida* 'Rubra', which flower well annually.

To the west of the Glade is the Rose Garden, a profusion of shrub and climbing roses in raised beds edged with stone and lavender; the climbing roses over the metal arches include 'New Dawn', 'Evangeline' and 'Pink Perpetue'. A stand of mixed beech and horse chestnut provides a magnificent backdrop to this small garden to the south-west, and just outside the Rose Garden to the west is one of Cholmondeley's most striking trees, an *Arbutus andrachnoides*, with brilliant cinnamon-red bark; there is another in the Temple Garden. Double herbaceous borders lead south out of the Rose Garden; in them two pairs of silver weeping pears hang over tulips in the spring and a mixture of herbaceous plants, more roses and other shrubs later in the year.

In comparison with these larger areas the scale of planting along the terrace round the south and east fronts is more intimate. Here are many of Lady Cholmondeley's most special plants, benefiting from the protection of the retaining wall or tumbling over its stonework. Among the most notable are *Daphne cneorum*, whose scented pink flowers drop over the wall, *Carpentaria californica*, *Clematis montana* 'Elizabeth', the gallica rose 'Tuscany Superba', abutilons, jasmine and ceanothus.

The huge open slope below the east terrace is a mass of daffodils in spring and from the far, east end is the Cherry Walk, a path leading down the hill beneath the overhanging branches of *Prunus* 'Shimidsu Sakura'. Immediately below the south front is a small formal Rose Garden; among the number of climbers and wall plants trained against the castle is, most appropriately, *Clematis* 'Mrs Cholmondeley'. A small flight of steps ascends to the Silver Jubilee Garden, below the south-east corner of the castle, where a series of small terraces are filled with a variety of silver-leafed plants such as santolina, senecio and artemisia. The beautiful wrought-iron of the steps leading up to the house from this little garden was worked by Robert Bakewell.

Since Lord and Lady Cholmondeley came here the scope and quality of the plants in the garden has expanded to match their scale and magnificent setting. Now the gardens are filled with a mixture of intimacy and grandeur, highlighted at different times of the year by the constantly changing patterns of colour.

CLYWD

CHIRK CASTLE

½ mile from Chirk off the A5
Tel. 0691 777 701
The National Trust

Open from Easter Sunday to October inclusive, on Sunday only in April, at weekends only in October, and all Bank Holidays; otherwise on Sunday, Tuesday, Wednesday and Thursday

High on an exposed hill on the borders of England and Wales, Chirk is exactly as one imagines a Marcher castle: built by Roger Mortimer in 1310, it was considerably altered during the Earl of Leicester's ownership between 1563 and 1588, but Chirk remains medieval rather than Tudor in appearance and atmosphere. The Myddelton family first came to Chirk in 1595; their influence, since the Civil War, in which both the family and Chirk were closely involved, has mellowed the brooding aspect of the castle and now, surrounded by its gardens and a landscaped park, Chirk tugs at one's sense of history from a more tranquil and picturesque existence.

The gardens were originally terraced during the early eighteenth century; some of the terracing still remains. The grounds were landscaped towards the end of that century by Emes, a pupil of 'Capability' Brown. It was then, in 1770, that the magnificent entrance gates and *clairvoyée* – made by two Welsh brothers, Robert and Thomas Davies of Bersham, between 1719 and 1721 – were moved from the Castle entrance, where they had formed the forecourt, to the New Hall Lodge. They were moved to their present position, at the entrance to the park, in 1888. During the mid-nineteenth century one of the great features of the garden, the yew hedges and topiary, were added to the east. Now well over a hundred years old, these have grown to huge proportions, and their dark forms echo the castle's still sombre bastions.

Between 1910 and 1946 Lord and Lady Howard de Walden were tenants at Chirk and made many additions to the gardens. They took advice from Mrs Norah Lindsay: it was she who suggested allowing the yew hedges and topiary to broaden out to their present dome-like shapes. Lady Howard de Walden made a very large herbaceous border along the north side of the Long Lawn, beyond the yew-enclosed main garden, which led to the Hawk House built for Lord Howard de Walden's hawks. Sadly this was almost destroyed by fire in 1977, but it is being restored by the National Trust, who have run Chirk for the Welsh Office since 1981. Soon the pink climbing Albertine rose will stretch up the walls and over a new thatched roof. On either side the small rock faces are planted with small shrubs and rock plants, and in front stands a bronze art-nouveau figure of Persephone, clasping a bunch of flowers and treading on a serpent, emerging from her six months' captivity in the Underworld to bring us back the Spring. Huge domes of yew in pairs on either side of the lawn here echo the pattern closer to the castle.

Much of the garden, particularly this lower area, was badly neglected during the Second World War; since then Lady Margaret Myddelton has worked very successfully to bring the gardens to their present high standard and beauty, by delightful and often adventurous planting, managing to enhance the already impressive setting.

The main Yew Walk across the garden, a wide gravel path with pairs of clipped domes of yew on either side, leads from the entrance gate to another female bronze statue. Two more grace the opening in the yew hedge which leads to the steps and the Long Lawn. Here Lady Margaret Myddelton's plantings of trees and shrubs have had perhaps the greatest influence of anywhere in the garden. The old herbaceous border to the north has been replaced by *Prunus* 'Kanzan' and shrubs, nearly all flowering varieties such as lilacs, magnolias, cherries, philadelphus, shrub roses and smaller azaleas and rhododendrons with hostas for groundcover and gentians. The contrasting light informality of scented blossom and flower from the dark yews is delightful. The opposite side of the Long Lawn is left unmown and here are many impressive standards such as the weeping lime, the whitebeam and the mature copper beech, cedar and European larch lower down, with grass paths winding between them. Simple but striking combinations have been created, such as the climbing hydrangea trained over an old tree stump, with a silver weeping pear close by. In spring daffodils throughout the long grass vie for attention with cherries and later with other flowering trees; amalanchiers, laburnums, philadelphus. One of the most unexpected finds is *Embothrium coccineum*, and one of the most spectacular a glorious *Cornus nuttallii*, grown from seed brought from Vancouver. At summer's end *Eucryphia glutinosa* is accompanied by several varieties of hydrangea. The Shrub Garden contains many types of rare shrubs dating from the last century, and in its midst is the rebuilt and enlarged pool.

Climbers and wall plants now draw the vast walls of the castle into the garden and soften the rather forbidding stone: climbing roses and a climbing hydrangea, together with the very large yellow honeysuckle, *Lonicera tragophyulla*, stretch up from the borders of shrub roses and peonies. The Rose Garden, originally made by Mr Algernon Myddelton-Biddulph, has been both considerably restored and altered; now its small, secluded area, with the walls of the castle above on one side and the outhouses and weather-vane on the other, has a totally different character from the more imposing lawns and yew. In its centre is a sundial from the now disused Kitchen Garden. To the south Lady Margaret Myddelton planted a hedge (to hide the Kitchen Garden) with a small herbaceous border.

After walking through the gardens at Chirk and arriving at the end of the long, gently sloping lawn, one would not dispute the claim that, looking east across the little ha-ha on a clear day, hills in many counties can been seen, a reminder of Chirk's origins and its metamorphosis from violence to beauty.

GWYSANEY HALL

1½ miles north-west of Mold on the A541

Tel. 0352 3034

Captain P. D. Davies-Cooke

Open on selected Sundays and by appointment

Gwysaney stands in Wales but very likely one of its raisons-d'être, and certainly one of its attractions today, is the panorama of views it commands from its hill position eastward into England across Cheshire and, slightly to the north-east, across Lancashire to the hills of the Lake District. The house, built of local stone, has been a home of the Davies-Cooke family since around 1600. Additions were made in 1850 and 1920 but the three periods here blend together unusually well.

The tree-lined drive leads up to a large lawn on the south front, with domes of clipped yew and a cut-leaf beech in the south corner. This restrained simplicity contrasts with the variety of plants trained against the walls of the house, including buddleias, roses, magnolias, wisteria, *Solanum crispum*, a summer-flowering jasmine and *Chaenomeles japonica*. One of a number of fine sets of wrought-iron gates leads to the East Terrace and its spectacular views across the park to the countryside. The terrace leads north to the Chapel Garden made after a wing of the house was pulled down in 1850; the mullioned windows were saved and rebuilt here into the walls of an eighteenth-century cottage. The stonework is covered in virginia creeper, and among the small plants inside the small enclosures are roses and nepeta. Beside the Chapel Garden is a fine arbutus, the 'Strawberry Tree'. Extending north from the Chapel Garden, along the east side of the garden are the twin borders which Captain Davies-Cooke's mother planted as outstanding herbaceous borders. They are now filled with shrubs in an attempt to reduce labour, but with some surviving herbaceous plants. They lead to another pair of gates, and one of the most interesting parts of the garden, the Arboretum, a long glade of about two hundred yards. The Arboretum was made by Captain Davies-Cooke's great-great-grandfather, one of the earliest examples of such a collection of coniferous trees. One of the nearest trees is *Abies cephalonica*, the Caucasian silver fir, first introduced into England in 1824, making this tree one of the earliest planted. There were large numbers of Douglas firs, possibly including some of the originals sent by David Douglas from America; now some of these have been thinned and replaced with young trees to avoid over-crowding and obscuring the views. There are also monkey-puzzles, redwoods, spruces and silver firs.

Between the Arboretum and the forecourt to the north of the house is the main flower garden, laid out formally in two areas divided by a mixed flower border containing carnations, pinks, ageratum, polyanthus and small azaleas. The lawn closest to the Arboretum has a central sundial with a circular rosebed on either side and four corner rosebeds. The farther area has a pattern of box-enclosed flowerbeds surrounding a central bell. Some of the outer beds are filled with roses, with lavender and round the bell are diagonally opposite beds of geraniums and antirrhinums. The effect is that of a parterre, an attractive patchwork of alternating colour.

In recent years Gwysaney's grounds have been successfully adapted to deal with the problems of reduced labour. While the alterations have not been drastic, they have made possible the maintenance of a most attractive and diverse garden, which will never lose the advantages of its position and setting.

GWYNEDD

BRYNHYDRYD

North of Machynlleth on the A487
Tel. 065 473 278
Mrs David Paish

Open all year by appointment

At first sight gardening in any kind of conventional sense of the word would seem to be impossible here. The house stands on a plateau part of the way down what can only be described as a precipice. Most people at this point are probably expecting a few alpines and climbers clinging to the bare rockfaces. But there is nothing conventional about most of this garden where many of the plants happily defy the elements, the soil – or lack of it – and, occasionally, gravity. This is a garden for the moderately intrepid visitor, undertaking an up-and-down progress of the series of stepped paths, all made by Mrs Paish's late husband and zig-zag, because of the slope's steepness. But the effort is certainly worthwhile for the host of interesting plants; and there is a certain sense of achievement, too, on reaching the top and pausing to catch one's breath – and enjoy the view.

The Paishes were past retirement age when they came to Brynhydryd. The only part of the garden that could be described as conventional lies below the house, where, many years before the Paishes arrived in 1961, there were fruit and vegetables and an old orchard. After clearing most of it they planted larches, birch, and Scots pines on the hillside as windbreaks and with this necessary shelter built up a collection of plants whose interest sets the standard for the rest of the garden. There are a number of surprises: a hoheria from New Zealand and crinodendron from Chile, both very tender, and a number of large-leafed rhododendrons, of which there are many in the garden; here are *Rhododendron calophytum* and *Rh. rex.*

Hardly surprisingly, there is only one small area of lawn in the garden, to one side of the house, shaded by a stand of three old beeches. Originally the Hill Garden was only directly behind the house but now it has been expanded on both sides. A steady pace is advised on these paths, not only to avoid tiring early but to be able fully to appreciate the ingenious planting and variety of plants. Rhododendrons and azaleas are perhaps the most widely represented family, both hybrid and specie plants. As well as their wonderful colours in spring and early summer, the foliage of many, particularly the large-leafed varieties such as *Rhododendron falconeri* and *R. sinogrande* is very effective seen against the grey stone of the hillside; many of the azaleas provide autumn colour too.

But there is much else besides these plants: among the many interesting conifers are a *Sciadopityus verticillata*, the Umbrella pine, and two Bhutan pines. And for the flowering trees such as *Halesia carolina*, aptly named the 'Snowdrop Tree', and *Arbutus menziesii*, one of the best 'Strawberry Trees', the steep slope allows the rare luxury of appreciating their display of flowers from above; elsewhere one finds *Styrax hemsleyana*, with its delicate bell-like flowers hanging beneath its branches. Two outstanding and unusual trees reveal the Paishes' discerning eye in their choice of plants: *Eucryphia lucida* and *Prunus subhirtella* 'Fukubana'. Both are among the best specimens in their respective families.

Mrs Paish is as philosophical about the problem of tidiness as she is about everything else in her garden. As she says, most of the things that grow wild are undeniably attractive, such as the numerous heathers and ferns and, more particularly, the little yellow pimpernel which has obligingly become beautiful groundcover in several areas. To most people the fact of the garden is as baffling as the pronunciation of its name, but to visit here, and learn, is a most rewarding experience.

PLAS NEWYDD

On the Isle of Anglesey, 1 mile south-west of Llanfairpwll on the B4080
Tel. 0248 714 795
The National Trust and the Marquess of Anglesey

Open daily except Saturday from April to October inclusive

With its outstanding rooms, re-modelled by James Wyatt in the Gothic and Classical style, Plas Newydd is one of the most important acquisitions by the National Trust in recent years. Thanks to the continuing attention of successive generations, its gardens are exceptionally rich both in history and in horticulture. In 1793 Lord Uxbridge consulted Wyatt about alterations to the house, and it was probably due to him that Humphry Repton was commissioned to landscape the surroundings. It must have been an enviable task, with the grounds round the house sloping gently east to the Menai Strait and the distant view of Snowdonia. Much of Repton's layout remains, to which subsequent additions were made: by the 1st Marquess of Anglesey after 1815, who planted a great many trees; by the 6th Marquess in the 1920s and 1930s; and finally by the present Marquess since the 1950s. Repton's work extended beyond the present garden boundaries, but within their area a number of mature oaks, beeches and sycamores were clearly planted as part of his design. Some of Repton's proposals were rejected by Lord Uxbridge, such as his plans for an octagonal summerhouse on one end of the house described in his *Red Book* (dated 1798–9) in the most beguiling terms: 'seen from the library on one of those warm summer evenings, when such a pavilion would tempt us to walk out by moonlight to enjoy the murmur of the waves, and the perfume of those plants which are most fragrant at that time.'

The first major additions to the gardens were made by the 6th Marquess between the two World Wars. To the existing woodlands to the south of the house, on that gentle slope to the Strait, he added a number of trees, including blue cedars, a ginkgo and a tulip tree; the site was ideally suited, too, for the large groups of azaleas, acers and various magnolias which he also planted. Beyond these, as well as a quantity of camellias from the second family home of Beaudesert in Staffordshire – they had been in greenhouses there but could easily survive in the unusually sheltered and mild conditions at Plas Newydd, due to its proximity to the sea and the influence of the Gulf Stream – he planted extensive groups of *Rhododendron* 'Praecox' and 'Jacksonii'. In complete contrast, he laid out the formal Italianate garden on the North side of the house: the top terrace already existed, lower ones were made out of the sloping lawns, and he planted Mediterranean cypresses and roses to complete the effect.

After serious neglect during the Second World War, the present Marquess has not only restored but greatly added to the planting in the gardens since the 1950s. As well as the standard trees, these plantings wind round the lawns so that the whole area, called the West Indies, is a series of open glades between banks of trees and shrubs. Some of the most spectacular additions are the huge hedges of *Viburnum tomentosum* 'Lanarth'; these are now one of the great features of the garden, but at present are under serious attack by honey fungus. Numerous varieties of magnolias were added here to the now very large *M. soulangiana* planted between the wars, and there are styraxs, eucryphias, *Kalmia latifolia*, *Osmanthus delavayi*, *Embothrium coccineum* and banks of hydrangeas too. After the late summer-flowering plants the acers, red oaks and cercidiphyllums in particular give magnificent autumn colour. At the south end of the West Indies an interesting avenue of *Chamaecyparis pisifera* 'Squarrosa' and yew leads abruptly down to the water.

In the Italianate Garden most of the rose borders have been replaced by herbaceous and shrub borders, but the formality of its layout is retained on the various terraces, enhanced by the stone ornaments and the statue of Mercury at the end. Against the wall of the lowest terrace honeysuckle is trained close along its whole length, with berberis hedges along the top and a long border of hydrangeas below. Opposite here the damage to a hedge of hardy fuchsias, which runs the length of the terrace, bears witness to the severity, even here, of the 1981–2 winter. In 1984, however, its total recovery is fully evident.

Beyond the Italianate Garden 'Lady Uxbridge's Walk' leads to the wild Rhododendron Garden some distance away along the strait. The original plantings of rhododendrons were made by the 6th Marquess in the 1930s, in the setting of Repton's trees, but it has taken considerable work to restore this area. To the old plants, which included *Rhododendron Thomsonii*, *R. fortunei* and *R. mollyanum*, the present Marquess added a great many others, some of which were a generous wedding present from Lord Aberconway and brought over from his garden at Bodnant. There are now many of the tender, scented varieties such as *Rh.* 'Fragrantissimum' and 'Lady Alice Fitzwilliam'.

Plas Newydd is a fine tribute to successive generations of gardeners and their various helpers and advisors; comparative inaccessability makes their stylish work the more impressive and a visit the more rewarding.

Looking across the lake and Edwardian rockery at Benington Lordship, Hertfordshire, between tall cypresses to the statue of Shylock; the stone steps beyond accentuate the axis.

Looking along the glade at Trewithen, Cornwall to the eighteenth-century house. In early springtime the view is enhanced by one of the garden's many superb magnolias.

Dinmore Manor, Herefordshire. Here the buildings and garden date from the 1930s on a site with ancient origins.

The formality of the avenue of clipped ilexs at Arley Hall, Cheshire is reflected in the clipped conifers round the square lily pool.

Alpines and other dwarf plants along one of the raised beds at the Manor House, Walton-in-Gordano, Avon.

Blickling, Norfolk; one of the Jacobean towers and cupolas framed by trees with, in front, the nineteenth-century parterre.

Looking from the terrace at Muncaster Castle, Cumbria across part of the garden to Eskdale and the Cumbrian hills in the background, a view which Ruskin called; 'the Gateway to Paradise'.

The gently rising terrace at Kepwick Hall, Yorkshire, with equally imposing mature trees and rhododendrons.

The Chapel Garden at Gwysaney Hall, Clwyd, the mullioned windows and walls picturesquely draped in Virginia Creeper and other Climbers.

Dundonnell House, Ross and Cromarty. Agapanthus are among the rich variety of plants which thrive in the box-edged borders of this Walled Garden on the wild north-west coast of Scotland.

The stream garden at Bidlake Mill, Devon and, in the background, the ancient mill.

Huge lysichitums and hostas in front of rhododendrons and azaleas along one of the paths in the Woodland Garden at Coverwood Cottage, Surrey.

NORTH POWYS

LLYSDINAM

South-west of Newbridge on Wye, off the A470
Tel. 0597 89200
Lady Delia Venables Llewelyn and the Llysdinam Charitable Trust

Open one day per year and by appointment

In its traditional appearance there is something akin to many Scottish gardens at Llysdinam – lawns round the house leading to a Woodland Garden, and with an old walled Kitchen Garden directly west of the house as the main feature. It seems likely that much of the Llysdinam's planning dates from the nineteenth century when the Rev. R. L. Venables lived here, whose curate was Francis Kilvert the diarist.

The stone house enjoys an enviable position above the upper valley of the River Wye, looking south-west to the distant Brecon hills. It is partly in order not to detract from the views that the gardens immediately in front of the house are kept simple: a set of stone steps, albeit intricately designed, breaks the terraced lawns which merge into open fields. The attractive bow windows at either end of the south front look out over the main lawn dominated by two old trees, a Turkey oak and a lime. The Woodland Garden begins at the lawn's end, its planting mainly rhododendrons and azaleas, some of which are very old, although a more varied selection of shrubs has been brought into some areas. There is a Water Garden here, and below its path a Bog Garden has recently been made with acers and a silver weeping pear, as well as peltiphyllum and hostas, all thriving in the damp conditions.

The long border, stretching south-west from the house, beneath the tall yew hedge boundary of the Kitchen Garden provides colour in later summer. Raised above the lawn by a low stone wall, it is filled with peonies, groups of tall delphiniums and small pinks, though the striking scarlet 'Flame Flower', *Tropaeolum speciosum*, is spreading with great rapidity among the other plants.

Central in the yew hedge is an attractive pair of wrought-iron gates, set between brick piers, which lead straight into the double herbaceous border flanking the path up the middle of the Kitchen Garden, in traditional style screening the vegetables and fruit. But to prove that man does not live by fruit and vegetables alone, the best view anywhere in the garden is to be found here, looking down the herbaceous border, through the gates, between the clipped yew domes to the valley and hills.

MAENLLWYD ISAF

Near Abermule, between Newtown and Welshpool on the B4368
Tel. 068 686 204

Mrs Denise Hatchard

Open one day per year and by appointment

Mrs Hatchard has restored the originally Elizabethan house and created most of the garden since she came here in the 1950s, making a series of varying island beds and a lawn out of a derelict scrubland as the main garden. On the other side of the house, between it and the Orangery, is a smaller area where old box hedges tell of an earlier garden of some sort, but even without this the spot would have instant attraction, with the picturesque wooded valley of the River Mule curving round two sides, on its way to join the Severn.

The garden is in typically cheerful cottage-garden style – many and varied plants mix freely in the borders – but there are moments of unlikely grandeur too: a pair of stone pillars at one end of the garden carry the eye to the prospect beyond in the best landscape tradition; a solitary but obliging peacock who spends much of his time posing close by an impressive terracotta urn; and an Orangery for tender plants which Mrs Hatchard converted out of an old pighouse, with classical door and eighteenth-century windows.

All the island beds contain a mixture of herbaceous plants, shrubs and small trees, with hardly any space between rhododendrons, peonies, drawf conifers and columnar conifers, bamboo, rugosa roses, and many others. One bed is planned round a small pond and rockery where hostas, gunnera and *Primula florindae* mix happily with miniature rock pinks, campanula and a variety of alpines, all beneath the canopy of a weeping cherry. Among the other trees, one of the most striking is the *Robinia* 'Frisia' and many small maples, at the far end of the lawn, near the bank sloping down to the river.

In the smaller garden Mrs Hatchard has clipped the old box hedges back into shape. Informality is retained in the planting: in the four small enclosures on either side of the central box-flanked path, vegetables have been replaced by a mixture of herbaceous and shrub roses, and tall eremuruses form an eccentric contrast with a more refined *Hydrangea villosa* in the little border below the house. Among a variety of clematis on the Orangery wall is the violet-purple 'Gypsy Queen'. As a change from the garden's busy atmosphere the walk along the wooded bank above the river where there has probably been little change for centuries, makes one more than ever aware of what has been achieved in quite a short space of time just a few yards away.

POWIS CASTLE

¾ mile south of Welshpool off the A483
Tel. 0938 4336
The National Trust

Open daily from July to August inclusive

Powis Castle has been deservedly admired and written about for many years, but nothing can fully prepare the visitor for, or minimize the overpowering effect of, the series of terraces falling away from the pink stone castle. They are, without question, one of the most spectacular sights of any garden in Britain. Christopher Hussey described them as 'reproducing more nearly an Italian baroque terraced garden than any other surviving in England'.

Perhaps the reason that Powis is one of Britain's foremost gardens is because the stunning visual effect is matched by richness and depth of detail. Of the former, whether one is standing on the terraces below the castle looking to the wooded slopes of Wilderness and to the Welsh border beyond, or looking back to the Babylonian prospect of ascending terraces surmounted by the castle, the effect is unforgettable. Of the detailed interest, be it the ceaseless profusion of plants with which these terraces and the rest of the garden are now filled, or the history stretching back to medieval days when the old castle was first built and to the late seventeenth century when the terraces were first made, there seems to be no limit.

The date and architect of the terraces are not exactly known. It might not be too unrealistic to suppose that the Earl of Rochford himself (who came to the castle at the end of the seventeenth century) may have been partly or largely responsible for their creation out of the bare rock-face of pink gritstone. One thinks of the description of the flying staircase at Kingstone Lyle Park in Berkshire (whose architect is also not definitely established), that it must have been designed by an amateur because a professional would not dare attempt such a feat, for the Powis terraces are comparable. Since the Earl's time they escaped the hand of 'Capability' Brown and others, although Brown did suggest that they should be returned to a slope of natural rock. Instead they have been steadily adorned: with the Loggia Orangery below – the architectural focus of the terraces; with the lead urns and figures which stand upon the balustrading and might have been made by Van Nost; with Irish yews and box, some of which have swelled to shapes and sizes far beyond their original purpose; and with the borders of herbaceous plants, climbers and wall plants, and ornamental trees along the lowest slope.

Far below the top terrace, and reached by a curving walk between nineteen-foot-high walls of box leading from the end of the Orangery Terrace, is the old Kitchen Garden, which has now been re-planned as a series of formal areas. It is still surrounded by the pyramid-shaped apples dating from 1908, and still divided by formal yew hedges. There are flower borders and a vine arch, but one feels the contents of this lower garden fight a losing battle against the temptation to turn away to the view of the terraces above. Beyond the raised terrace along one side of the lower garden is the open lawn at the bottom of the escarpment – the Water Garden in the original design – and along this terrace a long yew walk leads to the wooded slope, the Wilderness, opposite the castle and terraces. The paths lead through this among a limitless variety of trees: the old oaks and beeches, evergreen redwoods and ilex, flowering magnolias, rhododendrons and eucryphias, and an *Aesculus hillocastanum* 'Baumannii' and Caucasian firs – the former with an enormous canopy, the latter with enormous height.

The whole scale of Powis is uncompromisingly large, not so much in the area but in the conception and detail of such a remarkable landscape. You can go there for ideas for your back garden or you can go there to be thrilled, and in either quest you will be rewarded.

SHROPSHIRE

BENTHALL HALL

4 miles north-east of Much Wenlock, 8 miles south of Wellington, 1 mile north-west of Broseley off the B4375

Tel. 0952 882 254

The National Trust

Open from Easter Saturday three afternoons a week to the end of September

Despite its proximity to the popular Severn Gorge, Benthall has the air of a retreat. Nevertheless, like nearby Ironbridge, it had an active nineteenth-century life and in fact dates from a much earlier period. Built by the Benthall family the small Elizabethan house contains one of the finest sixteenth-century oak staircases in England, as well as exquisite panelling and plaster ceilings. It was with the eminent nineteenth-century botanist, George Maw, however, that the story of Benthall's garden began.

Maw and his brother Arthur rented Benthall in 1853, having started a tile factory close by. The tile factory eventually moved to another site in the Severn Valley and became the largest source of ornamental tiles in the world, but Maw based himself at Benthall for the next thirty-three years and increasingly devoted himself to scientific studies and interests, in particular botany and geology. A lot of time in each of his first twenty years at Benthall was spent searching for new and decorative species in various mountainous regions of the Mediterranean and although Benthall is on an exposed site at 600 feet, the garden became a repository for the plants he brought back. Many were what would now be termed 'alpines' and by 1870 there were between three and four thousand species at Benthall.

A rockery was made with boulders from a nearby quarry, and a large greenhouse built with coke-fired furnaces and hot water pipes. Maw employed seven gardeners, and it was they who dug the curving ditch that he covered with removable frames to protect those species that could not cope with the wetter English weather. Identification and naming of his plants understandably was almost an obsession with Maw. His method of labelling was unique. Flat terracotta pegs were made in his tile factory, and after he had inscribed them with the plant names and any other relevant details, they were fired in a kiln, thus making the ink truly indelible; some have been found in recent years with still legible writing. Despite his varied collection Maw was particularly interested in the single genus of crocus, and in 1886 he published *A Monograph of the Genus Crocus*, the result of many years' work and quite outstanding. He hand-painted each of the sixty-one colour plates in all the copies printed. As these only numbered twenty-seven the work is of unique interest and value.

After Maw's death some of his introductions managed to naturalize themselves at Benthall, but most of his plants disappeared. Part of the rockery survived, as did the ditch without its brick sides and covering frames, and most of the garden in its present form was laid out by Robert Bateman and his wife, who were tenants between 1890 and 1906. They laid out the terraced 'Pixie Garden' on the west side of the house beyond the rectangular pool, with topiary yew and box and an attractive dovecot against which cling various climbing plants. The main south front of the house looks out on to terraced lawns; here and to the east of the house are some fine trees including beech, oaks, Scots pines and a young Colorado blue spruce. A laburnum now spreads over Maw's ditch.

In 1934 the Benthall family returned to their ancestral home, and it is largely thanks to Sir Paul and Lady Benthall, the present occupants, that the remnants of the garden's distinguished Victorian past have survived. Scattered through the long grass and beneath the surrounding hedges are two spring varieties of crocus – *Crocus vernus* and *C. tommasinianus* – and three autumn ones – *C. speciosus*, *C. pulchellus*, and *C. nudiflorus*. As well as these Sir Paul considers there to be about twenty-five unusual plants which Maw introduced to Benthall, often from abroad. Not so unusual is the chionodoxa, which he introduced in 1877 and which is now widely known as *Chionodoxa luciliae* 'The Glory of the Snow'. This is in fact incorrect, as the true *Chionodoxa luciliae* was named by a French botanist called Boissier in 1844 and is quite rare in this country, though admittedly the difference between the plants is slight and both originate from the same mountainous area in Asia Minor.

Perhaps it is hardly surprising that so avid and questing a botanist as George Maw should have started a controversy. One thing, though, seems certain: the placid home where he did his work is disarmingly unaware of this or any other wrangle. Although it cannot be one of the National Trust's most frequented members it is one of its most charming monuments to botanical history.

THE DAIRY HOUSE

In Ludstone, 7 miles west of Wolverhampton and south of the A454
Tel. 074 66237
Miss N. E. Wood

Open on selected days in July, and by appointment

'The garden, such as it was, had become a wilderness breast-high with Michaelmas daisies, lupins and Flanders poppies. Self-sown ash and over-mature spruce, with brambles, ground-elder and nettles six feet or more high, formed about an acre of almost impenetrable woodland at the far end. Cattle roamed at will through neglected hedges. There was a massive collection of broken glass, china, tin cans, watertanks and other household debris, as well as boots, barbed wire, netting etc. left by the Home Guard when they vacated their local post in the woodland.'

Thus Miss Wood on the state of her garden when she moved here in 1956. The Dairy House had been, as its name suggests, the cottage for the adjacent dairy buildings on the estate of the Carolean Ludstone Hall which stands across the road. It was enlarged in 1854 and a Georgian façade was added. In the 1920s two bay windows were introduced on the south side looking over the present garden.

Having already renovated the cottage before taking up residence, Miss Wood was not to be daunted by the task before her and indeed was continually cheered by the obvious natural beauty of the site, particularly to the east where the ground sloped to a lake called the Pool, with two copper beeches on its far side. In the opposite direction the view crossed fields to the square tower of the Saxon church at Claverley.

The land on the south side of the house had originally been a gravel quarry and the soil had been thrown up to form banks, leaving a series of flat areas, hollows and steep slopes. The soil proved to be hungry, shallow, stony, compacted sand, with very little topsoil, and acid. The site was also a severe frost-pocket because of the proximity of the lake. Despite these and other problems, such as the lack of shelter, Miss

Wood has steadily built up the garden with plantings along the banks, following the lie of the land, and island beds on the lawns. In a number of places the plants have had to be almost exclusively drought-resistant and sun-loving, but an extensive irrigation system installed in 1969 has greatly helped. Despite this, the collection Miss Wood has built up throughout the garden is impressive.

Miss Wood was helped in her garden planning by Percy Cane, who suggested the terrace and paving round the house, and stressed the importance of keeping the basic nature of the garden simple, in harmony with its setting. As well as heather beds Miss Wood has made a magnolia bed and a viburnum bed. Other plants that have done well are a variety of trees, shrubs and smaller plants: junipers and cypresses, sorbus, golden elm Scots pine and birch, *Cornus kousa* 'Chinensis', yew hedges hosting *Tropaeolum speciosum*, *Cytisus battandieri*, hostas, cyclamen, lilies, nerines and many spring bulbs. The winter of 1981–2 inflicted terrible damage and buddleias, berberis, *Eucalyptus gunnii* and *Garrya elliptica* all perished.

Still, the effects of one disastrous winter cannot detract from Miss Wood's achievement or the natural attraction of the site. It is reassuring to look from the terrace to the Pool with its island, where Canada geese breed, and the copper beeches and park beyond, across the intervening beauty. The garden will remain an impressive testament of success against difficulty.

HODNET HALL

In Hodnet between Market Drayton and Shrewsbury on the A53 and A442
Tel. 063 084 202

Mr A. E. H. and The Hon. Mrs Heber-Percy

Open daily from Easter to September inclusive

When Brigadier Heber-Percy embarked on the creation of the gardens at Hodnet in 1922 it was possible that he was spurred on by the enormous proportions of his house, built of red brick in 1870 in Elizabethan style on a slope overlooking the valley he was to transform. The gardens that he created may not have been in the style of an eighteenth-century landscape but they were certainly on a scale that even 'Capability' Brown would have been proud of, covering some sixty acres, much of them, rather than open parkland, being instead areas of dense and varied planting. It was a size of project that has rarely been attempted in the twentieth century and is not likely to be undertaken again in the future.

When the Brigadier began work the valley contained many outstanding mature trees with a small stream flowing through marshy ground at the bottom. He put in a series of dams which allowed the water to build up into a chain of descending lakes, pools and streams starting well out of sight to the west and stretching down across the front of the house to the earlier Horse Wash Pool. Surrounded by beech woods and water meadows, they made an impressive prospect even before the pageant of planting on the banks and surrounding slopes. Lime-free soil, shelter, shade where necessary and moist positions, the sites were ideal for a wide variety of plants.

The main areas of planting stretch from the waterfalls and Water Garden across in front of the house to the Magnolia Walk and up towards the Garden Centre. The view from the terrace along the south side of the house looks across the Broad Walk and terracing to the Main Pool and the ground rising on its far side to the old brick dovecot, built in 1656. On the terraced slopes are acers, rhododendrons and other plants. On the east side of the terraces is an interesting Circular Garden, the Lower Rose Garden, with beds of peonies, Korresia floribunda roses and *Hydrangea paniculata* 'Grandiflora' in rings around the central statue. Close by is the Camellia Garden.

From the waterfalls the descending pools and streams, like some aquatic Pied Piper, trail countless numbers of plants: gunnera, primulas, astilbes and ferns close to the water's edge, large plantings of rhododendrons, azaleas, flowering cherries, and many smaller plants such as trilliums and daffodils on the banks behind. Different plantings continue from the series of small pools at the valley's end to the Stone Garden on the slope above. Close by *Cornus canadensis* spreads as ground-cover beneath a stand of oaks, a good example of the attention to detail to be found throughout these gardens. At the western end of the valley the gardens have a more 'natural' aspect and it would be a pity for any visitor to miss these more distant but tranquil areas to compare with the busy planting lower down the valley.

The appearance of Hodnet has been greatly changed in recent years by alterations to the house. Because of its unwieldly and enormous size the original roof, top floor and two large rooms which extended from the ground floor have been removed. The outer walls of the last two have been retained to form attractive small courtyards. It is a tragedy that

Hodnet was among the worst hit gardens during the winter of 1981–2. The task of clearing and replacing the casualties in gardens this size was daunting but even in the summer of 1982, when the effect of the winter on them was most apparent, interest did not seem noticeably diminished.

An exhaustive description of everything in the gardens would be overwhelming. It may surprise most visitors to know that originally the gardens were kept up by Brigadier Heber-Percy and three gardeners, and even now his son Algernon and Mrs Heber-Percy have only four gardeners to maintain Hodnet's park-like proportions. It is fitting that the proportions of a memorial to him reflect the grandeur of the brigadier's vision. To the north of the house, set at a distance across the main road, he had erected the columns of the portico from Apley Castle in Shropshire, which he bought when the castle was demolished in 1956. They have been a memorial since his death in 1962, by which time he had made Hodnet's reputation as one of the outstanding creations of twentieth-century gardening secure.

SWALLOW HAYES

In Rectory Road, Albrighton, 7 miles north-west of Wolverhampton off the A41
Tel. 0907 222 624

Mr and Mrs Michael Edwards

Open two Sundays a year, and by appointment for parties

This one-and-a-half acre garden, begun in 1968, contains well over fifteen hundred plants. The numbers partly stem from the fact that Mr and Mrs Edwards run a commercial nursery nearby, for which the garden provides some propagating material, but equally because a keen knowledge and enjoyment of numerous varieties has encouraged them to make maximum use of their ground. They have now begun work to extend the garden to four acres.

The plan is that of a fairly conventional modern garden – lawn winding between informally arranged beds and borders; what one would not normally see in a conventional garden are some of the unusual plants. Near the entrance of the garden are groups of acers and hamamelis, and spreading across the steps leading down from the little

Rose Garden beside the house to the main lawn is perhaps the most spectacular tree in the garden, *Prunus* 'Shidare Yoshino', a wonderful weeping cherry.

The main entrance to the garden leads past *Pinus strobus* to a collection of cherries which are also spectacular in the spring, including 'Yukon', 'Accolade', 'Pandora' and 'Shirotae'. Beyond here is a blue cedar – in fact the whole garden is full of outstanding trees including many magnolias, *Davidia involucrata*, *Metasequoia glyptostroboides*, *Cedrus deodara* 'Aurea', *Eucryphia glutinosa* and the rare *Fagus sylvatica* 'Tricolor', though difficulties may arise when some of them get much bigger.

In the various parts of the garden there is an easy balance between areas with a distinct theme and groupings of similar varieties, and those where there is complete variety. This is particularly noticeable looking over the main lawn from the house: one border opposite is dominated by rhododendrons and azaleas but also contains *Malus* 'Royalty' with purple leaves, *Acer* 'Brilliantissimum', and *Betula utilis* with unusually white bark. On the other side of a headland of lawn is an herbaceous border, of generous proportions for a small garden and backed by lilacs and standard cypresses.

Variety is continuous as one progresses round the garden, from a border of dwarf rhododendrons past some of the standard trees mentioned above to the damp bottom corner where willows drape over *Primula japonica* and hostas. What better contrast to the dwarf rhododendrons than *Clematis alpina* trained into one of the fastigiate cherries here? Towards the bottom corner is the Children's Garden, enclosed by birches. Inside dwarf conifers planted by the Edwards' son have replaced the camp of past years, with heathers in the dry higher part, and rhododendrons and azaleas, shaded by birches, lower down.

Many plants such as berberis, escallonias and *Osmanthus delavayi* were badly hit during the winter of 1981–2, but have now either completely recovered or been replaced. Even if conditions in some places do appear somewhat cramped this does not detract from the garden's interest, and works towards what has always been a major factor for the Edwards, ease of maintenance. Mrs Edwards spends an average eight hours a week working in the garden and receives, of course, the gardener's reward.

STAFFORDSHIRE

LITTLE ONN HALL

6 miles south-west of Stafford and 2 miles south of Church Eaton, midway between the A5 and the A518

Tel. 0785 840 154

Mr and Mrs I. H. Kidson

Open one Sunday in June

Little Onn Hall was built between 1850 and 1855 to replace a Queen Anne house to the north which was pulled down because it suffered from excessive damp. Further additions were made to the house in the 1890s and then the Misses Ashton, who lived at Little Onn at the time, commissioned Thomas Mawson to design extensive gardens to surround the house and encompass the ancient moat to the north-east. Mawson had earlier laid out the gardens at Graythwaite Manor in Cumbria (*see* pp 151–3) and would later add the main terrace to Wightwick Manor near Wolverhampton (*see* pp 206–8). His ambitious plans for Little Onn Hall were never fully carried out, but photographs of the garden in 1900 testify that those which were have remained virtually unchanged. Mr and Mrs Kidson bought Little Onn Hall in the early 1970s, and their twin aims have been to preserve Mawson's work while adding new planting in different areas of the garden.

Mawson's first major contribution was the formal Rose Garden to the west of the house, beyond the entrance forecourt. The large rectangular area is divided into three patterns of rosebeds, the central one arranged round a stone sundial and the outer two round clipped yews. It seems that most of the roses were originally old-fashioned varieties, but these have been replaced by hybrid teas and the old-fashioneds are continued to the border on either side of the steps leading down from the forecourt. The symmetry of the design is enhanced by the surrounding walls and in particular by the two stone gazebos with tiled roofs which Mawson placed on the north-west and south-west corners. The only major change in the Rose Garden has been the removal of the low box hedging which enclosed the rosebeds, and one feature has grown to dramatic proportions – the bank of rhododendrons along the far, west wall; they now spill over into the meadow beyond, rather than forming a neat boundary as when originally planned by Mawson.

Mawson's other large-scale plan was the double herbaceous borders, sixty yards long, along the entrance drive from the imposing gates right up to the forecourt. These now have a variety of shrubs mixed in with the herbaceous plants but retain their yew hedges behind; they make a dramatic introduction to the Hall when in full flower.

Mawson's plans for formal but open areas of lawn, hedges and paths between clipped yew and box for the south and east fronts were never fully carried out. Today the south front looks on to a croquet lawn and on the east side two grass terraces descend to the Tennis Court lawn. The problem of what to do with the uneven ground beyond here was solved in the 1920s when a series of shallow descending terraces was laid out from the imposing old beech tree in the south-east corner of the garden, near a central 'dog-bone'-shaped lily pond. The low wall which forms the east boundary between the garden and park is lined with rhododendrons.

From the north end of the terraced lawns a path between overhanging cherries makes the transition from formality to informal woodland, with the Moat Garden beyond. The moat, which dates from around 1400, surrounds a square area where parts of a medieval building remain; ancient yews have expanded to hang right down over the water. Around the outer sides of the moat contrastingly light-foliaged beeches shade close plantings of spring flowers – bluebells, primroses and daffodils. With its slightly overgrown trees, the Moat Garden has a secretive and picturesque appearance, but nature has not been allowed to take over completely: along the north side in front of the wall marking the boundary with the old Kitchen Garden, is a long mixed border of shrub roses and herbaceous plants; and at the west end of the moat is a small formal garden of rosebeds.

The Kidsons are restoring parts of the medieval building on the moat island. They have only limited part-time help to manage their ten-acre garden but have preserved the balance between Mawson's late Victorian formality and the secluded woodland areas, a formidable task successfully achieved.

WIGHTWICK MANOR

3 miles west of Wolverhampton off the A454
Tel. 0902 761 108
The National Trust

Open daily except Thursday, Saturday and Bank Holidays, and closed in February

In 1887 Samuel Theodore Mander, a Wolverhampton manufacturer, bought the manor of Wightwick and immediately commissioned designs for a new house from the architect Edward Ould, who specialized in half-timbered houses. Wightwick's exterior is richly varied, with elaborate carving, spiral Tudor chimneys and diverse building materials including oak, local red sandstone, brick and tile. Of far greater significance, however, are the interiors, the decoration of which Mander commissioned from William Morris and Company. Morris's company was strongly influenced by the work of the Pre-Raphaelites and it is this connection which gives Wightwick particular interest. Today, with the more recent acquisitions by Sir Geoffrey and Lady Mander, who gave the property to the National Trust in 1937, the manor is a unique treasure-house of the Pre-Raphaelites' work; their influence extends to the ten-acre garden, mostly laid out when the house was being built to designs by Alfred Parsons RA, with later additions designed by Thomas Mawson. Both the terrace and most of Parsons' work survive today to present a picture which combines a typically late Victorian appearance with a number of most distinctive features.

Parsons was better known as an artist and in particular for his paintings of roses which illustrated Ellen Willmott's enormous book *The Genus Rosa*. His designs for Wightwick were predominantly formal but the bold lines of yew hedges and topiary, and the bright colours in herbaceous borders and the formal Rose Garden, were ideally suited to the elaborate architecture of the house.

In 1910 Thomas Mawson laid out the broad flagged terrace along the south front. His intention of echoing the architecture of the house within the garden is obvious from the unusual oak balustrade with which he surmounted the retaining wall: it recalls at once the oak beams, gable-ends and carving.

A broad flight of stone steps breaks Mawson's wall and balustrade, leading down from the lawn to a narrow avenue of huge, cylindrical domes of yew which dominates this lower south garden. Around the perimeter of the lawn here are a number of interesting mature trees; these include a purple-twigged lime and a copper beech, planted by King George V and Queen Mary respectively in 1900 when they visited Wightwick as Duke and Duchess of York, and a hornbeam (William Morris's favourite tree), planted by Clement Attlee in 1953. To the east of the house is another lawn beyond which the road, which forms the garden's boundary on this side, is crossed by one of Wightwick's many oddities, a wooden replica of the 'Mathematical' bridge at Queen's College, Cambridge.

To the west of the house a broad slope, divided in the middle by a long narrow path between yew hedges, drops away from the entrance courtyard. The entrance to the path is flanked by two crowns on stone pedestals which were taken from the parapet of Big Ben's clock tower in 1933. The formality of Parsons' layout to the north of the central path contrasts with the peaceful informality of the open meadow which extends down the slope on the south side, akin to a miniature park with its mixture of trees – oak, lime, plane, tulip tree and a ginkgo. A narrow opening in one of the central yew hedges leads north between herbaceous borders to the area of Parsons' most intricate planting, the formal Rose Garden, a pattern of rosebeds surrounding huge specimens of yew topiary and a central octagonal arbour draped in climbing roses and clematis. Columns of alternating golden and green yew fill one side of this garden; on another are even larger yew drums surmounted by clipped yew birds. The Rose Garden is made even more impressive, if somewhat overpowering, by the tall yew hedges which enclose it.

From the north-west corner of the Rose Garden another path leads down the slope along the garden's north boundary flanked by alternating clipped golden hollies and yews. An informal apple orchard fills the space below the Rose Garden between this and the central yew-lined path. Another peculiarity in the Wightwick gardens is discovered at the bottom of the orchard – a curving path with a line of boulders along one side explained by a notice: 'These boulders from the Lake District and Scotland were left here about 45,000 years ago when the great glacier melted in the last Ice Age.' Each boulder is marked with its place of origin.

At the bottom of the west slope a more tranquil air prevails: two ponds with an informal planting of mixed rhododendrons, yellow scented azaleas, bluebells and striking red acers. A stream flows from the upper pond to the lower where the deep canopies of two copper beeches overhang the water. The mood of the garden becomes noticeably more formal, and the planting more pronounced, as one returns from here up the slope, almost certainly a response to the house's rich architecture and decoration. While it would perhaps be fanciful to suggest that the gardens are an horticultural attempt to portray the Pre-Raphaelite style that influence is unmistakable and very considerably enhances Wightwick's period atmosphere.

SOUTH WALES AND THE MARCHES

Dyfed
Glamorgan
Gwent
Herefordshire
South Powys
Worcestershire

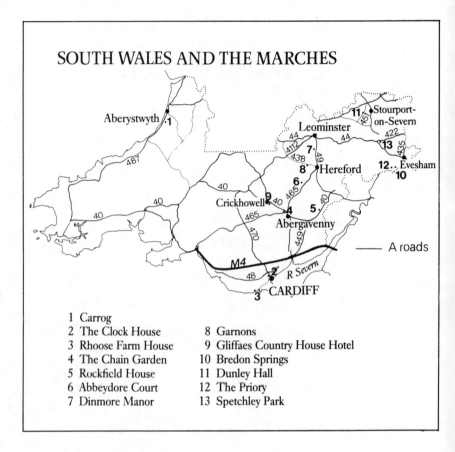

SOUTH WALES AND THE MARCHES

1 Carrog
2 The Clock House
3 Rhoose Farm House
4 The Chain Garden
5 Rockfield House
6 Abbeydore Court
7 Dinmore Manor

8 Garnons
9 Gliffaes Country House Hotel
10 Bredon Springs
11 Dunley Hall
12 The Priory
13 Spetchley Park

DYFED

CARROG

In Llanddeiniol, south of Aberystwyth, off the A487
Tel. 09748 369
Mr and Mrs Geoffrey Williams

Open one Sunday per year and by appointment

The immediately striking effect in this garden, made almost completely since 1970, is its subtle association of plants particularly for their foliage. Other than the small Walled Garden to the west of the two-hundred-year-old stone house, the main five acres were planned to minimize labour, with lawns, narrow paths, borders and island beds flowing in an unbroken sweep to the south and east of the house. As the trees and shrubs have matured the form of the garden has pulled together and now it provides all-year interest. A very basic plan for the layout was suggested by Notcutts of Woodbridge, and advice on planting was given by the late Basil Fox, curator of the Botany Garden at the University of Wales in Aberystwyth. But the garden is primarily the creation of Mrs Williams, made with help from her husband from the two fields where they kept ponies for their children; and they maintain it themselves. Unfortunately Carrog was badly hit in the winter of 1981–2, when many of the more tender plants were killed, but the Williams's are not gardeners who are easily demoralized and replacements are appearing.

Within the small Walled Garden a series of striking combinations set the tone: *Robinia pseudoacacia* 'Frisia', one of the most beautiful of any ornamental trees, has been positioned so that the cloud of delicate, golden pinnate leaves appears behind the dark screen of an old box hedge. In the background, beyond the robinia, is another equally graceful tree, *Styrax japonica*, and close by the branches of a weeping birch drape a golden acer beside the small pond.

Leaving the Walled Garden by the iron gate in the south wall – covered in various climbing plants as are all the walls – one sees clearly that it is not only the planting which is important at Carrog. From the gateway a beautiful view is revealed, across the garden to its lowest part where the Williams's have surrounded the existing pond with dense planting of hostas, primulas, metasequoias and swamp cypresses, which are such a good combination and well suited to the damp conditions. The large peat bed nearby contains more damp-loving plants closely grouped, including candelabra primulas, dwarf rhododendrons and azaleas. One of the greatest aids in reducing maintenance is the success of close planting, so that weeds do not have room to grow, and it is immediately recognizable in all the beds here.

In many places in the main garden, compact shrubs – olearias, senecios, hydrangeas, viburnums and hebes – contrast with the narrow vertical leaves of plants like *Aralia elata* 'Albo-variegata' and various irises. Everywhere they are highlighted by standard trees planted in borders or singly on the lawns. Some are mature specimens which the Williams's inherited, such as the oaks and beeches, but the majority are the huge variety which they themselves have added – various acers, sorbuses, rowans, birches and cercidiphyllums and, among the flowering trees, cherries and magnolias. The evergreens, often planted singly, range from the golden Monterey cypress and *Cupressus macrocarpa* 'Donard Gold', to the dark green, pendulous *Picea breweriana* 'Brewer's Weeping Spruce', and blue Atlantica cedars, whose foliage is excelled only by the wonderful blue-grey shades of a rare and tender Kashmir cypress. Two small, but superb, trees signify the quality of other trees planted as standards: *Fagus sylvatica* 'Rohanii', a purple form of the fern-leafed beech, and *Gleditsia triacanthos* 'Sunburst' whose brilliant golden leaves rival the robinia.

Not all the plants are large shrubs or trees: one border is a mass of small herbaceous plants, and another, at the top of the garden, in contrast to the widespread stress on foliage, contains large shrub roses – 'Buff Beauty', 'Blanc Double de Coubert' and others – planted close together to emphasize the effect when in flower. Shrub roses have also been planted along part of the drive on the edge of the garden, in front of a belt of protective pines.

Not only is there variety here, but Carrog seems to have all the vigour of youth and there is constant change, since the Williams's successful informal style allows for constant alteration. Carrog is a garden which is never static, perhaps a daunting undertaking at times, but always exciting.

GLAMORGAN

THE CLOCK HOUSE, LLANDAFF

Next to Llandaff Cathedral in Cardiff
Tel. 0222 564 565
Professor and Mrs B. M. Hibbard

Open one Sunday per year

Llandaff was a Roman settlement, even older than Cardiff itself of which it is now part. The Norman cathedral has been continually added to and restored, particularly since the Second World War when it was badly damaged by bombing; it stands just beyond the Clock House garden, partly screened by trees and partly by the walls of some old cathedral buildings.

Despite being a modern building, the Clock House has taken on the serenity typical of a cathedral close. Its garden was originally laid out by Roy Horley in the mid-1950s. Since Professor and Mrs Hibbard arrived in 1974 they have replanned much of the three-quarter-acre but have retained the basic concept, a series of enclosures, open àreas leading into each other, in which one can see the influence of Hidcote. The orderly layout belies some adventurous planting, particularly of old-fashioned roses, and in June and July the garden is a mass of colour, seen against the cathedral towers and spire with the ruins of Bishop's Castle on the hill beyond.

Part of the garden's charm is its irregularity of shape, proving that imaginative design can produce numerous vistas even in a small garden. The main west lawn is at an angle to the house, with rose borders in front and a small lily pond to one side enclosed by small acers, shrubs and roses again, including a small pink Macracantha rose. At the south end of the lawn columnar cypresses frame the entrance to a beautifully planned path leading to a small bench beneath one of the old walls. Behind the bench is the outstanding mature tree in the garden, a ginkgo, which came to the cathedral garden from the Duffryn Estate about seventy-five years ago in return for a wellingtonia. Along the path are small hedges of lavender, with standard 'Iceberg' roses and herbaceous plants behind.

On the north side of the lawn the cypresses are balanced by an arch smothered with the single pink 'Complicata' rose, leading to part of the garden which is like a baby Hidcote. A profusion of shrub roses, delphiniums and other herbaceous plants is divided up by grass and paved paths and closely clipped yew hedges of different heights. The north wall behind a little dovecot is covered with roses, including 'Madame Alfred Carrier', and clematis, which have been tamed from their customary riotous behaviour. There is a rewarding view east between the flowers, shrubs and yew hedges to a *Viburnum plicatum* 'Lanarth' on a far wall. Alongside this viburnum is a young *Ceanothus* 'Trewithen Blue' which is rapidly replacing a superb specimen tree killed in the winter of 1981–2.

In contrast to the almost cottage-garden roses and herbaceous borders is a small walled courtyard, just beyond the yew hedges in front of the north end of the house, formally planned with a central pool and fountain, standard 'Iceberg' roses and low clipped box hedges. The viburnum mentioned earlier is on one wall, and on the wall opposite the house a climbing hydrangea stakes its claim against a vigorous honeysuckle. Beyond the courtyard is the small part of the garden closest to the cathedral. It was overgrown with ivy and *Clematis vitalba* when the Hibbards arrived but it has been cleared, and filled with lilacs, camellias, azaleas and philadelphus.

On the far side of the longest, west, wall of the garden, beyond the lawn, are the playing fields of the cathedral choir school. Along this wall are various trees and shrubs – an old walnut, buddleias, kolkwitzias, cornuses and viburnums – planted as a screen though with some views through to the fields. On one part of the wall a Kiftsgate rose most effectively discourages the schoolboys, even the budding gardeners among them, from any adventurous climbing.

RHOOSE FARM HOUSE

In Rhoose, near Cardiff, on the B4265
Tel. 0446 710 276
Professor A. L. Cochrane

Open two days a year and by appointment

In building up the garden here since 1958, after he had bought the property in 1947, Professor Cochrane has shown a notable ability to overcome the limitations of the garden – a heavy and alkaline soil and exposure to sea winds – beginning by drawing up a plan for the garden's proposed finished appearance, thereby imposing a distinctive structure and pattern.

On one wall of the house is a fine yellow Banksia rose. Placed on a low wall nearby are seven seventeenth-century pig troughs filled with choice alpines – one is devoted to New Zealand alpines and another to alpines discovered by William Boyd, including *Salix Boydie*.

Looking from the house across the lowest lawn one is immediately presented with one of the outstanding features and most striking views at Rhoose – an abstract sculpture by Barbara Hepworth with a flowering cherry spreading above it. The sculpture is aligned with the garden's main axis, between mixed borders with informally curving edges up to the top of the garden sheltered by a high wall. In these borders are a number of plants from New Zealand – a special interest of Professor Cochrane's – including *Corokia cotoneaster*, *Sophora tetraptera* 'Microphylla', olearias and, in contrast to these compact shrubs and small trees, the New Zealand flax, *Phormium tenax*, with its huge sword-like leaves, strikingly positioned on a headland in one of the borders, challenging *Yucca filamentosa* opposite. The borders also contain hardy fuchsias and herbaceous plants, and an exotic Mediterranean 'Oleander' tree with dark evergreen leaves.

In contrast to these unusual and exotic plants is the parallel axis leading from the little summerhouse at the top between borders of shrub roses to the lowest lawn, where it is focused on a standard 'Little White Pet' rose. The colours in the rose borders progress from red through pink to yellow and white. There is also an attractive Rose Walk, edged with miniature pinks, leading from the house to the borders of shrub roses.

At the top of the garden are more sculptures – another Barbara Hepworth and a mother and child by Peter Nicholas, who lives in the beautifully restored and converted farmyard buildings; there are many of his sculptures throughout the garden. The sculptures here dominate a fine vista across the top of the garden with the ornamental pool and a huge *Clematis montana* 'Rubens' on the wall behind.

On the far side of the house the old farm buildings make an attractive background, in particular the series of unusual seventeenth-century arches. Professor Cochrane has stressed their importance by effective planting along the low wall dividing the farmyard: a thick lavender hedge along the top, and a different variety of lavender, alternating with standard 'Iceberg' roses, along the bottom. In the lower part of the old farmyard Professor Cochrane has made one of the particularly interesting features at Rhoose, a Scree Garden: a case, really, of making a virtue of necessity, since the ground was almost impossible – limestone and virtually no soil. Now established, the scree mixture has, after careful initial weeding, proved virtually weed-free and therefore labour-saving. There is enormous variety here, with the conifers, such as dwarf junipers, pines and a Cyprian cedar, giving constant shape, aided by the shrubs, some of which are for foliage effect – such as *Helichrysums* – and others for blooms, like *Convolvulus cneorum* with pink trumpet flowers. Throughout the year various alpines are in flower; among the more unusual ones are many varieties of the Californian fuchsia *Zauschneria*. Dwarf bulbs include various *Narcissus* and miniature tulips, and the whole area is greatly enhanced by the various cotoneasters which Professor Cochrane has trained close to the ground in winding trails between the other plants. Also in the farmyard garden is a small pond surrounded by low groundcover plants and various willows, among which are more of Peter Nicholas's sculptures and a copy of a Welsh seventeenth-century figure as a fountain.

Considering that the whole garden at Rhoose is only just over an acre and a half, there is an unexpectedly large collection of plants within its well-planned structure, and certainly the Scree Garden, the more unusual plants from New Zealand and the sculptures add a special zest to its pleasures.

GWENT

THE CHAIN GARDEN

In Chain Road, 1 mile north of Abergavenny, off the A40
Tel. 087 33825
Mr and Mrs C. F. R. Price

Open one or two days at the beginning of June, and by appointment from April to October inclusive

Perched on a hill on the outskirts of Abergavenny, the Chain Garden was originally laid out in about 1800 by the Baker Gabb family. The stone and brick walls which completely enclose the two-acre site date from about the turn of this century, the division of its west-facing slope into four levels disguising an overall drop. It is likely that some of the older trees date from the early nineteenth century, but Mr and Mrs Price have planted a variety of trees, shrubs and other plants themselves, using the existing features, in particular the small Cibi stream which flows through the garden and disappears underground at one point, only to re-emerge close by.

Where the stream flows into the garden through a small gully the banks are planted with a host of white daffodils, erythroniums and drum-head primulas in spring, with white foxgloves and phlox later in the year. As it flows on across the main garden the stream is adorned by constant variety: irises and day lilies; tree peonies; purple aubretia all over the walls where it flows through a little channel; spring and autumn cyclamen on the bank beneath two fine old oaks which, with the evergreen oak on the edge of the garden, date from the Baker Gabbs' days; syringas; mahonias and old musk roses. A large weeping willow spreads across the water by the wooden bridge, its pendulous form contrasting with the upright variegated hollies nearby.

Because of the informality of most of the planting and the abundance of open lawn on the various levels the garden does not appear over-planted at any point. The older trees and shrubs – the oaks, a very old medlar and a mulberry which are reputedly over three hundred years old, rhododendrons and two ninety-year-old camellias – have been joined by younger liquidambars, stewartias, acers, *Magnolia stellata*, a metasequoia and other trees and shrubs including a very pretty daphne, often planted as standards on the lawns to highlight their appearance and maintain the feeling of space.

Now that the main house has been converted into flats, the Prices maintain the Chain Garden from the smaller new house at the top of the slope. A narrow lawn leads past the new house to the Kitchen Garden and swimming pool, and this small area demonstrates the same flair for planting. An old walnut on the lawn has been joined by a recently planted one, and along one side of the lawn is a cheerfully haphazard border where spring flowers like polyanthus are followed by roses, a variety of herbaceous plants, smaller grey-leafed plants and clematis. At the far end, on the wall behind the swimming pool, is a magnolia and a lovely carpentaria. The Prices have named the new house Merys-wydden, the Welsh for 'Medlar', after one of the garden's most interesting and certainly oldest trees; looking to the future they have planted another to accompany the rest of the new generation they have brought to the garden.

ROCKFIELD HOUSE

2 miles north-west of Monmouth on the B4233
Tel. 0600 2874

Lieutenant-Colonel J. C. E. Harding-Rolls

Open one afternoon in June

A photograph taken shortly before 1959, when Colonel Harding-Rolls came here, shows cows grazing in a field just beyond the terrace round the house. There was no garden other than the old Walled Garden to the east and a number of fine trees to the south. The site did, however, enjoy many advantages, particularly in front of the house where the ground slopes steeply to the south from the terrace to a valley.

One of the first things Colonel Harding-Rolls did was to dam the small boggy stream in the valley so that it expanded to form the present lake, really the outstanding feature at Rockfield, and build a bridge across it to carry the new drive, incorporating the old lodge gates; the balustrade on one side of the bridge is today covered with a large wisteria. In building up the garden along the lake some of the old trees were an invaluable setting. The most striking tree in the garden is the columnar *Calocedrus decurrens* on the lawn above the lake, but also particularly good are the lime, cedar and wellingtonia to the west of the bridge, and a very tall wellingtonia by the path on the far, south, side of the lake. Further along this path is a wonderful weeping beech; its branches, which reach right to the ground, have been trained over the path to form an arched canopy. Around these trees smaller acers and a laburnum have been added, and at the far eastern end of the lake, where the stream flows in, a number of willows and an amelanchier give variety. Above here on the steep slope is an effective rockery, part of which, because of its imposing appearance, is known as 'The Maginot Line'.

Above this rockery in turn is one of the most effective additions to the garden, a terrace stretching along the outside of the Walled Garden. Called the Hermes Walk, it leads to a statue of Hermes with, in its stand, the inscription: 'This statue was originally erected in the Hendre rose garden in commemoration of the double flight across the Channel by the Hon. C. S. Rolls in June 1910 and was re-erected on this site in 1960'. (It is a replica of one at Dover.) Trained against the wall on one side of the path here are climbing roses, and in the border on the other side are standard roses and a spectacular display of lobelias in summer. Purple aubretia covers the top of the lower wall, draping over the edge to be visible from the lower gardens.

Colonel Harding-Rolls has completely converted the Walled Garden to be a paved Water Garden, a series of rectangular pools and fountains with a number of small statues and dwarf conifers round them. Coming from the Walled Garden towards the house, roses dominate the scene in front of the house. There is a semicircular Rose Garden with five beds, and on one side of the Croquet Lawn there are standard roses and peonies; on the far side is a deeper border of shrub roses and herbaceous plants. Both these areas are cleverly planted with bulbs for the spring – hyacinths in one, and a mass of daffodils in the other.

Beyond the Croquet Lawn is one of the most restful corners at Rockfield: a fine old stone bench, backed by purple-leafed acers and flowering cherries, looking on to a small pool with a very elegant central fountain of the Three Graces. From here again one looks down across the lake, perhaps at its most appealing in spring when the trees have just come into leaf, but a view with enormous attraction at any time of year.

HEREFORDSHIRE

ABBEYDORE COURT

In Abbey Dore, 11 miles south-west of Hereford off the A465
Tel. 0981 240 419
Mrs C. L. Ward

Open daily from March to October inclusive

Mrs Ward has revived Abbeydore from a very neglected Victorian garden, remnants of which are the two imposing wellingtonias on the lawn to the south-east of the house and the two remaining walls of an old walled garden. Today, after a great many dense alders were cleared from its banks the Dore river, flowing along the whole of one side has been restored as the garden's main feature and attraction. Along the river bank Mrs Ward has made an attractive Spring Walk with numerous bulbs and smaller flowers – daffodils, tulips, hellebores, primulas and fritillaries – beneath old Scots pines, as well as an interesting collection of ferns. These have all proved surprisingly adaptable to the vagaries of the river's flooding and drying up, as have the euphorbias which fill one of the borders close to the river.

Because of maintenance problems the garden has been kept simple: lawns in front of the house with surrounding borders. Most of these contain an informal mixture of spring flowers, shrubs and an interesting and unusual variety of herbaceous plants. An attractive feature just beyond the wellingtonias is the circular Herb Garden which Mrs Ward has made; in the old Walled Garden she has planted an orchard of mixed apple trees closely underplanted with daffodils.

The most ambitious part of the garden is the pool and Rock Garden opposite the south-west front of the house and on the far side of the river. The Rock Garden, begun in 1981 on a raised mound behind the pool, has already been planted with a wide range of plants, including many sedums, which Mrs Ward's daughter is particularly interested in. The National Sedum Collection is now at Abbeydore; there are over two hundred varieties throughout the garden. Once it has gained maturity in the next few years this area will be a delightful feature and will effectively extend the garden to the far side of the river. Mrs Ward has already made a striking bed here, planted with various meconopsis round a tall Scots pine.

A visit to the nearby Cistercian Dore Abbey is as worthwhile as to Abbeydore; the monks once owned the land and something of cloistered calm can still be felt here amid the riverside walks and vistas.

DINMORE MANOR

1 mile off the A49, 6 miles north of Hereford towards Leominster
Tel. 061 941 2313

G. H. Murray Esq.

Open daily except Christmas Day

Dinmore Manor's romantic and spectacular position at the head of a long valley with high wooded spurs on either side is matched by its early history when it was a commandery (county headquarters) of the Order of the Knights Hospitaller. The Hospitallers came to Dinmore in 1187 and remained until the dissolution of their order in 1540, but even before their arrival the natural advantages of the site, its strategic position in the Marches of England and Wales, made Dinmore a place of considerable importance. A gully running in front of the house marks the line of one of the major Roman roads from England into Wales.

Only the chapel, which stands in the garden to the south of the manor house, remains from the Hospitallers' occupancy. Part of its north wall is original twelfth-century but the majority of the interior dates from 1370, when it was rebuilt; the stained glass and present roof date from the nineteenth century. It is interesting that there are no windows on the long north side of the chapel; this is because other conventional buildings would have adjoined it. Today the chapel is the vital element in the garden, linking the twentieth century with Dinmore's distant past.

The manor house was originally built at the end of the sixteenth century and a section was added to its west end during the eighteenth. From the dissolution of the Hospitallers Dinmore was owned by three families until in 1927 it was sold to the late Richard Hollins Murray. Murray built up a considerable fortune through his invention of the reflecting lenses known as 'Cats' Eyes' for which he took out a patent in 1924. No expense was spared for his work at Dinmore. He built the Music Room with its timbered roof like a medieval hall on the west end of the house and the cloisters which stretch west then turn south to terminate in the octagonal South Room. The cloisters, too, are in medieval style, built of local stone and lined on the inside with golden Bath stone; their windows are filled with intricate stained glass executed by the William Morris company. In many ways the whole is character-istic of a 1930s fantasy, recreating Dinmore's historic past.

Murray also planned the garden in front of the cloisters, and it, too, is characteristic of the 1930s, with rockeries surrounding the stream which descends to a pool in front of the South Room and is crossed at one point by an impressive stone bridge. The rockeries are planted with a variety of very good acers and contrasting columnar cypresses with ferns, irises and yuccas among the smaller plants along the water.

On this south side of the house the primary appeal of the garden is the balance of the planting in the rockeries and other borders, and the open lawn with the chapel on its south side with the superb view as one looks east; the valley drops away between long wooded hills to the expanse of flat plains north of Hereford. The stone wall which forms a rampart on the eastern edge of the lawn heightens the dramatic effect.

The main consideration in gardening at Dinmore is the dryness of the soil and as a result plants which enjoy the often very dry conditions in summer have been planted extensively: cistus, hypericums and aubretia as well as the more unusual *Cytisus battandieri*, against the east-facing wall of the house. Spring flowers are also a feature, with daffodils, narcissi and auriculas filling the narrow borders round the chapel. In summer the Long Border between the South Terrace and the lawn is backed by climbing roses and clematis on the house walls, and a large wisteria which hangs picturesquely over the arches of the cloisters.

The other main area of the garden to the north of the cloisters has the Music Room on its south-east corner, and is dominated by the large circular pool, once a swimming pool; overhanging one side of it is a large fern-leaf. This area of the garden, partly enclosed by tall trees, has an especially strong air of secluded tranquillity which today is Dinmore's most appealing characteristic.

GARNONS

7 miles west of Hereford on the A438
Tel. 098 122 232
Sir John and Lady Cotterell

Open one or two Sundays per year

The landscape at Garnons – the house perched on a wooded hillside and open parkland below – immediately calls to mind the hand of Humphry Repton, who laid out the park and made alterations to the gardens. Repton moved the main road some half-mile, but the lake he proposed for the park was never made because of drainage problems and the expense of diverting the River Wye. Still, from the bottom of the park, from the wide terrace in front of the house and below the west side of the garden, the view is equally satisfying and reveals Repton's particular mastery of the siting of single parkland trees. Laid out round the Jacobean house, which was considerably extended at the same time, is one of the best preserved Repton landscapes in the country.

That the original Jacobean house was attractive can be seen from the Repton's Red Book, but by 1860 it was falling down, and a Victorian wing was added to the earlier nineteenth-century extensions. The gardens for this house were mainly to the east, in and around the Walled Garden moved there by Repton so that it did not interfere with his work round the house or intrude on the view from the park. This garden was intensely cultivated with numerous typically Victorian flowerbeds and borders, nearly all of which have been removed. Sir John's father, Sir Richard Cotterell, planted the trees and shrubs to the west of the house which mark the third phase in the garden's development and blend happily into the framework of Repton's mature trees. Among the older holm oaks and yew he also planted a mass of spring bulbs on the bank behind the lawn and a number of smaller trees such as sorbuses, flowering cherries, a *Betula jacquemontii*, a *Halesia carolia*, the 'Snowdrop Tree' and *Acer hersii*. Beyond, in the Old Garden, he placed rhododendrons and other shrubs. An intriguing vaulted tunnel leads beneath the drive to the garden on the east of the house, where some magnificent oaks and Lebanon cedars are the outstanding features. Beneath them Sir Richard planted an interesting mixture of trees, particularly in the area above the long yew hedge of the old Kitchen Garden: flowering amelanchiers and cherries with silver birch, liquidambars, a blue pine and tulip tree. One of the more unusual trees is *Sorbus scalaris*.

Not surprisingly the enormous house became unmanageable and Sir Richard pulled it down save for the wing which is the present house. Lady Cotterell plans to make more of the large paved terrace on its east side – where part of the old Victorian house stood – and so bring the garden closer. A Herb Garden will help solve the problem of the four-hundred-yard walk to the Kitchen Garden – obviously not considered a problem in Repton's day – and climbing roses will soften the imposing stone walls round the house. There is no doubt that the smaller house and this gentler style of planting which Sir Richard began, and Lady Cotterell is continuing, are admirably suited to the style of Repton's wonderful surroundings.

SOUTH POWYS

GLIFFAES COUNTRY HOUSE HOTEL

North-west of Crickhowell, 8 miles west of Abergavenny on the B4558
Tel. 0874 730 371
Mr and Mrs N. S. Brabner

Open daily from April to December inclusive

Since 1948, when the Brabners first came here, their strategy has been to simplify the mainly Victorian layout of formal, labour-intensive borders and to create a peaceful garden of shrubs and trees which also acts as a foil to the spectacular view from the southern aspect of the house down to the River Usk one hundred and fifty feet below. Help in the basic transformation came from Charles Taudevin, Mr Brabner's grandfather, who moved from Guernsey to Cheshire earlier this century and became an expert plantsman and landscape designer. His advice was invaluable in simplifying as well as in planting to take full advantage of the outstanding setting.

In spring and early summer the long drive is a colourful welcome to Gliffaes, lined by daffodils and banks of rhododendrons and azaleas, the woods round about giving protection from the westerly winds. The garden on the east and west of the house is mainly given over to lawns, shrubs and young trees planted among mature trees; as well as old cedars, beeches and chestnuts there are some more unusual specimens: *Pinus cembra*, *Cryptomeria japonica*, *Sequoia sempervirens*, *Sequoiadendron giganteum*, *Taxodium distichum*, *Liriodendron tulipifera*, *Ginkgo biloba*, a 'Lucombe' oak, various thujas, junipers and abies. Two specimen *Juniperus pfitzerana* cover almost a hundred square yards, and a beautiful *Acer palmatum var. septemlobum sanquinium* is among others planted almost a century ago.

Within this framework Mr and Mrs Brabner have added flowering shrubs and trees, many of which give outstanding autumn colour, such as the acers and the *Stewartia sinensis*. Magnolias flourish and, in a small Bog Garden, so do a *Metasequoia glyptostroboides* and another swamp cypress, placed together to point up the subtle difference in their similar foliage. Many flowering shrubs were killed to ground level in the winter of 1981–2, such as *Arbutus unedo*, *Abutilon vitifolium* and *A. megapotamicum*, camellias, *Carpentaria californica*, crinodendrons, eucryphia, pittosporums and sophora. All except *Solanum crispum* and *Fabiana imbracata* have now recovered and grow strongly, although some did not show any sign of life until August 1982.

An enviable setting, easy atmosphere and the understated quality of its planting make Gliffaes a pleasure to visit. The Brabners have demonstrated to perfection how a potentially burdensome garden can be successfully adapted and maintained rather than abandoned.

WORCESTERSHIRE

BREDON SPRINGS

Near Ashton-under-Hill, 6 miles south-west of Evesham off the A345
Tel. 038 688 1328

Ronald Sidwell Esq.

Open three days a week from April to October inclusive, and by appointment

Mr Sidwell describes the style of his small garden around an eighteenth-century stone cottage as 'controlled wilderness', and certainly there is something untamed and not unattractively so about its appearance. Unfortunately the winter of 1981–2 did extensive damage and killed a great many tender shrubs and climbers he had accumulated, many from New Zealand.

Much of the garden is very damp, the heavy soil fed by underground springs and so along the small stream on the east side of the garden primulas, lysitichums, ligularias, astilbes, *Gunnera manicata* and *Irish kaempferi* flourish. All that Mr Sidwell found flowering when he arrived here in 1948 were a number of fruit trees, and these are still doing well. They include two large malus and some old pears, and have been joined more recently by philadelphus, a ginkgo, a metasequoia, a *Thuja plicata* which, by the looks of things, will soon be the tallest tree in the garden, and various others. Beneath the trees are many attractive low plants, like lily of the valley; some of the most interesting are among a large variety of herbaceous plants in beds and borders.

The natural slope to the north-east of the house is covered with small trees and shrubs; from the top the view ranges across the garden to the village of Ashton-under-Hill below, affording, perhaps, a better opportunity to appreciate Mr Sidwell's skill as a plantsman in achieving an apparent liberalism in the how and where of his planting, as borders, trees and lawn ramble one to another. The 1981–2 winter has robbed the visitor of some of Bredon's quality, but Mr Sidwell quite clearly has the determination and the energy to regain lost ground.

DUNLEY HALL

In Dunley, 1¾ miles south-west of Stourport-on-Severn on the A451
Tel. 029 932 040

Mrs John Lea

Open one Sunday in April, and by appointment

'S.B.' are the initials carved in one of the old beech trees at Dunley – but they belonged to Stanley Baldwin in the days when he lived here as a newly-married man. The garden in its present form has taken shape since 1962 when the late Mr Lea introduced the lawns, flowering trees and shrub borders one sees today. These could be maintained with minimal labour so that he was able to concentrate on his main interest, the cultivation of daffodils, at which he was acknowledged to be the leading expert in the country. Mr Lea died suddenly in May 1984, a sad loss for the world of horticulture and in particular the breeding of daffodils.

The main garden is south-west of the partly sixteenth-century house and it is no surprise to see large drifts of daffodils round the lawn and beneath the old beech, oak and lime trees during spring. Magnolias predominate amongst the flowering trees, particularly in the south-west corner of the garden, where the lawn slopes over a bank down to a small dell: *Magnolia* 'Charles Raffill', a cross between *M. mollicomata* and *M. sargentiana robusta*, *M. hypoleuca*, *M. salicifolia* and *M. wilsonii*. Within the dell the planting of primulas round the base of a *Metasequoia glyptostroboides* is especially effective. Sadly, the *Arbutus andrachnoides*, one of the most beautiful 'Strawberry Trees', was badly damaged during the winter of 1981–2, but another interesting specimen is a tree with a long history – the young *Sorbus domestica*, the 'Service tree', which is a clone from the old tree at Arley, itself descended from the original growing wild in the Wyre Forest until it disappeared during the last century.

To the south, beyond the main garden, with its simple layout and striking individual trees and shrubs, is the area where Mr Lea raised his daffodils. A visit during spring is certainly worthwhile to see row upon row of numerous varieties. He won prizes at the Royal Horticultural Show with unfailing regularity – in 1982 he won the Engleheart Trophy for the best twelve daffodils in the show, a trophy he won nine times between 1971 and 1981, as well as the Wilson Memorial Trophy. Mr Lea achieved even greater landmarks in his work: he was the first man to raise a double pink daffodil. The names of his varieties, which so often baffle would-be buyers, are all taken from places in Scotland where he and his wife Betty used to fish for salmon and trout. The River Spey has produced a great many, including Ben Avon with a white trumpet, and Dailmanach, acknowledged to be the best pink daffodil in existence.

As well as the daffodils, Mr Lea's most recent interest was raising *Auratum* lilies; at Dunley there are many beautiful hybrids, in particular a cross with a *Speciosum* lily. Mr Postle will carry on Mr Lea's work of breeding daffodils which, one feels certain, will continue to be an intrinsic part of Dunley for many years to come.

THE PRIORY

In Kemerton 5½ miles north-east of Tewkesbury off the A438
Tel. 038 689 258

Mr Peter and the Hon. Mrs Healing

Open Thursday and on selected Sundays from May to September inclusive

To many people herbaceous borders are old-fashioned, boring and difficult, time-consuming to maintain and unsatisfactory in result because they flower for such a short spell in summer. All or some of these accusations may be true, but there are few gardens where they are less applicable than the Priory. The herbaceous borders which the Healings have planned and built up since they came here in 1938 would surely change the opinion of any but the most entrenched opponent. They are clearly the work of experts and make outstanding advertisements for this often-maligned style of gardening.

When the Healings came to the Priory there was little of character or real interest other than the picturesque sixteenth-century ruin with a huge clipped yew tree, now thirty feet high and possibly three hundred years old, at one end. Other than the yew the garden is almost exclusively post-Second World War. The house is mainly Georgian, though one part is sixteenth-century. The lawn to the west of the curving drive is planted with a few standard weeping trees, such as hornbeam and purple beech, but is otherwise left unadorned, in contrast to the more intensely-planted areas to the north and west of the house.

There are three main herbaceous borders, each with its different character, and each planted with clear emphasis on colour-grouping. In one the colour-grouping has been carried to the extreme; exclusively red in flower, foliage or stem, it stretches in front of the ruin and yew. The variety of plants ranges from shrubs to some small annuals and is certainly eye-catching, particularly in late summer when the flowering plants are at their peak. A mixed-colour border faces the west side of the house, and beyond this is the main border, 19 feet deep and 150 feet long, filled with mixed but carefully grouped colours. One of the most difficult effects to achieve in an herbaceous border – the plants descending in height from the back – is here achieved with seeming ease. Large roses and other shrubs, clematis trained up over supports and glorious giant thistles, form the backdrop for traditional herbaceous plants combined with many unusual ones; at the height of the season gaps are non-existent. The dense form and dark colour of the long yew hedge behind the border throws the colours into perfect relief.

A pergola trained with climbing roses, clematis and vines extends west from the main border, past an early summer garden, whose central stone path leads to a stone vase at the south end. On either side are borders filled with many small and low-growing plants of soft pastel colours – pinks, silver and mauve. At its best in June and July, this small garden, enclosed on three sides by yew hedges and trees, forms a gentle counterpoint to the more strident borders elsewhere. The pergola leads to a Water Garden, where the banks and stones round a small stream have recently been planted with bog and water plants: arums, primulas, gunnera, and ligularias; shrub roses form a screen along the garden's edge. In this part of the garden are some of the Priory's many attractive young trees, including a weeping purple beech and a *Cercidiphyllum japonicum* close to the small swimming pool.

In contrast to the main lawns and borders is the small Sunken Garden to the east of the house. Borders of hydrangeas, lilies, hostas and peonies surround a central square Lily Pond, with small pinks and campanulas in the rocks of the retaining walls. Overhung by cherry trees, it is an intimate corner, enlivened in the late summer by the *Tropaeolum speciosum* spreading across the wire netting behind, and by the trumpet flowers of two golden daturas on the small paved area to the north.

The flourishing appearance of these exotic and tender visitors reflects the high standard of plantsmanship seen everywhere at the Priory, the secret of this garden's success.

SPETCHLEY PARK

3 miles east of Worcester off the A422
Tel. 090 565 224
R. J. Berkeley Esq.

Open daily except Saturday from April to September inclusive

The Berkeleys are relative newcomers at Spetchley: though they have been at Berkeley Castle since the twelfth century, they purchased this thirty-acre estate only in 1605. It looked very different then, with a moated Tudor house, but this was burned down by Charles II's soldiers before the Battle of Worcester in 1651, though the Berkeleys were Royalists. The diarist John Evelyn was a regular visitor to the new house later in the seventeenth century, and is supposed to have suggested the siting of some of the old cedars still standing in the garden, and of an elm avenue in the park, now destroyed by disease.

The appearance of Spetchley was changed completely yet again in 1811 when the present Palladian house was built of golden Bath stone on a slightly higher position, looking southwards across wide lawns to a lake – originally part of the old moat – and the large deer park beyond. Further change came at the end of the nineteenth century, however. In 1891 Robert Berkeley married Rose Willmott and with the help of her sister Ellen Willmott, whose garden at Warley Place in Essex was famous, she gave Spetchley a garden to rival its park.

The main work took place in and around the old Walled Garden to the east of the house. Outside the walls Mrs Berkeley made deep borders filled mainly with herbaceous plants, although the south border, filled with the masses of polyanthus she hybridized, must have been particularly striking. South of this was Mrs Berkeley's chief contribution to Spetchley, the Fountain Garden. She laid it out with a central fountain and pool and cross-paths dividing four yew-enclosed gardens. Each of these she divided into a series of beds and paved paths, every bed devoted to one plant family. It is not hard to imagine the large and varied collection of plants which this garden soon contained. Captain Rob Berkeley, who took over the garden after his mother's death in 1922, maintained her high standards, continually adding to the plant collections throughout Spetchley and still managing operations, towards the end of his life, from a wheelchair. Tradition has been

231

continued by his son, John, who, despite all the problems of keeping up a large house and garden today, maintains not only the garden at Spetchley, with the help of three gardeners, but Berkeley Castle as well.

As much as possible of Mrs Berkeley's garden has been retained, though some of the borders have been changed. The old polyanthus border is now herbaceous, divided by low box hedges with a border of irises opposite. There are some interesting shrubs and climbers in the west border outside the Walled Garden – where daffodils and helle-bores are followed by tree peonies and mixed herbaceous, including *Rhus verniciflua* and *Jasminum stephanense* on the wall. The loggia to the north of the Fountain Garden and two lead figures at the entrance to the path add greatly to the Fountain Garden's charm. Although the pattern of strict division into families is not now maintained so closely there is still great variety between the various enclosures, with smaller plants growing beneath larger shrubs and trees: viburnums, magnolias and acers, and the tall, slender Serbian spruce, *Picea omorika*. Polyanthus beneath the yew hedges have been reintroduced here, on either side of the two main paths, followed by *Campanula lactifolia* in the summer.

One path leads out south into the Rose Garden. Many of the outstanding trees at Spetchley are roundabout – cedars, beech and copper beech and an old cork oak – and on one side of a nineteenth-century conservatory, filled with tender plants, is a large cut-leaf beech, one of the best trees in the entire garden. On the other side is one of Rose Berkeley's more unusual varieties to survive, *Berberis montana* from Chile. The diversity of Spetchley is further demonstrated as one continues from the Rose Garden to the Woodland Garden stretching beneath stands of mature Corsican and Austrian pines along the eastern boundary; rhododendrons, azaleas, primulas and acers are planted along a winding glade. Camellias and eucryphias here were badly hit during the winter of 1981–2.

Spring bulbs, so perfect anywhere in a setting of open grass and mature trees, are a great feature at Spetchley. Crocuses spread beneath the trees to the east of the main lawn, leading to the white ironwork bridge across the old moat. After them come fritillarias and daffodils, here and in the yew walk leading from the bridge to the statue of Apollo. Daffodils were a particular interest of Rose and Robert Berkeley; among the many hybrids they raised was 'Spetchley', mainly planted in the New Lawn where Mr Berkeley has recently planted a number of ornamental trees: sorbus, malus, acers and *Cercidiphyllum japonicum*. It is no wonder that Elgar, a friend of the Berkeleys, was particularly fond of Spetchley's very English setting; he regularly took the gardener's cottage during the summer and wrote some of his best known works there.

THE SOUTH WEST

Cornwall
Devon
Dorset
Somerset and Avon
Wiltshire

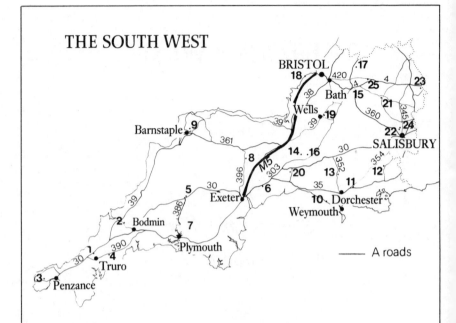

THE SOUTH WEST

1 Chyverton
2 Pencarrow
3 Trengwainton
4 Trewithen
5 Bidlake Mill
6 Fernwood
7 The Garden House
8 Knightshayes Court
9 Marwood Hill
10 Abbotsbury
11 Athelhampton
12 The Manor House, Cranborne
13 Minterne

14 Barrington Court
15 Crowe Hall
16 East Lambrook Manor
17 Essex House
18 The Manor House, Walton-in-Gordano
19 Milton Lodge
20 Wayford Manor
21 Broadleas
22 Heale House
23 Hillbarn House
24 Lake House
25 Sheldon Manor

CORNWALL

CHYVERTON

In Zelah, 5 miles north of Truro off the A30
Tel. 087 254 324
Nigel Holman, Esq.

Open selected Sundays in spring and by appointment all year

Chyverton is blessed with an enviable relationship between the house and garden inherited from the eighteenth century, which Nigel Holman and his father before him have exploited to great advantage in the making of this garden. The Georgian house sits above a wide grass slope, looking down to a long valley, originally the site of an old lead or silver mine. The boggy stream running along the bottom of the valley was dammed around 1800, when John Thomas originally laid out the garden, to make a wider pond ('Or lake, as our grander visitors call it', says Mr Holman). At the same time a picturesque arched bridge was raised across one end for the drive. In about 1870 *Rhododendron* 'Cornish Red' was planted along the water's edge; these have now attained a huge size, and in April their reflections turn the water a glorious magenta. Beyond these giants the main part of the garden stretches along the valley to where more 'Cornish Red' tower beside the drive, and in one place join to form an entrance archway to the garden from the surrounding woodland.

Mr Holman's father was particularly interested in magnolias and most of his work was devoted to building up what is now an outstanding collection. Numerous different magnolias have been planted throughout the garden, most of which flower freely. There are a number at the top of the hill, around the house, including a fine *Magnolia campbellii* 'Alba'. It stands in a small walled enclosure with some of the many camellias in the garden, including two new American varieties,

'Royalty' and 'William Hertrich', which won an Award of Merit in 1981, together with two great rarities, *Machilus thunbergii* from Korea, and *Craibiodendron yunnanense*, recently introduced into cultivation from China, both with attractive young growth in spring.

From the house a path leads down to the main part of the garden along the valley, past a remarkable hedge of *Myrtus luma*. Beside this path, below two of the best mature trees at Chyverton – a copper beech and a cedar – are *Rehderodendron macrocarpum* and *Edgworthia papyrifera*, with its clusters of delicately fragrant lemon-yellow and white flowers.

The advantage of having water stretching right along the garden is nowhere better shown than where the path from the house reaches the valley. Here are a number of fine magnolias – *Magnolia hypoleuca, M. campbellii, M. sargentiana robusta, M. cylindrica* and *M. globosa* – as well as some very large *Camellias* 'Donation' and the pendulous Huon pine from Tasmania, *Dacrydium franklinii*, one of the rarest trees in the garden. The beauty of all these plants is greatly enhanced by their waterside position and reflections.

Walking along the valley, one is immediately aware of the way in which Nigel Holman has tried to plan this part of the garden on axes so that one is constantly coming upon vistas leading to the focal-point of a tree or shrub. One such vista is a small glade leading from *Magnolia speciosa*, standing where the garden extends up the hill towards the woods, past a young *Nothofagus dombeyi* and various photinias, to the pond at the bottom. Further along a *Eucryphia nymensis* stands in the open as a focal-point for a vista from another angle. All along the valley are a number of different acers which Nigel Holman is building up into a considerable collection. Often these are most effectively planted close to large groups of azaleas. As well as the glorious old rhododendrons there are many younger plants of particular merit throughout the garden, including an award-winning plant of *Rhododendron spinuliferum, R. mallotum*, the scented *R. ciliatum, R. pachysarthum* and *R. schlippenbachii*, perhaps the most exquisite of all azaleas.

Across the drive from the main part of the valley a path leads to the small and intimate memorial garden beside a pond. Slightly enclosed, this little garden has a pretty arched wooden bridge across the water beneath which yellow and white *Lysitichums* have seeded themselves and grow with great vigour. Among the plants around the bridge are *Rhododendron* 'Ethel', whose bright scarlet flowers more than make up for its small stature, and a low spreading plant of *Camellia* 'Lady Clare'. Above this peaceful corner are protective large-leafed rhododendrons – *R. sinogra/nde* and *R. falconeri*.

Near the far end of the garden, where the drive leads out beneath the arch of 'Cornish Red', is a collection of magnolias of which two trees are very close to Nigel Holman's heart. One is a cross between *Magnolia sargeniana* and *mollicomata*, named 'Treve Holman' after his father. The other is an award-winning form of *M. dawsoniana* named 'Chyverton', over fifty feet tall. On the far side of the drive is the luckiest magnolia in the garden, a *Magnolia mollicamata* 'Lanarth' that only just survived a gale in which a tree fell on either side of it. Its large deep-purple flowers are now made even more effective by its solitary position in the surrounding woodland.

Since he inherited the garden Nigel Holman has built up both the quantity and variety of plants. Although the magnolia collection is Chyverton's outstanding feature, he likes to think that he is steadily creating a garden from which no tree or shrub is barred, so long as it is of particular interest or beauty, and in harmony with the informal woodland setting. Mrs Holman and himself maintain this very extensive garden with no help other than a keen knowledge and an eye for graceful planting. Chyverton is a garden where trees and shrubs can develop freely, with plenty of space, in what could be their natural setting.

PENCARROW

Near Camelford off the A39

Tel. 0409 27220

The Molesworth-St Aubyn Family

Open daily from March to September inclusive

The gardens of Cornwall are largely renowned as the homes of plants introduced by the famous collectors of the late nineteenth and early twentieth centuries from expeditions made to South-East Asia and China. By contrast Pencarrow's reputation rests on its collection of trees from the other side of the world, built up by Sir William Molesworth Bt, the Victorian politician, from around 1830. Much of the seed for Sir William's plantings was sent by the most famous of all plant-collectors in America, David Douglas, and later by a Cornishman, William Lobb, who was working for Veitch, the famous Exeter firm. Sir William did not, however, collect exclusively from America. He also received seed, particularly of rhododendrons, from Sir Joseph Hooker, collected on expeditions; from Nathaniel Wallich, the director of the Calcutta Gardens; and from his brother Francis in New Zealand. By the time of his death Sir William's collection was very extensive, and it is most encouraging that Lieutenant-Colonel J. A. Molesworth-St Aubyn is now clearing parts of the woodland garden which had become badly overgrown, and is embarking on considerable re-planting.

The Molesworth family have lived at Pencarrow since the sixteenth century and the mile-long drive, laid out by Sir William with a great many of his conifers and other species on either side, runs through the site of an ancient British settlement. The house is Georgian; in front of it Sir William made the Italian Garden with a raised rockery along one side, for which the great blocks of stone were dragged from Bodmin Moor in rough wooden carts. The layout of the Italian Garden has been greatly simplified; it is now dominated by a central fountain and domed cypresses on either side. Perhaps the outstanding tree close to the house is an enormous specimen of *Magnolia campbellii* but trees continue behind the rockery to the lawn opposite the entrance forecourt of the house; among them are *Pinus radiata*, many uncommon varieties of chamecyparis, *Calocedrus decurrens*, two fine cedars and *Cunninghamia lanceolata*.

These areas around the house are the most attractive for the garden visitor, but for the real tree enthusiast the two areas of woodland will be of greater interest. A broad field stretches away from the end of the Italian Garden with woods on either side. A path, recently cleared, leads from the rockery to the American Garden, which takes its name from a variety of American conifers. Best of the American conifers is *Pinus montezumae* from Mexico, which has been recorded by Alan Mitchell as the largest specimen in Britain. There is a davidia beside the pond, *Rhododendron falconieri*, an outstandingly large *Magnolia soulangiana* and another *Cunninghamia lanceolata* nearby. Also close to the pond are two wing-nuts – *Pterocarya fraxinus* from the Caucasus and *P. stenoptera* from China.

Across the large field, from where one enjoys a fine view of the house, with the land rolling into the small valley in front, is the other main area of woodland along the main entrance drive. Only a few trees remain of the avenue of 'Monkey-puzzles', *Araucaria araucana*, which flanked the top of the drive and now extend beyond the present entrance gates, but those which do are impressive and considerably more accessible now where the ground has been cleared around them. Cephalotaxus, podocarpus and taxodiums are particularly well-represented genera, but the variety of the collection is what one notices. Among the spruces are *Picea polita*, the 'Tiger-tail Spruce', and *P. breweriana*, 'Brewer's Weeping

Spruce', while *Pinus thunbergii* is one of the outstanding pines. Among the conifers are many rhododendrons and camellias, some of them old-established plants such as the *Rhododendron magnificum*, spectacular in early March.

It is most encouraging to see a garden like Pencarrow, where dedicated clearing and re-planting both display old specimens to the advantage they deserve, and build up a stock of interesting young trees for the future.

TRENGWAINTON

2 miles north-west of Penzance on the B3312
Tel. 0736 3106
The National Trust and Major Simon Bolitho

Open four days a week from March to October inclusive

The garden enthusiast should have no worries about feeling ignorant when visiting Trengwainton, for among its enormously diverse collection of tender and half-hardy plants are many which even established experts do not recognize. Rather he should marvel at the mildness of climate around this garden in the south-western extremity of Cornwall, which allows so many plants from warmer parts of the world to thrive.

Trengwainton in the old Cornish language means 'The House of the Spring' and there can be few gardens in Britain more aptly named. Frost-free winters are not unusual, severe frosts almost unheard of, and here spring starts anyway in late-February when the first of the huge Asiatic magnolias, usually *Magnolia campbellii*, come into flower – and when most of Britain is still firmly in the grip of winter. Certainly full advantage has been taken of these almost unique conditions – perhaps only bettered by those of Tresco Abbey on the Isles of Scilly – ever since Sir Edward Bolitho inherited Trengwainton in 1925. Today Trengwainton has one of the most unusual and extensive collections of plants from South-East Asia in Britain, and the garden's exotic appearance forms an intriguing contrast to the wild and remote Cornish countryside surrounding it.

At the beginning of the nineteenth century Trengwainton was owned by Rose Price, son of a wealthy Jamaican sugar planter who was later made a baronet. His most interesting addition to the gardens was the series of walled kitchen gardens near the lodge. Not only were these enormously expensive – they were made of brick which had to be brought from some distance away, there being no brick clay locally – but they were unusual, too, for the sloping raised beds he made in each against the south-west facing walls, to catch maximum sunlight. These beds still survive.

The Bolitho family acquired Trengwainton in 1867 when it was a part-Elizabethan house with a Georgian front added in carved granite. Robin Bolitho altered and considerably enlarged the house in 1881. What garden existed then was typically Victorian, with herbaceous borders and closely-planted flower beds. They planted a considerable number of trees, particularly the beeches round the house and in a long stretch down to the lodge; these later provided vital shelter for the collection from the often gale-force winds. When Sir Edward inherited from his uncle, his early changes in the gardens were greatly helped by Mr A. Creek, who had been head gardener since 1904 and who was an expert propagator. (In later years seeds were sent from Kew and other leading gardens with notes attached: 'If you cannot succeed with them no one can.') The developments at Trengwainton were encouraged by Sir Edward's gardening neighbours and in 1926 George Johnstone from nearby Trewithen suggested that he take shares in Kingdon Ward's expedition to North-East Assam and the Mishmi Hills of Burma planned for 1927–8. The trip was one of Ward's most successful, and the seeds brought back formed the basis of Trengwainton's rhododendron collection.

Sir Rose Price's walled enclosures made ideally sheltered homes for the new arrivals and combined with Mr Creek's skills to ensure some spectacular successes. Among the most tender seedlings were *Rhododendron macabeanum* and *R. elliottii*, flowering for the first time in this country. In 1928 the Trengwainton plant of *Rhododendron macabeanum* was awarded a First Class Certificate by the Royal Horticultural Society. At the same time as establishing the collection Sir Edward embarked on opening up what has become the other main part of the gardens, the stream flowing between the present drive and the long beech wood. Sir Edward brought the stream out of its underground culvert and began the planting of candelabra primulas, lilies and other moisture-loving plants which make this long garden winding up towards the house such a rewarding sight. In the damp and shady woodland areas are New Zealand tree ferns and various meconopses as well as tender rhododendrons and large-leafed varieties such as *Rhododendron falconeri*, *R. sinogrande* and *R. macabeanum*.

In 1961 two important events occurred. Sir Edward was awarded the Victoria Medal of Honour and he gave the gardens, with an endowment, to the National Trust. Right up to his death in 1969 Sir Edward devoted himself to building up his collection of plants and developing the various areas of the gardens. The gardens are now maintained jointly by the Trust and Sir Edward's son, Major Simon Bolitho, who lives at Trengwainton and shares his father's knowledge and enthusiasm. He is helped by Peter Horder, the present head gardener.

It is in the five walled enclosures that there is the greatest concentration of plants. On entering one is immediately greeted by one of the finest trees in the gardens, *Magnolia x veitchii*, a hybrid of *M. campbellii* and *M. denudata*, which was planted in 1949. Other outstanding magnolias in the walled gardens are *Magnolia campbellii*, planted in 1926; *M. mollicomata* and *M. mollicomata* 'Lanarth', *M. sprengeri diva* and *M. cylindrica*. Because of their size the magnolias are a most impressive sight; when in flower they dominate the enclosures. But the succession of colour, both of flower and foliage, is maintained by numerous other varieties, some of which flower with the magnolias, others later in the year. Even with some of the specimens, which can also be seen elsewhere, it is often their size or vigorous growth which is most impressive, such as the huge *Styrax japonica* beside the entrance into the second enclosure. But many other plants are rarely seen elsewhere because of the mild climate from which they originate: *Michelia excelsa* and *M. doltsopa*, Himalayan evergreens related to magnolias; *Eucryphia moorei* from New South Wales; and *Myosotidium hortensia*, the Chatham Island Forget-me-not. There are others, too, which one would normally only see in a glasshouse in this country, such as *Clematis indivisa*, a tender New Zealand climber; *Abutilon globosum* 'Canary Bird'; and *Passiflora caerulea*, one of the climbing Passion Flowers. One can immediately see that the walled enclosures were planned for both contrast and balance, an important combination when one is dealing with so many different plants.

Outside the walled enclosures the atmosphere is different; there is not the feeling of intimacy nor intense concentration of plants in the broad sweep of the drive, stream garden and beech wood up towards the house. On the right of the drive are more rhododendrons and also the Queen's Meadow, where Queen Elizabeth the Queen Mother planted a Bhutan pine, *Pinus wallichiana*, in 1962. Princess Anne added a more tender Mexican *Pinus patula* close by in 1972.

One might think that Trengwainton is known chiefly for its outstanding collection of plants, but on reaching the top lawn in front of the house, the visitor realizes that it also boasts one of the finest views from any garden in the country. Through a specially made cutting in the beech trees below the house St Michael's Mount can be seen in the far distance. The view has been only slightly affected by the recent loss in a gale of some of the beeches on one side. It is the Atlantic gales which pose the greatest threat to the gardens, particularly now that many of the mature trees, such as the beeches, are at a vulnerable age. Considerable damage was done by a very severe gale in the Magnolia Garden beyond the top lawn which contains possibly Trengwainton's outstanding magnolia, a huge specimen of *M. sargentiana* 'Robusta', as well as a very large *M. delavayi*.

· The variety of plants at Trengwainton ensures that the garden is outstandingly impressive whenever one visits, be it at magnolia time, later when the rhododendrons and camellias are at their best, or towards the end of the summer when the beech wood is filled with the various shades of blue hydrangeas. It is also important that the plants do not just form a collection, interesting only because of their rarity or individual merit, but form a real garden with its own character and atmosphere. It is to be hoped that the National Trust will ensure it does not disappear.

TREWITHEN

Between Probus and Grampound, north-east of Truro off the A390
Tel. 0726 882 418

Mr and Mrs Michael Galsworthy

Open daily except Sunday from March to September inclusive

To visit Trewithen in March or April when the many outstanding Asiatic magnolias are in flower is to witness one of the most impressive sights to be found in any garden in Britain. They are perhaps the showpiece of this garden created by George Johnstone between the beginning of the century and his death in 1960. His achievement was the more remarkable because during the last thirty years of his life he was confined by a hunting accident to a wheelchair.

When George Johnstone inherited Trewithen in 1904 there was no real garden. As he himself said, the colour in the eighteenth-century walled garden on one side of the house depended on the shades of the washing hung out by the maids. The stone house, built by Philip Hawkins between 1715 and 1730, was however surrounded by mature beeches and a landscaped park. This was probably the work of Philip's son Thomas, a keen and expert dendrologist. His diary and a contemporary print both record (beech) woods to the south and south-west of the house, and avenues radiating to the north and east. One interesting addition to the park during the nineteenth century was a number of holm oaks, many of which survive today. They were grown from acorns collected at Bignor Park in Sussex, the seat of John Hawkins, whose son inherited Trewithen from his unmarried uncle. When George Johnstone inherited he thus found a park ready to form the setting for his garden and the beech trees to provide shelter – a vital factor, as he was determined to populate his garden with many tender species, for which the mild Cornish climate is perhaps the most acceptable in Britain.

Work started before the First World War but it was the felling of three hundred trees by government order during the war which enabled George Johnstone to plan what has become the backbone of the garden: the great glade stretching over 200 yards from the south front of the house. It was a masterpiece of design, rivalling those of his eighteenth-century predecessors. Not only does it provide unforgettable vistas both away from and towards the house, but it also allows the various trees and shrubs planted on either side of its winding edges to present themselves to maximum advantage from many viewpoints.

George Johnstone was lucky in that his collecting of plants for the Trewithen garden was greatly helped by a number of gardening friends who soon recognized his talent and enthusiasm. One of these, J. C. Williams, was particularly generous with plants from his remarkable collection at nearby Caerhays Castle. (He also picked a different flower each day from the Caerhays garden and sent it to Johnstone during the months when he was lying immobile after his hunting accident.)

Magnolias were always George Johnstone's first love, perhaps because they flower early in the year, often starting in late February, and because their size and their luxuriant shades of pink, purple and white make them so spectacular a sight. The huge tree of *Magnolia mollicomata* which towers over the right-hand side of the great glade as one looks from the house is magnificent. Throughout the garden many varieties present their subtly different shades of colour and shapes of flower – sometimes with branches hanging almost to the ground, or just with splashes of colour in the uppermost branches where the trees have had to stretch upward for the light. The majority of Asiatic magnolias are well represented. In 1955 the Royal Horticultural Society published

Johnstone's outstanding book, *Asiatic Magnolias in Cultivation*, a work in the great tradition of botanical books and now very rare.

Trewithen also has an outstanding collection of camellias; in the Camellia Walk alone are numerous forms of *C. saluensis*, *C. reticulata* and *C. williamsii*. There is an outstanding plant of that most popular of camellias, 'Donation', which was a cutting given by Colonel Stephenson Clarke from the original plant of 'Donation' which he raised at his garden, Borde Hill in Sussex. George Johnstone raised a number of camellias himself, naming one 'Elizabeth Johnstone' after his daughter and naming as 'Glenn's Orbit' one which first flowered on the day that John Glenn completed his space orbit of earth.

Rhododendrons are Trewithen's other most widely found plants, both specie and hybrid. The outstanding specimen is another generous legacy from one of George Johnstone's gardening friends. It was a seedling of *Rhododendron macabeanum* given to him by Sir Edward Bolitho from the first plant of this species to be raised in Britain, Sir Edward's own at Trengwainton near Penzance, after receiving seed from Kingdon Ward's expedition of 1927–8. Now the Trewithen plant stands about twenty feet high with a diameter of thirty feet. When in flower it is weighed down by up to five hundred trusses of brilliant sulphur-yellow flowers, and is considered to be the outstanding rhododendron specimen in Europe. Never one to rely on the fruits of other people's labours, George Johnstone raised a number of rhododendron hybrids himself. There can be few of more intriguing and brilliant colour than *Rh.* 'Trewithen Orange' while 'Alison Johnstone', named after his wife, and 'Jack Skelton', named after his head gardener, have special charms as tokens of personal affection and gratitude.

If magnolias, camellias and rhododendrons are the mainstays of Trewithen in quantity there are numerous other plants of both interest and beauty. Throughout the garden there is a subtle balance in the variety; without a hint of uniformity different areas reveal themselves and blend one to another as one progresses along the numerous paths. A large *Davidia involucrata* stands at the top of the great glade on the corner of a narrow path which is surrounded by plants of interest: on one side a hedge of *Myrtus lechleriana* is complemented by the bank of brilliant *Pieris formosa var. forestii* opposite. Beneath the wall on the right of the path are a number of tender plants, including one of the most striking camellias, *Camellia* 'Benton' with vivid variegated foliage and small single pink flowers, and a very rare visitor from Georgia, USA, *Franklina alatamaha*. This path leads into the small Walled Garden where among the plants trained on the walls are the homegrown *Ceanothus arboreus*, 'Trewithen Blue', and the bright red 'Lobster's Claw' from New Zealand, *Clianthus punicens*.

Down the great glade the visitor has to be busy not to miss things; on one side the *Rehderodendron macrocarpum*, with flowers similar to a styrax; introduced from China in 1934, it is one of only two mature such trees in England. Beyond, around the area named after Alison Johnstone, are birches and stewartii with their striking barks and, among some smaller magnolias, the brilliant 'Fire Bush' from Chile, *Embothrium coccineum*. In fact it seems that most areas of the temperate world have envoys at Trewithen: nearby in this one part of the garden are representatives from Australia, Tasmania and China. A path can be taken to the edge of the garden overlooking the park. Here is variety, subdued but still typical of Trewithen: on one side an old avenue of towering sycamores and on the other a row of those two most primitive trees, *Ginkgo biloba* and *Metasequoia glyptostroboides*.

Returning across the bottom of the great glade the house is once again revealed centre-stage, its grey stone a foil for the constant variety of colour and form in the wings along either side of the lawn. Beyond the Camellia Walk in one corner of the garden is the Cock Pit, a small sunken area not to be missed when the rhododendrons and primulas with which it is filled are in flower. One of the landmarks on this side of the garden is the huge screen of *Eucryphia cordifolia* which protects tender plants such as *Michelia doltopsa*, a cousin of the magnolias. One of the most peaceful paths at Trewithen leads to the Water Garden, which is being restored in accordance with the original plans, still in existence. On the way down the sloping path is the Coronation Plantation with *Magnolia sprengeri diva* and *M.* 'Charles Raffill' and, to welcome you at the bottom, another large *Davidia involucrata*.

While the walled garden retains the same tranquillity it probably had in the eighteenth century, one could well reflect that Trewithen has come a long way since the days of the maids' washing. For many years after George Johnstone's death the gardens were nurtured and improved by his widow, Alison Johnstone, and his daughter, Miss Elizabeth Johnstone. When the latter retired in 1978, Trewithen became the home of George Johnstone's grandson and his wife, Michael and Charlotte Galsworthy. In their care, with the expert help of Michael Taylor, the present head gardener, the garden is certainly not standing still. Some of the changes are involuntary, such as the felling by a severe gale of a large number of beeches on one side of the great glade. Others are truly adventurous, such as the area of new planting above the path to the Water Garden. It seems certain that Trewithen will retain its qualities as a tribute to one of the outstanding plantsmen and gardeners of this century.

DEVON

BIDLAKE MILL

In Combebow Bridge, off the A30 between Bridestowe and Lewdown
Tel. 083 786 323
Mrs E. Wollocombe

Open daily by appointment

Although the garden of Bidlake Mill today is quite young – it was started by Mrs Wollocombe and her husband in 1956 – it was made on a very ancient site which has been in the family's possession since 1268. The sense of antiquity pervading the whole of the small cottage garden focuses on the feature in it of greatest interest, a medieval corn mill, with its original water-wheel, dating from about 1100. What makes the mill unique is that it has been in continual use since that date, and although it no longer mills corn it has been adapted to a saw which Mrs Wollocombe uses to cut her logs. Since 1970 it has been a scheduled building of the Department of the Environment.

It is simplicity which gives the garden at Bidlake Mill its appeal for it has grown up naturally around the small house on the slopes leading down to the River Lew at the bottom of the garden and the mill leat which drives the water wheel. In typical cottage-garden style there is a steady development of colour from the spring right through the summer; daffodils in the borders and areas of long grass, and later on delphiniums and sweet williams together in the long border above the house, then lupins followed by phlox in the large island bed on the lawn below it. The Rock Garden, which is also below the house, is perhaps at its best in the spring when the various heathers are brightened by gentians and many different bog plants.

Above the house, too, Mrs Wollocombe has removed part of the orchard at the top of the garden to make three more island beds in the grass for small rhododendrons, azaleas, mahonias and hellebores, and some very effective ground cover, in particular a white periwinkle which has spread itself all around the larger plants. Mrs Wollocombe has cleverly linked this garden and the orchard with primroses on a grass bank – simple and natural and in perfect keeping with the atmosphere of the garden.

In a gale in December 1981 the garden suffered the disastrous loss of two trees – an oak, which stood beside the stream at the bottom of the garden and, more importantly, a huge beech which stood over the Water Garden beside the mill. Not only did the falling beech do considerable damage, but the loss of so large a tree from so small a garden meant the loss of important protection and the creation of a difficult gap to fill appropriately. Mrs Wollocombe has planted two new beech and a nothofagus in its place, and one hopes that the newly planted primulas will soon restore the Water Garden's appearance. Luckily the second water garden along the stream did not suffer; here water flows between banks smothered with primulas and a small collection of camellias and azaleas, which seem to thrive despite the frost that settles in this low-lying area.

Bidlake has all the unpretentious charm of the small traditional garden; one, moreover, in especial harmony with its surroundings, and the age-long service of the old mill.

FERNWOOD

Toadspit Lane, 1 mile west of Ottery St Mary off the A30 between Exeter and Honiton
Tel. 040481 2820
Mrs and Mrs H. Hollinrake

Open daily from April to September inclusive

A dense wood of Scots pines could not have been a very inviting place in which to set up gardening, but twenty years ago Fernwood's two acres were exactly that; indeed the wood still surrounds part of the garden. Having cleared some areas and carefully thinned the trees from others, Mr Hollinrake steadily built up his collection of plants round an open lawn in front of the house, and preserved the original woodland character with paths winding away from the lawn between borders and individual trees and shrubs.

Rhododendrons are Mr Hollinrake's main interest and the garden now contains an impressive quantity of them, over four hundred, in fact. Nearly all the specie rhododendrons have been raised from seed from Edinburgh and Wisley, and he has raised some seedlings of his own. In addition to these there are over a hundred camellias. The sheer number of plants in a relatively small area has made their positioning and grouping all the more important, and one immediately recognizes that these potential problems are major successes in the garden. A small but effective combination is immediately visible as one crosses the lawn, in the border along its foot where *Pieris japonica* 'Variegata' and *Euonymous* 'Silver Queen' are planted together. Throughout the garden there are a number of open areas with an individual plant as a focal point. One such view is from the corner of the lawn past a *Magnolia stellata* to an eye-catching plant of the hybrid *Rhododendron Barclayi* 'Robert Fox', with its scarlet flowers.

The preponderence of rhododendrons and camellias means that spring and early summer are the seasons when Fernwood is at its most colourful. As well as many *williamsii* and *japonica* varieties of camellia there are a number of interesting ones from America, such as 'Guilio Nuccio' and reticulata hybrids. At this time of the year, too, the garden is filled with daffodils, polyanthus and erythroniums, the most attractive of which is the small pink *Erythronium revolutum* from nearby Knights-hayes (discussed later in this Devon chapter). Two trees that flower very well considering that they are both less than twenty years old are *Magnolia mollicomata* near the top of the garden and *M. sargentiana robusta*, which stands lower down. This latter tree is an important feature in another effective group; nearby is a beautiful example of the contrasting evergreen *Picea breweriana* with a screen of camellias behind it – the pink 'Rosemary Williams' and white 'Nobilissima'.

In any garden, but especially when in one surrounded by tall woodland trees, it is clearly important to retain some open areas which are best filled with low plants. Throughout this garden various heathers are effectively used as ground cover, and one of the most beautiful small glades is in front of two plants of *Rhododendron macabeanum* where, in the late spring, there is a frost of lily-of-the-valley. Of the two macabeanum plants it is interesting that only one has yet flowered in eighteen years. One of Mr Hollinrake's greatest successes with planting up the small glades has been the *Cyclamen libanoticum* round the trunks of one group of Scots pines. The survival of this cyclamen, not normally hardy, points to the mildness of Fernwood's climate and the shelter of its situation, as does the healthy appearance of the tender *crinodendron hookeranum*.

Mr Hollinrake summed up his achievement at Fernwood very succinctly when he said that his aim from the start had been to 'create a garden in an old pine wood trying to avoid being either purist or pedantic in the plantings or layout.' The balance he has successfully created between the trees, shrubs and smaller flowers easily avoids these faults, and produces features of continual interest in what might have been considered an inauspicious setting.

THE GARDEN HOUSE

In Buckland Monachorum. West of Yelverton off the A386, 10 miles north of Plymouth
Tel. 0822 854 769

The Fortescue Garden Trust

Open three days a week from April to September inclusive

Lionel Fortescue, who created the garden here in the thirty years before his death in 1981, was famously acquisitive of plants and a ruthless perfectionist in what he allowed in his garden. During his lifetime the garden was subject to daily scrutiny; today the quality resulting from that rigorous inspection is clearly recognizable. One hopes that the trust which has been set up to ensure the garden's future will maintain these standards, for the Garden House really is a tribute to a true perfectionist.

The place is well named: although the main area of garden is on the north-west-facing slope below, the house is virtually surrounded by plantings. Above the house is a long border of rhododendrons and azaleas, with *Pieris japonica*, hellebores and pink erythroniums sheltering beneath. Curving away up the drive, the border leads to a mass of camellias, particularly 'Donation', and the two most impressive mature trees in the garden, a beech and copper beech, each underplanted with daffodils and crocus. With the camellias, bulbs and many cherries on the far side from the house, the driveway is a most welcoming sight in spring. It is, however, in a fairly exposed position on the western edge of Dartmoor. Protection comes from the walls which enclose the eastern side and bottom section of the garden, and from a tall hedge of *Cupressocyparis leylandii* extending down the slope on the western side. The slope is divided into a series of descending terraces providing further shelter, a framework for planting and an obvious opportunity for variety. Hedges on the different levels form strong axes up and down the slope and across the garden, ensuring a succession of surprises as one reaches areas hidden from view.

At the bottom of the slope is the door to an old Walled Garden, originally a vegetable garden and now filled with herbaceous plants. The combination of traditional planting with an old thatched barn and stone tower give this area the look of a cottage garden. At right-angles to the main path across the Walled Garden is a narrow path, enclosed by hedges, leading under an arch of cypress to a short flight of stone steps and a small, sheltered terrace belonging to the stone tower. Above the steps is *Eucryphia milliganii*, whose size is perfectly suited to the scale of this part of the garden. Along the back of the terrace is a hedge of *Cotoneaster lacteus*; mixing with the herbaceous plants here are various shrubs, such as cornus and kolkwitzia.

Above the tower is the largest terrace with a thuya hedge at its western end. Borders surrounding the central lawn have a balanced variety of planting: as well as herbaceous plants flowering from April through the summer there are some striking larger trees and shrubs, in particular three *Magnolia soulangiana*, a *Hoheria glabrata* 'Lyallii', whose healthy existence testifies to the degree of shelter achieved in the garden, and *Cornus kousa* 'Chinensis'. A partially hidden flight of steps at the top of this terrace leads to the paved path above the lawn. As well as tree peonies, hibiscus and *Eucryphia glutinosa* closely-planted *Camellia japonicas* have formed a dense hedge about ten feet high behind the path. It is easy to imagine how spectacular a sight this is when the camellias are in flower.

On either side of the path are a number of rhododendrons, of which there are many outstanding plants throughout the garden. One would expect so single-minded a gardener as Lionel Fortescue to raise plants of one species or another, and two of his most successful hybrid rhododendrons are 'Katherine Fortescue', named after his wife, which won an Award of Merit in 1981, and *Rh.* 'Lionel Fortescue'. Both are particularly notable for their superb yellow flowers. More hybrid rhododendrons are concentrated outside the terraces in a triangular area between the western *leylandii* hedge and another planted at a slight angle; these include *Rh.* 'Elizabeth' and *Rh.* 'Queen Elizabeth II', with contrasting scarlet and yellow flowers; and the cream-flowered *Rh.* 'Jack Skelton' raised by George Johnstone at Trewithen (discussed in the

Cornwall chapter of this book). Also thriving in this sheltered position is
Leptospermum scoparium.

One of the most inspired pieces of planting was the magnolia which is
actually outside the garden on the far side of the stream at the bottom of
the valley but is the perfect focal point in the small gap where these
hedges come to a point. Undoubtedly the finest magnolia within the
garden is the *M. salicifolia* on the uppermost terrace; the abundance of
fragrant white flowers seem almost to defy the winds to which they are
exposed by virtue of the tree's height, over thirty feet. *M.* 'Leonard
Messel' close by never attains any great height but is a most attractive
hybrid. Perhaps one of the most unexpected finds here is round the
corner from these two trees, on the west-facing wall of the house. Here,
trained in a sheltered corner, is *Clematis indivisa*, a most tender visitor
from New Zealand. Stretching along this wall from it and matching its
creamy-white flowers, is a large *Wisteria floribunda* 'Alba'.

In total contrast to horticultural interest all around is the tale behind
the 'Ten Trees' field beyond the cherries; it takes its name from a line of
ten lime trees planted for the ten children of a past vicar of the parish. It
is a pleasantly simple note on which to dwell as one leaves the Garden
House, where a visit always demands concentration if one is to appreciate the variety and quality of plants.

KNIGHTSHAYES COURT

2 miles north of Tiverton off the A396; dual carriageway from Junction 27 on
the M5
Tel. 0884 255 438
The National Trust and Lady Heathcoat Amory

Open daily from April to October inclusive

For many people Knightshayes possesses that rare and indefinable
blend of qualities which make a great garden. When Sir John and Lady
Amory inherited in 1937 they found themselves the possessors of a large
Victorian house surrounded by wonderful Devon hills and by a park that
stretched half a mile from the front of the house down to the valley of the
River Exe.

There are outstanding trees throughout the park, many of which were planted by Sir John's grandfather, the first baronet. In the Scottish tradition his grandmother made a large Walled Garden (no longer part of the pleasure gardens) away from the house, with yew hedges, espalier fruit trees and herbaceous borders. Beyond the Walled Garden is one of Knightshayes' outstanding legacies, the Douglas Walk; the Douglas firs there, some of which are over 140 feet tall, have been compared with the columns in Salisbury Cathedral, and were probably planted by Sir John Heathcoat Amory for whom William Burges built the house in the 1870s.

All the surrounding trees, planted at the same time, provided the Amorys with foundations and a setting, and it will encourage many people to hear that two people who will always be thought of as one of gardening's most successful partnerships had at the start only limited knowledge and experience, as Lady Amory is the first person to admit.

She had been the outstanding lady golfer of her day, and she tells how when they first moved to Knightshayes the only purpose the flowerbeds in front of the house served for her husband were as a focus for his golf balls when driving up from the park. Alteration to these flowerbeds provided Lady Amory's first lesson in making her garden: she replaced the fussy pattern of beds filled with antirrhinums with a formal Rose Garden. It was the realization that even this spoiled the specifically designed view down across the park that taught Lady Amory both the importance of being able to appreciate an established setting without feeling the urge to alter or add to it, and also to endeavour to blend and balance whatever alterations and additions she did make with that existing framework.

In their determination to avoid disharmony the Amorys gave the garden at Knightshayes the two qualities which are perhaps the secret of its character and appeal, taste and restraint. Everywhere these two most elusive influences are evident. Thus tiny plants are as highly valued as huge flowering trees, open spaces are balanced with areas of detailed planting linked by paths and vistas, harsh and vibrant colours are banished and the values of simplicity and naturalness are constantly revealed.

They began by scaling down the formality of the Victorian terraces round the house. Near the end of the terrace which leads to the present Woodland Garden, was a small Paved Garden surrounded by high clipped yew hedges and filled with roses. This was transformed by replacing the roses with slightly raised beds filled with low prostrate plants, particularly those with soft grey and silver foliage, complementing the high hedges and two standard wisterias in the back beds. Four small charming figures of the seasons and a lead waterbutt dated 1727 also at the back complete a picture of balanced formality. Immediately between here and the Woodland Garden a bowling green, again surrounded by high yew hedges, was replaced by the Pool Garden, now the quintessence of tranquillity. A weeping silver pear, thinned regularly to maintain a delicate and truly pendulous form, hangs over the circular pool. A stone statue set in a recess in the far yew hedge contemplates the scene and the visitors encouraged by stone seats to sit and enjoy this garden's atmosphere of timeless simplicity. .

It is the Woodland Garden, or the Garden in the Wood, as it has always been called, which will certainly be the Amorys' greatest achievement. By the time they tackled this their knowledge and confidence had increased; Sir John, in particular, was becoming an avid collector of plants, while Lady Amory took special interest in positioning and grouping them. In the early years Sir Eric Savill, creator of the gardens in Windsor Great Park, gave advice and encouragement, with so many other gardening friends over the years. So, too, since his arrival as head gardener in 1963 has Michael Hickson, still head gardener and a major contributor to the development of the gardens.

Despite the quantity of plants the Garden in the Wood is easy for any visitor to enjoy and appreciate. The thinning of mature trees was selective, with the best specimens and those in prominent positions being retained so that the natural woodland atmosphere survived. Within this framework the areas of planting are not overcrowded and are balanced with generous glades and areas of open space. Just the size of the area involved, well over twenty acres, is impressive in itself, although it was not all taken in at once. Rather, as Lady Amory says, the development of the garden brought them continually to the boundary fence, which was continually moved back as the temptation to expand proved irresistible.

One of the outstanding features of the Garden in the Wood is the balance and unity between plants of all sizes, from hellebores, hostas and anemones to the highest standard trees. Many of the magnolias are impressively large; at one end of the long open glade running along the north side of the original Woodland Garden is a particularly well-positioned group. Perhaps the best specimen is the *M. campbellii mollicomata* which stands above the main path leading from the terrace through the centre of this garden. There are interest and surprises on every side and round every corner if one follows this path or one of the smaller ones winding amongst the beds on either side. Spring and early summer are perhaps the most rewarding seasons when the many rhododendrons, azaleas and camellias are in flower, and when there is fresh foliage on the trees, for instance the various acers. Beneath these are smaller plants. In one typical corner the ground beneath a chestnut tree is covered with the delicate flowers of yellow and pink erythroniums, primroses, pink cyclamen, blue Muscari and fritillaries. Erythroniums are a great feature at Knightshayes; in another part of the Woodland Garden is a path beneath larches and firs with the ground either side of it covered with drifts of their pink and white flowers.

Beyond the original Garden in the Wood is a large glade that can be enjoyed from a beautiful stone seat badly in need of restoration. Round about are various borders and a long hedge of philadelphus, an impressive sight later in the summer when many other plants, such as the striking *Stachyurus praecox* with its distinctive racemes of yellow flowers in March, have finished flowering. This glade leads to the areas of more recent planting – Holly's Wood; Sir John's Wood, where *Primula japonica* 'Postford White' is a feature; and Michael's Wood (named after Michael Hickson), where there are many large-leafed rhododendrons. To avoid any possible conflict in the styles of planting the space between Sir John's Wood and Michael's Wood was designated No Man's Land, the name by which it has been known ever since. Above Michael's Wood is the arboretum, where recently planted trees of interest will grow up to replace older ones in the Woodland Garden.

Although the Amorys did leave the view in front of the house unbroken down to the park, they developed the South Garden to one side. Here, amid open areas of grass filled with daffodils in spring, are various trees and shrubs planted singly or in groups: rhododendrons, *Viburnum tomentosum* 'Lanarth', *Acer palmatum* 'Senkaki' and, close to a group of mature conifers, *Picea breweriana* and the evergreen *Nothofagus betuloides*. The most recent area of planting is to the west of the house, where a collection of willows has been built up round a large pool. Old-fashioned azaleas were retained when the existing *Rhododendron ponticum* were removed and these now blend effectively with the willows.

After the death of Sir John Amory in 1972 the National Trust took on Knightshayes, and now run the garden with Lady Amory. Visitors come and return to appreciate the plants, their relationships and their setting, and the Amorys' creative achievement. One hopes that they will also continue to sense the enjoyment and devotion which was such a part of their work.

MARWOOD HILL

In Marwood village, 4 miles north-west of Barnstaple
Tel. 027 142 528

Dr J. A. Smart

Open daily except Christmas Day

Dr Smart estimates that his garden at Marwood Hill now contains over three thousand different varieties of plants. He began the twelve-acre garden in 1960, building it up on the fairly steep slopes of a valley along the bottom of which a small stream originally flowed. In 1969 this was dammed to form three lakes; further along the valley it flows out of the bottom lake. Dr Smart showed his particular sense of priorities by building his house after he had built up much of the garden, thus siting it to maximum advantage with the best possible view. Now he has the satisfaction of being able to see almost every corner of his garden from his drawing-room windows, with the exception of some of the most far-flung outposts down the valley. Recently he has taken on another two acres, a move which he compares with Hitler's last territorial aim in Europe.

Marwood Hill now has one of the most interesting collections of trees and shrubs to be found anywhere and it might be easy to forget in a garden of such general interest that it also has a leading reputation for its camellias, particularly the collection which fill the large Camellia House near the top of the garden where the blooms attain quite spectacular size. There are many prize-winning plants among them, and special interest in some of the new American hybrids of *Camellia reticulata.* Many of the plants seen at Marwood may be purchased in a sales area in the garden.

The terrace in front of the house is perhaps the best place from which to view the garden as a whole, for one can see the unity given to the groups of plants and the individual trees and shrubs as well as the particular features of various specimens. Close to the dwarf rhododendrons and heathers on the bank in front of the house is *Cornus alternifolia* 'Argentea', whose silver-variegated foliage stands out immediately. Between the house and the Walled Garden is a small formal Rose Garden, whose blooms follow on from the mainly spring and early-summer flowering plants in the main garden. On the small lawn beside the house is perhaps the outstanding magnolia of the garden's large and impressive collection. A tree of the hybrid *Magnolia loebneri* 'Merrill', planted in 1964, it is a fast-growing variety with exquisitely scented white flowers. Elsewhere in the garden are *Magnolia sargentiana robusta* and *M. sprengeri* 'Diva'; one of the most eye-catching trees is *Magnolia dawsoniana*, on the far side of the lakes.

As well as the Camellia House there is another, equally large, glasshouse in the garden, the Australia House, with a collection of plants that has been built up from regular visits Dr Smart has made over many years to Australia, Tasmania and New Zealand. A number of wonderful mimosas fill the whole house with their scent when in flower; among a host of other plants are *Correa harrisii*, a member of the small family of Australian and Tasmanian evergreens with spectacular red funnel-shaped flowers, and an *Indigofera australis*. Obviously many of these plants could not survive outside the glasshouse, but in many parts of his garden Dr Smart has succeeded in growing a number of tender plants, the most vulnerable of which are along the ten-foot-high buttressed wall on the south side of the Walled Garden. As well as a wide variety of clematis and ceanothus there are more unusual visitors from Australia, such as the *Billardieras*, *Acacia dealbata*, *A. pravissima* and *A. riceana*, and from other parts of the world. Dr Smart's spirit of gardener's adventure continually leads him to experiment in this way with plants, for despite their healthy appearance none of these specimens survives easily in climatic conditions which are at times fairly hostile, compared with their normal habitat. Everywhere, however, one immediately recognizes an uncompromisingly critical attitude in his choice of plants, and a discerning eye in their positioning and grouping.

There are some fine standard trees near the lakes: *Picea brewerana* close to the upper lake and, between this and the middle lake, one of the most beautiful and distinctive Japanese cherries, *Prunus shirotae* 'Mount Fuji'. Quite close by is an interesting clump of black bamboo and a collection of willows, whose well-trimmed stems are outstanding in the winter but one of the most effective groups is on the far side of the lakes, where a silver-leafed weeping pear has *Clematis alpina* 'Frances Rivis' and *C. 'Ernest Markham'* trained into its branches; this is flanked by two *Acer* 'Senkaki', again good in winter, when their twigs are bright red. This far slope beyond the lakes has been specially planted to be seen from the advantage of the area round the house; among the magnolias are many rhododendrons, including a very good plant of *Rhododendron macabeanum*. Beyond this a conifer glade leads to the top of the garden on the far side of the lakes and a tree of which Dr Smart is particularly fond, *Abies spectabilis*, grown from seed collected in Nepal. Other trees of which he has good specimens are embothriums, eucryphias and, as to be expected from someone with a particular interest in Australia, eucalyptus.

At either end of the garden are two widely contrasting areas. At the top Dr Smart has converted an old quarry into a Rock Garden, with many alpines and a lovely little yellow erythronium. Above the stream at the far end, planted with primulas and with other damp-loving plants, is one of Dr Smart's most ambitious projects, for he has planted the whole slope with trees with a wide variety of interesting flowers and foliage. Fastigiate trees stand at the entrance to various rides leading at all angles across the slope; all are focused on a distinctive feature, such as the church tower on top of the hill. Because of its youth Dr Smart compares this wood at the moment with Heathrow Airport, 'with rides cutting like runways between the young trees'.

With its formidable collection of plants Marwood Hill is of particular interest to the connoisseur and expert, but nevertheless its wide variety means that there is something for everyone. And any visitor will immediately feel the boundless energy, enthusiasm and expertise with which the garden has been created, and for this alone it is worth visiting.

DORSET

ABBOTSBURY

West of Abbotsbury Village, off the B3157 between Weymouth and Bridport
Tel. 03058 7387
Strangways Estate

Open daily from mid-March to mid-October

The aptly-named 'sub-tropical' gardens at Abbotsbury are one of the
spectacles of English gardens, containing as they do great numbers of
rare and tender plants, many now of great age and enormous size. The
exotic appearance of the gardens would no doubt surprise Elizabeth,
Countess of Ilchester, who in 1765 built Abbotsbury Castle on a
protected hill overlooking the sea, and who made the original small
garden within high stone walls. Over the centuries the gardens have
suffered many setbacks, particularly enforced neglect during the two
World Wars, but thanks to devoted restoration by Lady Teresa Agnew,
her late husband Viscount Galway, their head gardener, John Hussey,
and the present curator John Kelly, they have been brought back to a
glory one hopes will also bring deserved popularity with the public, both
horticultural and holiday-making.

The original modest Walled Garden was first expanded by the wife
of the 2nd Earl, and more particularly by her son, William Fox-
Strangways, 4th Earl of Ilchester. A respected botanist after whom the
genus *Stranvaesia* was named, he realized that his garden was an ideal
site for the many unusual and often tender plants being introduced from
America, China, the Himalayas and other parts of the temperate world.
The hollow is sheltered on all sides by hills, further protection is given
by belts of evergreen oaks, and proximity to the sea and the prevailing
warm south-westerly winds mean that Abbotsbury has the rare luxury of

an almost frost-free climate. During the winter of 1981–2 the gardens suffered minimal, if any, damage compared with the devastation wreaked throughout most of the country.

It seems that when describing plants at Abbotsbury, 'the largest in England' or 'among the largest of England' are almost compulsory terms. Many of the largest specimens in the gardens, particularly around the original walled area, were planted during the 4th Earl's time. These include *Trachycarpus fortunei*, 'Chusan Palms', which are forty feet tall; and many enormous camellias, particularly *japonica* varieties, and *C. reticulata*. The *Pterocarya fraxinifolia*, the 'Caucasian Wing Nut', perhaps the best specimen in Europe, dates from even earlier. One of the garden's most spectacular trees, *Magnolia campbellii*, now over sixty feet high and only rivalled by one or two in the most southerly Cornish gardens, was planted in 1864, just a year before the 4th Earl's death. It is a fitting memorial to his contribution to the gardens.

Adventurous additions continued through the late-nineteenth and early-twentieth centuries. In 1877 one of the rarest of the garden's many varieties of oak was planted, the hybrid *Quercus hispanica* – a cross between the 'Turkey' and 'Cork' oaks – in its 'Diversifolia' form; the two *Cupressus macrocarpa*, now of gargantuan proportions, were added in about 1895; and in 1911, to commemorate the coronation of King George V, a stand of *Pinus radiata*, the Monterey pine. Many of the rhododendrons and azaleas were also planted then.

In 1913 Abbotsbury Castle burned down, and in 1936 the replacement building was demolished. It was not until after the Second World War that any serious attempt was made to tame the rapacious growth through the gardens and expand the collection. Two of the most recent additions have been the Peat Garden and the Rose Corner, both made during the winter of 1981–2 and both interesting, if not in the true 'Abbotsbury' style of gardening, which normally involves a combination of size and tender rarity. From the West Lawn, surrounded by cannons from a wrecked ship, past the old Walled Garden, to the Valley Garden and the slopes around, the progression of plants continues in marvellous variety throughout the year. Among the best and most unusual plants are cornuses – *C. controversa* for its size, *C.* 'Ormonde', a rare hybrid between *C. nutallii* and *C. florida*, and *C. capitata* for their rarity; *Osmanthus yunnanensis*; *Magnolia veitchii* 'Isca', over sixty feet tall; many acacias including, as well as the better-known *A. dealbaba, A. baileyana*, all with their yellow flowers; and *Myrtus apiculata* (*M. luma*), the best of the myrtle family, with flowering cinnamon trunk and branches but too tender to thrive in anything but the very mildest of British climates. Most of these flower in the spring or early summer, though the myrtle is good all the year round. Later in the summer huge drifts of hydrangeas flower throughout the gardens, together with various *Hoherias* from New Zealand, *Eucryphias* and *Clerodendrums*. The display is endless, the scents are almost overpowering, and their combination cannot fail to impress any visitor.

ATHELHAMPTON

Near Puddletown, north-east of Dorchester on the A35
Tel. 030 584 363
Sir Robert Cooke

Open Wednesday, Thursday, Sunday from mid-April to mid-October, and every day except Monday and Saturday in August

---

It is hard to believe that the building of the earliest parts of the house and the making of much of the present garden at Athelhampton were separated by four hundred years, such is the harmony between the battlemented and gabled stone manor house and the series of gardens and walks which surround it. The house was started in 1485 and virtually completed by the mid-sixteenth century, but the series of formal enclosed gardens to the south and east of the house were the work of Inigo Thomas (with suggestions from Thomas Mawson) in the 1890s, and there have been substantial recent additions. They are full of surprise and intimacy. Their architecture gives a great sense of establishment and so, too, does the ever-present sound of water in the series of fountains and pools supplied by the River Piddle, which encloses two sides of the gardens in a large curve.

The main focus of the gardens is the Corona, a small circular enclosure with gateways on four sides. Tall yew hedges grow behind the walls surrounding the central circular pool, vase and fountain. The walls are surmounted with stone obelisks and bordered in front with eucryphias, fuchsias and abutilons, but the overpowering effect is one of clipped yew, stonework and water. From the Corona views through four narrow gateways are tempting on all sides, inviting curiosity as to what lies beyond, heightened by the fountains glimpsed through the ironwork and perpetually audible.

Steps to the south of the Corona lead up to the largest area of the

Great Court, whose style mirrors that of the Corona on a larger scale. A raised walk leading to the Great Terrace surrounds a sunken lawn containing another ornamental pool with marble basin and fountain; around the lawn like sentinels are twelve obelisks of clipped yew, now over twenty feet tall, their shape complementing the stone obelisks of the Corona and echoed by the pointed roofs of the two summerhouses, of 'Joy and Summer' and 'Sorrow and Winter'. The terrace wall cascades water into stone troughs as at Villa d'Este. To the north of the Corona is the Private Garden, on the east side of the house. Here again is a sunken lawn this time with rectangular pool and fountain, and in front of the house is an open, balustraded terrace. In the borders beneath its walls are summer flowers and shrubs; syringa, carpentaria, callstemon, hydrangea magnolias and *Azara lanceolata*.

This series of three was Thomas's most inspired piece of garden design, a variation on a theme in descending levels, linked by pools, fountains and enticing gateways. The idea is continued through a gateway on the far (north) side of the Private Garden into the White Garden, with its marble group, 'Il Giuocatore', from the Exhibition of 1862 and the shaded River Piddle beyond. A long river terrace has been made here, to give views of open fields and distant hills. This main axis from the Great Terrace to the White Garden is complemented by others, parallel and at right-angles, leading off the Corona, the Private Garden and the White Garden. A new Cloister Garden – pleached limes backed by beech hedges surrounding an octagonal pool and fountain – joins the White to the walled Kitchen Garden; through the gateway into this is an apple and laburnum walk leading to a pool surrounded by yew.

From the Private Garden the Bell Gate, flanked by statues of Don Juan and Don Cesar, opens on to a prospect of the long walled rectangular canal made in 1969–70. *Magnolia grandiflora* and *M. delavayi* are trained on the walls which lead to the statue of Cupid and Psyche at the far end. It is a masterly piece of seventeenth-century-style formality, one day to be completed by the addition of a summerhouse beyond the statue.

The third of the eastward axes leads out of the Corona to the Dry Garden with a lion's head fountain in its far wall. In this, the most sheltered enclosure, grow palms and other sub-tropical plants. Beyond is a long grass path; at one end is a statue of Hygea, and at the other is a more imposing one of Queen Victoria who, dare one say it, looks a shade incongruous in this setting. The path leading to her has been closely planted with shrubs on either side – hydrangeas, shrub roses, amalanchiers, tree peonies, *Sycopsis sinensis* and *Callicarpa bodinieri*. Beyond

Queen Victoria, at the end of a parallel lime walk, is a statue of Venus and Cupid. This walk completes the symmetry of the design; it crosses the path from the Private Garden to the Canal at right-angles, from where a recently added extension of pleached limes brings one back to the Cloister Garden. A sense of grace and movement is perfectly rendered by Athelhampton's gardens, and it is clear that the works in progress will enhance them further.

THE MANOR HOUSE, CRANBORNE

In Cranborne on the B3078, off the A354 between Salisbury and Blandford
Tel. 07254 248
The Marquess of Salisbury

Open the first Saturday and Sunday in each month, Bank Holidays and by appointment

---

Where most of its contemporaries have succumbed to Palladianism, the Landscape Movement, High Victorianism or plain neglect, Cranborne overflows with the genius of Elizabethan and Jacobean England. It dates from the time of King John, for whom the manor was a hunting-lodge and was given to Robert Cecil, 1st Earl of Salisbury by King James I. Cranborne's gardens have been maintained and enhanced by successive generations of Cecils, in particular by the present Marquess and his wife, as well as his parents, but it is that earlier genius of understatement, with the occasional flourish in perfect taste, that pervades the whole.

Perhaps because he had his great palace at Hatfield Robert Cecil was happy just to add to Cranborne rather than rebuild it. Nowhere in his work on the house is there a trace of grandeur, but the harmony between his gatehouse towers and the twin towers of the house behind, his Italianate arched porches on the main north and south fronts, subtly prefiguring the Renaissance architecture, and above, the tall brick chimneys – all are full of the confidence of his age. John Tradescant the Elder was his gardener, as well as the King's, and the gardens he laid out round the house in their sympathy with its architecture reflect through formality of terraces and clipped yew the sense of order so important to the Elizabethan and early Stuart mind. With order established the mixed plantings of fruit and flowers were allowed a measure of informality, a blend of scent and colour whose carefree and restful effect is so often forgotten today in the quest for plantsmanship. Tradescant was a superb plantsman – as were many of his contemporaries – but to him a garden was first and foremost a place of beauty and repose.

Some of Tradescant's original design has survived and provides the framework and inspiration for the garden's present style and appearance. On the west side of the house the Bowling Green leads to the bank and Mount Garden raised up at its far end with yew hedges behind, and a clipped yew allée stretching along one side. To the south is the main courtyard bounded by brick walls with the arch of the gatehouse opening on to a long beech avenue. To the north the original pattern is similar, with a Walled Garden below the balustraded terrace in front of the house, and stretching up the slope on the far side of the river an avenue, originally of Cornish elms and now young planes.

A great deal of work re-planting was done by Lord Salisbury's parents, before whose time Cranborne had slightly suffered from being a second home. The pleached Lime Walk along the east of the main courtyard was planted by his father. Since 1954, when they came to live at Cranborne, the present Lady Salisbury has had to cope with the practicalities of maintaining over eleven acres with three gardeners – fewer than half the number her parents-in-law had. Cranborne held a fascination for her since childhood acquaintance with it that has grown to deep affection, and she has built up the garden with a rare sensitivity for period.

Throughout the gardens Lady Salisbury has used old and traditional plants, and particularly those that would have been used in the original garden. This is especially true of her Knot Garden, where there are only plants grown in the sixteenth and seventeenth centuries filling the pattern of clipped box hedges and low topiary – pinks, double primroses and crown imperials. The main courtyard is now paved and cobbled, but there are climbers on the walls such as *Solanum crispum*, and climbing roses adorn the brickwork of the gatehouse. Elsewhere in the garden lady Salisbury has added her mother-in-law's collection of old-fashioned roses.

Some herbaceous and bedding plants have been replaced; now below the terrace on the north side of the house is the White Garden, still with its old éspalier apples. Away from the house is Lady Salisbury's Herb Garden, enclosed by old walls and high yew hedges, and approached through a cool enclosure of lawn and beech hedges and a narrow arch in the yew. Shrubs abound, including many old but rarely seen varieties, such as *Abelia triflora*, with its gloriously scented clusters of white flowers tinged with pink. There are collections of old tulips, dianthus and violas, many of which are in the borders along the Church Walk, which has low apple hedges and other fruit trees behind. And growing wild beneath the beeches and in the orchard are daffodils, narcissus, primroses, cowslips and crocus, both spring and autumn varieties.

Few of the great gardens in England do not rely wholly or in part on the influences of styles from abroad, or more particularly on the arrival of plants from foreign parts. In its happy communion with the past Cranborne is a place of enchantment and, though many of its qualities are intangible and unobtrusive, they are not so modest as to disguise the fact that it is a superb example of the truly English tradition.

MINTERNE

In Minterne Magna, 2 miles north of Cerne Abbas on the A352
Tel. 03003 370
The Lord Digby

Open from April to end of autumn colouring, and by appointment

---

The building up of the landscape at Minterne has been a virtually uninterrupted process since the eighteenth century. Historical connections abound. The property, at one stage owned by the Warden and Scholars of Winchester College, passed to the Churchill family, and it was the brother of the 1st Duke of Marlborough who sold Minterne to Admiral the Hon. Robert Digby in 1768. He laid out the park, on the rising ground to the east of the house, having first planted sheltering trees along the tops of the surrounding hills no doubt, taking occasional advice from his brother, Lord Digby, for whom 'Capability' Brown was laying out the park of Sherborne Castle at the same time. The present house, built in 1903, is one of the outstanding Edwardian houses in the country; the earlier Manor was the model for Great Hintock House in *The Woodlanders* by Thomas Hardy.

Admiral Digby made one of the most attractive areas at Minterne, the lakes, ponds, cascades and balustraded stone bridge along the eastern edge of the garden. Below this bridge the water separates into more than one stream, and at one point a pretty wooden bridge is overhung almost to the point of being rendered invisible by an enormous *Parrotia persica*.

With the cercydiphyllums, particularly *C. sinensis*, nearby and many acers, the autumn colour in this part of the garden is outstanding.

But it is the Woodland Garden, stretching in a great horseshoe round the park on the south side of the house, and in particular the collection of rhododendrons which are perhaps Minterne's most prized possession. The rhododendron collection was started in the mid-nineteenth century, and is one of the best established in the country, steadily built up and maintained by four generations of the Digby family. They were fortunate to inherit a well-wooded site and, in parts of the curving wood, spectacular terrain, particularly on the east side of the neck of parkland where an almost sheer bank drops to the ground around the series of streams flowing out of the lakes and ponds. Many of the rhododendrons have been grown from seed collected on various expeditions to China and the Himalayas, starting with some of the very earliest. These specie rhododendrons are interesting because many are unnamed; they bear just a number and tag with the name and date of the expedition. Perhaps those of Kingdon Ward and George Forrest in the early part of this century are best represented at Minterne, but there are certainly many older plants. It was only recently that a plant of *R. arboreum* was removed because it completely obscured two far finer specimens. Lord Digby's father never would remove it because it was planted in the 1850s which, he said, was a sign of an original rhododendron garden. Now *R. griffithianum* and *Rh.* 'Penjerrick' make an unforgettable sight, high on the steep east-facing bank with, towering above them, a huge beech from an earlier date.

Some of the best early plants came in the 1890s, including *R. thomsonii, R. campylocarpum*, and in particular *R. falconeri*. Later hybrids have been added to the collection, many of them raised at Minterne. Although the flow of plants here has been almost continuous since those early days, with much of outstanding interest among the more recent introductions, it is understandably some of the oldest and largest plants which are the most impressive.

Rhododendrons are important at Minterne, but throughout the Woodland Garden there is much else besides both to provide variety and to blend with their varying colours and evergreen foliage. Along the west of the central park is the simple beauty of a thickly-carpeted bluebell bank beneath beeches. With the beeches and pines – dominant among the mature trees – are a number of interesting specimens: *Picea brewiana*, 'Brewer's Weeping Spruce' and, close by, a large Californian redwood, and two large and venerable *Davidia involucratas*. Among the magnolias *Magnolia campbellii* and *M. mollicomata* are the most impressive, but Lord Digby's favourite is the more delicate *M. wilsonii*, with its scented, hanging flowers. At the far end of the horseshoe from the house, a group of acers leads to what was a cherry avenue along the path; most of the original trees have died but Lord Digby has replanted many.

Inevitably, though it is the huge variety of rhododendrons, specie, hybrid and azaleas that focus one's attention. A special feature at Minterne are the early flowering varieties. There can be nothing more heartening than to walk into the garden in December and see the white and pink flowers of *Rh.* 'Nobleanum' or the pink blooms of *Rh.* 'Christmas Cheer'.

SOMERSET AND AVON

BARRINGTON COURT

3 miles north-east of Ilminster off the A303, ½ mile east of the B3168
Tel. 046 052 242

The National Trust

Open Sunday to Wednesday, afternoons only from Easter to September
inclusive

Barrington Court was acquired by the National Trust in 1907, through
the generosity of Miss J. L. Woodward, and was one of their first great
houses. At that time, however, there was little to recommend the place –
the house was in a state of dilapidation and there was no garden. The
restoration of the one and creation of the other date from 1920, when
Colonel A. A. Lyle became the National Trust's tenant. Colonel Lyle,
whose grandson lives at Barrington today, had been wounded during the
First World War and devoted the rest of his life – and the considerable
financial resources he acquired from the family's sugar company – to
Barrington.

There is some argument whether Barrington Court was built by
Henry, Lord Daubeney, Henry VII's Chamberlain, or by William
Clifton, who bought the estate in 1552. However, confusion cannot
obscure the fact that this is one of our foremost Tudor houses. Built of
Ham stone in the characteristic sixteenth-century 'E' shape, there is yet
an element of dynamic energy in its proportions and the spiralling
chimneys and finials which is quite individual. The house passed from
the Clifton family to Thomas Phelps of nearby Montacute House and
then at the end of the seventeenth century to William Strode, who built
the imposing stable block immediately adjacent, to the west. The Strode
family sold Barrington during the eighteenth century and from then
until the National Trust took it on its history was unsettled.

Despite the considerable architectural qualities of both the house and the stable block there is no evidence of any significant gardens at Barrington until, shortly after taking on the lease, Colonel Lyle employed the architects Forbes and Tate to renovate the house, convert the stable block to be lived in and draw up plans for extensive gardens. No expense was spared and as if to atone for Barrington's time in the wilderness, some 400 men were employed to work on the estate. Forbes and Tate also designed immaculate cottages and farm buildings in a traditional style.

To clothe the designs of his architects Colonel Lyle consulted the most eminent English gardener of his time – Gertrude Jekyll. Miss Jekyll was by this time in her eighties and probably never visited Barrington, but she supplied detailed plans for planting in various parts of the garden, especially in the walled areas immediately to the west of the stable block. In some parts the combinations of plants she suggested were not used, or have subsequently been changed, but the style and character of her work, especially the blending of colours in the borders, is immediately recognizable.

Forbes' original plans were elaborate and covered about ten acres. Some parts of them, such as his designs for the large orchard west beyond the small enclosed gardens and south of the walled kitchen garden, were rejected. Forbes also planned an intricate pattern of yew hedges for the south front but this area was wisely left as a large open lawn in front of both house and stables, showing both buildings to their best advantage, with the park rising beyond. On the lawn's west side three old oaks are the only survivors of what was Barrington's entrance avenue, leading from the imposing wrought-iron gates in the west boundary wall to the south front.

The entrance was moved by Colonel Lyle to the north front where an avenue of stately horse chestnuts approaches a forecourt of lawns and yew hedges. Midway, this avenue is crossed by another at right-angles; such grandeur heightens the contrast with the restrained expanse of the south front and the intimacy of the walled gardens to the west and north-west.

It is remarkable to think that these enclosed gardens were a farmyard in 1907. Now each garden has its own character and appearance. Intricately patterned paths of brick, so typical of Gertrude Jekyll's work, lead between them, lined by borders or closely clipped hedges of box and lavender. Outside the long wall the western boundary of this area is marked by one stretch of the moat – not a moat in the true sense, in that it does not enclose the house, but a stream enclosed by walls which appears to mark a boundary in different parts of the gardens.

Immediately below the west front of the stables is the Lily Garden. Gertrude Jekyll's influence is again quite clear here, with raised beds of azaleas, set in imported lime-free soil, surrounding a central pool, with deep mixed shrub and flower borders round the walls. A brick path leads north through wrought-iron gates between the Irish Garden on the west and the Rose Garden on the east. In the former the flag irises which fill a formal pattern of beds are a now important collection, and roses that were once here have given way to lavender and clematis. The pattern of the Rose Garden is also formal, beds forming a circle within the square boundaries. Along the north side is a recently added pergola, its style reminiscent of those which feature in many Jekyll-Lutyens combinations, and on the far side of a small lawn is Barrington's most picturesque range of buildings – a line of seventeenth- or eighteenth-century ox-byres which have been carefully restored and incorporated into the gardens.

A small doorway leads out of the enclosed gardens across a wooden bridge over the moat on the west side. In front, stretching along a south-facing outside Kitchen Garden wall is Barrington's most impressive border. Ironically, perhaps, this was not planned by Gertrude Jekyll but by Colonel Lyle's wife, Elsie, herself an expert gardener. About twelve feet deep, the border in summer is filled with a luxurious variety of herbaceous plants. Behind, to the north, is the immaculately maintained Kitchen Garden, divided into four squares and with a variety of fruit trees covering all four walls.

On the far, east side of the gardens stretches a wide grass path, flanked by columnar yews and pleached limes. On either side Sir Ian Lyle, Colonel and Mrs Lyle's son who took over at Barrington after his mother's death in 1947, planted an Arboretum filled with a variety of deciduous and coniferous trees, adding yet another aspect to Barrington's gardens but, as always here, entirely in character with the existing features. Today the gardens are maintained to an extremely high standard by four gardeners and it is largely thanks to the management of Christine Middleton, the young head gardener, that they are arguably as good now as in their earlier heyday.

CROWE HALL

In Widcombe, 1 mile south-east of Bath
Tel. 0225 310 322
John Barratt Esq.

Open two Sundays a year

The situation alone of Crowe Hall would satisfy most people. The Georgian house, built of the richly coloured local stone, stands on one of the seven hills encircling Bath, looking down on to the city to the north-west. It is the view from the other side of the house which is the more soul-stirring: out across the valley to Prior Park and 'Capability' Brown's landscaped park dropping gently to the Palladian bridge over one of the two lakes. Anyone who yearns for the romantic will find balm in the combination of this aspect with the presence of the garden near at hand.

The ambitious conception of a garden on such a steep slope, belonged to the Tugwell family, who occupied Crowe Hall in the nineteenth century. The construction of descending terraces and huge retaining walls have given the garden an Italian appearance within its English setting, a dual impression especially evident from the main South Terrace overlooking Prior Park. The Tugwells also planted the yews along the path beneath the western retaining wall here, and their huge frames, hung with Russian vine and *Clematis armandii*, obscure virtually all light. The other narrow paths along this very steep and closely wooded slope have the same atmosphere of gloom and it seems inevitable that at the end of the lowest path a scene of sombre stone tombs in an abandoned graveyard, many of them cracked and broken, should be revealed.

Much of the garden derives its atmosphere from an appearance of gently decaying antiquity in true Picturesque tradition, and nowhere more so than in the old Rock Garden and Grotto which the Tugwells built into the slope at the south end of the main terrace. Treacherously steep steps descend beside the old Water Garden where clumps of bamboo and ferns survive among rough rocks. The arched stone entrance of the Grotto is weirdly overhung with creepers; the darkness seems to lead deep into the hillside, an unconscious masterpiece of the grotesque.

But one must not make too much of the over-maturity in the Victorian parts of the garden, however appealing it is. After they bought Crowe Hall in 1961, Sir Sydney and Lady Barratt undertook an enormous amount of very necessary clearing and restoration. Many of the small terraces on the west-facing slope below the house have been improved – paths cleared, lawns made and borders planted, some with spring bulbs or roses, others with flowering trees and shrubs. Almost every young tree and border in the garden has been planted by Lady Barratt, a very considerable achievement considering the size and inaccessible nature of the garden.

As well as the restoration and planting work, one of Sir Sydney's main additions to the garden was his impressive collection of statuary and urns which now stand throughout the garden as focal points on lawns, at the end of paths, or adorning the various terrace walls. Most of the urns are filled with flowers. One of the most impressive of the statues is Neptune opposite the main east-facing pillared entrance to the house; he stands behind a small pool and trickling fountain in a surround of heathers and dwarf conifers clinging to the bank. Two other particularly attractive lead statues stand on the South Terrace against a backdrop of wisteria and magnolias trained against the house. The formal pool in the middle of the sunken lawn was put in by the Maconochies, the Barratt's predecessors, and Sir Sydney Barratt added the fountain.

Stretching away from the house, behind Neptune, is one of the Barratts' most successful areas, the wide sweep of grass backed by a narrow wood, which curves up the hill, and which in the spring is covered in daffodils. From the top of this walk Brown's landscape and the Palladian bridge are revealed from a new angle.

One could hardly believe that somewhere like Crowe Hall exists so close to the edge of a city, surrounded as it is on two sides by houses and busy streets, but this only serves to enhance its particular and fascinating appeal. John Barratt's own work continues to balance the elements of picturesque antiquity and preserve a treasure among England's gardens.

EAST LAMBROOK MANOR

2 miles north of South Petherton on the B3165, 4 miles from the A303
Tel. 046 040 763

F. H. Boyd-Carpenter, Esq.

Open daily all year

It is hard for any garden to survive the loss of its creator, but if the garden is small, busy and intimate in character, and that creator was one of the most legendary personalities of twentieth-century gardening, then survival is all the more difficult. A visit to East Lambrook Manor in the spring at hellebore and blossom time, or later when the borders and beds are full of summer plants and the climbing roses in full flower high up in the appletrees, is both a reassurance and an opportunity to enjoy much of what Margery Fish created and made famous worldwide in her unrivalled gardening books. It also says a great deal for the noble efforts of the Boyd-Carpenters in maintaining this garden's appearance and atmosphere, so much the product of one style and mind which have been as widely influential as those of any other garden since the Second World War.

Margery Fish began at East Lambrook from a position of relative horticultural ignorance but was blessed with originality and an instinctive, almost uncanny appreciation of an affinity with the plants she used, a combination which never flagged until her death in 1969. In the early days she was greatly helped by her husband Walter, and until his death in 1947 it was his influence which dictated the garden's strong framework which her originality and informality of planting needed, in order to appear to greatest effect. His help was recognized in Margery Fish's first book *We Made a Garden*, which would have been called *Gardening with Walter* had he lived.

It was always Margery Fish's ambition to make a traditional cottage garden, and what emerged at East Lambrook is certainly in the cottage-garden style. Around the bones of the old stone house and malthouse, the boundary walls, small lawns and paths, that were generally fairly narrow she built up a pattern of planting in the various beds and borders of often ingenuous complexity and busyness. And she did not limit the plants she either raised or popularized but spread them far and wide, a dissemination faithfully maintained by the garden and nursery staff, as the continuing enormous plant sales from the garden show.

The intensity of planting within a small area has brought obvious changes to East Lambrook since Mrs Fish's death, aimed at controlling over-crowding, but many ideas remain – the series of densely-planted beds on either side of the path to one side of the house flanked by clipped domes of *Chamaecyparis lawsoniana* 'Fletcheri'; and the enclosed area of small silver-leafed plants and herbs – thyme, artemsis, dianthus and wormwood 'Lambrook Silver' – although this little corner was badly hit by the winter frosts of 1981–2. Elsewhere hellebores are still perhaps the main feature in the spring, with numerous varieties throughout the garden accompanied by polyanthus, primroses and daffodils, and followed by euphorbias, irises and geraniums. The back garden wall is still closely planted with climbers and wall shrubs, many roses and clematis, *Rubus* 'Tridel', ceanothuses and a *Cytisus ratisbonensia*. Now there are more recently planted ornamental trees in the garden – birches, *Magnolia stellata* and *Acer capillipes* – to add to the older fruit trees, some of which, particularly the apples, have died and been given over to rapacious climbing roses.

All in all, even if disciples of Mrs Fish might notice slightly less success with the various weed-controlling perennials which she used to such great effect (and by so doing gave great help to the now ever-present problem of how to reduce labour in a garden), it would be churlish to complain about changes which are bound to occur in any garden. Through the efforts of the Boyd-Carpenters and their staff this garden is continuing to evolve, something the founding spirit of Mrs Fish would no doubt appreciate.

ESSEX HOUSE

In Badminton, 5 miles east of Chipping Sodbury and north-east of the M4 (Junction 18)

Tel. 045 421 288

Mr and Mrs James Lees-Milne

Open on one Sunday and Monday in late June or early July, and by written appointment

---

Essex House was built in 1680 for Mary, 1st Duchess of Beaufort, one of the leading lady gardeners of the seventeenth century whose almost total ignorance of Latin did not prevent her from collecting and propagating many rare plants, and corresponding at length with the leading botanists of her day. Essex House still belongs to the Badminton estate, and stands beside one of the gates into the great park of Badminton House, but three hundred years later it is now the home of another eminent lady gardener and garden-writer, Mrs James Lees-Milne. Since she and her husband came here in 1975 the small garden has been transformed from a scene of neglected dereliction to one of satisfying order, full of ingenuity and eclectic charm.

Mrs Lees-Milne's achievement has been not only to draw on her considerable experience from her two previous gardens, one in the South of France and the other at Alderley Grange, close to Badminton, but also to create in the relatively small space of about half an acre a garden totally in harmony with its own charming house, neither manor nor cottage, with its seventeenth-century origins. The bold coat-of-arms of the 1st Duchess on one wall of the house – Somerset, her married name, impaling Capel, her maiden name – is an effective reminder of her enthusiasm and discerning interest in botany, two characteristics that are evident again in Mrs Lees-Milne's garden.

It may not be wishful thinking that the three old Cedars of Lebanon, which stand at the far, south-west end from the house and dominate the garden, are a direct link with the 1st Duchess. Because of their shade and the dryness of sail they cause, the garden has been partly planned round them. The area directly beneath is roughly-mown grass, now planted with daffodils and cyclamen, and an eighteenth-century stone Apollo, the copy of a Greek statue, stands at the end of a flagged path leading across the grass.

. Looking from the small terrace in the 'L' of the house on this south-west facing side, restraint is obviously the keynote sounded in the garden. On the walls of the house it's a different matter: roses such as 'Madame Abel Chatenay', several late-flowering clematis like C. viticella 'Royal Velours' and a Golden Hop remind one that order does not always have the last word. The same vigour is shown by the climbers trained against the east boundary wall of the garden: more clematis – summer and autumn flowering varieties – and honeysuckle mixing with abutilons and ceanothus. In the raised border in front of the wall the roses, which are such a feature throughout the garden, are chosen here for their upright habit, so that the many smaller plants – santolinas, artemisias and senecios – which spread below, selected for their foliage, are not obscured. The border is cleverly divided by a square of flagstones and a white bench.

The 1st Duchess of Beaufort would have been quite at home in the small parterre which Mrs Lees-Milne has laid out in the centre of the garden's main lawn, where low box hedging with standard clipped hollies on the corners encloses a pattern of flagstones and low grey-foliaged plants. Dividing the parterre is a flagged path which stretches the length of the lawn to a flight of steps leading up to rough grass beneath the cedars. Pyramids of clipped variegated box line this path; throughout the garden columnar, fastigiate and standard plants, whose vertical growth is invaluable in limited space, are used extensively. Where the gravel path beside the east border continues, dividing the area round the cedars from the little Pond Garden in the south-east corner of the garden, it is lined with elegant columnar junipers, effectively alternating with osmarea.

In the Pond Garden, a surprise discovery since it is out of sight from much of the rest of the garden, columns of clipped box stand on the corners of the central rectangular pond, and fastigiate cherries flank the white seat on the far, east side. The orderly atmosphere in this garden is accentuated by the standard roses, honeysuckles and plants of clipped box in white tubs. This is one of the few damp corners of the garden, where primulus and *Iris silurica* are doing well, but Mrs Lees-Milne's careful blending of colours is as recognizable here as everywhere else: the Pond Garden is limited to pale yellows, whites and greys.

An eye for detail and for simple plant combinations are vital in a small garden and have obviously been ever-present in the creation of the Essex House garden. Each corner of the main lawn is marked by two silver weeping pears; in the west corner white roses and an elaeagnus grow behind the trees, and two *Amelanchier canadensis* with standard 'Little White Pet' roses flourish beneath them. Again, variety is given to the dark green yew hedge along the garden's west boundary by a low hedge of Jackman's Blue Rut in front of it.

Essex House garden contains many instances of symmetry and formality, such as the clipped box and hollies and clipped plants in tubs, which hark back to its seventeenth-century origins, but these are blended with much exuberance, showing that Mrs Lees-Milne is not always adamant about containing a plant which is getting above its allotted station, and cannot always resist planting something she really likes. Considering that this garden was only begun in 1975 and that the site is on a fairly high, exposed limestone ridge, extremely cold in winter, it already has an air of establishment which is completely disproportion-ate to its size and position, and disguises the fact that Mrs Lees-Milne has only occasional help with its maintenance.

THE MANOR HOUSE

In Walton-in-Gordano, 2 miles north-east of Clevedon on the B3124
Tel. 0272 872 067

Mr and Mrs Simon Wills

Open three days a week from April to September inclusive, and by appointment

Mr and Mrs Wills bought the Manor House in 1976 and since then have created a garden of considerable horticultural interest. Looking across the mouth of the River Severn to Wales, Walton-in-Gordano is cut off on the west coast by the valley of Gordano and the M5 motorway, a detached position which lends an air of accustomed tranquillity to the gardens round the Manor House, despite their relative youthfulness. The gardens total about five acres and although certain limitations are imposed by the light sandy soil, the quantity and variety of plants is most impressive.

The Manor House was built around 1705 and added to in about 1780. The gardens are consequently blessed with a number of outstanding mature trees, including beech and chestnut, and the large London plane immediately to the east of the drive may be the tree shown on a drawing by Peter Grimes dated 1781. These old trees are complemented by numerous younger specimens planted by Mr and Mrs Wills, such as the fastigiate English oaks along the drive leading to the south front. In this area, enclosed by trees on east and west but open to the Gordano valley to the south, the two principal characteristics of the gardens can be seen straight away: the rich variety and the balance between standard ornamental or flowering trees and mixed beds.

A small lawn immediately to the west of the drive is simply planted with four standard trees, each unusual and striking: 'Golden Dawyck Beech', *Acer griseum*, *Magnolia mollicomata* and *Cornus controversa* 'Variegata'. On the other side of the drive is a large horse chestnut and younger trees planted by the Wills's for their striking bark or autumn colour: *Prunus serrula* and *Acer sieboldianum*. This is essentially a spring area, so in addition to the yellow erythroniums planted round the prunus, thick dark thujas planted in the nineteenth century have been cut right back to allow space for a border filled with hellebores, fritillaries and primulas planted beneath standard whitebeams.

Mr and Mrs Wills combine their love of gardening with a love of travel, and the warm, south-facing beds on either side of the front door are filled with many plants collected on their peregrinations, especially in the Mediterranean. *Melia azedarach*, the 'Indian Bead Tree', which is trained against the wall of the house and is very tender, was grown from seed collected in Crete; most of the various forms of iris have been collected in Crete, Rhodes and the Peleponnese. The dry, sunny position of these beds suits the many euphorbias and daphnes, too, as well as *Carpentaria californica*.

The garden to the south is in a sense a welcome, as the main area is on the other side, covering the slope stretching uphill to the north and north-west. When the Wills's came to the Manor House this area was just lawns broken by rosebeds, but they have completely replanned it in impressive style. Now the lawn closest to the house, which forms a north- and west-facing 'L', is broken by a series of long beds. Beyond it is the only truly formal area in the gardens, known as the Fragrant Garden, where the ground was levelled into a large rectangle designed by Desmond Evans and laid out in 1982. Beyond this the slope is now lawn planted with a quantity of flowering and ornamental trees, sheltered by the mature trees round the perimeters.

Although still very young the beds closest to the house are already full of interest because of their huge variety of small trees, shrubs, herbaceous plants and spring bulbs, including many unusual plants. The Fragrant Garden provides an immediate contrast, with its pools, flagged paths and lines of lavender, which will soon grow into clipped hedges. The raised beds along its north and west edges which are filled with small plants and Alpines, many collected by the Wills's on their travels. The enclosed atmosphere here will be even more pronounced when the yew hedges are grown up on all sides. The soft pinks, blues and whites which will fill the Fragrant Garden will continue in the Asia Bank at its southern end, where only plants which originate from Asia will be grown.

The raised bed along the upper, west side of the Fragrant Garden is broken by a flight of steps effectively flanked by *Cornus kousa*. The note of formality continues a small way up the slope with 'Purple Dawyck Beech' on either side of the path, but beyond the lawn opens out to each side and is only broken by the informally planted trees – blue cedar and weeping cedar, *Davidia involucrata*, *Metasequoia glyptostroboides* among others; there are a number of malus, prunus and cercis, too, of which the garden holds the National Reference Collection.

The interest of this garden can only grow with its increasing maturity.

Careful grouping and combinations of plants have not only given the beds and borders varying and distinctive characters, but also mean that there is always something of interest in the garden throughout most of the year. The ambitious nature of the planting, considering the garden's size, is accommodated by many techniques of maintenance, such as regular mulching with bark which minimizes labour, and allows Mr and Mrs Wills's energy to be concentrated on building up their plant collections.

MILTON LODGE

½ mile north of Wells off the A39
Tel. 0749 72168
Mr and Mrs D. C. Tudway-Quilter

Open on selected Sundays in spring and summer, and by appointment

When Mr Tudway-Quilter's grandfather Charles Tudway planned the present gardens he designed them to take advantage of the view south from the edge of the Mendip Hills over the city of Wells. He made a series of terraces with marvellous prospects to the towers of Wells Cathedral, and to the Vale of Avalon ending at Glastonbury Tor and the ruined abbey where, according to legend, King Arthur and Queen Guinevere are buried.

The terraces, of different shapes and sizes, are linked by flights of stone steps and divided by stone walls and yew hedges which provide both shelter and sunny corners. Mature woods also provide shelter, especially from the north and east. Much of the garden was in need of restoration when Mr and Mrs Tudway-Quilter came to Milton Lodge in 1962; they re-seeded the lawns and clipped the overgrown hedges as well as making considerable additions to the planting.

At Milton the planting along the front of the house focuses the eye on the garden's ordered details while the views continually lead it away. Trained against the stone house are the yellow rose, 'Lawrence Johnston', clematis, vines, jasmines and ceanothus, above a narrow border filled with senecio, olearia, phlomis, rosemary, fuchsias and hypericums. Four cannons – relics from the Napoleonic Wars – point from the edge of the Upper Terrace. Looking out from beside these the cathedral

278

towers are framed by *Ginkgo biloba* and *Crataegus lavellei*, two of a variety of specimen trees planted on the slope below. A pink rugosa rose hedge accompanies the walk leading away from the front of the house and overlooking the main terraces in place of the huge old box hedge which was part of the original planting, greatly improving the view of the three descending terraces.

On the first of these terraces the wide lawn has a mixed border of shrubs and herbaceous plants against the high upper retaining wall, with low shrub roses along the lower wall. Abutilons are an outstanding feature throughout the garden and many – both blue and white – bask in the sun against the upper wall along with feijoas, *Abelia grandiflora* escallonias and thriving *Romneya coulteri*. Against the stone wall of the old stables at the east end roses 'Purity' and 'Parade' look down upon a wide mixed border of shrubs and herbaceous plants. Next to this is a formal Lily Pool; the steps leading down to the next terrace are covered with one of the most attractive roses at Milton, the rambler 'Thelma' with small pink flowers.

The middle terrace is the narrowest and possibly the best conceived in the garden, the effect of its midsummer exuberance heightened by its very concentration. Beneath the upper wall is a deep border of shrub roses – rugosas, hybrid musks and a few old-fashioned varieties – underplanted with smaller helianthemums, geraniums and fuchsias. Trained on to the wall is another medley of climbers: *Solanum crispum*, clematis, ceanothus, and a large *Garrya elliptica*. The clipped yew hedge along the opposite side of the lawn, above the lower wall, sets off the colour display admirably. At the west end of this terrace is the Pavilion, built in 1906, the stonework of which is highlighted by the bright variegated foliage of *Elaeagnus pungens* 'Maculata', the blue of clematis and ceanothus and the pink 'New Dawn' rose. Grouped around the Pavilion is perhaps the best display of *Clerodendrum trichotomum*, which happily seed themselves throughout the summer. The Pavilion conveniently serves as a changing-room for the swimming pool at the bottom of the garden, with a large yew hedge on the lower side.

Beyond the Pavilion end of the terraces on the site of an old orchard is a recently planted area of specimen trees – whitebeam, cut-leaf beech, acers, and cedars – planted in company with enormous hebes. Along the retaining wall stretching away from the Pavilion is a mixed border predominantly blue, yellow, silver, grey and white: tall agapanthus, astrantias and penstemon stretch above dome-shaped senecio and potentilla, with clematis effectively trained into the yew hedge which surmounts the wall.

Some distance away from the gardens round the house, down the hill towards Wells, is a woodland area called the Coombe, which was originally planted for the earlier family home, the Cedars, built in 1758 and now part of the Cathedral School. The Coombe is a glorious natural valley, its banks full of old oaks, horse-chestnuts, beech, limes and cedars. Among these Mr Tudway-Quilter has added birch, rowan, sorbus, crataegus and a variety of flowering trees, including a davidia and a paulownia, increasing the freer woodland contrast with the architectural terraces and hedges of the main garden. Together they make a perfect foil for Milton's glamorous setting.

WAYFORD MANOR

South-west of Crewkerne between the A30 and the B3165
Tel. 0460 73253
Robin L. Goffe Esq.

Open on selected Sundays in spring, and by appointment

An Italianate garden made at the beginning of the twentieth century is not what one would normally expect to find in the almost archaically rural countryside of the Dorset–Somerset borders. Wayford Manor was reported to have a 'fair garden' in the seventeenth century and one feels that parts of the surrounding landscape haven't changed much since then. But at the beginning of this century the setting of the mainly Elizabethan manor house was transformed by the plantings of its owner, Mr Lawrence Ingham Baker, and by the designs advised by his wife's brother, Harold Peto, leading protagonist of the Italian Renaissance style of gardening. Lawrence Baker died in 1921 and afterwards his son Humphrey extended the Rock Garden with the help of Gavin Jones, and added to the Wild Garden. He also planted a Woodland Garden nearby (which is now separate property). Now the courtyard of the 'E'-shaped house looks on to formal yew enclosures; and along the top of the steep south-east-facing slope – so suitable for Peto's style – is a wide balustraded terrace leading to an arched loggia added to the south-east end of the house. The slope below the garden was also re-planned, becoming progressively more informal as distance from the house increased.

The relatively mild conditions at Wayford are testified to by the presence of *Clerodendrum bungei* on the walls of the house, as well as ceanothus, acacia and *Magnolia grandiflora*. At the west end of the loggia terrace are a pair of enormous horse-chestnuts, growing together almost as one tree. Beneath them Peto laid out a formal Lily Pool, with a boy and dolphin fountain, surrounded by topiary. His most successful use of water in the garden lies just below here, reached through a gate in the wall at the west end of the lower, wide grass terrace; only the sound of water betrays the presence of this secret garden, with a rectangular lily pond and cherub fountain, shaded by two unusually large specimens of *Acer palmatum*. On the grass terrace are formal rosebeds and clipped yew, large magnolias, including *M. soulangiana* with, beneath the balustraded, retaining wall, a mixed border in the Robinsonian tradition, but of recent planting. A *Solanum crispum* behind has successfully assaulted the wall and gone over the balustrade.

The next area lower down the slope retains some formality – another terrace with a path leading west to the Kitchen Garden. Below this terrace is a Rock Garden planted originally with dwarf conifers – few of which have retained their dwarf proportions – and small shade-loving cyclamen and *lithospermum*. The Rock Garden in turn descends to a small Japanese Garden, complete with stone Buddha, a stone lantern, small Japanese acers, bamboo and a series of small streams.

From this point the garden opens into informality in an area which also contains the greatest variety of Mr Baker's plantings. At the very bottom the Water Garden and its aquatic plants have returned to a wonderful semi-wild state amid a grove of *Acer palmatum* 'Shishigashira'. In the long grass of what was a cider apple orchard are daffodils and crocus, as well as naturalized Martagon and Leopard lilies and fritillaries. Among the trees are more magnolias, huge Japanese acers everywhere including more 'Shishigashira', *Embothrium coccineum* and a liquidambar. On the west side, in a more densely wooded area, acers vie with old cherries and rhododendrons: specie *R. sutchuenense* and *R. campanulatum* and, among the hybrids, 'Loder's White' and 'Penjerrick'.

The garden at Wayford Manor was made at a time of great affluence and readily available labour. The Goffes, who have lived here since 1966, have concentrated on retaining the style of the upper terraces while allowing an increasingly 'natural' look on the lower slope, to which they are ideally suited. Full of surprises and with its romantic combination of Italianate architecture and rich plantings, Wayford is a fascinating garden, not only as an unusually good and little-known example of Harold Peto's work, but of an early twentieth-century landscape in close concord with an Elizabethan manor house.

WILTSHIRE

BROADLEAS

South of Devizes off the A360
Tel. 0380 2035
Lady Anne Cowdray

Open on Wednesday, Thursday and Sunday from April to October inclusive

---

The Broadleas of 1946, when Lady Anne Cowdray bought the house, was a place which had suffered badly from neglect during the war years. As well as restoring the main garden, and filling it with new plants, Lady Anne's main interest has been the creation of the Dell in the steeply sloping valley on one side of the lawn to the south of the house. Its shape possibly derives from ancient British encampments made on either side of a river valley; now the river flows underground.

In many ways the site is ideally suited to the planting of flowering trees and shrubs. Lady Anne has used it to good advantage: on the naturally sheltering slopes are trees and shrubs which like a light, well-drained position, and their canopies protect those plants lower down which prefer a less sunny and damper site. Some wonderful mature oaks and Scots pines on the slopes give additional protection; hills and the fact that the cold air drains out of the bottom of the Dell has encouraged Lady Anne to grow a wide variety of interesting and often tender plants which are suited to the greensand soil.

This is immediately evident as one approaches the Dell from the house. Near the top are some of the many fine magnolias in the garden: *Magnolia sargentiana* and *M. sargentiana* 'Robusta', the smaller and more unusual *M. cylindrica* and, lower down, *M. sprengeri* 'Diva'. Round their trunks, and those of a nearby weeping pear are most effective groups of pink and yellow erythroniums. As one descends more interesting plants present themselves, particularly the rhododendrons. Lady Anne has built up an extensive collection of these, although some of the tender varieties such as the large-leafed *Rhododendron macabeanum* and *Rh. falconeri*, the varied group of pittosporums and many eucalpytuses were badly hit in the disastrous 1981–2 winter.

Bulbs add so much character to a woodland garden, and the Dell is no exception – daffodils, anenomes and primroses cover the ground between rhododendrons, camellias and other densely leafed shrubs, carrying the eye up above them to the graceful forms of flowering and ornamental trees: *Stewartia serrata*, *Cercidiphyllum japonicum*, *Styrax obassia*, *Davidia involucrata*, a very large *Magnolia mollicomata* and a very small *Nyssa sylvatica*, planted in 1979.

At its southern end the Dell slopes down into open meadowland. Lady Anne solved the problem of getting from the bottom of the valley to the path which runs along the top of the valley's eastern slope by designing a path which zig-zags up the hill with weeping trees on each bend: lime, ash, prunus, birch and purple beech. From the top path many of the flowering trees are seen in spring to their best advantage as one looks down into their canopies. Stretching along the path's opposite, eastern side is a bank thick with daffodils.

Though the Dell is perhaps the area of greatest interest at Broadleas, other smaller parts of the garden close to the house have great attraction. The walled Rose Garden below the east side is entered through an archway on the South Terrace: shrub roses divided by paths in which Alpine strawberries and aubretia have pushed their way between the paving stones, trained against the house is an especially beautiful climber – *Rosa chinensis* 'Mutabilis' – as well as *Syringa pinnatifolia*, providing a constant guessing game for visitors while its pinnate leaves conceal its true identity. To the east of the Rose Garden, beyond a border of herbaceous and rock plants, backed by shrub roses and a large acer, is another small enclosed corner, the Secret Garden. A lot of its charm is owed to the hedge of Prunus x blireana, which has pink flowers in the spring and copper-coloured leaves. Among the plants inside are a number of small shrubs and acers, many with clematis trained into them, and large groups of euphorbias.

These pretty hideaways and borders make telling contrast with the spacious South Terrace stretching between Irish yews at either end, the open lawns on three sides of the house, and with the Dell. It is sad that the 1981–2 winter caused such setbacks just as the garden was reaching maturity, but with help from such a determined gardener, recovery is undoubtedly under way.

HEALE HOUSE

Near Woodford, 4 miles north of Salisbury off the A345
Tel. 072 273 207

Major David and Lady Anne Rasch

Open Monday to Saturday, and on the first Sunday in each month from Easter to September inclusive

Heale House is a tribute to two periods, the seventeenth century when the original house was built, and the Edwardian era when the building was enlarged and the garden laid out. Tucked unobtrusively in the Avon valley, there is an immediate charm to Heale – the well-proportioned house of softly shaded brick and stone, the gardens with the river flowing silently by, the water meadows beyond – all with a slight air of understatement and of being at one with the surrounding countryside.

The Hon. Louis Greville, great-uncle of Major Rasch, bought Heale House in 1890 and he commissioned the architect Detmar Blow to add a wing, thus giving the house an 'L' shape. In building up the gardens round the house Greville was advised by Harold Peto in 1906; the result was a simple but definite form which has been easy to retain – a series of different levels and terraces divided by low balustraded walls. To the west of the house Greville made the main garden vista, with a wide paved path leading away from the paved terrace up a slope to a wrought-iron gate set in the old yew hedges of the garden boundary. From here is a most rewarding view of the house's main seventeenth-century façade. Another large paved area lies in the angle of the house to the east; double flights of balustraded stone steps lead down to the water at one point and the river front is balustraded too. A stone and flint retaining wall link this area with the main South Lawn, which is on a slightly higher level. Where the ground drops away at the far end of the lawn another balustraded wall was built, with a bordered path below. The extent of the garden to the south was dictated by the Avon which curves to form a second boundary side.

An old stable block stands on the south west of the house, and Greville extended his garden through a pair of wrought-iron gates beyond it. Here, having diverted a channel from the obliging Avon, he gave Heale its most intriguing corner, the Japanese Garden; a love of things Japanese had been fostered during his time there as a diplomat.

In typically Edwardian style Greville employed no half measures and brought in gardeners from Japan. The main features are the red Nikko bridge; the tea-house, the largest and certainly one of the most authentic in Britain, beneath which two channels of water flow at right-angles on two levels; and a large stone ornament from a Temple garden in Japan. With its trees and water-loving plants, this garden is a delightful little bit of eccentricity such as one expects to find in most old country houses, and stands in perfect contrast to the nearby traditional Kitchen Garden, surrounded on three sides by tile-topped brick walls.

The fact that the gardens at Heale were almost all designed as part of a larger picture including the house and Avon valley setting, has meant that they have survived broadly unchanged from the affluent Edwardian days of their creation and can be maintained by Major and Lady Anne Rasch and one gardener. Nevertheless, although the garden has been reduced – the area closest to the river on the south front has become a meadow of daffodils and cherries in which only the stone Italian wellhead bears witness that it was originally part of Greville's garden – it still covers eight acres. Some of the planting, in the borders and the Japanese Garden, has been simplified but as well as shrub and climbing roses there is an interesting variety of plants, again grown not so much for their individual merits but as to fit in with and enhance the general appearance and atmosphere of the garden within the landscape.

Good examples of this appear in the South Lawn border and in those to the west of the house. In the former, hybrid musk roses, some trained on wooden frames, mix with weigela, a weeping silver pear and standard wisteria, and with herbaceous plants on the other side of the path; in the latter, alongside the steps leading up from the terrace 'Spek's Yellow' and 'Rambling Rector' roses are trained with clematis and honeysuckle on wooden pyramids. The wide paved path runs between lawns and laburnum trees – originally planted by Greville but now mainly more recent replacements – up to the four boundary borders where shrub roses 'Nevada' and 'Fantin-Latour' are planted with flowering cherries, wisteria, a weeping silver pear and *Viburnum plicatum* 'Mareisii'. The whole picture – yew hedges and gates, stone seats, borders and a large copper vat at the cross-paths – is especially well put together.

The Japanese Garden has retained its character too; *Magnolia soulangiana* hangs over the water between the bridge and the tea-house, with an unusually large *Cercidiphyllum japonicum* nearby. In the Kitchen Garden the four plots of fruit and vegetables are divided by box-edged paths meeting at the central circular Lily Pond surrounded with domes of more clipped box. Three paths are covered by pergolas of éspalier apples and pears and the fourth by a wonderful mixture of laburnum, wisteria and climbing roses. The 'random' planting in the border beneath the east wall here, which Lady Anne disarmingly calls 'a home for everything', is totally appropriate, confirming the impression of Heale as part of the tradition of country houses and gardens whose beauty is quite unpretentious and, as a result, seems to be achieved with unconscious ease.

HILLBARN HOUSE

In Great Bedwyn, south-west of Hungerford off the A4
Tel. 0672 870 207
Mr and Mrs A. J. Buchanan

Open two Sundays in summer

One of the joys of visiting the garden of a house in the middle of a village is that so often the façade, however large or small, looks out blandly, disclosing little or nothing about what lies behind. This is certainly true of Hillbarn House: only the tops of the pleached limes just above the south roadside wall give an inkling of the garden beyond the little entrance gate. Once inside the formal symmetry of this, the smallest part of the grounds, displays the garden's characteristic – a stately, measured layout of regular shapes and architectural form.

Such is the continuity of style that no visitor would guess Hillbarn has had three owners in the short space of time since the 1950s when the Earl of Wilton bought the dilapidated house and cottage, restored them and started the gardens.

Lord Wilton enclosed the lawn on the south front with pleached limes at the end and along the village street wall. The tone of restrained formality he set here has been maintained. Now beneath the limes are narrow borders of spring bulbs, foxgloves, Japanese anemones, hostas and lilies of the valley; on the paved terrace in front of the house here are clipped bay trees and tubs of agapanthus. On the side of the lawn facing west to the village street is a raised shrub border beside steps leading round the corner of the house to the large East Lawn, stretching to two old yew trees which are about the only survivors from the days before Lord Wilton's ownership. On the northern side of the East Lawn he laid out the original Parterre Garden, on either side of a white weatherboarded summerhouse, which has been subsequently altered and is now a major feature of this part of the garden.

During Lord Wilton's time this lawn and the garden to the south of the house were the only two parts of the garden, forming an 'L'-shape on two levels. In 1962 Hillbarn was bought by Lord and Lady Bruntisfield, who at the same time bought the land between the two sides of the existing garden. The different levels of the new area called for more walls and flights of steps, further accentuating the garden's architectural formality. The Bruntisfields decided to repeat the pleached trees and clipped hedges here. Much of their layout and planting, particularly of the new area, was done for them by Lanning Roper and included some delightful borders.

A swimming pool was put into the low protected area at the west end of the new garden. Above the high wall to one side of it Hornbeam hedges were planted along the gravel path which led from the East Lawn steps to a hornbeam arbour. From here another gravel path was made to the east end of the new garden, with éspalier pear trees trained over metal arches at regular intervals and a border outside the path with a hornbeam hedge behind. At this east end they built a tennis court, with a border and path along one side, but the most effective feature here is the split hornbeam hedge: a low hedge on one side of the path and on the other, against the tennis court, a higher hedge with trunks clipped up to the height of the lower hedge. The largest border was made beneath the East Lawn's retaining wall, and a nut walk along this border's path effectively screens the end of the court. In the central rectangle of the new garden they made a box-edged potager.

Mr and Mrs Buchanan, who bought Hillbarn in 1971, have made some changes to the garden but the basic structure they inherited has remained. In front of the Parterre Garden are now two box-enclosed mixed borders and large domes of clipped box now flank the gravel path to the summerhouse. Within the garden they have filled part of the box-edged pattern with a Rose Garden on one side of the path and a Peony Garden on the other, but they have retained the central beds of irises and tulips followed by annuals. Characteristic pleached limes and a yew hedge screen the boarding fence at the back of the parterre.

The East Lawn steps now lead to one of the garden's most impressive features. The Bruntisfields' hornbeam hedges have been trained together by Mr Last, the Buchanans' gardener, to form a tunnel to the hornbeam arbour where small 'windows' are now cut in either side; there are similar 'windows' at intervals along the tunnel looking down on to the swimming pool. The border along the path of éspaliered pear arches is now devoted to shrub roses, with other plants such as phlox, hardy geraniums and sedums in carefully arranged groups. The border in front of the tennis court shows how effective large groups of selected varieties – shrub roses, day lilies, peonies and agapanthus – can be, with smaller grey-leafed plants beneath. The long border beneath the East Lawn's retaining wall is the most informally planted, with floribunda and shrub roses, and plants of subdued pinks, mauves and blues blending together. On the wall behind are climbing roses and fruit trees.

The old central potager has been made into a chess-board Herb Garden by the Buchanans, the low, carpet-like pattern of herbs enclosed by little hedges effectively offset by standard roses. To either side quinces are trained over metal arches.

As well as adding features of their own the Buchanans and Mr Last have maintained the previous high standards that such a garden demands, a daunting task but a rewarding one, most especially in summer when the clipped hedges and borders are in their full glory.

.LAKE HOUSE

In Lake, 7 miles north of Salisbury off the A345
Tel. 098 022 138

Captain O. N. Bailey

Open on selected days in April and July, and by appointment for parties

---

The main part of Lake House was built by George Duke in 1578 during the height of the Wiltshire wool and cloth trade, its appearance greatly enhanced by the chequered pattern of flint and a mixture of chalk known as 'clunch' in which the house was built (similar to nearby Longford Castle being built at the same time). But in 1912 Lake suffered a disastrous fire which gutted the house, and it is since the subsequent restoration and additions made by Captain Bailey's parents, Colonel and Lady Janet Bailey, that the extensive gardens to the east and south of the house date. Mr Darcy Braddell, the architect who worked for the Baileys, gave considerable advice on the gardens too.

The five-gabled north entrance front with central porch and two-storey battlemented bays on either side is the outstanding feature that remains of the original house. The yew hedges, estimated to be over two hundred years old, which had originally enclosed a bowling green

An imposing, Victorian statue of two angels at Duxford Mill, Cambridgeshire.

A hidden gateway shrouded in climbers at Carrog, Dyfed.

The Dutch Garden at Ilmington Manor, Warwickshire. Enclosed by yew hedges, an informal mixture of small summer flowers surround the central statue of two children.

Athelhampton Manor, Dorset; the Corona, the focus of the gardens, whose balance of architecture, water and planting is continued in the other areas reached through narrow gateways.

Vann, Surrey; looking to the house from the area of informal planting round the pond, whose appearance was influenced by Gertrude Jekyll's advice.

The pool at Walpole house, Chiswick, adorned with irises, water lilies and other acquatic plants. The garden's size and appearance disguise the fact that it is in central London.

A stone statue of 'Summer', one of a set which Lord and Lady Haddington brought from Vicenza in Italy to their garden at Tyninghame, East Lothian, is the centrepiece of Lady Haddington's Secret Garden, a luxuriant mixture of old-fashioned roses, clematis and shrubs.

Looking across from the Walled Garden to the Norman towers of Raby Castle, Durham with, on the left, one of the two-hundred-year-old yew hedges.

Looking down from the roof of Broughton Castle, Oxfordshire to the 'fleur-de-lys' pattern of box-enclosed rose beds in the Lady's Garden.

Looking from the terrace across the largest parterre at Dunrobin Castle, Sutherland. Between the wars the beds were filled with 16,000 dahlias; now they are planted with roses. In the background is the North Sea.

A section of the amazing parterre at Drummond Castle, Perthshire, its effect heightened by being seen from the terraces and castle above.

The view from the central path between herbaceous borders dividing the Kitchen Garden at Llysdinam, Powys, through the delicate wrought-iron gates to the valley of the River Wye and the Welsh hills.

The trunk of one of a number of stately beeches at Plas Newydd, Gwynedd, which date from Humphry Repton's early nineteenth-century landscaping. Along the front of the belt of shrubs are *Viburnum tomentosum* 'Lanarth', now one of the garden's outstanding features; the Menai Straits can be glimpsed in the distance.

In the Walled Garden at Goodnestone Park, Kent mixed borders, containing in particular peonies, old-fashioned roses and pillars of clematis, flank the central path leading down to the wall beneath the tower of the parish church.

immediately to the east of the house were largely retained but cut away on the green's east side to open up the view and allow access to other parts of the garden.

There was plenty of scope for the Baileys' ambitious plans and with three or four gardeners, Lake House gardens enjoyed a hey-day during their ownership. As well as putting in many immaculately maintained borders, they added a number of most interesting features. Round the old tennis court at the far end of the wide East Lawn they made a pleached lime allée on the near and north sides, with a clipped yew hedge at the east end; Colonel Bailey built the curved wall of the old Walled Garden with a summer border outside it. Further along this wall the Baileys indulged another of their interests – exotic birds – with an aviary of wonderfully elegant proportions. A semicircle of columns curve away from the Walled Garden, and from a distance, when the netting between the columns and glass roof was invisible it appeared more like a graceful loggia. Inside the birds enjoyed a luxurious existence, with plenty of space to fly about, bushes and trees to roost in, and heating in winter.

To the south of the house, the ground slopes gently down to the Avon, and here the Baileys made some of their most successful additions to the garden. By diverting a series of small channels they had the basis of a Water Garden of islands which they filled with flowering cherries, birches, weeping willows and many spring bulbs, particularly daffodils. Across the streams, to give access to the islets, they made two stone balustraded bridges and a charming arched brick bridge, but it was the hand of the architect, Darcy Braddell, which so effectively linked the Water Garden to the house by a path leading from one of the balustraded bridges to a flight of stone steps between flowering cherries and spring borders, and so up to the terrace beneath the bay window of the new dining-room.

The Baileys left Lake House surrounded by gardens that were a more than fitting setting and which, other than a number of unavoidable labour-saving alterations, their son Captain Bailey maintains today.

The old bowling green on the east side of the house is kept simple – stone benches and stone urns on either side of the lawn in the centre of which a stone baluster is surrounded by a circular flowerbed. Steps also flanked by a fine pair of lead urns lead east from here to a small Circular Garden enclosed by yew hedges and flowerbeds devoted mainly to summer plants; beyond is the large East Lawn, bordered on its top side by a long shrub border. The pleached lime allée at the end of the lawn has been retained, as has the yew hedge on the far side of the old tennis court which has now been put down to lawn. The labour-intensive borders in front of the pleached limes and yew hedge have been removed but not the summer border of shrub roses, delphiniums, peonies, potentilla and smaller grey-leafed plants along the outside of the Walled Garden. With climbing roses and a coronilla on the wall behind it leads to the pillared summerhouse at the end of the wall looking on to the new hard tennis court. From this far eastern end of the garden a path leads to the Woodland Garden made by Captain Bailey's parents – carpets of aconites and snowdrops followed by rhododendrons and azaleas. Peacocks survive from the numerous exotic birds which used to fill this woodland; alas, the wallabies which also lived here and in the park have gone.

Inside the old Walled Garden the Baileys' original plan has also been slightly adapted. The entrance, now through a fine pair of wrought-iron gates, led to a pattern of one rectangular and two square pools in line with four flowerbeds, all surrounded by yew hedges; plum and pear trees were trained on the top wall. One of the pools has been filled in and the centre one made into a swimming pool; the flowerbeds have been grassed over, leaving only the four standard cherries which used to stand in their centres.

Along the outside of the Walled Garden facing west towards the Water Garden is the yew hedge that is one of the garden's most interesting features. Originally this was one of two lines of yew trees but now the tops of the trees have been trained together and their trunks kept clipped so that they form a line of yew columns joined by arches with a solid hedge up to fifteen feet above. The yews are probably the same age as those round the old bowling green.

Most of the garden on the south side of the house has been kept as it was, with the beautiful view from the house across the lawn to a huge copper beech and the river and Water Garden beyond, and one of the most attractive views at Lake House is west from the Water Garden along the path to wrought-iron gates leading to a thatched cottage. Between the Water Garden and the main house is a small Circular Garden made in front of a curving wall that screens some outbuildings: a yew hedge completes the circle from the end of the wall and together they enclose a fan-shaped pattern of rosebeds, focusing on a small rotunda.

Lake House is of particular interest as an example of an early twentieth-century garden made in an ambitious and varied style to incorporate existing advantages, such as the proximity to the river and the old Walled Garden, and of particular merit as an example of later twentieth-century adaptability to the problems of running a garden of this size without diminishing its appearance and character.

SHELDON MANOR

Near Allington, 1½ miles west of Chippenham off the A420
Tel. 0249 653 120

Major and Mrs M. A. Gibbs

Open on Thursday, Sunday, and Bank Holidays from Palm Sunday to the first
Sunday in October inclusive

Neglect, restoration and renewal have formed a continual cycle in the
long history of this medieval manor house. Over the centuries there have
been a number of different gardens surrounding it and the three yew
trees which dominate the grass entrance court are estimated to be about
seven hundred years old; they date from one of the earliest gardens,
perhaps originally having been part of a hedge.

Since he has been at Sheldon Major Gibbs has planted many trees
and shrubs. Much of the garden was a wilderness after the Second
World War, particularly the area below the terrace in front of the house,
which was given over to growing potatoes and keeping pigs. Steadily he
has built up a varied and interesting collection of plants, particularly of
shrub roses, but without making the garden fussy and destroying the
strongly medieval atmosphere which surrounds the manor.

The earliest parts of the house date from the thirteenth century,
including the main porch looking out over the entrance court and past
an impressive pair of eighteenth-century stone gate-piers and the
cobbled terrace to the yew walk beyond the drive. The grey stone of the
walls – along the terrace on either side of the main gate-piers, of the
house and of other buildings – lend itself to climbers and wall plants;
trained on the terrace wall are some very old climbing roses, including a
plant of 'Alberic Barbier' planted in 1911, while on the wall of the
building opposite are 'Madame Alfred Carrièn' and the Hidcote yellow
form of 'Lawrence Johnston'. Along with the roses are ceanothuses, a
Carpentaria californica, and a spectacularly vigorous *Akebia quinata* which
has stretched itself into the branches of one of the three ancient yews.
The walls are also home for many of the most interesting plants in the
garden, although sadly some of them were lost during the winter of
1981–2: two tender Australian plants, *Grevillea rosmarinifolia* and *G.
sulphurea* bearing racemes of scarlet and yellow flowers respectively, and

the equally tender Australian bottle-brush plant died, and have now been replaced.

The lower level of the main garden is divided by the yew walk that leads from the gate-piers. At the far end of the walk the garden is protected from wind by a tall hedge of Lawson's cypresses; many shrub roses have been planted here among ornamental trees such as an *Acer* 'Brilliantissimum', a catalpa and a rare white Judas tree. Extending beyond the yew walk is another lawn similarly enclosed by yew on one side, by a stone wall on the house side and by hornbeam hedges on the other two. This lawn is dominated by the enormous trunk of a fallen elm and is filled with daffodils in spring. There are more roses and among them three striking snake-bark maples; magnolias, including *Magnolia stellata* and *M. soulangiana* 'Lennei' have been planted beyond these. A gap in the bottom hornbeam hedge leads to the Water Garden, a direct contrast to the general informality of Sheldon, with the strong architectural lines of the stone pool surrounded by pleached hornbeams.

Although the garden was very run down when Major Gibbs came to Sheldon, there were still some old herbaceous borders. These have now disappeared and the garden's colour is found among the trees and shrubs. In the orchard the old apple trees are now hung with climbing roses and other trees have been planted amongst them: eucalyptus, which all died down to the ground in the 1981–2 frost, but have now shot up again, a taxodium, a metasequoia and two American cockspur thorns, both of which have grown into dense domes. Below the pond the same style continues down to the boundary hornbeam hedge – flowering cherries and *Prunus serrata* with its distinctive red bark, another Judas tree (grown from seed collected at the Petit Trianon at Versailles), a ginkgo and *Viburnum tomentosa*. The field beyond the hedge is inhabited by one of Sheldon's non-horticultural features, a pair of llamas from South America.

By his imaginative plantings of shrubs and of trees in particular, Major Gibbs has somehow caught Sheldon's medieval atmosphere and set a style in which house and garden respond to one another as the best achieved themes always do.

THE THAMES VALLEY
AND THE SOUTH

Berkshire
Buckinghamshire
Hampshire
The Isle of Wight
Oxfordshire

THE THAMES VALLEY AND THE SOUTH

1 Englefield House
2 Hazelby House
3 The Old Rectory, Burghfield
4 The Old Rectory, Farnborough
5 West Woodhay House
6 Chenies Manor House
7 The Manor House, Bledlow
8 Turn End
9 Bramdean House
10 Exbury
11 Fairfield House
12 Jenkyn Place
13 Mottisfont Abbey
14 Cedar Lodge
15 23 Beechcroft Road, Oxford
16 Brook Cottage
17 Broughton Castle
18 Kingston Lisle Park
19 Marndhill
20 The Mill House
21 Pusey House
22 Rousham House

16
17
421
361
423
5
413
34
43
22
41
40
OXFORD
420
34
15
40
4129
418
8
413
404
Thame
7
6
Faringdon
417
21
Abingdon
M40
18
20
Wantage
19
423
4
4
Hungerford
Newbury
1
Reading
M4
417
34
4
3
340
5
2
30
343
303
30
30
12
Bentley
303
34
31
31
3057
272
9
13
Winchester
Romsey
31
Hambledon
11
32
3
SOUTHAMPTON
27
31
Beaulieu
10
Ryde
14
ISLE OF
WIGHT

—— A roads

BERKSHIRE

ENGLEFIELD HOUSE

6 miles west of Reading off the M4 (Junction 12). Entrance is off the A340 between Pangbourne and the A4

Tel. 0734 302 221

Mr and Mrs W. R. Benyon

Open every Monday and one Sunday in May

Looking out south across the open panorama of parkland to the valley of the River Kennet, one can see why this site was of strategic importance long before the present house was built at the end of the sixteenth century. At that time it was owned by the Englefield family, but after Sir Francis Englefield was arraigned for treason for pursuing the Catholic cause and giving his allegiance to Queen Mary, it was acquired for Queen Elizabeth I by Act of Parliament. The Queen gave it to Lord Walsingham, whose daughter lived there briefly; the Norris family were the next occupants. After the Civil War the Marquess of Winchester made it his home; his descendant, the widowed Mary Powlett-Wright, married in 1744 Richard Benyon, lately retired from the East India Company. The last major rebuilding was undertaken in 1860 by a later Richard Benyon. It is interesting to compare the house as it is today with the painting made by John Constable in 1832.

Like the house the gardens have seen gradual change over the centuries. The spacious terraces to the south date from the seventeenth century. There is little evidence of what they looked like then but we know that during the nineteenth century their enclosing and retaining walls were given the impressive stone balustrading and urns, as well as the raised prospect corners at the east and west ends of the long south terrace. The park, which provides a wonderful setting for the house and gardens on all sides, was laid out in the eighteenth century. The most significant addition to the gardens came in the 1930s when the area of rising wooded ground to the north of the west terrace was expertly landscaped and planted by Wallace of Tunbridge Wells as a Woodland Garden extending to seven acres, and it is this combination of old-established formal terraces and informal woodland which give Englefield its special character.

Approaching the house along the drive from the south-east one sees the outstanding mature trees which are such a hallmark of Englefield. Particularly impressive are the copper beech and horse chestnut close to the east front, but most interesting is the huge ginkgo to the east of the drive, close to the wrought-iron gates leading into the old brick-walled kitchen gardens; it is reputed to rival for size the famous specimen at Kew. One of the kitchen gardens is now run commercially, another is an all-weather school for horses, and the third, retained for its original use, is approached by an iron gate from the drive through an avenue of standard wisterias, whose gnarled and twisted trunks give an impression of great age.

The terrace below the south front is broken by a grass bank. The simplicity of grass and stone balustrading is only enlivened in spring when the bank is a mass of daffodils: the view from here over the park would make any other garden adornment superfluous. From the south terrace a wide gravel path extends right away to the far end of the wider, west terrace. At this far end a bank rises from the terrace, dominated by a very large red acer, and in the south-west corner of the smaller raised terrace beyond the bank is a tiny Blue and Grey Garden.

The main area of the west terrace used to be filled with a large formal Rose Garden, laid out in the nineteenth century. Mr and Mrs Benyon, during their twenty years at Englefield, have removed this and left the area as a wide lawn planted with standard flowering and ornamental trees. The huge herbaceous border which used to stretch the length of the north retaining wall is now a mixed border, mainly filled with shrubs, shrub roses and small trees, such as a fastigiate cherry and strikingly large elaeagnus.

Wide flights of stone steps in the north retaining wall lead up to the Woodland Garden. On the main flight of steps is a charming inscription, taken from a letter signed by Sir Edward Norris and dated 1601: 'If you help towards Englefield garden, either in flowers or invention, you shall be welcome thither.'

The Woodland Garden slopes from west and east into the valley of a small stream flowing from north to south into a small pool. Its undulating terrain provides the ideal framework for mixed plantings of trees and shrubs, many of which were established in the 1930s. The slopes and areas of long grass are thickly planted with bulbs – daffodils and bluebells in particular – and the whole area is at its colourful best in spring and early summer, with rhododendrons, azaleas, camellias, cherries and magnolias in flower. More unusual trees include the davidia which has attained handsome size, and a variety of eucryphia.

The original plans for the Woodland Garden, which survive from the 1930s, show clearly how the natural advantages of the site have been fully used. Many mature trees were obviously cleared but a number of outstanding specimens have been retained: towards the north-west corner is a large open lawn shaded by a huge oak and an equally impressive *Cryptomeria japonica*. In the north-east corner are two handsome *Cedrus atlantica* 'Glauca'.

Because many open vistas have been retained there are a number of rewarding views to be enjoyed out over the terraces to the park. Two full-time gardeners and a student help the Benyons maintain more than ten acres; the orderliness of the terraces and the wealth of plants in the Woodland Garden testify to their care.

HAZELBY HOUSE

At North End, 6 miles south-west of Newbury off the A343, towards Ball Hill
Tel. 0635 253 265

Mr and Mrs M. J. Lane Fox

Open on one Sunday in July and by written appointment

When Mr and Mrs Lane Fox bought Hazelby House in 1974 it was surrounded by a wilderness; the only definable elements were parts of an old walled kitchen garden to the the north-west of the house and, to the south, a park extending from east to west which had some fine trees and an overgrown lake.

Mr Lane Fox has devised the layout and planting of the whole four acres and his achievement is quite remarkable. Despite its youth the garden has already achieved a marked degree of establishment and Mr Lane Fox is already reaping the benefits of building it up round a strongly delineated framework, which he can soften at will by his plantings. Retaining walls support the different levels created from an uneven terrain. The areas of varying character are regular in shape, and firmly – but also enticingly – enclosed and separated by hedges and walls. Paths lead from one enclosure to the next by flights of stone and brick steps and through narrow openings or wrought-iron gateways in the hedges.

The main area of the new enclosures is to the west of the house. The division from the old kitchen garden is a strong double axis of a long grass path enclosed by a thuja hedge on the north and holly hedge on the south, with a double border immediately on the other side of the holly hedge. Leading up to a stone statue this double border is already one of the garden's main features. On either side of its central grass path the borders are divided into bays by alternating brick and stone paving; between the south side bays stand stone vases and between the north side ones, lead figures. The planting is mainly shrubs; roses, euphorbias, ceanothus, magnolias, eucryphias, lilies and abutilons are among the most prominent plants.

A white gate leads from the hedge-lined grass path into the old Walled Garden, now transformed. From the gate double herbaceous borders on either side of a gravel path stretch north the length of the garden past a central white, wooden lattice-work arbour clothed in 'New Dawn' rose. The borders are backed by high beech hedges, among the first things planted in the garden. An opening to the east leads into a small formal White Garden, also enclosed by beech hedges, and an opening in the north hedge leads to the swimming pool garden. From here another axis extends west through the rose arbour, at right-angles to the double borders, to borders of roses backed by apple trees which divide the large squares of vegetables here.

From the main double border leading away west of the house an opening brings one to the main Rose Garden, directly beyond the flagged terrace in front of the house. Within the yew hedges there is a formal pattern of borders divided by patterned brick paths; those borders facing the hedges are lined with box and divided by alternating brick and stone bays which support wooden arbours for climbing roses. But all formality is flouted when the exuberant mixture of old-fashioned shrubs and climbers, thickly underplanted with a wide range of herbaceous plants, is in full flower, and the effect is greatly increased by the garden's enclosed, secretive aspect. The large square lawn decorated only by a white bench immediately to the west, also enclosed by yew hedges, nevertheless feels completely open, a feeling reinforced by an area to the south of similar size and formal shape, but informally planted with a mixture of individually planted trees and shrubs round a central metal arbour already partly covered by 'Bobby James' roses.

The garden is continually developing, particularly towards the south-west, and some of the most recent planting is to the south towards the lake. Here Mr Lane Fox has landscaped in the grand style: a vista between wide double borders backed by lines of sorbus leads to the rotunda he has put up on the island on the lake. Halfway down the borders is an equally impressive but contrasting axis, with the bland façade of a classical temple with pillars and pediment looking from the east side across the water of a rectangular formal canal.

Mr Lane Fox is balancing a variety of styles and characters with an overall quality and interest of plants. With the conscious formality of its enclosures and axes and the softening shades of colour, Hazelby is in the tradition of some of the most delightful twentieth-century gardens.

THE OLD RECTORY

In Burghfield, 5½ miles south-west of Reading off the A4
Tel. 073 529 2206

Mr and Mrs Ralph Merton

Open on selected days and by appointment

Since moving to the Old Rectory in 1950 Mrs Merton has developed a garden whose character clearly reflects the unending pleasure it has given. Shrubs and climbing roses are the outstanding feature, at their best in late June and July. They are mainly old-fashioned varieties, their scent, pastel shades and exuberant growth more than making up for their comparatively short flowering period. They surround the swimming pool, stretch along one wall of the garden and on either side of a pillared summerhouse designed by Ralph Merton and the architect Claude Phillimore (whose own garden at Rymans in Sussex is also included in this book). Some of the most effective features of the garden are combinations of roses with small spreading plants beneath, either grown for their silver or grey foliage or their delicate, soft-coloured flowers.

The Old Rectory's lovely Georgian façade, added to the older house in 1720 and built of similar red brick, has been left unadorned by roses or anything else. Behind the house is the old kitchen garden and a number of outbuildings smothered by climbing roses whose origins are often obscure. A lawn to one side of the house, shaded by an old cedar, ends in a long double herbaceous border, which is in flower from daffodil-time through the summer, admirably set off by the yew hedges behind it. The central path leads to the main pond at the bottom of the garden with a stone statue of Antinous in the middle of the water. The pond is surrounded by roses, cherries and water-loving plants and a dense shrubbery on the far bank has helped to replace nearly a hundred and forty elms lost to disease.

Mrs Merton is a compulsive collector of roses and may stop to ask for a cutting from any roadside garden in England or abroad. The result of this serendipity is a variety of glorious plants in luxuriant and apparently untrammelled growth that disguises Mrs Merton's skilfully chosen combinations of colour and type. This is well illustrated by the variety of plants and blend of soft colours in the curving herbaceous border beneath the south-facing boundary walls. As well as the climbing roses there are many clematis and other climbers, such as *Solanum crispum*, *Actinidia kolomikta*, and wall plants such as the outstanding *Carpentaria californica* 'Ladhams Variety', so that nowhere are the brick walls round the garden bare of colour.

Although the soil here is heavy London clay in parts, which causes problems with drying out, its neutrality allows azaleas and many ericaceous plants, some from Japan and China, to do unexpectedly well.

Fast becoming another major feature of the garden are the many sinks filled with small plants, in the Sink Garden and also a sink-enclosed Herb Garden which Mrs Merton is making with all her customary flair and verve. Enthusiasm for plants brings with it acceptance of the numerous hazards they may face, and though the winter of 1981–2 brought setbacks to some parts of her garden, one can see already how these are being used positively by Mrs Merton to bring in new life and colour. It is delightful to go to a garden that so obviously reflects its owner's style and personality.

THE OLD RECTORY

In Farnborough, 4 miles south-east of Wantage, off the B4494
Tel. 048 82298

Mrs Michael Todhunter

Open on two Sundays and by appointment

The Old Rectory was built in 1749, at a time when English domestic architecture was at its most attractive and elegant. Like the Old Rectory at Burghfield, it is of mellow red brick and its proportions are exquisite. The house stands at eight hundred feet, with superb views across the Berkshire Downs, but, unfortunately, exposed to the often blasting winds of winter, when the surrounding beech trees and some limes provide very necessary shelter. John Betjeman lived here between 1945 and 1950, but most of the planting has been done by Mrs Todhunter since she and her husband came here in 1965, building up the four acres with the help of one gardener.

The main façade of the house supports wisteria, climbing roses and clematis and looks onto a wide lawn enclosed by beech trees. Mrs Todhunter inherited the double herbaceous borders leading off to one side of the lawn to which she has added a number of shrub roses. Concealed from the drive by a yew hedge, the borders lead invitingly to a seat. The simplicity of lawn and trees continues on one side of the house; yew hedges here enclose an oval pool – modelled on one at Westonbirt – with a central fountain and statue and the scene is completed by a summerhouse, in a corner of the lawn, especially notable for its interior murals by Molly Bishop.

The note of eighteenth-century restraint is continued by the small courtyard in the main garden – there are lemon trees in tubs and small-flowered *Clematis tangutica* and *C.* 'Bill Mackenzie' on the brick walls – but disappears in the garden of old-fashioned roses straight opposite, where colours and scents mix together and the roses almost conceal the low artemesias and other foliage plants, even the seat at the far end of the central path. The 'Kiftsgate' rose on the lawn beside the Rose Garden is unrestrained to the point of completely obscuring the old apple tree it has invaded.

In the old orchard on the far side of the lawn from the Rose Garden are a tulip tree, philadelphus, magnolias and a ginkgo. Above, to one side of the house, the picturesque stables are draped with climbing roses and *Hydrangea petiolaris*. Below, a clipped beech hedge hides the vegetable garden but through its wrought-iron entrance gate the Downs can be seen stretching away. The vegetables are mixed with still more shrub roses and some striking trees: a variegated acer, cherries and, best of all, *Liriodendron aureomarginatum*, with variegated foliage. The tennis court to one side of the orchard is effectively screened by *Rosa* 'Nevada' and Lawson cypress. The swimming pool, far from being disguised, has become the centrepiece for a part of the garden which, as Mrs Todhunter says, 'is a world of its own'.

A group of standard shrub roses, including voluptuous pink 'Constance Spry', leads to the pool's surrounding wall and arched white doors flanked by large 'Cerise Bouquet' roses. Inside the effect is more oriental than of an English garden. At the far end of the pool daturas and lilies stand in tubs in front of the part-Gothic, part-Indian summer-house; its large arched window looks out onto the Downs. *Cytisus battandieri*, climbing roses – 'Golden Wings', 'Sombreuil', 'Paul's Lemon Pillar' and 'Alister Stellar Gray', all white-gold or yellow, and deliciously scented – blend with blue ceanothus and *Solanum crispum*. Everywhere the effect is one of luxurious, self-delighting beauty; not, perhaps, what an eighteenth-century rector would have countenanced, but for today's visitor it provides a delectable retreat.

WEST WOODHAY HOUSE

6 miles south-west of Newbury, between the A4 and the A343
Tel. 048 84271

J. Henderson Esq.

Open on one or two Sundays in April, May or June

The setting for the gardens at West Woodhay could hardly be bettered: an architecturally outstanding house and parkland surroundings which include a memorable view south to the rising ground of the Downs in the far distance. The house was built in 1635 by Inigo Jones for Benjamin Rudyard, a close friend of Charles I, and its restrained red-brick architecture, especially the east- and south-facing fronts, show many hallmarks of Jones's genius. Late Victorian additions to the south and west fronts doubled the size of the house but these were skilfully removed by Mr Henderson in 1950, returning the building to its original Carolean symmetry.

Mr Henderson's grandfather had bought West Woodhay in 1921 and commissioned Percy Cane to lay out extensive gardens. Parts of Cane's work survive today, but the gardens went into a serious decline during the 1939–45 war years when the house was occupied as offices.

Beyond the east entrance forecourt the ground slopes down to the lake then rises into the park on the far side. The view in this direction focuses on the tower of 'new' West Woodhay church on the top of the hill in the distance; (new in that) it was built at the end of the nineteenth century to replace the old church which had stood in the gardens of West Woodhay, very close to the house to the south-east.

Percy Cane added a large Bog Garden round the south end of the lake, but this has been removed. The rest of his work, mainly to the south and west of the house, shows in its surviving parts a characteristic balanced formality. To the west of the house he laid out the formal Rose Garden, which today is filled with many varieties of shrub roses. It is likely that he planned the simple, broad grass terrace beneath the south front of the house, too, and the wide flagged path stretching west across the terrace to a flight of steps. These lead up to a walk between tall, clipped Irish yews, backed on the north side by a yew hedge, dividing it from the Rose Garden. Cane probably also planted the Churchyard Garden close to the house, although much of the planting has been changed here.

Immediately after the war Mr Henderson was preoccupied with alterations to the house. Since turning his attention in the 1950s to the gardens he has made some sympathetic alterations, most of which were virtually obligatory as a result of the garden's decline, but these have reduced labour demands and together with a number of notable additions have brought the gardens back to a very high standard. Jim Russell advised on the grouping of trees in the park which now frame the marvellous view. The south terrace is bounded by a low wall and central steps beyond which a huge lawn, unbroken by any tree, shrub, border or other distraction, stretches to the ha-ha boundary. The gardener estimates that he walks eight miles behind his cylinder mower when mowing this main south lawn.

Jim Russell also suggested much of the planting in the informal area of Woodland Garden along the west side of the south lawn, from the Yew Walk. Here an outcrop of greensand, comparatively rare in this predominantly chalky part of Berkshire, has enabled a number of acid-loving plants to flourish and give West Woodhay spring and early summer colour. Outstanding mature beech and oak provide the framework for rhododendrons, azaleas, camellias, pieris and magnolias. In spring daffodils are scattered right through this woodland area, along with a number of other smaller bulbs and wild flowers.

The east side of the south lawn is bounded by a clipped yew hedge, a legacy of Percy Cane's formality. Immediately beyond the hedge is the Churchyard Garden, its secluded tranquillity in character with an old-established, godly past. Round a central sundial are narrow raised beds containing mainly low or grey foliage plants, such as senecio, beneath cherries, laburnum and an old cedar. It would surprise many visitors, who presume that the group of gravestones in one corner mark the resting place of family pets, to know that in fact they mark human graves. Below the Churchyard Garden and tennis court a wide grass slope extends east down to the lake.

In 1960 Mr Henderson added the south-facing Garden Room to the west of the house; its appearance is akin to a seventeenth- or eighteenth-century orangery, totally harmonious with the rest of the building. In spring and early summer the Garden Room contains Mr Henderson's great pride: superb, scented rhododendrons such as 'Fragrantissimum' and 'Countess of Haddington', which are too tender to live out-of-doors and spend the rest of the year in the greenhouses of the kitchen garden.

BUCKINGHAMSHIRE

CHENIES MANOR HOUSE

In Chenies, off the A404 between Amersham and Rickmansworth
Tel. 02404 2888

Lt Col. and Mrs MacLeod Matthews

Open two days a week from April to October inclusive

Venerable Chenies was mentioned in the Domesday Book as a Demesne manor. Of the present building the most important work was carried out for John Russell, 1st Earl of Bedford, who married the heiress of Chenies after she had inherited in 1523; parts of the house, however, do date from the thirteenth and mid-fifteenth century. The Russells continued to use Chenies as their principal home for a hundred years. Henry VIII came frequently; the house was one of the scenes of Katherine Howard's adultery with Thomas Culpepper, which led to her execution; and Elizabeth I was a frequent visitor. Just before the Civil War the Russells established themselves at Woburn Abbey, their present home, and although Chenies was retained it was leased to successive tenants and not fully occupied until Colonel and Mrs MacLeod Matthews bought the house in the 1950s.

While the Russells were living at Chenies the present gardens to the west of the house were known as the 'little' gardens and the main area or 'great' garden was to the north of the house. Although most of the original layout here has disappeared the area now contains the most historically interesting feature at Chenies, a small labyrinth or maze, reconstructed by the MacLeod Matthews from a picture at Woburn Abbey dated about 1580. During late medieval times these were popular features in gardens but today – in an original or reconstructed state – they are very rare.

Both in the courtyard north of the long east range of the house and in the main areas of garden to the west and south-west, the layout and planting have been done by Colonel and Mrs MacLeod Matthews. Remnants of older gardens did survive but they had not been maintained. Now both the style and character of the gardens are perfectly suited to the late medieval and Tudor architecture of the red brick house, the steep gables and tall decorative chimneys of which the latter reputedly rival those at Hampton Court as the best examples of their period. Tudor character is most strongly retained in the Sunken Garden to the west of the house and the Physic Garden which lies beyond.

The large courtyard which greets visitors to Chenies sets the tone with its restrained formality. Layout and planting are ideally simple. The courtyard has the house on its west and south sides, a brick wall with the village church beyond to the east and another wall to the north, in which wrought-iron gates lead to the labyrinth. The large lawn has a central raised stone bed round a fountain, and on the corners of the lawn fastigiate yews are enclosed by clipped box. Beneath the brick wall which marks the boundary with the churchyard is a mixed shrub and herbaceous border.

The main gardens beyond the west front of the house are divided by hedges and walls. A narrow grass path enclosed by mixed cypress and yew hedges with tall domes of clipped yew at intervals forms a strong axis through the middle of the garden. The path leads enticingly to a doorway in the wall at the far west end, beyond which lies the Physic Garden, a formal pattern of beds filled with a variety of herbs. Climbing roses are trained on the walls here and on the north side is a charming octagonal building, built of brick with a steep tiled roof, which covers a medieval well.

Immediately to the north of the central path is the Sunken Garden, which is remarkably similar to that at Hampton Court. It may originally date from the same Tudor period, for although its present appearance is the work of the Macleod Matthews there was a sunken area of some description here when they came to Chenies. The garden is rectangular, small terraces of lawn with narrow beds and low retaining walls descending to the central lawn divided by flagged paths. The main east–west path is lined by domes of clipped box and at the far west end is a boundary of pleached limes. The partly ruined building immediately to the north-west of the Sunken Garden was built around 1525 as a nursery for the Russells' children. The daffodils and tulips which fill the beds round the terraces in spring are followed by herbaceous plants in summer and by summer bedding.

Immediately to the south-west of the house is a fine Chinese weeping ash which is known to have been planted about 1770. To the west of here an arch in wooden trellis-work, which stretches from the central path to the southern edge of the garden, leads to the Formal Garden, a rectangular area corresponding to the Sunken Garden. The lawn here is broken by clipped yew topiary surrounded by low clipped box round a central statue of a child. The borders round the lawn in the Formal Garden are again filled with a refreshing variety of spring bulbs and later herbaceous plants; in summer the roses climbing over the wooden trellis-work contrast with the formality of shape and colour in the hedges and topiary. A secluded grass path lined by pleached limes marks the southern boundary of the Formal Garden. Immediately to the west is the small White Garden which Mrs Macleod Matthews recently planned with the help of Jamie Garnock, a young garden designer.

Formality of design balanced by a carefree note in the planting and colours of the borders are the hallmark of Tudor gardens. One feels certain that the gardens which adorned Chenies four hundred years ago had many similar characteristics to those of today; fine proof of sensitive restoration.

THE MANOR HOUSE

In Bledlow, 2½ miles west of Princes Risborough off the B4009
Tel. 08444 3499
The Lord and Lady Carrington

Open one Sunday, and by appointment

Originally built in 1648 and added to in 1714 and 1802, the Manor House has for much of its life been a farmhouse. It was the loss of a large barn in a fire in 1968 which prompted many of the alterations to the garden. The barn stood close to the south side of the house, and now the area between the house and other farm buildings has for the first time been designed and planted by Lord and Lady Carrington as part of the garden.

The garden is on three sides of the house, to the north, east and south. The yew and beech hedges in many parts of it give a period look and provide an essential element of surprise – the style of each enclosure is a secret until its narrow gateway or opening is passed.

Planting is largely dictated by the high lime content of the chalk soil. Beyond the main entrance forecourt, to the north of the house, the lawn is planted with a selection of standard trees, among them two beech, replacing the backdrop of elms the garden enjoyed until they were killed by Dutch elm disease and leading to the pleached limes which flank the drive and Walled Garden. Many of the garden's thriving clematis are in this part but no doubt the dominating feature is the five-hundred-year-old yew tree.

To the north-east of the forecourt a narrow opening leads to the first of three gardens designed by Robert Adam. High yew hedges enclose an intricate pattern of clipped yew and box round gravel and brick paths, with a central astrolabe. Through another small opening in the yew hedge is a garden of formal box-enclosed beds filled, at the moment, with miniature fuchsias and lavender, santolina, araphalis and dwarf hostas. In one corner is a stone statue of St Peter which originally stood against the south-east wall of the Houses of Parliament and which Lord and Lady Carrington bought from the Department of the Environment. The third enclosure is paved and planted in part with small shrub roses, but its most striking feature is the wide central carpet of lavender.

To the east of the house the swimming pool and its surrounding garden were made out of an old orchard, part of which has been retained in one corner. Here the style is open and unrestrained in comparison with the formal enclosures, with mixed borders of scented, colourful shrubs and herbaceous plants, lilacs and laburnum leading to an eighteenth-century urn. Nevertheless, yew and beech hedges combine with an immaculate croquet lawn to restore a note of order even here. An opening in the tall beech hedge along one side leads back to the lawn beyond the north forecourt and a mixed border of shrub roses and peonies along the wall of the traditional Kitchen Garden.

The courtyard below the south front of the house is divided by an avenue of *Viburnum carlesii* leading to a sunken lily pond enclosed by beech hedges and brick walls. On one side pleached limes have been planted on a raised mound and against the far wall is a border of old-fashioned shrub roses, beside which a path leads to an enchanting gazebo beneath the steep bank at the back of the garden, on top of which more shrub roses have been planted as a screen.

This courtyard and sunken garden are two of the recently designed parts of the garden, reflecting the overall concept of complementary enclosures and open spaces. Lord and Lady Carrington have successfully achieved a balance between design and planting, reciprocal harmony between form and order, and variety.

TURN END

In Haddenham, 3 miles north-east of Thame, between the A418 and the A4129
Tel. 0844 291 228

Mr and Mrs Peter Aldington

Open one or two Sundays each year

Turn End is one of three award-winning houses designed by architect
Peter Aldington and built in what used to be the orchard and vegetable
garden of the large house next door, part of which is now his office. Its
one-acre garden retains some of the old features – mature trees and
walls with tiled tops built of a local clay called Wychert – and so sustains
a transition in style to that of the modern house it surrounds on two
sides. The idea behind the garden originated in the courtyard built as
part of the house and now echoed in a series of enclosed spaces. Not
surprisingly, parts of the garden have a definitely 'architectural' character, and the detail in many of the features, such as the flight of steps, the
brick paving and the raised beds, all of which Peter Aldington has made
himself, is exceptional.

Among the mature trees on the long lawn are a chestnut, an evergreen
oak, and a wellingtonia at one end. The last survivors of the old orchard,
now supporting a 'Kiftsgate' and other climbing roses, provide the
framework for a Spring Garden. More recent additions among the trees
are striking silver birches whose barks stand out at the back of the lower
lawn. The planting in this lower area reflects the informal style which
blends with the architecture; hostas and foxgloves follow the path along
the brick boundary wall and round the lawn near the wellingtonia, in
notable combinations of colour, the plants are blue, mauve and yellow,
with roses adding an occasional touch of pink. Mixed herbaceous plants
are placed near a square pergola now covered with the bright red
climbing rose 'Parkdirektor Riggers' and a red-leaved vine.

The contrast is immediate as one descends further to the small paved
courtyard, enclosed with hedges of yew and beech, on one side of an old
coach house and stable which has become a central feature of the
garden. The coach house is open on this side, with a small archway
leading into another courtyard with tiled walls on its far side, with little
box-edged beds and an immaculate fan-trained plum and cooking

cherries on the walls. Steps go down into yet another courtyard in front of Peter Aldington's office. The effect is almost one of walking through a set of neat conjuror's boxes.

On the other side of the house, beyond the original courtyard with a pool now shaded by mature acacias, an archway leads from the main part of the garden into a miniature courtyard of cream walls topped by the customary tiles. A 'Felicité et Perpetue' climbing rose entwined with a honeysuckle add to the almost Mediterranean brightness. An old wooden trough, originally used for laying out dough in a bakery and now filled with alpines, brings in some softer hues. Another archway leads into a larger, recently made court, sunnier than the rest of the garden. A series of raised beds made with old railway sleepers, and a pergola on the far side will form the basis for an area of climbing roses and clematis, and more roses mixed with sun-loving plants, using soft with stronger colours to give yet another element of contrast in Turn End's enduring garden.

HAMPSHIRE

BRAMDEAN HOUSE

In Bramdean, midway between Petersfield and Winchester on the A272
Tel. 0962 79214
Mr and Mrs H. Wakefield

Open on selected Sundays for one week in summer, and by appointment

At first sight Bramdean's position is anything but enviable: the traffic of a busy main road zooms past within yards of the front door, the sight of it kept at bay by a huge and ancient hedge of yew and box with central wrought-iron gates. But this disadvantage, real as it is, only heightens the effect of the garden on the far side of the house from the road, a haven of tranquillity for the Wakefield family since 1944.

From the garden door a vista of some three hundred yards stretches gently uphill between herbaceous borders, an exquisite wrought-iron gateway, the central borders of an old-fashioned Kitchen Garden, another gateway and through the orchard to the old cupola-mounted Apple House. Through the seasons the details constantly change, so that the effect of each section at its peak is intensified in a way that plantings for a more permanent picture could not achieve.

The deep, luxuriant herbaceous borders are the overture to the whole and the main theme of the first section of the garden: lawns and mature beeches, limes and a cedar, raised terraces and borders. Great attention is paid to their shape and colour grouping to maximize their impact in high summer. Other, smaller borders are filled with a host of plants for different seasons including some special alpines and rockplants, many varieties of snowdrops and aconites. There is continual interest if one wanders here, but the temptation is very strong to take the main path up the steps through the wrought-iron gateway into the Walled Garden.

Here is a Kitchen Garden *par excellence*, with a traditional mixture of flowers, fruit and vegetables. The path, with a central stone sundial surrounded by a circle of lawn and clipped yew, is flanked by triangular beds filled alternately with antirrhinums and floribunda roses. Behind are trained climbing roses and a variety of cotoneasters, and a tempting array of vegetables planted out in attractive orderliness. Another set of wrought-iron gates lead from the Walled Garden into the orchard and informality: springtime blossom, daffodils by the central path and spread under the trees with many varieties of snowdrops and aconites; later on the apple trees are garlanded with climbing roses, clematis or honeysuckle. At the top it was an inspired decision in the eighteenth century to make the simple necessity in any orchard for somewhere to store the fruit into the enchanting focus of the garden. The height of the brick Apple House and tiled roof is almost doubled by its decorative adornments of clock, cupola and weather-vane. In winter, when the trees are bare, the blue door and matching clock-face invite one through the garden; during summer, when these are obscured from the bottom of the garden, the cupola and weather-vane can be seen peeping over the fruit trees.

The mid-summer weeks are a just reward for the work involved in maintaining Bramdean's labour-intensive style of gardening over four acres with just one full-time gardener and an under-gardener. When the borders are in full flower they form an image visitors are unlikely to forget.

EXBURY

15 miles south-west of Southampton, off the B3054 between Beaulieu and Dibden Purlieu
Tel. 0703 891 203
E. L. de Rothschild, Esq.

Open daily from early March to mid July

Lionel de Rothschild, who bought the Exbury Estate in 1919, immersed himself in a life-long love affair with rhododendrons, the offspring of which was not only one of England's most spectacular rhododendron gardens but also one of the finest collections of rhododendrons and azaleas anywhere in the world. He always maintained that he was 'a banker by hobby and a gardener by profession', and looking at what he achieved as a gardener one hardly dares disagree.

Exbury is situated on a small neck of land between the Solent and the Beaulieu river. When Lionel de Rothschild bought the property the eighteenth-century red-brick house was surrounded by extensive and dense woodland. The house was transformed into an elegant neo-Georgian mansion faced in stone, then the clearing of undergrowth, leaving only mature standard oaks, beech, Scots pines and other conifers, and the preparation of the ground, were alike carried out in characteristic Rothschild style. The final site extended to two hundred acres forming three adjoining woods: Home Wood, to the south-west of the house towards the Beaulieu river; Witcher's Wood to the north of this; and Yard Wood, further to the north again, the latter originally cut off from the rest by a road, but linked by the balustraded Exbury bridge which Rothschild built. The woods were criss-crossed by over twenty miles of paths, and watered by twenty-six miles of underground piping.

Soon the views along woodland glades and across the ponds in Home Wood were framed by quantities of plants, particularly rhododendrons and azaleas. Many of these were raised from seed collected on expeditions to the Himalayas and other parts of Asia, of which Rothschild was one of the main financial backers between the world wars. By the time of his death in 1942 he had planted over one million rhododendrons at Exbury and raised 1210 new hybrid rhododendrons and azaleas, of which he deemed 462 worthy to be registered as new varieties. Among these the best known are the Exbury strain of hybrid azaleas, but there were quantities of outstanding rhododendrons of rarely achieved qualities, particularly purity of colour. 'Naomi', named after his youngest daughter, was perhaps the finest all-round plant he raised; it never fails to produce a rich display of pink flowers. In his quest for a perfect yellow rhododendron Rothschild produced 'Hawk' and 'Hawk' variety 'Crest', whose colour is unrivalled.

After the Second World War Rothschild's eldest son Edmund returned to administrate Exbury, as he does today. Rather than live in the main house he returned to his father's original home, Inchmery, on the edge of the estate, and concentrated his attentions on the gardens which were badly in need of restoration after the enforced neglect of the war years. The Arboretum to the east of the main gardens was completely overgrown and as a result returned to farmland. His two-acre Rock Garden on the north edge of the gardens, which he had constructed with the aid of a miniature railway through the woods to carry the huge boulders, was a similar jungle. Through the rhododendron woods, undergrowth had steadily encroached. Clearance and replanting, to replace old plants or introduce new varieties, have been slow processes but have steadily quickened pace in recent years. Since 1976 the watering system has been completely renewed and in 1980 the Rock Garden – the most ambitious piece of restoration – was replanted.

Today the gardens are fully restored to their former glory, older rhododendrons blending with the succession of later introductions. A stand at the bottom of Home Wood of one of Lionel de Rothschild's most striking hybrids, 'Fortune', produced by crossing the two large-leafed varieties, *R. falconieri* and *R. sinogrande*, contains towering plants of over twenty feet, and in different parts of the woods younger generations all produced from 'Naomi' crosses can be found: 'Carita', 'Idealist' and 'Lionel's Triumph' to name just a few. From his father's Exbury strain of azaleas Edmund de Rothschild himself has made further crosses to produce the 'Solent' range which now line Lover's Lane, the long avenue through Witcher's Wood which leads south-west towards the Beaulieu river. New names are constantly appearing in the garden and Fred Wynniatt, the head gardener for most of the post-war period, has given his name to one of the best recent hybrids.

Still, Exbury is not, and never has been, just a rhododendron garden. For much of the year their foliage – be it the deciduous azaleas in Witcher's Wood, or the bright, evergreen Kurume ones round the Home Wood ponds, or the huge leaves of 'Fortune' – blends with the softer leaves of beech, acers and other deciduous trees, or the flowers of other species, notably magnolias and camellias. The original framework of oaks and Scots pines has been greatly enhanced by numerous more unusual trees, including the huge swamp cypress on the island on the upper pond, many 'Brewer's Weeping Spruce' and different varieties of nothofagus. After the main, rather exotic flowering period in the woods is over, summer beauty and stillness can be found in the Rose Garden between Home Wood and Witcher's Wood, planted in memory of Edmund de Rothschild's late wife, Elizabeth.

FAIRFIELD HOUSE

In Hambledon, 10 miles south-west of Petersfield
Tel. 070 132 431
Mr and Mrs Peter Wake

Open for eight days in June, and by appointment

The white house was built in typical Georgian style in the 1820s. At that time the now outstanding Lebanon cedars, beech, copper beech, yews and lime trees were planted on the south entrance front and to the west, and the walled gardens on the north and east sides were also laid out. Within this framework virtually all of the present garden dates from 1970 when Mr and Mrs Wake bought Fairfield House; their work proves how quickly a young garden can attain maturity, especially if built up as part of an older setting. The soil on the edge of the Hampshire downs is chalky, but this has not inhibited Mr Wake's primary interest, the shrub and climbing roses that are the main feature of the garden. There is variety on each side of the house and small enclosed corners contrast with the wider areas of lawn and long grass beneath the mature trees.

Mr and Mrs Wake have left the south and west gardens open, dominated by the various trees. The copper beech in particular, close to the drive in the south-west corner, is of outstanding spread, the lower branches spanning some 110 feet. An interest in roses is immediately revealed by the carefully-chosen climbers trained up the slender pillars of the verandah on the south and west sides of the house; mixing with wisteria and clematis they draw the two façades – the Ionic entrance and the bows of the west front – into the garden. Part of the garden to the west had been enclosed by yew hedges; the Wakes removed these and now the lawn stretches up the slope to where mature beeches sweep the long grass beneath them, planted with spring bulbs. Younger trees planted by the Wakes here include a fern-leafed beech, a blue cedar and a number of sorbus.

The Wild Garden to the north is bordered on one side by a long brick wall stretching back down to the house. Through a Gothic arch is a two-acre Walled Garden, originally the Kitchen Garden but completely re-planned by the Wakes in 1971–2. Once the garden had been cleared the

315

whole area was grassed down save for borders beneath the walls. Now it is planted with a variety of trees and shrubs, in particular over a hundred outstanding specie and old-fashioned shrub and climbing roses. Mr Wake takes enormous care with his roses and it shows. Every year the ramblers and climbers, numbering over sixty varieties, are taken off the wires before pruning and re-training in an immaculate fan shape. Among the shrub roses are marvellous *Rosa californica* 'Plena', 'Cerise Bouquet' and 'Marguerite Hilling' (the pink form of 'Nevada').

The fact that the shrub roses are free-standing single specimens would normally reveal defects, but at Fairfield it only highlights their qualities. There are some good trees among the roses, including a *Metasequoia gliptostroboides*, damson, malus, sorbus crataegus, *Prunus robinia* and a Dawyck beech. The only plants retained from the old garden were a cut-leaf elder against the top wall and, close by in a sheltered corner, an old brown Turkey fig. The informal rose planting with plenty of space between them and mown paths winding through the long grass, gives the garden the appearance of a decorative orchard, particularly in June and July. A second Gothic arch, opposite the other, leads east to a narrow strip with a low flint wall on the far side. This is partly for vegetables but there are more climbing roses on the outside of the brick wall.

At the bottom of the Walled Garden an oval swimming pool has been incorporated with no sense of incongruity. In the curving border round it roses mix with hibiscus, lavenders and rue. The pool is surrounded by brick to echo the main walls; steps lead to a small pavilion whose pointed arches recall those of entrances. The brick-piered pergola in front is draped with 'The Garland', 'François Jouranville' and 'Rambling Rector' roses; 'Albertine', 'Rambling Rector' and *Solanum jasminoides* grow on the wall. More recently a tennis court has been incorporated with similar success, surrounded by brick walls, and with brick pillars supporting the wires on which climb more roses, including 'Felicité et Perpétué', and clematis.

In the smaller East Walled Garden the Wakes re-planned what was a rose garden with central beds and borders to give a central lawn and borders beneath the walls. Because of early-morning sun there are mainly evergreens along the east-facing side in front of the house. There is a vinehouse lightly screened by a *Genista aetnensis* and in the borders shrub roses mix with a variety of plants: small trees, such as a snake-bark maple, many shrubs, hebes, berberis, and smaller plants all with a stress on yellow, blue and grey, such as santolinas and helichrysums. Along one wall the many climbing roses are challenged by a large wisteria which flowers outstandingly.

Perhaps more than anywhere else the busy variety in the East Garden demonstrates the energy put into those four-and-a-half acres by Mr and Mrs Wake, who maintain the gardens themselves, with occasional help from their children.

Spring bulbs and blossom and much autumn colour contribute great interest through much of the year, but it is undeniably the roses that make Fairfield irresistible for a summer treat.

JENKYN PLACE

In Bentley, 400 yards north of the crossroads in Bentley (sign to Condall)
Tel. 0420 23118

Mr and Mrs G. E. Coke

Open alternate Sundays from May to August inclusive, and by appointment on
Wednesday and Thursday for parties

It is arguable that the style of gardening immortalized by Hidcote Manor and Sissinghurst is regarded as *the* modern tradition, developed through the twentieth century. The style has many advantages: rather than providing a standard formula, it calls for a personal interpretation of an overall idea; development of areas with different characters and appearances, and a variety of planting within a formal or semi-formal design. Enclosures are linked by gateways or pathways, and to walk round such a garden is like reading a story, the different personae and places steadily being revealed and given continuity by the overall design or plot. The possibilities are limitless and can be adapted to any site or ambition.

Since the Second World War Jenkyn Place has grown up to become a leading exponent of this style. Admittedly it is on a scale not everyone can aspire to, and is maintained by the owners with three gardeners, but the composition, as a whole and in its various parts, is immediately impressive. Architecture is balanced with plantsmanship, intimacy with grand design and as the story unfolds the depth of detail steadily becomes apparent.

The Cokes came to Jenkyn Place in 1941. The site had the advantage of being on upper greensand and on a south-east facing aspect on the north side of a valley, of the River Wey. Around the house traces of an

Edwardian garden were integrated into the far larger overall design stretching away from the house to the south and west. It is difficult to simplify the pattern, but essentially the smaller and more formal areas were built up closer to the house and interlinking, while the individual areas beyond these were surrounded and joined by wider grass paths and lawns. There is also a natural progression through these areas to the far end of the garden, from where the main vista, bordered by the belt of mature trees along the roadside, stretches majestically back between standard trees and shrubs to the south front of the house.

The names which all areas of the garden are given enhance the sense of formal progression pattern and point up the variety. The Dutch Garden, a small enclosure through the entrance gate, is the visitor's introduction. As well as admiration for the climbing roses, such as 'Madame Gregoire Staechelin', on one wall, the tender *Trachelospermum jasminoides* 'Variegatum' on another and the picturesque remains of an old dairy to one side, one has a strong sense of expectancy as glimpses over walls and through an archway give some inkling of what lies beyond. To the west is the Sundial Garden, a small paved area filled mainly with pot-plants. With its beautiful peacock-pattern wrought-iron gates on either side, the Sundial Garden is in a sense a small crossroads. Continuing to the west lie the Bowling Green and formal Rose Garden: rose beds, some filled with hybrid teas, others with specie and old-fashioned varieties – also on the walls – around a central rectangular pool with a boy and swan fountain. Variation is given by the unusual shrubs on the north wall, such as *Caesalpinia japonica*. It is typical of the many different areas of Jenkyn Place – self-sufficient in its appearance and interest, but linked to the whole.

Taking the lower gate out of the Sundial Garden into the double herbaceous border, the visitor has 'arrived' at Jenkyn Place. Just the proportions of this border are impressive, accentuated by the dark yew hedges behind and the generous width of the central grass path. Their most dramatic effect is achieved by entering through the large wrought-iron gates at the end closest to the house. But it is the luxury of a large garden with unlimited seasonal variety that they are planned for flowering 'en masse' in high summer, and not for colour for as long as possible which only diminishes the overall effect. One may admire them at ease from a stone seat, backed by a curved clipped yew hedge at the far end from the house.

Parallel to the border is the Long Walk. With a narrow Rock Garden along one side, where the succession of small plants and alpines is continuous through the year, it forms a cleverly placed division between the herbaceous border and the series of gardens beyond, again in an axis across the garden – the Italian Garden, the old-fashioned Rose Garden and the Yew Garden, the first two shaded by enormous old limes. The rectangular area occupied by these three gardens is especially notable for a central path between borders of massed peonies and two apple walks, one underplanted with crinums, the other with alpine strawberries.

Below the Old-fashioned Rose Garden the circular Herb Garden, enclosed by a hedge of cider apples and centred on a statue of Bacchus, continues the theme of small enclosures, but below the Kitchen Garden the intensity is relaxed somewhat in the more informal and open Leaf Garden, a mixture of herbaceous, shrubs and trees with, as to be expected from its name, a stress throughout on foliage especially, in the lower part, on autumn colour. This is a fairly recent addition at Jenkyn Place, made in 1976, but already it contains the largest concentration of varied plants of any of the small areas. Two striking and unusual varieties of shrubs better-known in their normal form are *Aralia argento* 'Variegata' and *Rhus typhina* 'Laciniata'.

The naming of parts reaches a glorious climax at the Armillary Sphere Garden, an area of seventeenth-century formality that has as its centrepiece the 'skeleton celestial globe of metal rings representing the equator and the tropics'.

Pleached limes hedge the north and west sides and herringbone brick paths divide the area into four small lawns, each with a single tree: *Morus alba*, the white mulberry; *Diospyrus lotus*, the date plum; a medlar; a *Prunus serrula* with polished, mahogany bark. The south and east sides are enclosed by hedges of lilac and hedgehog holly, beyond which is the Lion Garden. Here formality is again relaxed in mixed plantings of trees and shrubs, including rugosa roses, sorbuses and *Cornus controversa*, but kept in mind by the pair of eighteenth-century lions beside the steps down to the garden, and by the pattern of the beds of hostas and hardy fuchsias. Restrained formality is the mood in the parallel Lion Walk, a most rewarding vista to come upon at the bottom of the garden, leading between high hedges of mixed green and copper beech to the eponymous recumbant stone beast.

The Sunken Garden on the other side of the Lion Walk reveals distant views of the house higher up the valley, the approach to which is mapped out by the lines of perfectly mown lawn yet constantly interrupted by attractions on either side: *Abelia triflora*, a variegated cornus, a weeping lime, *Styrax hemsleyana*, *Gleditsia triacanthos* 'Sunburst', *Hoheria glabrata* and many others. It is difficult to find anything to criticize at Jenkyn Place; certainly being almost too perfect is not a fault.

MOTTISFONT ABBEY

In Mottisfont, 4½ miles north-west of Romsey off the A3057
Tel. 0983 526 445
The National Trust

Open afternoons Tuesday to Saturday from April to September inclusive

Since the 1970s Mottisfont Abbey has been chiefly renowned for its Rose Garden filled with roses from the eighteenth and nineteenth century. But the Rose Garden is only the latest addition to a garden which has long provided an appropriate setting for the building, part-medieval, part-Tudor and part-eighteenth-century – indeed, since 1201, when the Priory of Holy Trinity was founded.

The south front looks on to surroundings most of which have changed little since this side of the house was rebuilt in the 1740s by Sir Richard Mill. The red-brick façade represents a transition from strict Palladianism to a more romantic interpretation of classicism, a sympathy that is echoed by the eighteenth-century Gothick summerhouse in the north-east corner of the garden. But of the gardens to the south of the house, it is the trees that dominate; beech and copper beech, cedars, sweet chestnuts and the enormous London plane – in fact two trees growing together – which is reputed to have the largest canopy of any tree in Britain. To the west of these sloping lawns is the spring which first brought the monks to Mottisfont – it still gushes at a rate of two hundred gallons per minute – and beyond are more recently planted flowering trees: a tulip tree, a paulownia and catalpa. The main drive on this side of the house is lined by an avenue of cedars.

The main alteration to the South Garden is the small parterre added by Mr and Mrs Gilbert Russell, who bought Mottisfont in 1934. Two years later they commissioned Geoffrey Jellicoe to design the gardens on the north front. Here the façade is radically different; with very little alteration it is the nave and tower of the Augustinian church of the medieval priory. Originally Jellicoe put a pool in the centre of the lawn but that has since been removed; now the grass stretches unbroken to two low walls, between which the perspective is narrowed, and beyond to the ha-ha and park. Along the west side of the lawn he raised a pleached-lime walk with nineteenth-century vases along the retaining wall; in the spring the ground beneath the bare trees is covered with blue chionodoxa, the little Flower-of-the-Snow. The walk leads to a yew enclosure close by the house, with steps up from the lawn and away on the other side to the small area behind the stables where there are a number of magnolias.

The house and its setting are somewhat detached from the Rose Garden, which is some distance away in one of the old brick-walled kitchen gardens, an ideal site with a large rectangular area and box-edged paths. Most of the roses it contains were collected by Graham Stuart Thomas who, at the time this work was begun, was Gardens Advisor to the National Trust. The various beds and borders now contain well over three hundred forms of roses, all old shrub roses with climbers and ramblers covering the walls. When in flower the garden is a wonderful sight – a mist of blending colour undisturbed by the often jarring shades of many modern varieties. Before and after the roses flower small spring plants along the border-edges and the central double herbaceous border both give variety and stress the factor which make the Rose Garden so instantly attractive as well as impressive – it is a garden and not just a collection.

ISLE OF WIGHT

CEDAR LODGE

In Puckpool near Ryde

Tel. 09836 2604

Mr and Mrs George Harris

Open on selected Sundays in May and by appointment

.The mild maritime climate of much of the Isle of Wight has its drawbacks, as the Grimaldis – the Harris's immediate predecessors – discovered when they came to Cedar Lodge in the late 1940s – the existing garden had become a jungle. Since then they have capitalized on its advantages, and built up a garden containing many very tender plants

The garden is mainly on a south-east-facing slope, with a large lawn in front of the house; on one side a grass bank descends to the lower, tennis court lawn and the bottom of the garden, where there are west and south-facing boundary walls. Of great value were the number of outstanding trees, including a Lebanon cedar from which the house takes its name, a cork oak, a weeping beech and a superb free-standing *Magnolia grandiflora* at the far end of the main lawn which may be about a hundred years old. Along the top of the main lawn is the only area of flower garden at Cedar Lodge, a long, mixed summer border. Below, near the tennis court lawn, are some of a number of magnolias, most of which have shown exceptionally vigorous growth: *Magnolia obovata, M. mollicomata* and, nearer the bottom of the garden, *M. campbellii* and *M. veitchii.*

Mr Grimaldi was fortunate in recently being able to acquire a one-acre triangle at the top of the garden. Along the boundary he planted ash trees and a berberis hedge which effectively block out the housing estate built on the far side. Like most of the garden this top area is simply and informally planted, the main interest often being in the plants themselves. Here are many eucalyptus, including *E. pauciflora* and *E. niphophila*, and *Parrotia persica*. These, like most of the plants in the garden, show unusually rapid growth: behind the *grandiflora*, for example, a weeping willow which was planted in 1950 already towers above the magnolia at a height of over sixty feet. Another thing one immediately notices, though it seems hardly credible, is that *Acacia dealbata* grows, as Mr Grimaldi remarked, 'like a weed'.

When Mr Grimaldi started collecting plants for his garden many of the earliest were rhododendrons and camellias. Although some are planted as single plants, most of these are now thriving along the west side of the garden, where tall trees give the necessary shade. He was very lucky at one stage, for when nearby Appley Hall was being demolished – to make way for an earlier housing estate – he was able to collect from the garden as many plants as he could take away, and the peaty earth that abounded. Many of his best rhododendrons came from there, including the two plants of *R. macabeanum* near the weeping beech.

It is along the west- and south-facing walls that many of the most interesting plants are to be found – mostly very tender, but apparently thriving here. Among the west-facing are: *Koelreuteria paniculata*, the 'Goldenrain tree' from China, *Crinodendron hookeranum*, *Pittosporum tobira*, and *Viburnum odoratissimum*, the last two noticeable for glossy, obovate leaves. Further along the wall are *Trachelospermum asiaticum* and the wonderful pink 'Bottle-brush', *Callistemon speciosum*, while freestanding away from the wall are *Acacia melanoxylon* and *A. verticillata*, *Cornus capitata*, *Hoheria populneis* and *H. lanceolata*. Joined with a Banksian rose and ceanothuses on the south-facing wall are *Acacia armata*, *Cestrum elegana*, and three plants with uninvitingly large spikes – *Acacia pravissima*, and a South American duo *Colletia armata* from Paraguay and *C. cruciata* from Uruguay. It is clear that many rare foreign visitors flourish in this island garden, while more usual plants, such as the *Paulownia tomentosa*, grow to prodigious height.

After the sad death of her husband in 1983 Mrs Grimaldi sold Cedar Lodge to Mr and Mrs Harris. They are both enthusiastic gardeners and as well as developing the planting around two existing pools at the far end of the main lawn from the house they have added a third pool on the lower, tennis court lawn level. Also now complementing the rich variety of plants are a number of Italian marble fountains and statues which Mr and Mrs Harris have brought to the garden. It is a warm tribute to Mr Grimaldi's work that his garden is thus being maintained and given the interest of new features.

OXFORDSHIRE

---

23 BEECHCROFT ROAD

In Oxford
Tel. 086 556 020
Mrs Anne Dexter

Open by appointment only

Mrs Dexter's garden is twenty-three yards long and seven yards wide, enclosed by brick walls on either side and by a fence at the far end. Hers is a typical terraced house which needed considerable repair when she bought it in 1959, and the garden was a rubbish dump enlivened by a few old gooseberry bushes. Since then she has made a garden which at times threatens to burst out of the tiny area like a child who has outgrown the nursery. But with coaxing and occasionally more radical reprimands, the more wayward members are kept in check before they succeed in annexing Mrs Dexter's neighbours.

Despite the quantity of plants the garden is thoroughly orderly; Mrs Dexter has concentrated on training the plants upwards, realizing that virulent growth by some of them would obscure and suffocate smaller and more delicate varieties. Soft colours – because there is not enough space to accommodate bright splashes – and numerous foliage plants play major parts in the garden's success, due, in truth, to Mrs Dexter's continual planning and work which are almost disproportionate to her garden's size.

A paved path two feet wide divides the plants and leads to an oak door in the far fence, giving the illusion that the garden continues beyond it. In a sense it does, for the trees in the adjoining ground shade the bottom of the garden where, in the damp soil, Mrs Dexter has planted trilliums, hostas, primulas, spring bulbs and a large collection of ferns. It was important, too, to have eye-catching features at the far end, such as the variegated gold and green ivy, the pink climbing rose 'New Dawn', 'Golden Wings' rose and *Robinia* 'Frisia'.

The brick walls, whose height of around eight feet has been extended with poles and trellis, are swathed in climbers, including a collection of over thirty clematis which in many places have entwined themselves into the shrubs below. The red *Clematis texensis* 'Etoile Rose' is particularly very expansive, as is *C. Durandii* falling over a large shrub of lonicera. The clematis flower from spring through to late summer and their ambitious growth is rivalled only occasionally by the climbing roses with whom they mix companiably, like the *Clematis* 'William Kennett' with the pink rose 'Mary Wallace'. The shrubs along the walls demonstrate the importance of foliage as a backdrop to these colours: elaeagnus, a golden ribes, *Rosa rubrifolia* and photinia. Occasionally such evergreen and variegated foliage is effectively off-set, for instance by the delicate white deutzia near the house.

Towards the far end of the garden herbaceous plants do not leave an inch of space, and closer to the house rock-beds, stone sinks and basins are filled with alpines. These are an outstanding feature, planted in great quantities yet in continually harmonious combinations. It is their combination of leaf and flower, always changing around a few constant evergreens, which make the smaller plants so telling. Without a visit to 23 Beechcroft Road one would not believe either in the quantity or in the clever grouping of its hosts of plants. For anyone with a small garden it will suggest dozens of ideas, but the conception and overall planning will reward any garden owner.

BROOK COTTAGE

In Alkerton, 6 miles west of Banbury off the A422
Tel. 029 587 303
Mr and Mrs David Hodges

Open on selected Saturdays and Sundays throughout the year and daily by appointment from April to October inclusive

Mr and Mrs Hodges came to Brook Cottage in 1962 and two years later started to make a garden which, over a twenty-year period has been expanded and developed until now it covers four acres of a west facing hill-side site in the valley dividing the villages of Alkerton and Shenington.

It is hard to imagine that in 1962 the 'garden' consisted of rough pasture and a dilapidated barn, and that the narrow lane alongside the house ended in a gravel yard. The combination of Mr Hodges' knowledge and experience as an architect and his wife's flair as a plantswoman has resulted in a remarkably successful transformation, in which the arrangement of banks and levelled ground, the retention where appropriate of natural slopes, and the siting of new trees and hedges create winding routes through the garden converging at focal points and linking areas of widely different character.

From the forecourt by the house a narrow gateway in a high stone wall leads into a terrace enclosed by walls on two sides, and on the other two by clipped yew hedges. The south- and west-facing walls give shelter to many of the less hardy shrubs such as *Cytisus battandieri*, *Carpenteria californica*, *Passiflora caerulea*, and *Solanum jasminoides* 'Album'. In the borders the colour theme is pink and red offset by the bright magenta of *Geranium* 'Armenicum', blue agapanthus and the subtle violet shades of the rambler rose 'Veilchenblau' climbing into the silver foliage of *Pyrus salicifolia* 'Pendula' on the lawn above.

A broad flight of steps descends from the terrace to the central lawn, enclosed on the west side by a continuation of the series of yew hedges and on the east by a stone faced bank which is separated from the lawn by a diverted watercourse. The stones are laid on black polythene (to keep down the weeds) through which is planted a wide selection of perennial plants and shrubs.

At the far end a yellow border is dominated by a column of the variegated ivy *Hedera colchica* 'Dentata Variegata' at the start of a long view down the lawn, which contrasts superbly with a background of copper beech hedge.

Following the hedge down the slope towards the brook from which the house takes its name, one finds a tunnel formed where two curving lines of hedge overlap. An overflow from a pond above keeps the ground permanently damp and within a circular enclosure primulas, astilbes and *Iris sibirica* have been planted. Nearby a *Salix purpurea* 'Pendula' spreads its delicate grey foliage and a group of *Picea omorika* raise their slender dark green spires far above the surrounding hedge.

Continuing along the brook, which forms the western boundary of the garden below the tennis court, made at a distance from the house in 1963 in what was then a field, the comparative formality of the central area gives way to less formal planting of quite large groups of *Viburnum tomentosum* 'Mariesii', *Aesculus parviflora* and *Sorbaria* 'Aitchisonii', with climbing roses on the tennis court netting above and, closing the view, a dense group of Leyland cypress interspersed with *Salix daphnoides* and *Populus alba*, planted to provide shelter from the south-west wind. The autumn colours of *parrotia persica*, the bright pink foliage of *Acer* 'Brilliantissimum' in spring and the summer brilliance of *Robinia* 'Frisia' show up vividly against the evergreens.

Beyond the tennis court shrub roses planted individually in the grass are seen rising up the steep hillside. Here there is room to allow the large species roses to grow to their full potential; there are many old-fashioned varieties and some modern shrubs to lengthen the flowering period. These give way to a more informal area towards the southern boundary where groups of sorbus, crataegus and betula and dense plantings of *Viburnum tomentosum* and *V. opulus* on the steepest bank make a natural transition between garden and countryside, exemplifying once again one of Mr and Mrs Hodges' guiding principles, that of blending garden naturally with landscape.

Above the tennis court and below a steep bank planted with *Viburnum opulus*, *Rubus* 'Tridel', *Cornus alba* 'Spaethii', varieties of berberis and many other shrubs, and bright with daffodils in spring, another focal point is reached, a pond fed by spring water seeping through the hillside, where cattle used to drink.

The boggy ground around the pond is densely planted with primulas – yellow *P. florindae* and scarlet *P.* 'Inverewe' – lysichitums, iris, astilbes, hostas and *Euphorbia griffithii*.

An avenue of the spreading *Prunus* 'Shirotae' makes a canopy of double white flowers in May and a cool shady walk in summer, leading back to the top level of the garden above the house. The original garden has been re-planned and re-planted and a new stone wall on the eastern boundary provides the backing for an herbaceous border and support for various climbers. From here one can look down into the courtyard below, bright with campanulas and hostas planted between the paving stones and backed with clematis and climbing roses on the stone walls of the house.

Below the house a slender curving pond is one of the latest additions to the garden. Here various watercourses are brought together and channelled through a terra-cotta lion's head set in the stone wall of a circular raised platform, where a central quatrefoil stone seat surmounted by a sundial provides a pleasant resting place.

The planting in this area near the brook is again restrained, but further up the hill against the background of the yew hedges are colourful borders. One is white and silver, another contains a somewhat random mixture and is dominated by the giant thistle *Onopordum arabicum* standing out against the yew. The south facing wall of the garage provides protection for a mixed planting, with hebes and the blue-grey grass *Helictotrichon sempervirens* giving strong foliage contrasts while cistus, ceanothus, hibiscus and *Convolvulus althaeoides* provide a wide range of colour. *Tropaeolum polyphyllum* trails its silver foliage and yellow nasturtium-like flowers over dark green mounds of *Berberis irwinii* 'Corallina Compacta'.

Much remains unmentioned, but a garden with such depth, detail, quantity and diversity of plants and striking colour combinations may be fully appreciated only by a visit.

Maintained by Mr and Mrs Hodges and one gardener, Brook Cottage garden reaches a standard of appearance as admirable as its design and horticultural quality deserves.

BROUGHTON CASTLE

In Broughton, 2½ miles west of Banbury on the B4035
Tel. 0295 62624
The Lord and Lady Saye and Sele

Open on Wednesday and Sunday from mid-May to mid-September inclusive, on Thursday in July and August, on Bank Holiday Sundays and Mondays and by appointment for parties

First sight of Broughton Castle is stunning, a marvellous uprising of gables, chimneys and battlements set within park and moat and reflected in the water. The original early fourteenth-century manor house at Broughton was partly transformed into a stone Tudor mansion in the second half of the sixteenth century, and today it is a rare and wonderful example of those two periods of architecture.

Such a bold, stylish building requires a special kind of garden to complement it, and what has been achieved is very much in keeping with both the periods represented here. The lawns between house and moat somehow convey a medieval air better than any flower or shrub garden could do, and balance the building's strong upward surge. An herbaceous border stretches from the gatehouse along the outside of the west-facing courtyard wall, down to the north entrance front. The courtyard below the south front of the house contains the Lady's Garden, a 'fleur-de-lys' pattern of box-enclosed rosebeds and borders beneath the enclosing stone walls corresponding more to the Tudor age. Colours are subdued – many of the roses are soft pinks – a scheme which is continued on the walls among climbers such as *Clematis* 'Hagley Hybrid'. Borders are planted to east and west of the Lady's garden along the outside of the walls – mixed shrub roses and herbaceous plants and on the west again predominantly herbaceous.

All these borders were possibly planned by Gertrude Jekyll, but have been subsequently extensively replanted. They subtly reinforce the intimacy of the Lady's Garden, the secure, enclosed atmosphere given to the whole place by the encircling water. The balance between the moat and the area it encloses was most carefully planned for both are exactly three acres in size. As a result it is the impression of harmony between house, lawn and moat which the visitor will find hard to forget at Broughton.

KINGSTON LISLE PARK

5 miles west of Wantage off the B4507
Tel. 036 782 223
Captain and Mrs T. L. Lonsdale

Open on Tuesday, Thursday and Sunday in August, on Bank Holiday weekends, on Thursday and Sunday in October, and by appointment

Kingston Lisle always used to be in Berkshire; it stands at the foot of the Berkshire Downs, surrounded by superb parkland. The owners of one of Oxfordshire's most recent attractions came here in 1945, when parts of the garden were Victorian and others just overgrown. Since then Captain and Mrs Lonsdale have made a number of additions and alterations, endowing Kingston Lisle with an air of spaciousness as well as many interesting garden features.

The original, centre, block of the house was built by George Hyde in 1677. The two wings were added around 1812 but their architect is not known for certain – Basevi and Cockerell (who also designed Sezincote, discussed in the Gloucestershire chapter) have been suggested. Perhaps the most intriguing unanswered architectural question is who designed the unparalleled flying staircase in the main hall. The north front is dominated by tall and very old clipped yew trees extending round to the terrace along the east side: from here one gains an outstanding view across the park, sloping down to the large lake.

Beyond the north entrance forecourt, Captain and Mrs Lonsdale have replaced an overgrown wilderness with a collection of standard trees which has steadily expanded into the area across the drive. There are a number of outstanding beeches, including a copper beech, a cut-leaf beech and a Dawyck beech. Another feature here are the varieties of cupressus, over twenty-five of them. The trees are highlighted by shrubs – roses, philadelphus and lilacs – with acers and cercidiphyllums providing outstanding autumn colour.

When Captain and Mrs Lonsdale came to Kingston Lisle the main garden was the Victorian flower garden on the south front, where the entrance used to be, planted in a typical pattern of box-enclosed rosebeds, with an unsuitable rockery to one side. Both flower garden and rockery have been replaced by a simple lawn with central pool and fountain, greatly improving the view south across the long lawn to the park which stretches round from the east. At the far end of the lawn a pair of wrought-iron gates, bought by Captain Lonsdale, open first on to a lime avenue and beyond an avenue of Cambrian elms, planted for the Lonsdales by the late Earl of Bradford, acknowledged during his lifetime to be one of Britain's leading tree experts. At its far end the lawn is bordered on its west side by pleached lime with undulating tops, an idea brought back by Mrs Lonsdale from a Belgian garden designed by André le Nôtre. Their formality and foliage is ideally suited to the aim of this part of the garden, a balance between lawn, trees and parkland setting. Mrs Lonsdale designed the walls and yew hedges which enclose a path edged with lavender leading further west to steps and another pair of gates – these were found in a junkyard in Seville – and they bring one to the Croquet Lawn and the Rose Garden.

Entered beneath a rose arbour, the Rose Garden was planted in honour of Queen Mary, Mrs Lonsdale's godmother, and the pattern of rosebeds is the same as that of Queen Mary's Garden in Regent's Park. Some of the beds are underplanted with lavender, and along the west edge climbing roses are trained up poles and along the encircling chains. The lawn behind the climbing roses is dominated by a wonderful Cedar of Lebanon; its trunk is only just smaller than that of a nearby vicarage garden specimen recorded as the largest Cedar of Lebanon in England. Close by is another of the trees which have become such a feature at Kingston Lisle, a scarlet oak planted by the Lonsdales in 1947 to celebrate the twenty-first birthday of their son, Norman.

The particular care which Captain and Mrs Lonsdale lavish on their trees is perhaps best embodied in the avenue stretching from west to east across the lawn beside the Rose Garden, leading back to the new lawn and pool on the south side of the house. An old avenue of elms, out of alignment with urns and steps down to the lower lawn had been on this site but because of their great age these were replaced with limes – and this time aligned symmetrically with the steps. To the north of this avenue more lawn with trees extends to the Walled Garden gates. A long south-facing herbaceous border is planted beneath the brick wall to one side of them and to the other side is a deep border of iris.

The expansive garden at Kingston is a tribute not only to the Lonsdales' 'eye' for balance and proportion on a fairly large scale but to their zest and patience in restoring the gardens with many slow-growing trees. Their reward is the harmony between house and garden and the parkland setting beyond.

MARNDHILL

In Ardington 1½ miles east of Wantage and south of the A417
Tel. 023 588 273

The Viscount Chelsea

Open one Sunday and Monday per year, and by appointment

Marndhill was a Victorian rectory; yew trees were the overriding feature, leaving the flower garden to one side and the lawns in front of the house as also-rans. Since Lord and Lady Chelsea arrived Marndhill has lost much of its somewhat claustrophobic atmosphere and gained considerably in variety and brightness without losing its air of establishment. Reformation began in front of the house where the plants include a number of tender and exotic varieties: *Abutilon vitifolium*; *Carpenteria californica*, *Fremontodendron californicum*, various clematis and hebes. Lawns on this main south-facing garden front of the house are on two levels, divided by a balustraded brick wall. A central path with a Grey Border leads down steps to the lower lawn. Only standard 'Iceberg' roses stand out in this border from the spread of alchemilla, potentilla, lavender and other low-foliage plants but tall columnar yews beside the balustrade provide a striking contrast. Below the brick wall the steps are flanked by the main herbaceous border; beyond the Croquet Lawn stretches south towards the bottom of the garden. To one side of the lawn the Victorian summerhouse is now hung with wisteria, and there are philadelphus along the edge of the summerhouse lawn in anticipation of the splendid group at its far end, providing a wonderful concentration of flower and scent beside an old walnut tree. The lawn is kept simple, trees and shrubs extended in places into island beds of viburnum and acers with a delightful variegated strawberry as ground-cover. At the bottom of this lawn an overgrown area has recently been reclaimed and planted with a selection of standard trees: a metasequoia, a ginkgo, acers, robinias, and most spectacular, a *Gleditsia* 'Sunburst'.

Lady Chelsea who was responsible for the recreation of the garden before her sudden death in 1984 made the old Orchard and Kitchen Garden to the east of the house part of the picture, and not purely productive. It is now divided by a long path running east–west flanked by éspalier apple trees with clematis trained into them. The trees are underplanted in cottage-garden style with wallflowers, peonies, roses, pinks and pansies. At a central sundial a cross-path leads towards the front of the house. Vegetables are confined to three of the squares, and in the fourth the apples and cherries of the old orchard have been joined by a variegated acer, a golden cut-leaf elder, with lilacs and philadelphus along the north-facing lower edge in front of a dense bank of yews. Beyond the yews, beneath the south-east corner of the house is Lady Chelsea's conservatory, with a semi-circle of shrub roses planted to its east as a foil to the background of evergreen yews.

On the far side of the Vegetable Garden from the house a swimming pool has been incorporated with unusual easc into the garden scheme. The steps up to the pool are flanked by silver weeping pears. On the garden side veiling white trelliswork is echoed in the summerhouse at one end; the other side of the pool is sheltered by Marndhill's brick boundary wall. The whole effect shows how easily an often intrusive garden feature can be accommodated.

To the south of the pool a long shrub border along the west-facing boundary wall leads to a group of camellias. Sadly ceanothus and other wall plants were among many that were badly hit during the winter of 1981–2. Major new planting schemes have been begun, partly to make up for these losses and also to bring more autumn colour to the garden. In much of their original planning of alterations and additions to the garden such as the siting of the swimming pool, the Herb Garden and the Grey Border, Lord and Lady Chelsea were greatly helped by Peter Coats. Now, in place of its disjointed appearance, Marndhill has a sense of ease and oneness appropriate to an old rectory garden, with its view of the church spire.

THE MILL HOUSE

In Sutton Courtenay, off the B4016, south of Abingdon and the A415
Tel. 02358 2219

Mrs Jane Stevens

Open on selected Sundays in summer, and by appointment

For most of the year the garden at the Mill House is idyllic: two tree-shaded islands, totalling about eight acres, between the River Thames flowing lazily around the northern edge and to the south, the stream originally diverted from the Thames to feed the old mill. For the month of March parts of the garden are flooded, a fact which has partly dictated the 'meadow' style of much of the gardens.

For a period before the First World War the house was owned by H. H. and Margot Asquith before he became the Liberal Prime Minister and, in 1925, was made Earl of Oxford and Asquith. They also owned The Wharf, the house next door. In his introduction to Margot Asquith's autobiography, their grandson, the Hon. Mark Bonham Carter, recalls holidays at the Mill House and 'a charming walled garden full of hollyhocks and roses, a private bridge over the Thames, and a pair of resident kingfishers'. Mrs Stevens has been here since 1981 but the outstanding garden was the work of her predecessors, Colonel and Mrs Peter Laycock, who lived at the Mill House for twenty-five years. They planted nearly all the trees and shrubs though some of the mature trees do date from when the islands were originally cleared. They also laid out the formal Rose Garden beneath the west-facing front of the house, and the lawn and long Mixed Border beneath the perimeter wall on its east side. Mrs Stevens has added new features herself, until 1983 with the help of Thomas Berens, the extremely capable and equally enthusiastic young gardener from the Laycocks' days.

The focal point of the gardens is the large millpond, to the north of the house, through which the stream flows. An enormous 'Kiftsgate' rose cascades from the old mill building down to the water at one end while lesser musk and rambler roses surround the pond's low retaining wall. Behind the 'Kiftsgate' curtain the old buildings of the mill have been made into a small Courtyard Garden with another, smaller

333

'Kiftsgate' on the back wall. In the middle *Prunus* 'Shirofugen' covers the whole courtyard with an umberella of pink flowers in May. There are also *Hydrangea* 'White Wave', hostas and fuchsias, with a statue standing in front of an effective reflecting mirror.

The lawn and garden to the east of the house are safe from flooding. The main feature here is the long mixed shrub and herbaceous border, beneath the perimeter wall, which contains an extensive variety of well-grouped plants. Two old yew trees command the lawn. Closer to the house is a small box parterre filled with herbs, fuchsias and purple wall-flowers, a very pleasant contrast; alongside this are a group of lilacs. At the far end of the lawn pleached limes make a fine screen along the wall built out from the house.

From the mill a path leads west between yew hedges to the main part of one island which stretches from the west around the north side of the pond to another small dividing stream. A striking combination of plants grows to one side of the yew walk, backed by a yew hedge: the pink rose 'Kathleen Ferrier' has been placed in front of *Aralia elata* 'Aureovarie-gata' and *Hydrangea aspera*. Ornamental trees and shrubs are planted throughout the hummocky ground of the island – sorbus, robinia, davidia, *Sophora japonica* and *Acer griseum* – as well as a number of shrub roses. The only feature which brings a note of formality is an avenue of malus leading to the summerhouse, hidden away in the far north-west corner and decorated with clematis, *Cytisus battandieri* and *Actinidia kolomikta*, which Mrs Stevens has planted. In front are more roses.

On the pond's north side a bridge swathed in wisteria surmounts the high brick wall out of which water gushes again from a gargoyle into the small stream dividing the two islands. Along the second island's millstream bank to the east of the pond Colonel Laycock planted willows and metasequoias, a wonderful combination, with other interesting trees such as the cut-leaf alder. There are three large metasequoias at the top of the mill stream close to the pond, and among the mature trees are two enormous horse chestnuts. In all directions across this island there are open views between the trees and shrubs. The spring bulbs that carpet much of the grass are followed later in the year by virburnums, cornus and roses, while *Parrotia persica* planted beneath silver birch is a most effective combination, particularly in autumn and winter. On the far north side of the island, towards the Thames, two weeping beech have been trained into an arch over the path leading to an avenue of green and golden yews; beyond this is a spring corner of malus and cherries. At the eastern extremity the island ends where the millstream flows back into the Thames.

The rambling, natural appearance of the Mill House gardens lend it a relaxed and friendly atmosphere, water so much a part of its design that the difficulties it creates slide past the visitor almost unnoticed. Few people could fail to feel affection for the Mill House and Mrs Stevens is maintaining that tradition with devotion and hard work.

PUSEY HOUSE

12 miles west of Oxford and 5 miles east of Faringdon, ½ mile south of the A420
Tel. 036 787 222

Mr and Mrs Michael Hornby

Open on Wednesday, Thursday and Sunday afternoon in April and May, and every afternoon except Monday and Friday from June to October inclusive

---

When Mr and Mrs Hornby bought Pusey House in 1935 the eighteenth-century landscape which stretched away from the south front was overgrown and partially obscured by dense, evergreen Victorian shrubberies. Since then they have sympathetically and expertly cleared, restored and added to the garden to produce a rare harmony between the old-established setting and twentieth-century plantsmanship and design. The setting is indeed enviable: the south front of the grey stone house, built in 1748, looks across a wide terrace to a huge lawn sloping down to the lake which stretches from east to west through the middle of the garden. On the other, south side of the lake lawn rises gently between trees to the ha-ha and the far view of the Downs. Unlike many twentieth-century gardens, which are characterized by their division by hedges and walls into a series of enclosures, Pusey has never lost its confident, large-scale openness which was such a hallmark of eighteenth-century landscapes. Its outstanding quality is the fluid equilibrium between the detail and the overall picture.

A number of mature trees have provided the framework for Mr and Mrs Hornby's planting in certain areas of the garden, particularly on the far side of the lake, on either side of the lawn. A huge copper beech dominates the small island and nearby an Oriental plane spreads its wide canopy over the water, close to the eighteenth-century white Chinese bridge which crosses the lake near this east end. At the west end of the lake is a London plane of equally grand proportions; also of note is the taxodium towards the south-east corner of the shrubberies where the lake curves to the south.

Having cleared the monotonous Victorian evergreens, Mr and Mrs Hornby have steadily replanted these shrubberies with a large variety of flowering and ornamental trees and shrubs: cornus, of which a number of varieties are especially good throughout the gardens, acers, cercidiphyllums, magnolias, sorbus, prunus and many others, which combine to give colour of flower or foliage throughout much of the year. To the east of the Chinese bridge are the Water Gardens, where numerous damp-loving plants thrive along the lakeside. As one moves from the shrubberies to the Water Gardens and on from the Chinese bridge to the shrub Rose Garden which lies towards the house, the variety of planting at Pusey becomes evident. Considering that other than round the lake the soil is light, alkaline and free-draining, the scope is remarkable.

When the Hornbys came to Pusey there was only a rough grass bank between the terrace in front of the house and the sloping lawn. In 1936 they commissioned Geoffrey Jellicoe to redesign this area, which he did to great effect. The terrace and lawn are now divided by a stone wall broken in the middle by stone steps of majestic width. The south-facing wall and border in front of it support a host of interesting plants: *Osmanthus delavayi*, *Carpentaria californica* and *Rubus* 'Tridel', as well as a number of jasmines, vines, clematis and abutilons.

To the west of the house the main herbaceous border, one of Pusey's most memorable features, curves gently for a hundred yards to the classical temple at the far end. The border is backed by a ten-foot-high wall of Cotswold stone; its proportions and the balanced blending of plants make the border a spectacular sight in full flower. It is a measure of Mr and Mrs Hornby's work at Pusey that when they bought the house there was no border, only a huge, overgrown box hedge which completely obscured the wall.

Elegant wrought-iron gates break the wall about halfway along and open on to a path, between double herbaceous borders, which leads to the garden's public entrance, north-west of the house. Further along the main border towards the temple a smaller arched opening leads into Lady Emily's Garden, a secluded enclosure surrounded by brick walls. In 1822 Lady Emily Herbert married Philip Pusey, whose younger brother Edward was one of the great religious figures of the nineteenth century; he became Canon of Christ Church and one of the leaders of the Oxford Movement. Lady Emily's little garden is formally laid out in a pattern of eight beds round a central sundial, divided by flagged paths. In the central four beds are hybrid tea roses, 'Violinista Costa'; irises and peonies mix with smaller plants in the outer four. As one might expect, the brick walls are enlivened with a rich variety of climbing and wall plants; clematis, roses, ceanothus, *Hydrangea sargentiana*, *Magnolia soulangiana* 'Alba Superba' and a huge *Cydonia japonica*, to name but a few.

From the temple the view across the lake, past low water-side plants and the over-hanging mature trees to the Chinese bridge is one of the most rewarding at Pusey. A path leads from the temple into open beech wood, judiciously thinned and now underplanted – as are all the open glades in the shrubberies – with a carpet of daffodils, bluebells and other spring bulbs. As from the east shrubberies, so from this south-west part of the garden one emerges on to the central swathe of grass leading up to the ha-ha with views in the one direction to the house, framed by green and copper beech, and in the other away to the distant hills.

In his book *Oxford Apostles* Geoffrey Faber described Pusey: '. . . standing where manor house has followed manor house for a thousand years, looking over water and trees and the miles of Pusey land to the unchanged outline of the downs, house and church and tiny village keeping company together as they had done for centuries. . .' Visiting Pusey today there is still that feeling of established continuity which he wrote about. The gardens which Mr and Mrs Hornby have created both fit in with its timeless framework and have added a new, enriching dimension. The twenty-odd acres are maintained by four gardeners to a standard which matches the garden's horticultural interest.

ROUSHAM HOUSE

12 miles north of Oxford, east of the A423 at Hopcrofts Holt Hotel.
Tel. 0869 47110
Charles Cottrell-Dormer Esq.

Open daily

The garden at Rousham House is of immense historical importance in that it is the only work of William Kent to have survived unscathed by later eighteenth- or nineteenth-century alterations. It is sad that we cannot enjoy comparisons with his other achievements as did his contemporary Horace Walpole, who described Rousham as Kent's 'most engaging work'. At the time Rousham was a revolutionary novelty amid the formality of the seventeenth century and, with a small number of contemporary gardens, laid the foundations for the landscape movement which followed and dominated garden design for over a century.

Rousham House was originally built of local Oxford stone by Sir Robert Dormer in 1635, and its appearance was typically late Jacobean. At the beginning of the eighteenth century Charles Bridgeman, who also worked at Kensington Palace, Stowe and Claremont, was employed to lay out the gardens and it was his designs, still predominantly formal, which Kent was to alter and expand. It was Bridgeman's work that Horace Walpole mentioned in a letter of 1728 when he described Rousham as 'the prettiest place for water-falls, jetts, ponds inclosed with beautiful scenes of green and hanging wood, that ever I saw'. The gardens lay to the north of the house, beyond Bridgeman's bowling green, where the ground drops to the River Cherwell, first flowing south and then round in a lazy curve to the east.

It is a reflection of Kent's extraordinary all-round ability that he was originally employed as an architect to enlarge the house, and redesign and redecorate the interiors by General James Dormer. Only afterwards did he turn his attention to the gardens, drawing up a plan in 1738 to soften Bridgeman's terraces and walks with serpentine rather than straight lines, and to enhance them with statues, buildings and other ornaments.

Notes of order were clearly retained by Kent, particularly in the way in which he planned the gardens to be seen by taking a set route so that the paths and features were revealed in a carefully conceived manner. Kent highlighted the view from the house across the bowling green with a wonderful group of a lion and horse by Peter Scheemakers, and beyond landscaped the ground to slope down to the river. From the north-west corner of the bowling green Kent's path into the woodland leads off down the sloping ground. A stone statue by Scheemakers of a Dying Gladiator reclines on a terrace from where views extend north across the river.

Beyond, to the west, is Venus's Vale, a small valley enclosed by trees where cascades feed a large octagonal pool. The upper cascade supports a lead statue of Venus and originally there were two more ponds above here. From the valley a path winds through the woodland along the course of a serpentine rill laid by Kent. At the far end is a Doric temple and from here the path leads east, downhill, to the statue of Apollo. Again, Kent carefully planned the views from here, looking north along the river to Heyford Bridge, transforming the old mill and building the sham ruin or 'eyecatcher' on the skyline.

From the statue of Apollo the path begins a return journey through the woodland along the Long Walk. At the far end one of Kent's most masterly additions to the gardens is revealed, the arcade with seven pediments which he built beneath the terrace with the Dying Gladiator and which is entirely invisible when passing along the terrace above; the surprise of its appearance as one returns is exactly as Kent intended. He called the terrace and arcade Praeneste. Beyond Praeneste, just above the river which is now flowing east, is the 'theatre' which Bridgeman made, and two lead statues of satyrs by Jan van Nost. From this slope one continues east to Kent's Pyramid and into the Walled Gardens on the east of the house, or back by a winding path to the north-east corner of the bowling green.

The red-brick Walled Gardens are in complete contrast to Kent's wooded landscape and contain many impressive features. A long herbaceous border stretches along the south side of the largest walled garden and is broken by a path leading south into the small formal Rose Garden, where beds of hybrid tea roses are enclosed by low box-hedging. This little garden is given considerable charm by the old circular pigeon house, built of stone with a steep tiled roof, and surmounted by a cupola dated 1685.

Today the significance of Kent's work at Rousham is disguised by the simplicity of its harmony between winding paths, ponds and cascades, statues and buildings. Indeed, to many people who are used to gardens created in the nineteenth and twentieth century it is not so much garden as landscaped woodland. And yet a contemporary description of Kent's 1738 plan clearly pinpoints the importance of his work here, both in terms of its own achievement and of the effect it was to have on garden design for the rest of the eighteenth century. It was 'a rarity, an organic yet disciplined design, applying order loosely, yet lucidly, to a slice of English country, achieving an effect crystalling Nature'.

YORKSHIRE AND
THE EAST MIDLANDS

Derbyshire
Leicestershire
Lincolnshire
Nottinghamshire
Yorkshire

YORKSHIRE AND THE EAST MIDLANDS

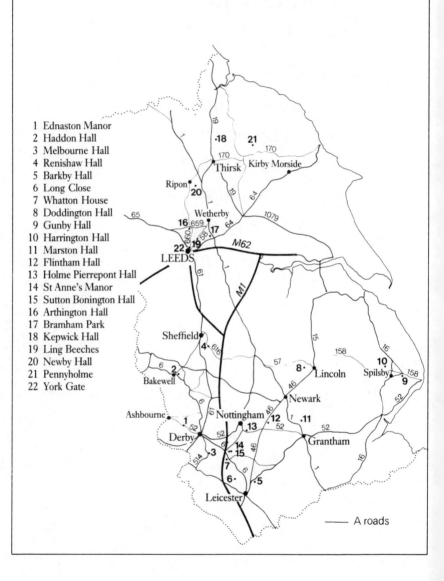

1 Ednaston Manor
2 Haddon Hall
3 Melbourne Hall
4 Renishaw Hall
5 Barkby Hall
6 Long Close
7 Whatton House
8 Doddington Hall
9 Gunby Hall
10 Harrington Hall
11 Marston Hall
12 Flintham Hall
13 Holme Pierrepont Hall
14 St Anne's Manor
15 Sutton Bonington Hall
16 Arthington Hall
17 Bramham Park
18 Kepwick Hall
19 Ling Beeches
20 Newby Hall
21 Pennyholme
22 York Gate

— A roads

DERBYSHIRE

EDNASTON MANOR

Near Brailsford, off the A52 between Derby and Ashbourne
Tel. 033 528 325
L. V. Pickering, Esq.

Open daily except Saturday and Sunday from Easter to September inclusive

---

Ednaston Manor is not one of Lutyens' largest houses, but the symmetry of its proportions, and the fine detail of its construction, such as the small, specially-made bricks, made it one of the last generation of British country houses created with an air of establishment and permanence. The work was carried out between 1913 and 1919, with a break in construction during the First World War, but by the time Lutyens had finished at Ednaston he had built a complete country-house unit in the style of the eighteenth and nineteenth centuries, something rarely done since: the house, the garden framework, the terrace and ha-ha look out on to a new park with, at the end of a new avenue, a model farm in the same style as the house. The farm buildings have recently been converted into cottages.

Ednaston was built for W. G. Player, son of the tobacco empire's founder, and no doubt the formal appearance of house and garden was very much to his own taste. Since 1948 a lot of planting was done by Mr and Mrs Stephen Player, W.G.'s son and daughter-in-law; this has softened the formality of the house's appearance and the architectural aspect of the garden, but in a way which disguised their relative youth. Five years ago Mrs Player sold Ednaston to Mr and Mrs Pickering.

Ednaston Manor stands on an exposed hill at 560 feet above sea-level, so that the provision of shelter was obviously a vital part of the early garden planning. To the north and west Scots pines and Leyland cypress were planted and a yew hedge, which has grown to an unusual height; Stephen Player was particularly fond of very high hedges. The east façade of the house is the most severe; here Lutyens levelled the ground in front into a series of terraces with brick retaining walls and balustrades. On the west front of the house Lutyens planted three chestnut avenues extending from the three entrances to the semi-circular forecourt enclosed by brick walls. The avenues both reinforce the strong formality of this front and recall the *patte d'oies* of the seventeenth century. One of them flanks the drive, and the centre one eventually forms the south boundary of the woodland garden into which the third entrance leads. On the south front Lutyens made perhaps his most attractive addition to the gardens, a small terrace with summer-houses at either end and paths in herringbone patterns of brick dividing the square flowerbeds. Opposite the house the ha-ha divided the terrace from the park beyond.

Before her marriage Mrs Stephen Player was a Miss Loder of the well-known gardening family, and to her the garden at Ednaston was an exciting challenge. A group of four blue cedars were among the few trees planted between completion of Lutyens' work and her arrival. She and her husband steadily reduced the dominance of the chestnut avenues over the Woodland Garden with a series of large beds planted with trees and shrubs and low ground cover, greatly enhancing the vistas. Their planting, now filled out to maturity, includes extensive collections of many varieties: rhododendrons and azaleas – particularly the older mollis varieties and the scented yellow azalea – viburnums, acers, magnolias, shrub roses, and hydrangeas. The *Hydrangea pani-culatas*, with cones of creamy-white flowers, are especially good, as are the camellias which fill one of the beds. One of the most beguiling vistas lies between rhododendrons, azaleas and acers to a small paved square with a rustic seat between two columnar Irish yews and overhung by a *Magnolia sieboldii*.

There are some unexpected trees here, an area certainly not noted for its mildness: *Embothrium coccineum* and *Eucryphia nymanensis* are two – the latter surviving severe frost-damage in the winter of 1981–2 to flower triumphantly later in the year. Other good trees are *Fagus heterophylla laciniata*, the fern-leafed beech, a davidia and a metasequoia. Labels on the various trees which give the date of planting and thus reveal their often unusually rapid growth are of great interest to visitors.

Another feature of the woodland garden are the clematis and climbing roses trained into some of the trees. In one place a *Clematis montana* covers a blue cedar, but most spectacular is the vigorous climbing rose, given to Mrs Player by Mrs Cavendish from Holker Hall in Cumbria. Uncertain of the rose's name they decided to call it the 'Ednaston' rose. The curving walls of the entrance courtyard and the west and south fronts of the house are now draped in climbing roses, and clematis. Tucked away in a sheltered corner on the outside of the south-west wall of the courtyard, *Cytisus battandieri* has defied both the often unwelcoming climate and the exuberant clematis and honeysuckle with which it competes. The summerhouses, too, bear roses and clematis, and on the main south front facing them the house also supports a jasmine and two *Carpentaria californica*. Mrs Player replaced bedding plants in the square terrace beds with far more interesting small shrubs and miniature flowers – China roses, potentilla, violas and pinks – a delightful contrast to the regimented patterns of the herringbone brick paths. The combination of Lutyens' original layout and the later planting makes this terrace one of the most successful areas of the gardens.

On the east front of the house *Actinidia kolomikta* mingles with clematis and roses and from their top level, paved with Derbyshire Hopton stone, the terraces descend with lawns and formal yew hedges. An uncharacteristic lapse in the quality of the work caused one of the main retaining walls partially to collapse recently; it has been rebuilt by the Pickerings and the divisions of the lawns have been reduced. Mrs Player planted shrub roses, agapanthus and lilies here in strong colour groups, contrasting with the mixed borders in other places around the lawns. This part of the garden descends to the vegetable garden; the plots were originally all enclosed with box hedges, but now the central path is flanked by borders of old-fashioned and shrub roses.

To one side of this east garden an old orchard has been mostly replaced with more ornamental trees; *Magnolia watsonii*, the strongly-scented variety with hanging flowers, is one of a number of magnolias. There is also a Rock Garden; the narrow area is enclosed by beech hedges. It is the least intensely planted area of the garden and, cut off by the hedges, it remains as it was originally intended, a separate section belonging to the old farmhouse. It embodies the sympathetic treatment given to Lutyens' strong lines by gardeners who understand both how to preserve and how to temper.

HADDON HALL

5 miles south-east of Bakewell off the A6
Tel. 0629 812 855
The Duke of Rutland

Open Monday to Saturday from April to September inclusive

Haddon seems to have drifted through centuries in an air of medieval antiquity. Parts of the surrounding wall, built under Royal License in the 1190s, still survive, but the low, castellated building on a wooded limestone hill above the Derbyshire Wye in the heart of the Peak District is an almost unique example of medieval building from the period between earlier castles built for defensive purposes and later country houses. Haddon was owned by the Vernon family for four hundred years, from whom it passed to the Manners by marriage in 1567. There are two courtyards and the present house was built up round these between the reigns of Edward III and Elizabeth I. In 1641 John Manners, who was living at Haddon, succeeded to the Earldom of Rutland, but by 1703, when a dukedom was conferred on the 9th Earl, the family was living at Belvoir Castle, always their main residence. Between 1701 and 1912 the house was not lived in at all and only maintained in a state of repair, though a series of terraced gardens was added in the seventeenth century. In 1912 the 9th Duke, while still the Marquess of Granby, returned to Haddon and began the extensive renovation which became a lifetime's devoted work; he restored the house and gardens to a status they had not enjoyed for over two hundred years.

The gardens are a series of seven spectacular terraces on the east and south sides of the house, descending to the banks of the Wye where it passes closest to the house. The three lowest terraces, below what were the Earl's apartments, may date from the mid-sixteenth century when the oriel windows were added to this range, but the main work of garden construction, including the larger upper terraces dates from the mid-seventeenth century.

This was a feat of engineering, achieved, of course, by manual labour. The drop from the main, Fountain Terrace, beneath the windows of the Long Gallery is almost vertical, calling for massive retaining walls and

346

supporting buttresses. The long balustrade extending from the corner of the house across the top of the Fountain Terrace and dividing it from the higher Bowling Alley Terrace was also added in the seventeenth century, as were the similar balustrades on either side of the central steps.

The highest level of the garden, above the Bowling Alley Terrace, was originally a narrow avenue of sycamores called Dorothy Vernon's Walk. Some old houses have their ghosts; others have their heroines, and Dorothy Vernon was Haddon's. Daughter of Sir George Vernon (nicknamed 'King of the Peak', who lived at Haddon between 1517 and 1567), she is reputed to have eloped with John Manners during her sister's wedding. She escaped to the narrow pack-horse bridge across the Wye – thereafter called Dorothy Vernon's Bridge – where Manners was waiting with horses. Their subsequent marriage ensured that Haddon passed to the Manners family on the death of her father.

When the 9th Duke began his task of restoration the gardens had become uncontrollably overgrown. The sycamores in Dorothy Vernon's Walk were enormous; the yews on the Bowling Alley Terrace had grown from their neatly-clipped state into huge trees; the walls of the house and terrace were cloaked in ivy. In 1949, Christopher Hussey wrote in an article in *Country Life*: 'The late Duke, as part of his reconditioning of Haddon, decided to clear all away. The loss of picturesque atmosphere is no doubt considerable, but justified and prudent.' Today he might agree that the picturesque atmosphere has been restored, and that the roses which fill the garden and tumble from the walls are Haddon's perfect adornment. A number of the older climbing roses suffered badly in the winter of 1981–2, and there is concern about the development of rose-sickness in the soil, but in June and July the display is still superb.

The visitor's first view of the garden is from the Bowling Alley Terrace and thus the gardens are seen as always intended, from the top downwards. Immediately in front of Dorothy Vernon's Door on the east side of the house is a small Rose Garden, with hybrid tea varieties and the larger 'Honorine de Brabant' in the centre of the beds. The sycamores have gone from Dorothy Vernon's Walk along the top of the garden; in their place are borders of floribunda roses and herbaceous plants, with more climbers on the wall behind: 'Parkdirektor Riggers', 'Colonel Poole' and 'Kordesii Dortmund'. There are also two plants of one of Haddon's most treasured roses, the white 'Mary Manners' rose, named after the present Lady John Manners.

The old giant yews surrounding the lawn which fills the rest of the Bowling Alley Terrace have been replaced by clipped yews and beneath the wall along the top side is a long mixed herbaceous border with climbing roses on the wall, including an old plant of the yellow 'La Reve', and 'Excelsa'.

From the Bowling Alley Terrace the wide flight of balustraded steps lead down to the Fountain Terrace, with its central pool and fountain surrounded by lawn. Roses again dominate the planting but are mixed here to great effect, as they are on the walls of the house, with many clematis; Clematis 'Mrs Cholmondeley', C. Lazurstorn and C. Henryii on the house and C. jackmanii superba on the balustrade. The avenue of cherries along the west side of the terrace has slightly outgrown its station; its future is under review.

It is only from the three lower terraces below the Fountain Terrace that the enormous proportions of the retaining walls and sloping buttresses can be fully appreciated. The buttresses are covered for their whole height in places by climbers – 'New Dawn', 'Boursault Rambler Amadis', 'Mme Gregoire Staechelin', 'Conrad F. Meyer' and 'Caroline Testout' – with borders of peonies and buddleias between them. The only ancient yew which has been allowed to remain in the gardens is in the middle of these terraces, a staging post between the twentieth-century gardens and Haddon's medieval origins.

MELBOURNE HALL

In Melbourne, 8 miles south-east of Derby on the A514
Tel. 033 162 502
The Marquess of Lothian

Open daily

Like most extant gardens of their period, those laid out at Melbourne Hall by Thomas Coke between 1696 and 1725 owe their survival to neglect. On Coke's death Melbourne passed to the Lamb family who never used the house regularly. The sweeping hand of the eighteenth-century landscaping passed by and Melbourne declined undisturbed until Lord Walter Kerr and his wife, Lady Annabel Cowper, to whose family the house had passed through marriage with the Lambs, made it their home in 1906. Lord Walter carried out extensive restoration in the gardens, adding trees and shrubs, but without disturbing Coke's seventeenth-century design with its division into two conjoined areas.

Coke's grandfather, Sir John, had settled at Melbourne in 1629. His gardens consisted of a terrace on the east front leading down to a rectangular kitchen garden, and beyond that a similar rectangle divided by canals filled from a nearby stream. His son, Captain Coke, extended the terrace as far as the original boundary wall, and built the dovecote to the north-east of the house. When Thomas Coke inherited Melbourne he had already travelled extensively in Holland and France. Taking a keen interest in architecture and garden design, he was strongly influenced by the work of André le Nôtre. Among the earliest additions were the two walks parallel to the yew hedges and brick walls on either side of the old East Garden, broken at the descending levels by flights of steps. One of the great features of the Melbourne gardens is a yew tunnel on the outside of the south wall, most of which probably dates from before Thomas Coke's time; it was originally planted 100 yards long and later extended to its present length of nearly 200 yards. At the far, eastern, end, Coke placed a circular pool and fountain, with an identical pool at the bottom of the walk outside the north wall.

In 1704 Coke obtained the leasehold of Melbourne by Act of Parliament, and from then on felt free to develop the gardens as he wished. His grandfather's rectangular kitchen garden beyond the East Garden was replaced with parterres descending the terraces and the canals in the lower part of the garden were replaced with the Great Basin. On the far side of the Great Basin the view from the house down the centre of the garden was closed off with the domed and highly decorative Birdcage Arbour, made by Robert Bakewell. Bakewell learnt his trade from Jean Tijou, the unquestioned master of wrought-iron work; although the arbour was one of Bakewell's earliest works it is his masterpiece, and is unrivalled in England.

After these alterations had been completed Coke consulted George London and Henry Wise, the leading garden designers of his day, and as a result ordered William Cooke to draw up plans to expand the gardens to the south. The form of the new garden was partly dictated by the uneven, wooded ground and showed some sympathy with the ideas of Addison and Switzer, who were combining the formality of le Nôtre's work with a more natural style anticipating the landscapes of the eighteenth century.

A series of allées flanked by hedges of beech and hornbeam were laid out from a line of three circular pools with fountains along one edge of the old East Garden and from the raised grass plateau at its southern end. Crow Walk is the main axis; from the Birdcage Arbour one sees across the central of the three pools to the Four Seasons urn on the plateau. This urn is the most notable of all the statues and ornaments which Jan van Nost, the master-craftsman of lead work, made for these gardens and is reckoned among his best pieces. Lead figures of boys surmount the fountains in the various pools. Van Nost also made four pairs of *amorini*, or winged boys, and four cupids, set in bays in the yew hedges of the East Garden; the north and south walks there lead to life-size figures of Perseus and Andromeda also set in yew bays. In the centre of the East Garden is the figure of Mercury and higher up on the lawns two kneeling slaves support globes; otherwise the lawns are broken only by the clipped domes of evergreens and pairs of trees, such as catalpas, magnolias and young copper beeches. The statues reinforce the twin themes of motion and repose found throughout the gardens: the mass of the Great Basin and the figure of Perseus contrasting with the restlessness of the fountains and Andromeda, the headlong vista of Crow Walk at length arrested by the Four Seasons urn.

Although most of the hedges in the South Garden have had to be restored or re-planted the old trees at Melbourne have grown to impressive maturity, in particular the beech and copper beech by one of the paths leading to the Four Seasons urn, and the plane and fern-leafed beech which spread above one of the banks beyond the yew tunnel. The restoration work at Melbourne begun by Lord Walter Kerr was continued by the Marquis of Lothian's mother, Mrs Kerr, who died in 1980, and it is as much thanks to them as well as to the longevity of the original plantings, that this seventeenth-century formal garden has survived against the odds of history.

RENISHAW HALL

Near Eckington, 7 miles south-east of Sheffield on the A616, and 3 miles west of the M1 (Junction 30)
Tel. 0346 432 042

Mr and Mrs Reresby Sitwell

Visitors by written appointment

Most of Sir George Sitwell's life was spent devising and expounding theories and innovations, and researching a select group of mainly obscure subjects in which his interest was fanatical. He will be best remembered for his eccentricity as recounted in the volumes of his elder son Osbert's autobiography *Left Hand, Right Hand*. Few of his projects ever got further than the drawing-board, but one that did, with spectacular success, was the Italian-style gardens at Renishaw Hall. Sir George's knowledge of gardens, and in particular of Italian gardens, was prodigious. Between the end of the nineteenth century and the 1930s, when he left England to spend most of each year at Montegufoni, his enormous castle near Florence, he applied his knowledge and flair to make Renishaw what his elder grandson has described as 'an oasis in an industrial wasteland'.

The original H-shaped stone house was built by the first George Sitwell of Renishaw in 1625. At the end of the eighteenth century substantial additions by Sir Sitwell Sitwell brought the house to its present size. Sir Sitwell bred racehorses, and kept his own pack of harriers; as a result he felt a need to build the outstanding stable block to the west of the house. He also employed the Rev. Christopher Alderson, rector of Eckington, to landscape the park (Alderson later worked for Queen Charlotte, at Frogmore in Windsor Great Park).

Family fortunes declined during the nineteenth century, and Sir George was brought up in a restrictive atmosphere. His own extremes of meanness and extravagance revealed the conflicting influences of his upbringing and his free-spending ancestors, of whom he was acutely aware. The Renishaw garden was one of his extravagances. In many ways the site was well-suited to an Italian-style garden. The house set on top of a hill with ground sloping to the south; the well-wooded surroundings concealing most of the nineteenth-century industrial landscape with which Renishaw was by then enclosed. The landscape-architect William Milner helped with the planting of trees on the south slope below the gardens. At the foot of this Sir George planned a lake – seventeen acres in size – and dug by hundreds of unemployed men from his Scarborough constituency.

Apart from Milner's advice just mentioned, the conception and creation of the gardens were Sir George's alone. He planned them as a series of enclosures on the different levels to which they were terraced. Today the yews he planted to divide and surround the various areas have grown into mature hedges that are an intrinsic part of the gardens' character, with tall pyramids of yew at the end of each hedge. Between the pyramids openings for flights of stone steps lead through the gardens and from one level to another. The large square of the gardens is bordered by a wood to the east and a brick retaining wall to the west, above which the garden continues.

The feature which more than any other complements the architectural setting of yew hedges and lawns, and enhances its atmosphere, is the collection of statues and ornaments which Sir George brought to the gardens from Italy. Among the statues are three superb pairs of stone figures. Neptune and Diana, reputedly by Caligari, are the most treasured. They stand either side of the central stone steps leading down from the lawn in front of the house to the main terrace walk and border; the steps extend across the garden to the lawn round the swimming pool. To the east, Warrior and Amazon stand sentinel by the gate into the wood. Here the present owners have recently created a new woodland walk that embraces two fine sweet chestnuts, a handsome Turkey oak and another magnificent beech, all now set around with many interesting new shrubs. Again, the yews have gone from their mound and many smaller plants, dwarf conifers and flowering shrubs have taken their place.

Each side of the circular steps descending from the garden to the park are the Giants. The positioning of these two figures, gazing out from the edge of the gardens was clear evidence of Sir George's strongly held belief, discussed at length in his essay, 'On the Making of Gardens', that a vital part of a garden's character was dictated by its relationship with the surrounding landscape: 'It is only a part of the garden which lies within the boundary walls, and a great scheme planned for dull or commonplace surroundings is a faulty conception, as it were to propose to build half a house or to paint half a picture . . .; it is Nature which should call the tune, and the melody is to be found in the prospect of blue hill or shimmering lake, or mystery-haunted plain, in the aerial (*sic*) perspective of great trees beyond the boundary, in the green cliffs of leafy woodland which wall us in on either hand.'

Osbert Sitwell inherited Renishaw and lived there until he, too, left England to spend the last years of his life at Montegufoni. Despite his life-long series of differences with his father, Osbert knew that Sir George's gardens were a unique creation. He made no alterations, and since Osbert's nephew Reresby and his wife have been at Renishaw the few that they have made have been only to remove labour-intensive borders and flowerbeds, and to simplify some of the planting with shrubs. The borders along the hedges flanking the main lawn have been kept, as has the main mixed shrub border, along the retaining wall beneath Diana and Neptune, at its peak in late summer. In 1967 Reresby Sitwell enhanced the main view of the gardens from the house by the addition of a fountain jet in the swimming pool. The house itself has ceanothus, climbing roses and a climbing hydrangea trained on its walls.

On either side of the main central lawn are two smaller lawns, reached between the customary yew pyramids. Central in these lawns are the

First and Second Candles, a pair of Veronese marble fountains. Beyond the smaller lawn to the right is a grass slope which, halfway along the garden to the south, joins the main retaining wall; above to the west is the higher, more informal part of the gardens. Along the top of the terrace a lime avenue is full of daffodils in the spring.

As well as a number of rhododendrons there is also an immense sessile oak, planted in 1815 to commemorate the Battle of Waterloo, *Metasequoia glyptostroboides*, *Ginkgo biloba*, *Liriodendron tulipifera* and *Davidia involucrata*. Most striking of all is the free-standing *Cytisus battandieri*, raised from seed from one of the two such plants trained against the walls of the house. The main feature of this area, however, is the Gothic Temple which, unlike the Italian ornaments, is built of the same stone as the house and echoes its castellated architecture. The one ornament which Sir Osbert brought to the gardens has recently been re-sited at the end of the lime avenue: a statue, raised on a large pedestal of 'Fame blowing the praises of English poets'.

Around the other lawn to the east is the predominantly white Rose Garden, reduced from its original size. The garden further to the east of the house is dominated by a marvellous mature fern-leafed beech, probably planted by Sir Sitwell Sitwell, as was the oak on a raised grass platform nearby, beneath which his most famous racehorse, Clinker, is buried. Also on the east side is the Secret Garden, completely enclosed by yew hedges and entered by a narrow flight of steps. It is filled with the foliage and seasonal flowers of Ponticum rhododendrons round three flowering trees: *Catalpa bignonioides*, *Paulownia tomentosa* and a larger *Davidia involucrata*.

Below the Secret Garden, on the same level as the swimming pool, is the Water Garden, Sir George's last addition and completed after he had left for Italy (he returned once a year to review developments). The design of the Water Garden is unique; a narrow causeway crossing the formal square canal to a yew-enclosed island planted with shrub roses but dominated by two *Eucryphia glutinosa*, possibly Renishaw's finest flowering trees, proving that the climate is milder than might be expected in north-east Derbyshire.

On the far side of the swimming pool is the Buttress Garden, taking its name from the western buttressed retaining wall. In the border below it are euphorbia, berberis and rugosa roses, while other roses tumble over the wall from the terrace, where they are planted with philadelphus and buddleias.

In the summer the soft colours of the borders that Sir George insisted upon link the parts of the garden as the lawns and hedges do throughout the year. Spacious in some places and intimate in others, the gardens at

353

Renishaw achieve a diversity within their overall style and formality that heightens the visitor's appreciation of their design, and of the spirit they represent. They combine with the long, castellated façade of the house in a manner which is unforgettably evocative.

LEICESTERSHIRE

BARKBY HALL

North-east of Leicester off the A46
Tel. 0533 692 247
Mrs Peacock Pochin

Open one Sunday per year, and by appointment

Barkby has been a family home since the fifteenth century. Since Mrs Pochin and her late husband came here in 1973 she has successfully improved its garden from the typically late Victorian or Edwardian regimented and labour-intensive flowerbeds, most of them filled with bedding plants, to one of adventurous design with both interesting and evocative planting.

The severe architecture of the large Regency house is softened at one point by a 'Cecile Brunner' rose on the wall, and the first lawn of the mostly flat site reveals the careful planning that has gone into relating the garden to its setting – the park on one side of the house, the old walls and the village church beyond one of them. Mrs Pochin has added a number of trees to the park, including fastigiate oaks, golden poplars, a copper beech and other specimen trees, and this simple style of standard trees has been extended on to the lawn, where there are many fine modern cultivars: a selection of prunus, weeping copper beech, the weeping aspen, *Populus tremula pendula*, *Betula jacquemontii* with its peeling bark, a liquidambar and *Sorbus cashmiriana*.

Most of the garden stretches away from this lawn to the north, with the far areas subtly concealed. The first part of the main garden has the style of a traditional flower garden with roses in beds and trained over arches, and closely-grouped irises of mauve and blue, white and yellow. Smaller plants bring colour at other times – purple aubretia is followed

355

by blue campanulas, and also in the spring there is a yellow violet, which
Mrs Pochin collected from Switzerland. The main lawn, continuing to
the north and east, is broken by many island beds, some designed for
autumn interest; low shrubs such as *Daphne cneorum* and prostrate
conifers contrast with prominently planted trees – *Gleditsia triacanthus*
'Sunburst' and the similar *Robinia pseudoacacia* 'Frisia'.

Wrought-iron gates lead east into the Woodland Garden, a total
contrast to most of the border planting. Here there are rhododendrons
and azaleas beneath the mature woodland trees, with small daffodils and
trilliums among the spring flowers, all informally planted. On the site of
an old orangery Mrs Pochin has made another Rose Garden, with
lavender surrounding the central twelfth-century font. From here one
can look across to other parts of the garden – the heather bed
interspersed with columnar dwarf conifers, and the herbaceous border,
along the kitchen garden wall covered with climbing roses, that includes
a summerhouse with brick pillars and sloping slate roof. The border
continues round a corner in the wall and merges into shrubs: hibiscus,
elaeagnus and potentilla; the bell-shaped yellow flowers of *Clematis
orientalis* on the wall blend ideally with the blue of a ceanothus. In front
of the large greenhouse low, grey-leaved plants surround roses and
distinctive purple-leafed shrubs, and at the far northern end of the
garden is the old-fashioned Rose Garden: beds of old shrub roses
forming a rectangle round a central lawn, with smaller beds of lavender
and a sundial.

The whole of this main area of the garden has the advantage of being
surrounded by old brick walls. The Walled Gardens behind the
greenhouse are mainly given over to flowers for cutting, but the old
Vinery and Peach House contain impressive displays of cool-house
plants: camellias, fuchsias, *Lilium auratum* and *L. speciosum*. Towards
the Spring Garden a revolving summerhouse has been replaced by a
semi-circular stone seat backed by a yew hedge and the mass of a copper
beech.

As the quantity of plants and labour-intensive nature of much of the
garden would suggest, there are two gardeners, and a head gardener
who shares Mrs Pochin's particular interest in Barkby's specialist
plants. It is a happy coincidence that he is one of four members of a
family working for Mrs Pochin who rejoice in the name of Flowers.

LONG CLOSE

In Woodhouse Eaves, south of Loughborough, off the B591 between the A6
and the M1 (Junctions 22 and 23)
Tel. 0509 890 376
Mrs George Johnson

Open one or two Sundays per year, and by appointment

When Mrs Johnson and her husband bought Long Close in 1949 the
garden had been neglected for ten years, but steady restoration revealed
both the excellent framework and the potential their predecessor,
Colonel Gerald Heygate, had left. Colonel Heygate bought Long Close
in 1925 and immediately expanded the garden beyond its existing size to
five acres. He made the four terraces beyond the Irish yews marking the
original boundary of the garden, and cleared and planted the further
new area, retaining many of the mature trees around the perimeters. His
mark has been most clearly left in the large banks of various rhododendrons stretching down one side of the garden, including many different
hybrids and specie plants. His remarkable knowledge of these was
revealed when he visited the house long afterwards: standing with the
Johnsons at the top of the garden he named from memory every
rhododendron in the garden in succession from the top. Taking
advantage of the lime-free loam the Johnsons built on Coloney Heygate's foundations, and the garden now contains an outstanding collection of plants, mainly trees and shrubs.

The garden follows a natural pattern from the more formally planned
areas near the house to the large informal area below, where the trees
and shrubs are planted in groups or individually. One of the most
important combined achievements of Mr and Mrs Johnson and their
predecessor has been to overcome the potential limitations of the
garden's long, rectangular shape. The upper lawn, with one of the large
banks of old rhododendrons on one side, slopes down to a flight of steps
between two narrow rose beds and then the main flight of steps to the
first terrace. In the centre of the terrace lawn is a fountain pool; one of
the interesting trees here is a free-standing *Magnolia grandiflora*. The
border along the far side of this lawn is kept purposely low and contains
an attractive mixture of agapanthus, penstemons, hebes, dianthus, sage,

357

lavender and, most striking of all, the dwarf morning glory, *Convolvulus tricolor*.

The Johnsons replaced the long herbaceous border along the left-hand side of the garden with various shrubs which, as well as being easier to maintain, have the advantage of differing shapes and sizes. Among them is *Poncirus trifoliata*, the 'Japanese Bitter Orange' which carries white flowers in the spring, beautifully scented like orange blossom. Behind one section of this shrub border *Actinidia chinensis* is trained along wooden trellis-work and has proved extremely headstrong despite a severe pruning every year. At the bottom of the border is a lily pond, surrounded mainly by camellias and backed by a yew hedge twenty-five feet high and three feet thick.

Below the terraces, the garden becomes noticeably more informal, with a number of striking trees: *Halesia monticata*, perhaps the best of this small family, paulownia, various acers and conifers, including *Pinus nobilis*, and a eucryphia. Next, another group typifies the thoughtful plantings found throughout the garden: liquidambar, scarlet oak and *Parrotia persica* combine to provide autumn colour, in contrast to a blue cedar with a large shrub *Rosa multibracteata* in front.

A handsome poplar tree dominates the bottom of the garden close to the small pond; in complete contrast is *Lathrea clandestina*, a small creeping ground-cover plant with crocus-like flowers which lives off the roots of other plants. From the bottom of the garden the main path curves to continue up the other side, while smaller ones lead to central areas with long views back towards the house.

Old rhododendrons stretch in a solid bank along one side of the main path, usually planted in large groups of one variety to increase the effect when in flower. The variety of other plants is continuous. *Cornus kousa* has achieved a fine size and flowers outstandingly. Nevertheless, it is outshone by three plants of *Viburnum plicatum tomentosum* 'Mariesii' placed singly along this side of the garden and improving in quality to the plant nearest the house, which is superb. There are a number of magnolias including a large *Magnolia kobus* and *M. salicifolia*.

It would be difficult to describe all the plants this garden now contains. The small entrance courtyard plays its part too: among the plants trained against the sheltered walls are two *Sophora tetraptera* and a *Crinodendron hookeranum*, whose contrasting yellow and red flowers are both produced in May and are equally spectacular. Mrs Johnson says her garden takes a lot of thought and time, something evident throughout. Spring and early summer see Long Close at its peak, but with such a variety of plants there is hardly a time of the year when the garden is not full of interest.

WHATTON HOUSE

Midway between Kegworth and Hathern on west side of A6. 1 mile from M1 (Junction 24)

Tel. 0509 842 268

The Lord Crawshaw

Open Sundays and Bank Holidays from April to September inclusive, and for parties by appointment

Whatton House was originally built for Edward Dawson in 1802 and in his *History and Antiquities of Leicestershire* John Nichols writes that Dawson had 'erected a handsome mansion about a mile from the village on a fine situation near unto the London road, commanding many extensive and picturesque views; itself, together with the surrounding grounds, being a handsome ornament to the adjacent Country'. After being extensively damaged by fire the house was sold to the 1st Lord Crawshaw in 1876 who rebuilt the house in a far more massive style, but still in its prominent hill-top position. He laid out the gardens in their present form, and although much of the planting has changed, the unique Chinese Garden, with its fantastic selection of bronze statues and ornaments, has been retained in all its originality.

The south front of the house looks on to a terrace now planted as a formal Rose Garden divided by clipped Irish yews, but most of the gardens lie to the west, extending from the walled Kitchen Garden to the surrounding woodland. The south terrace is linked to the main area by a wide path called the Broad Walk, parallel to which is a long herbaceous border beneath the south-facing outside wall of the Kitchen Garden. The style of the wrought-iron gate which breaks the border and leads into the Walled Garden gives a taste of the Oriental extravagance which appears, quite unexpectedly, along the north side of the main area. On the other side of the Broad Walk shrub borders lead west to another small formal Rose Garden, sheltered by a huge copper beech.

The largest area of the garden is the open lawn to the south west, which the present Lord Crawshaw has planted as an Arboretum. Inspiration was already there in the form of some outstanding mature trees, including a blue cedar, an evergreen oak and a tulip tree, and to these he has added acers, cercidiphyllums, nothofagus, a ginkgo and a metasequoia and various cherries. In spring the lawn is brought to life by their varying shades of flower and leaf, as well as the ornamental barks of some such as the *Prunus serrula* and the spring bulbs planted beneath the trees.

The Woodland Garden stretches along the north side of the Arboretum Lawn and round the west end. It contains a number of varying areas and features: ponds surrounded by azaleas and bamboos, the dog cemetery, a network of little brick channels which can be filled with running water, the Canyon Garden built of local Derbyshire stone and a small hidden Rose Garden laid out in 1898. One of the winding paths leads towards its northern edge where an *art nouveau* gateway in the enclosing laurel hedge leads into the Chinese Garden. Here one is transported into a different world made even more surprising by its natural woodland surroundings.

On every side are bronze ornaments of all shapes and sizes which the 1st Lord Crawshaw brought from China: Buddhist memorial lamps, a wonderful Chinese Koro with dolphin handles and the Three Wise Men of China on top, pagodas and a tall ornament surmounted by an eagle. The original significance of most of the ornaments would pass unnoticed by most visitors, entranced by their appearance, but we do know that the deity beneath an umbrella who is holding a miniature pagoda is demonstrating the Karake legend of standing on a child to squeeze the mischief out of him; beside the path out of the east end of the Chinese Garden two Indian storks stand sentinel, their presence signifying long life. The path leads back towards the west end of the Walled Garden but even the elaborate carving on the stone temple to one side seems plain after the sights of the Chinese Garden, one of the most memorable Edwardian eccentricities to be found in any English garden.

LINCOLNSHIRE

DODDINGTON HALL

In Doddington on the B1190, south-west of Lincoln off the A46
Tel. 0522 694 227
Antony Jarvis Esq.

Open Wednesday and Sunday from May to September inclusive, and on Bank
Holidays

Doddington Hall has remained virtually unaltered since it was completed by Robert Smythson in 1600. The walls of the east entrance
courtyard, between the three-gabled gatehouse and the house, and of
the Walled Garden to the west of the house are mainly contemporary
with it, survivors of the extensive formal gardens which surrounded
Doddington and shown in an engraving of 1707 by Kip. The whole has
been considerably remodelled since the Victorian era, when it seems to
have been extensively over-planted with sombre evergreens obscuring
the house and dominating the garden.

The courtyard was filled with four enormous Cedars of Lebanon,
planted in 1839. These were replaced in 1972 with the restrained
formality of lawns, square tubs of flowers and young ornamental trees,
far more sympathetic with the courtyard's Elizabethan origins without
distracting attention from the architecture of house and gatehouse. To
the west of the house the main Walled Garden has a more detailed
formality. In 1900 the garden was re-designed by Kew Gardens and
Country Life in Elizabethan style. The centre of the garden is occupied
by a four-part Knot Garden, planted with flag iris and bedding roses in
soft pinks, cream, yellow and crimson; the upper half in dwarf box
edging, the lower half set in lawns.

Along the sunny bank below the house is a border of old fashioned pinks, intermedia and dwarf iris, cistus, and helianthemum, with low growing shrub roses. On the other three sides, the long wall borders had, in the 1960s, become rose sick and in one case infected with honey fungus. They were cleared out and the soil was sterilized with Basamid. Replanting followed, using the old rose varieties pioneered by Mr Jarvis's parents together with flag iris and a wide range of herbaceous plants with an emphasis on white, silver, grey and mauve colours and the pink and crimson of the roses. Many traditional varieties of pansy, pink and iris have been used, though the planting is in no way limited to historical precedents.

On the far side of the Walled Garden from the house a pair of eighteenth-century Italian wrought-iron gates open on to an avenue, the same main axis as shown in Kip's drawing. The avenue of dark Irish yews immediately beyond the gates continues into lines of Lombardy poplars. Formality disappears to the north of the yew avenue, where a path leads into the Wild Garden, also planted mainly by Mr Jarvis's parents, with a variety of shrubs among the older trees. The interesting collection of rhododendrons came from a cousin of Mr Jarvis's father who took part in Kingdon Ward's last plant-collecting expedition to Asia in the 1930s. Elsewhere are various cornus, viburnums, elaeagnus and shrub roses planted informally in groups in unmown grass. In spring the garden is filled with bulbs and the blossom of many cherries; other ornamental trees include an avenue of catalpas and a davidia. Some of the old trees have climbing roses like 'Rambling Rector' trained into them. One of these is especially interesting, a hybrid Cork oak; beyond it, near the corner of the garden, is a Cedar of Lebanon planted in 1837. The octagonal Tuscan 'Temple of the Winds', built by Mr Jarvis in the 1960s, provides a turning point at the furthest corner of the garden.

Along the west edge of the Wild Garden bordered by the wall of the old Kitchen Garden is a walk planned by Mr Jarvis's parents, shaded by an avenue of cherries. *Cytisus battandieri*, trained on the wall, adds its distinctive pineapple scent to the variety of old-fashioned climbing roses in mid-summer. On the other side of the walk is an impressive *Cryptomeris japonica*, which one would not normally expect to find in east England, and three very old sweet chestnuts, *Castanea sativa*, an unusual contorted variety. These trees appear in Kip's drawing and possibly date from the original garden. At the end of the walk a grass tennis court has been made into a croquet lawn, with a low rose hedge along the low wall dividing it from the Wild Garden. Through the doorway into the corner of the Kitchen Garden the enclosed Herb Garden recalls the style of the original Elizabethan garden.

The balance between the Elizabethan parts of the garden and the more recent areas of informal planting is very well-handled, and although maintenance of the very large house and gardens is a daunting task, they undoubtedly possess strong enough atmosphere and interest to merit such effort.

GUNBY HALL

2½ miles north-west of Burgh-le-Marsh, south of the A158

Tel. 075 485 212

The National Trust

Open on Thursday afternoon from April to September inclusive, and by written appointment three days a week

Tennyson wrote of Gunby that it was 'a haunt of ancient peace', and today this feeling remains, protected by Gunby's remote position in east Lincolnshire, with most people hurrying past on their way to holidays on the coast. The gardens round the red-brick house, built in 1700 by Sir William Massingberd, 2nd Bt, were built up by successive generations until 1944, when Lady Montgomery-Massingberd gave the property to the National Trust. Since then the Trust have made certain additions in the old walled gardens and the larger areas of lawn and trees around the house.

The Gunby Tree Book, preserved in the house, records the sustained family interest in planting trees, which reached its height in the late eighteenth and early nineteenth century with Bennet Langton's son, Peregrine Langton, who took his wife Elizabeth's name of Massingberd. Peregrine planted tens of thousands of trees on the Gunby estate; he was fanatical too about their preservation. On the lawn to the east of the house is a Cedar of Lebanon, only survivor of the five he planted in 1812. His wife Elizabeth appears to have had ambitious ideas for altering both the house and the gardens, all of which were intensely impractical and romantic.

The formal garden beyond the west entrance front of the house was laid out by Mrs Stephen Massingberd around 1900, when the gardens took much of their present shape. The Trust have added to the trees on the east lawn – which include an old mulberry, a weeping lime and a liquidambar in particular – a young Cedar of Lebanon as a replacement for the others. The lawn extends to the Wild Garden when shrubs are planted with wild flowers; in many of the beds specie shrub roses are surrounded by the mauve wild geranium as ground-cover.

These areas provide an ideal setting for the house, but the main interest and character is to be found in the two walled gardens which lie to its north-east. An archway leads from the east lawn between herbaceous borders either side along the south-facing wall of the smaller garden. These are a prelude to the liberal mixture of plants to be found within it, whose effect is heightened by the enclosed atmosphere. The architectural features – the clocktower of the eighteenth-century stables visible in one direction; the dovecot surmounted by its cupola and weather-vane, which is probably older than the stables; and the apple house – all contribute to the kitchen garden ideal.

The late Field-Marshal Sir Archibald Montgomery-Massingberd continued the family interest in trees, specializing in fruit trees in these two gardens: in the smaller one they mixed with herbaceous plants, and in the larger one beyond, with vegetables. In the small Walled Garden an Apple Walk survives along one of the paths, and in summer the vigorous herbaceous plants, mainly blue, yellow and white, seem almost too tall for the limited space and threaten to crowd out their neighbours in an assertive but picturesque manner. The Trust have increased the quantity of roses here; now climbing varieties mix with clematis on the walls. Another recent addition is the Herb Garden – once rumoured to be the only one in Lincolnshire – but the dovecot reigns supreme within these walls, its homely appearance so attuned to the general atmosphere.

Along the outside of the main Walled Garden is a long path leading to the church beside a rectangular pond. Known as the Ghost Walk, it is reputed to be haunted by a female member of the family, thought to be eloping with the postillion, who was murdered (together with the butler) by a jealous relative. Old pear trees survive from Sir Archibald's time in the Vegetable Garden whose central cross-paths in the lawn are bordered by herbaceous plants and shrub roses. A number of roses here, and in the smaller garden, are quite unusual, such as 'Reine Marie Henriette' and 'Mrs Oakley Fisher', which has come to be known as the 'National Trust' rose. Vegetables in fact are confined to square plots in two of the four large areas of lawn, thus reducing the work in what is generally a labour-intensive garden.

The National Trust tenants, Mr and Mrs J. D. Wrisdale, have enormous sympathy for the very particular character of the Hall, and maintain the gardens in an appropriately random, yet not formless, style without which much of Gunby's charm would be lost.

HARRINGTON HALL

6 miles north-west of Spilsby off the A158

Tel. 0790 52281

Lady Maitland

Open on eight Sundays through summer, on Wednesday and Thursday
afternoons from April to October inclusive, and by appointment

> Maud has a garden of roses
> And lilies fair on a lawn;
> There she walks in her state
> And tends upon bed and bower,
> And thither I climb'd at dawn
> And stood by her garden-gate;
> A lion ramps at the top,
> He is claspt by a passion-flower.

So Alfred, Lord Tennyson immortalized the garden at Harrington Hall
with this and many other verses of his poem *Maud*. Maud was Rosa
Baring, ward of Admiral Eden who was living at Harrington in the early
nineteenth century, and Tennyson, whose birthplace Somersby is two
miles away, fell in love with her. The associations of Harrington give its
Walled Garden a romantic air harking back those poetic days and
beyond, to the seventeenth century.

In 1678 Vincent Amcotts made the last alterations to the long red-
brick house, fortunately maintaining the central Elizabethan porch
tower which dominates the front today. The house had replaced a
medieval building – Harrington is mentioned in the Doomsday Book.
The house looks across the oval lawn of the forecourt, enclosed by walls
on the north and south sides, to the gates mentioned by Tennyson and
the park beyond the ha-ha. These last were part of the eighteenth-
century additions to Harrington which included the brick walls surrounding the main area of garden south of the house, adjacent to the
forecourt.

Nearly all the planting in the borders round the oval lawn in the
forecourt and the croquet lawn in the Walled Garden has been done by
Lady Maitland and her late husband, Sir John, since they came to
Harrington after the Second World War. The mellow appearance of the

365

red-brick house, walls and gateways is closely echoed by the plants, which in many places have soft colours and scents and could have been used in the eighteenth-century garden. Only the old-fashioned shrub roses have been used among them. The forecourt borders have plants of delicate shades – mauve, pink, blue, white – and the climbing roses and clematis trained on the walls reinforce the general feeling of 'Fairer than aught in the world beside'.

One notable feature in the south Walled Garden is the raised Jacobean Terrace which forms the boundary on the west, park side. The terrace was supposedly built with the rubble from the medieval house, and its raised position continues to give rewarding views across the garden to the house, for which it was originally designed; the steps up to the terrace were built in 1722. Lady Maitland and her head gardener for twenty-six years, Mr Arnold Knights, have bordered the brick path along the top with aromatic dwarf shrubs and small rock plants. The main borders are beneath the wall extending from the house on the east side, and beneath the terrace; in both the plants are mixed shrubs and herbaceous. In the terrace border the shades are mostly of yellow and gold, and particularly striking are the clipped domes of *Ilex aquifolium* 'Ferox Argentea' at either end. In the north border many of the plant-shades are of red and pink; the climbers on the south wall of the house include the small deep rose pink flowers of the 'Debutante' rose, parent of 'Dorothy Perkins', *Rosa Banksia lutescens*, 'White Cockade', *ceanothus* 'Gloire de Versailles' and jasmine 'Revolution'. On the west-facing wall the old red 'Hiawatha', 'Bobby James' and 'New Dawn' contrast with 'Violetta' and *Clematis* 'Ville de Lyon'. A summerhouse is set in the far wall of the garden between narrow borders of peonies with lavender hedges; both it and the old pear tree behind it are in serious danger of being smothered by the white climbing rose 'Wedding Day'. An opening in the back of the summerhouse leads to a long south-facing border of larger shrubs and trees made by the Maitlands against the wall. The border replaced old dog kennels and chicken runs; now this part of the garden is made resplendent with cherry blossom and the scent of lilacs and philadelphus.

Hidden beyond the little road which comes up past the south-facing border is the Recess Garden, planned by Sir John, who was the local Member of Parliament, for those times when he was at Harrington during the parliamentary recess. Large white hebes screen the path which leads into the garden, whose plan is simple – outer beech hedges and a lawn round a central paved square enclosed with hedges and lavender. An opening in the variegated beech hedge on the far side leads to an area planted for autumn colour, with a selection of weeping trees around a central group containing *Robinia pseudoacacia* 'Frisia' and a variegated elaeagnus.

There is a sense of artless ease throughout the gardens at Harrington at one with its traditional character which is so charming, an overall mood that yet combines with the diverse features: the walls and gates, the view from the house framed by old ilex and yew beyond the ha-ha, the raised terrace, the many combinations of plants. The practical hard work all this means for Lady Maitland and her two gardeners is both increased and offset by the large kitchen garden; it supplies most of the plants for the garden centre which they run to help with costs.

MARSTON HALL

In Marston, 6 miles north of Grantham off the A1
Tel. 04004 225
The Reverend Henry Thorold

Open selected Sundays from April to October inclusive, and by appointment

---

Despite having been the Thorolds' family home for centuries, Marston was deserted by its owners when they moved into a new and far grander house nearby, Syston. It is ironic that the smaller Marston survives while Syston has been demolished as has its conservatory, which was the largest in England. The Thorolds did not leave Marston before they had made considerable alterations; today one sees the structure of the medieval great hall with Georgian additions and interiors. During the family's absence Marston was used as a Dower House and by the agent but it was not until the return of the present owner's parents that the house and its garden were restored.

The garden contains two old features of interest. A picturesque wych elm in front of the house is estimated to be about four hundred years old. Although devastated by elm disease, the old tree is now putting out new shoots and suckers; meantime its huge gnarled trunk is adorned in summer with a 'Kiftsgate' climbing rose and *clematis montana*. Beyond the wych elm a shrubbery leads to the path into the adjoining church-yard. Over the gate is a laburnum tree whose own size is partially hidden by the surrounding trees but whose age is unquestioned: it is reckoned to be the largest and possibly the oldest laburnum in England.

The rest of the gardens are small and shelter beneath two sides of the house. The Reverend Henry Thorold, an eminent antiquarian and architectural historian, laid out a Rose Garden at one end of the house around a sundial whose stand is a baluster from the old Waterloo Bridge. The Rose Garden has a most attractive design, leading naturally to the edge of the garden. Beyond low, wrought-iron gates is an avenue of limes, planted in 1953 to mark the Queen's accession. Much of Mr Thorold's garden-planning is aimed at leading the eye outward beyond the boundaries. In the garden to the east of the house a path leads to another wrought-iron gate looking out to recently planted trees.

This garden contains a traditional mixture of vegetables with herbaceous borders in front and was originally partially divided by climbing roses on trelliswork. The roses have now been mainly replaced by beech, although the survivors mix their flowers with the beech leaves in an attractive, random manner. The striking white wooden pyramids in which Mr Thorold has trained climbers is an idea he got from Nancy Lancaster's garden in Oxfordshire. At the end of an alley between tall thorn hedges is an eighteenth-century Garden House, restored in 1961 with a Gothick façade to a design by Mr John Partridge; it is decorated inside with murals by Barbara Jones.

One of the latest additions to the gardens is the Lancing Avenue on the north side of the house; the tall Lombardy poplars were given to Mr Thorold when he retired from teaching at Lancing College. The idea of using the poplars and planting the two lines close together came from a book on the gardens of Palladian villas round Venice, but it is not coincidental that the slender trunks and the branches which stretch together like old vaulting echo the lofty interiors of Lancing College Chapel. Mr Thorold derives great pleasure from planting for the future, an exciting prospect in a garden whose roots are deep in the past.

NOTTINGHAMSHIRE

FLINTHAM HALL

6 miles south-west of Newark on the A46
Tel. 0636 85214
Myles Thoroton Hildyard, Esq.

Open by appointment from April to October inclusive and on one or two
Sundays

Flintham's unique feature is its conservatory, the finest surviving
example of what became a widespread Victorian fashion. Between 1853
and 1857 the appearance of the house, rebuilt in 1798, was totally
altered by T. C. Hine, an architect from Nottingham. Hine was
employed by Thomas Hildyard, whose father Colonel Thomas
Thoroton had married the niece and heiress of Sir Robert D'Arcy
Hildyard in 1815 and adopted the name of Hildyard. Thorotons had
lived in the vicinity of Flintham since the Middle Ages. The brick
façades were encased in highly decorated stonework surmounted by a
balustrade, and a tower was added at the west end over the front door. At
the other end of the house are Hine's most notable contributions: the
tall windows of his library with a gallery to give views from above, look
out into the conservatory.

Hine's conservatory was strongly influenced by Paxton's Crystal
Palace, built for the Great Exhibition of 1851, and its proportions are
similarly massive, with tall arched windows and a rounded glass roof.
The Dorothea lily gaslights inside in fact came from the Great Exhibition. Two large camellias frame the door and decorative iron-work
baskets hang from the roof. Palms originally surrounded the central
fountain but Mr Hildyard has replaced them with a more interesting and
colourful selection of plants, including jasmines, tree salvias, plumbago,
bignonias and a mimosa tree, which now threatens to burst through the
roof. All in all, the conservatory is a fascinating survivor from the

nineteenth century and one of the great showpieces of Victorian garden architecture left in Britain.

After such exotica the rest of the gardens have an air of repose. Victorianism did not encroach beyond the balustraded terrace along the south front now planted with lavender, alchemilla, catmint and tobacco plants, beyond which a wide lawn with a central fountain leads to the eighteenth-century park and its lake. Both lawn and park contain many fine trees – beech, copper beech and cedars. To the south-west of the house two cedars stand close to a weeping copper beech near the Spring Garden, outstanding for its snowdrops as well as the old trees: more cedars, including two Cedars of Lebanon, four unusual Lucombe oaks and a Turkey oak. The path winding among them leads to the figure of a cloaked girl whose name, 'Modesty', is carved on the statue's base.

On the east side of the main lawn is the old brick-walled garden. Both inside it and in the areas around many traditional varieties have been planted. One of the best vistas at Flintham is looking south along the border outside the Walled Garden with old trees drawing the eye to a classical statue and the lake beyond. The border itself is divided by two classical busts on tall stone pedestals, and is filled with a mixture of herbaceous plants and roses, set against clematis and climbing roses on the wall behind. Beyond the statue the path turns the corner of this upper Walled Garden and moves through old-fashioned shrub roses, lilacs and philadelphus to the Regency pheasantry.

Along the long top wall of the lower Walled Garden is a border of shrub roses. Classical statues stand at either end of the path along this border, one surrounded with columnar cypresses, the other before a large group of 'Lace-cap' hydrangeas. Clematis and vines have appropriated the wall, in competition with a large *Magnolia grandiflora*. To one side of the shrubbery is a garden of grass and wild flowers, in charming contrast to the somewhat more ordered shrubs and paths. A third statue in the shrubbery acts as the focal point of the central path in the upper Walled Garden, visible from there through the gate joining the two gardens. Traditional appearance is preserved in the upper Walled Garden by the herbaceous borders, enclosed by box hedges and backed by éspalier apples and pears, which attend the central path leading from the shrub garden to a classical statue beneath an arch of 'Cupid' climbing roses. The north wall was heated in the nineteenth century, and the arches which held the stoves are still visible. Along the path parallel to the north wall, and also box-enclosed, are roses and irises, but this walled garden's most striking display is produced by mingling 'Morning Glories' and sweet peas trained up the slender poles in the vinery.

Devotees of Victoriana who visit Flintham to see the house and, more especially, the conservatory, will find much else of differing character in the gardens to attract them, but undeniably there are few places in Britain where eighteenth- and nineteenth-century styles of park and architecture co-exist so happily, and in company with a traditional flower garden.

HOLME PIERREPONT HALL

5 miles south-east of Nottingham off the A52
Tel. 060 732 371
Mr and Mrs Robin Brackenbury

Open on Bank Holidays and on Tuesday, Thursday, Friday and Sunday from June to August inclusive, and on Sunday in September; also by appointment for groups

The house and gardens at Holme Pierrepont were nearing dereliction when Mr and Mrs Brackenbury began their work of restoration in the 1970s. Divided from its estates, the house had been lived in only sporadically for well over a century before it was requisitioned by the army during the First World War and again in the Second, after which it was quite properly invalided out. The fortunes of the place had changed considerably since the days when the Pierrepont family held a dukedom and the Hall was a Jacobean mansion, which had been added to the older building but was pulled down during the 1730s. The present house is medieval in its oldest parts; its most striking feature is the Tudor front, built by Sir Henry Pierrepont in the late fifteenth century when the family fortunes were beginning to climb.

From the beginning of the eighteenth century Holme Pierrepont suffered from being a second home to the family, who also owned Thoresby Park. Nevertheless the most interesting part of the garden, the now restored courtyard with a parterre was made in about 1875 for Lord Newark (who later became the 4th Earl Manvers) during one of the family's stays at Holme Pierrepont. Lord Newark also built the attractive colonnaded cloister round the courtyard, part of which survives, but once he succeeded to the earldom and left for the enormous replacement house which Salvin had built at Thoresby, occupation of Holme Pierrepont once again became irregular. Only the return of Lady Sibell Argles, one of his daughters, after the Second World War ended the neglect and since her death Mr and Mrs Brackenbury (who is a great-niece of the 4th Earl) have continued the work.

The 3rd Earl's wife had been the daughter of the French Duc de Coigny, and the intricate pattern of the box parterre is clearly French-inspired. The hedging has been restored and the parterre is now flanked by two small rose gardens. An herbaceous border follows the courtyard wall; an attractive scene. The other main area of garden is to the east of the Hall, on the site of the old seventeenth-century gardens, but restoration is still under way here; at the moment the vista down the lawn enclosed by yew hedges is the main feature. It is a marvel, though, that either the house or any part of the gardens has survived, and the re-emergence of this piece of Nottinghamshire history is both testimony to and reward for its owners' efforts.

ST ANNE'S MANOR

In Sutton Bonington, 5 miles north-west of Loughborough
Tel. 050 972 280

Barbara, Lady Buchanan

Open one Sunday in June, and by appointment

Sir Charles and Lady Buchanan began the garden at St Anne's Manor after the Second World War, and built up a diverse collection of plants. The original mid-Victorian house was extensively rebuilt after a serious fire in 1907; positioned on a slight hill above the village of Sutton Bonington, surrounded on three sides by its garden, it enjoys attractive views of Charnwood Forest to the south.

Gloomy yews and hollies dominated the Edwardian garden the Buchanans inherited: possibly their most useful purpose was to deaden the sound of trains speeding through the cutting to one side of the garden on the main London to Scotland line. Different areas of the garden have been cleverly developed, linking them with views to give a combination of open spaces and unexpected, secret corners.

The garden is relatively narrow in front of St Anne's south-facing entrance façade, and the Buchanans kept it simple in order to give prominence to the view out: a low wall with an unusual pattern of herringbone bricks divides a narrow border of floribunda roses. To the east of the front door, the Library Border contains interesting shrubs: *Garrya elliptica*, *Schizophragma viburnoides*, *Chimonanthus fragrans*, *Carpentaria californica*, *Hoheria lyallii* and others, filled in with fuchsias, mostly hardy, and some annuals. To the west of the house the terrace between the house and the large lawn has a narrow border of tree peonies and hardy fuchsias; these survived the severe frosts of 1963 and 1982 and are now underplanted with *Nerine bowdenii*. At the north-west corner of the lawn are three full-grown purple beeches, very much a feature of the garden. To the north of the lawn is the Bank and its border, planted with shrubs and herbaceous plants such as Jerusalem sage, a blue cedar provides contrasting colour and form. On the far, west, side of the lawn from the house are further shrub borders containing mahonias, rhus and junipers. In autumn here the eucryphias, euonymus and *Parrotia persica* provide a mass of pink and crimson leaves. Close by a peat bed has provided a home for small rhododendrons, and among the striking trees on the lawn are a eucryphia, a ginkgo, *Parrotia persica* and *Acer griseum*. Most of the borders round the lawn are planted with different snowdrops.

To the east of the house the Buchanans replaced twelve elm trees with an open cherry orchard where many varieties of narcissus appear as a prelude to the blossom. Along the south side of the orchard is a large border of mixed shrubs where a variety of small spreading geraniums provide effective ground cover. Large philadelphus and lilacs stand at the back of the border. At the east end of the garden an old wall is draped with climbing roses and clematis 'Perle d'Azur'.

The most striking areas of the garden lie to the north of the orchard. In the formal Rose Garden floribunda varieties and grass paths surround a summerhouse and are in turn enclosed by yew hedges on two sides and a brick wall at the north end. Immediately west of the Rose Garden a small partly paved enclosure contains the main peony border with modern shrub roses behind – 'Fritz Nobis' and 'Cerise Bouquet' – a spectacular sight in June. Lawn continues to the west with a selection of trees including a good variety of magnolias, such as *Magnolia veitchii*, under which hydrangeas are grouped for late summer colour. Among the other trees here is a tall Dawyck beech, with its characteristic fastigiate habit. Stretching away north from this lawn is the wide double herbaceous border. Enclosed by a beech hedge on one side and a brick wall bearing ceanothus, honeysuckle and *Actinidia kolomikta* on the other, it is perhaps the outstanding feature of the gardens. At its top the

373

quality and variety of plants in this border are characteristic of St Anne's throughout, and help to make it a garden for enjoyment at almost any time of the year.

SUTTON BONINGTON HALL

In Sutton Bonington, 5 miles north-west of Loughborough
Tel. 0509 72355
The Lady Elton

Open one Sunday in June and by appointment

The garden at Sutton Bonington Hall was originally laid out by Lady Elton's great-grandmother Lady Paget, but has been simplified since then, especially by Lady Elton, who maintains the garden herself with no full-time help. Fine cedars and Scots pines in the paddock sloping up to the north of the attractive red-brick house hark back to the time when this whole area was part of the garden. Now the garden stretches in a wide vista mainly to the south-east, through the parterre where Lady Elton has filled the beds with roses, to mature trees, lawn and a shrub border at the far end.

It is likely that Lady Paget added the conservatory, one of the Hall's best features, to the north end of the Queen Anne house. In its conception, though not in its style, the conservatory is similar to its far larger neighbour at Flintham Hall – designed to be looked into from the drawing-room to which it formed an extension, and to make an attractive addition to the house when seen from the garden. Its roof is in the interesting 'ridge-and-furrow' pattern which Joseph Paxton developed and which can also be seen at Somerleyton Hall in Suffolk. Inside, most of the present plants have been added by Lady Elton, including three white jasmines, passion flower, white clematis, plumbago, daturas, mimosa and white tobacco plants. In the centre is a fountain with statue, and the combination of water, predominantly pale colours and mixture of scents is most attractive.

The Georgian bow window and arches on fluted columns with a balustrade built on to the east facing garden front of the house add considerably to its character. The old parterre beyond the terrace is still enclosed by a balustrade, and is dominated by four shrub rose beds,

374

each in an 'M' pattern with the 'arms' pointing in towards the central grass path and each with roses of alternating white, pale yellow and gold. Clipped yews among the rose beds add to the formality and the fountain on the north side is surrounded by four clipped domes of golden yew. Lady Elton has planted an avenue of delicate variegated acers and a line of standard white roses on the outer, northern side of the parterre balustrade beyond the fountain. There is a very pretty view from the small statue behind the fountain, across an attractive white herbaceous border which Lady Elton is building up, to a metal arbour set over an opening in the yew hedge behind and a larger statue to the south beyond. A silver border adds yet another delicate air to this part of the garden.

Beyond the parterre to the east the garden becomes more informal with a wide lawn stretching past an old holm oak to a blue cedar and Scots pines. In the shrub border beyond are rhododendrons, azaleas – the scented yellow variety – and a striking acer 'Brilliantissimum', with a wide variety of hostas as ground cover. Seen here the harmonious balance between garden and house is at its most pronounced. The character of the building allows for simplicity in its setting; and in the retention of this balance, while still developing areas of special interest, Lady Elton is most successful.

YORKSHIRE

ARTHINGTON HALL

In Arthington, 5 miles east of Otley on the A659
Tel. 0532 842 115
Mr and Mrs C. E. W. Sheepshanks

Open one Sunday per year, and by appointment

Arthington is blessed with a spectacular view to the north-west down to the River Wharfe and the arches of the nineteenth-century railway viaduct in the middle distance, and on this side of the house low heathers and conifers have been planted so as not to obscure the view. The main area of gardens to the east and south-east of the Georgian house have been equally blessed by Mr Sheepshanks' seemingly random planting to achieve a charmingly informal effect, full of variety and surprise. Mr Sheepshanks has special interests in trees, in blending colour and in the challenge of rearing good specimens to provide interest through much of the year. Maintenance is sometimes a problem, particularly as Mr Sheepshanks' gardener for fifty-two years has recently retired; but help is obtained from the village sexton, who still hand-digs all the beds and borders.

To the south-east of the house shrubberies surround the paths leading to other parts of the garden. Many of the azaleas and rhododendrons here were brought from Mr Sheepshanks' garden in Sunningdale, where he was a schoolmaster, and have prospered happily. Planted among them are various cornus, shrub roses and acers. Mr Sheepshanks has in twenty years built up a fine collection of over forty of these last, most of them in the Arboretum; particularly good are the different snake-barks, such as *Acer pensylvanicum*. Among others trees, in the Arboretum are a ginkgo, a metasequoia, a tulip tree, a golden poplar, a copper cut-leaf beech, a paulownia, *Styrax japonica*, *Eucalyptus niphophila* and, a special pride, *Nissa sylvatica* which, maintains Mr Sheepshanks, is not supposed to grow north of Nottingham.

East of the house is the large Walled Garden, and outside its ten-foot brick wall along the south side is the main border. Here one can see Mr Sheepshanks' liberal philosophy put gloriously into practice with a mixture of shrubs, roses, peonies, agapanthus, delphiniums and other herbaceous and annuals. Fruit trees are trained on the walls and on the other side of the path are shrub roses, *Cotinus coggygria*, the 'Smoke Bush' and *Cornus alba* 'Elegantissima' and some acers. Further along are rather more formal beds of roses, with behind them a rapacious honeysuckle clambering the tennis court netting. At the far, eastern end is a dahlia border, a blaze of colour which can be seen across the fields from the village street. More retiring surroundings are to be found in the Woodland Walk curving away north-east from this end of the garden along a chestnut avenue leading to lovely old beeches. Initially one looks out to the distant woods round Harewood House, but where the double ha-ha – an unusual feature – begins, the views open out in all directions over Wharfedale.

A pedimented stone gateway, a typically simple but effective eighteenth-century feature, leads into the Walled Garden, a traditional mixture of fruit, vegetables and flowers. Climbing roses are trained over the wooden arches along the main path, with small shrub roses on either side and other climbers trained along wire behind them. The various greenhouses are maintained to a very high standard; as well as nectarines, peaches, figs and grapes there are exotic flowering plants such as the red climbing geranium, bougainvillea, passion-flower and a mimosa. Behind the larger greenhouse is a Camellia House, containing a mass of flowers in the early spring.

Mr Sheepshanks' enthusiasm for exotics, despite the work they entail, reflects his belief in gardening for enjoyment. Though most of the garden at Arthington is undeniably traditional, it has the fizz of individuality which not even the splendour of its site can efface.

BRAMHAM PARK

5 miles south of Wetherby on the A1
Tel. 0937 844 265
Mr and Mrs George Lane Fox

Open on Sunday, Tuesday, Wednesday and Thursday from mid-June to August inclusive and Bank Holiday weekends

Bramham Park is one of the outstanding French-style formal gardens surviving in England. Although small compared with André le Nôtre's works at Versailles and Vaux-le-Vicomte which were its inspiration, Bramham is considerably larger than its surviving English contemporaries such as Melbourne Hall and St Paul's Walden Bury.

Robert Benson, later 1st Lord Bingley, built the house between 1700 and 1710, and he also laid out the gardens probably with some advice from his gardener, Fleming. Sir John Reresby described Benson's father as 'one of no birth' but Robert was by all accounts a remarkable man, who had not only inherited his father's financial acumen but in addition turned to politics – he was Chancellor of the Exchequer; to diplomacy – he was later an Ambassador; and to architecture, where his work as an amateur was held in highest esteem.

Bramham's survival so comparatively unchanged is largely due to vicissitudes in the family fortune. At the beginning of the nineteenth century it was inherited by George Lane Fox, a member of the Prince Regent's set whose gambling and high living, combined with the disastrous extravagance of his notorious wife, Georgina Buckley, left little to expend on either upkeep or alteration. A serious fire in 1828 partially destroyed the house but until the beginning of the twentieth century, although the gardens and pleasure grounds were maintained there was no possibility of restoring the house or making changes in the grounds. Bramham's most recent setback was a gale in February 1962, during which hurricane-force winds blew down some four hundred trees in the garden alone. After clearance of the debris, replanting was immediately started, both of the standard trees and the beech hedges, and it is now possible to see half the sixty-six-acre garden more or less as its eighteenth-century designer conceived it.

The style is typical of the French landscape formality that preceded the more 'natural' English landscape school ushered in by William Kent. A series of hedge-enclosed allées and wide avenues of beech were laid out to the south-west of the house, with woodland filling the spaces between, and a separate area of woodland was planted to the south, known as the Black Fen pleasure grounds. The woodland is mainly beech, lime and sycamore and the avenues and allées all lead to focal points of statues, temples (most of which were designed by the architect James Paine), or another architectural feature. Formal and ornamental water, in the shape of a small T-shaped lake, added to the main area in 1728, and a series of ponds and cascades were, and still are, important parts of the design. Just before the fire of 1828 the parterre below the west-facing garden front of the house contained a 'Pleasaunce', or decorative orchard. Early this century it was made into a Rose Garden, with obelisks of clipped yew among the rosebeds, but the main vistas and axes through the woodland remain virtually as they were two hundred and fifty years ago.

One of the main vistas stretched from a temple along the Broad Walk on the garden front of the house. The temple has a portico, Ionic pillars and fine stucco work inside. Originally it may have been an Orangery but at the beginning of this century it was consecrated as a chapel. From the Broad Walk the vista extends south past the Obelisk Ponds and Cascade through a beech avenue to the Round House on the edge of Black Fen pleasure grounds. This building may have been modelled on Kent's Temple of Ancient Virtues at Stowe; beyond it, at the junction of many avenues in Black Fen, is the Obelisk, surmounted by an urn, which George and Harriet Lane Fox (she was Robert Benson's daughter) had erected in memory of their son, Robert. Closing another vista to the south-west from the Round House into Black Fen, is the 'Lead Lads' Temple, so-called because of the lead statuettes that once adorned its portico. On a broad stretch of grass looking down to the Obelisk Ponds is the octagonal Gothick Temple, a telling contrast to the other, classical creations.

Looking north from the 'Lead Lads' Temple, another vista extends back to the main gardens and across the short arm of the T-Lake to the Four Faces urn on the far north side, the focus of a number of paths. This large stone urn represents the four seasons, similar to the famous Four Seasons lead urn at Melbourne Hall by Jan van Nost. One of the paths leads east past the Stone Nymph statue back to the chapel. In a different direction a walk continues round a corner to the Open Temple on the west edge of the garden, again with Ionic pillars, which faces east along a broad avenue to a point near the house. One of the main avenues radiating from the house leads south-west to the long arm of the T-Lake and the curved belvoir on the edge of the garden overlooking the parkland.

The overall impression of the garden is of formal harmony – trees, walks and temples – but the area round the Dogs' Graves close to the Gothick Temple has been replanted with variety with ilex and magnolias, and in spring snowdrops, daffodils and other bulbs and wild flowers bring refreshing contrast. In summer the Rose Garden and long herbaceous border bring warmth to the area round the house, but all these later features only serve, in fact, to enhance the original design, an inheritance really worth safeguarding.

KEPWICK HALL

7 miles north of Thirsk off the A19
Tel. 0845 537 242
Mrs Julius Guthe

Open on selected Sundays in spring and summer

A chance conversation in a train in 1936 between Julius Guthe, a shipping magnate, and Robert Wallace, a garden designer was the starting point of Kepwick's gardens. It must have been a challenging task (and very different from Wallace's native Kent) to plan within the imposing setting of the North Yorkshire moors and Hambleton Hills. The result, on different levels round the house, was a great success and today the gardens are a fine addition to the landscape. There is a suitably majestic air about some of Wallace's work – the long terraces and wide flights of stone steps – but there is informality, too, in smaller areas with a succession of colours through much of the year.

Wallace linked the various levels with low walls of distinctive flat stones and flights of stone steps, lending an architectural air which is greatly augmented on one side of the house by the imposing grass terrace stretching for two hundred yards to white wrought-iron gates and the wooded hill at the boundary. Sloping gently upwards from the house and broken at intervals by flights of shallow stone steps, it was designed both to exploit the view over the park below, and to divide this part of the garden from the park, accomplished by a low retaining wall on the upper side and a higher wall dropping to the park. From midway to the boundary on one side is an herbaceous border, which adds to the terrace's spacious appearance.

The rhododendrons and azaleas on the long slope above are spectacular in spring, whether in the large groups round the various paths or more widely spaced with shrub roses in the meadow at the east end. Mature trees in this part include chestnuts and copper beech, set off by daffodils then bluebells. Among the rhododendrons and azaleas are many other interesting trees and shrubs, including acers, pittosporums and *Nothofagus obliqua*. Along the top of the bank the path runs between azaleas and passes a circular pool with a semi-circular wall and fountain behind. From here Wallace planned a narrow path through rhododendrons to the long terrace, achieving a contrasting effect of secluded paths and open areas of long grass with views to the park below, especially telling in the clearing with a central stone statue of the Three Graces. The various paths lead back towards the house where a Heather Garden, laid out in a series of raised terraces, surrounds part of the main lawn.

North of the house the mood of the garden changes from the open planting of trees and shrubs to the more detailed formality of flower borders. A circular Rose Garden, filled with various hybrid tea roses, is surrounded by clipped yew hedges; smaller beds behind are filled with hostas, gentians and meconopsis, and to one side is a Japanese cherry covered with *Clematis montana*. A double herbaceous border with a central circular lawn stretches down the slope between yew hedges to the old Kitchen Garden, an old-fashioned mixture of flowers, fruit and vegetables carefully arranged with the main path leading between éspalier apples and pears to a second more formal Rose Garden planted with floribundas, including 'Elizabeth of Glamis'. Hostas make a striking edge either side of the path beyond here. The large greenhouses are full of interest, containing many tender and scented plants.

All in all, though one of Yorkshire's lesser known gardens, Kepwick, both in scale and quality of design, deserves to be counted among its assets.

LING BEECHES

In Ling Lane, Scarcroft, 7 miles north-east of Leeds off the A458
Tel. 0532 892 450

Mrs Arnold Rakusen

Open on selected Sundays and by appointment

The site of Ling Beeches was originally thick woodland, mainly beech, belonging to the Bramham Park estate, and the house was built between 1935 and 1937 when the land was sold off. Originally sufficient space was cleared in the wood for the house only, but since then the garden has steadily expanded. Early work was perforce slow, as the hungry woodland had leeched out the soil to a thin grey dust. Some soil and leaf-mould were imported but a great deal was obtained from compost which Mrs Rakusen continues to make in abundant supply. The varying foliages and forms, and the interplay of light and shade give the garden its character; floral colour is of secondary importance but is used subtly to enhance the secluded woodland atmosphere.

Thyme and other rock plants fill the narrow spaces between the paving stones along the terrace in front of the house, against the walls of which a number of tender plants are trained, including *Solanum crispum* 'Glasnevin' and *Nandina domestica*. This terrace looks out on to the main lawn, the only really open area in the garden. Along one side is a border of old-fashioned shrub roses and at the far end from the house large old rhododendrons. On the other side from the border a single silver weeping pear is a typically restrained piece of planting, with only winter aconites as company.

The Woodland Garden surrounds three sides of the house and lawn, with paths winding between the mature beech and Scots pines and more recent plants. Some of the hungrier plants in the garden occupy three peat beds; close by autumn cyclamen cover the ground beneath two beeches. In fact, small groundcover plants, beneath the larger shrubs and along the paths, are one of the garden's outstanding features: they include spring bulbs and lily-of-the-valley, but best of all are the baby *Cornus canadensis*, which have colonized one path, though proving rather reluctant to get established elsewhere in the garden. With the trees, climbers and smaller plants are many shrubs; including azaleas, mahonias, olearias, hebes and specie rhododendrons. Ferns and Solomon's Seal, both with their distinctive leaves, thrive in the damp and shady parts of the garden, and hellebores are outstanding in early spring.

Some of the old woodland trees have been replaced by ornamental ones including acers, sorbuses, eucryphias, *Pittosporum tenuifolium* and prunuses. Where others have been removed their stumps have been left as hosts for a variety of climbers: *Vitis coignetiae, Hydrangea petiolaris* and *Humulus lupulus* 'Aureus'. Two climbers that have annexed whole trees in characteristic style are a 'Kiftsgate' rose, well over thirty feet high, and a *Clematis montana* stretching over fifty feet into a Scots pine. Other clematis, often trained over the tree-stumps, are *C. chrysocoma, C. orientalis* and *C. tangutica*.

Carefully chosen as the individual plants are it is their collective appearance which is important: Mrs Rakusen remarks that while her plants are not expected to stand to attention they are asked to play their part in the total effect. She is a very experienced gardener, and is also Honorary Director of the Harlow Car Gardens of the Northern Horticultural Society – a very interesting modern garden of over sixty acres made since 1948 near Harrogate. At Ling Beeches, much of the garden is planned to keep maintenance to a minimum, an abundance of seats adding to its restful atmosphere.

NEWBY HALL

4 miles south of Ripon on the B6265
Tel. 09012 2583
R. E. J. Compton, Esq.

Open daily from April to September inclusive (not Mondays except Bank Holidays)

Newby Hall is a country house of rare quality. It was originally built in the 1690s for Sir Edward Blackett, and the restrained south and west front are virtually unchanged except for the stone balustrade and central carved pediments added between 1760 and 1774 by Robert Adam. Adam was employed by William Weddell, one of the great English collectors of the eighteenth century who during his lifetime filled Newby with superb paintings, furniture, tapestries and classical sculpture which today may be seen in the interiors Adam planned.

The gardens are no less outstanding than the house. They were largely created by Major Edward Compton from 1923 on the existing nineteenth-century framework and have been restored by his son and daughter-in-law, Mr and Mrs Robin Compton. They have done considerable replanting and added a degree of simplification, largely to enable five gardeners to maintain what was formerly tended by twelve.

The paved forecourt with its fountain and four Adam vases set in yew niches, and the terrace below the south front, with curving balustraded stone steps leading from each side to the gardens, were planned by William Burges in the 1870s. Burges also designed the Statue Walk, to the south of the terrace, stretching east–west across the garden between unusually fine stone seats at either end. The walk was designed for a collection of Venetian statues which stand between dark Irish yews, and it crosses at right-angles the Long Border which Major Compton planned as the garden's main axis and outstanding feature.

The view from the south front down this sloping double herbaceous border three hundred yards long, to the River Ure at the bottom, is justly famous and unforgettable. It was a supremely ambitious design which few gardens can rival. Backed by clipped yew hedges, some of the plant grouping remains as planned by Major Compton with hosts of unusual herbaceous plants. Although the maintenance demanded by the border is in proportion to its size a few carefully chosen shrubs have been added to relieve its labour intensive nature.

On either side of the border, Major Compton developed a series of formal gardens each with its own theme and containing a large variety of plants, many of which one is surprised to find in the often inhospitable Yorkshire climate. These formal gardens were designed to be at their best at different seasons. A rose walk to the west, planted by Robin Compton and called 'The Wars of the Roses' since it is planted with the 'White Rose of York' and 'Red Rose of Lancaster', leads to Sylvia's Garden, a sunken garden named after Robin Compton's mother. It is enclosed by yew hedges and the raised beds between paved paths are now filled with many of Mrs Robin Compton's favourite plants of soft colours and silver foliage including pinks, aubretia and lavender. On the same side are the sunken formal Rose Garden, surrounded by a copper beech hedge and re-planted with old-fashioned roses, and the July Garden, filled with midsummer flowering plants.

Along the far west perimeter of this side of the gardens is an exciting recent discovery, a lime avenue, formerly hidden by a thicket of trees and undergrowth which leads down to the river and continues on the other side. It has been cleared and the gaps filled with more lime trees. On the east side of the Long Border is the Autumn Garden, planted with late flowering and foliage plants. Lower down the Long Border, back on the west side, a path leads to the curving Pergola, clad with laburnum and Japanese quince, both spectacular in flower. There are many fine laburnum trees throughout the gardens. Below the Pergola is the Rock Garden, made by Ellen Wilmott (she also worked at Spetchley Park in Worcestershire, and her own garden at Warley Place in Essex was famous). This is a rock garden on the grand scale. Small, damp loving plants thrive around the waterfall and streams joining the various ponds, all recently restored.

Other paths lead from the Long Border through informal glades and shrubberies. As well as a wide variety of specie and hybrid rhododendrons, many of which are rarely found in the north-east of England, there are outstanding trees and shrubs everywhere. Copper beeches, a variegated sycamore and unusual pines are among the large mature trees. Flowering trees include a Swedish white beam of over seventy feet high and many magnolias: *Magnolia dawsoniana, M. sargentiana* 'Robusta' and *M. sprengeri* 'Diva' all well grown and rarely seen in these parts; also *M. kobus, M. salicifolia*; and the loebneri hybrids *M. 'Merrill'* and *M. 'Leonard Messel'* and the soulangeiana hybrid *M. 'Brozzonii'*. Eucryphias and *Embothrium lanceolatum* are among other unusual exotics in this region. Camellias, too, are well represented, planted in a circular garden with azaleas and primulas.

There are other features such as the Rose Pergola and Orchard Garden, and many other shrubs and trees which have not been mentioned. Throughout the twenty-five acres of garden the variety of content matches the quality of design, making it a place no garden enthusiasts, be they plantsmen, historians or just appreciative visitors, should miss. An occasional whistle from the small gauge train running along the bottom of the garden is a reminder of Newby's other entertainments for those not engrossed by the beauties of house and gardens.

PENNYHOLME

At Sleightholmedale near Fadmoor, 5 miles north-west of Kirby Morside off the A170

Tel. 075 131 500

C. J. Wills, Esq.

Open on one or two days in June, and by appointment

The narrow road to Pennyholme travels through some wild countryside in the Yorkshire Moors – beautiful but remote and bleak at many times of the year, certainly not everybody's idea of the perfect setting for a garden. The Earl of Feversham, however, decided to make a garden along the rushing river below the old farmhouse at the end of the road. It was the second garden that he had made, the other being at Nawton Tower, the Fevershams' larger home a few miles away across the moors. After her husband's death in 1963, Lady Feversham went to live permanently at Pennyholme.

It was the presence of the river, and its potential as the main feature of a garden, which had stirred Lord Feversham's ambitions during the conversion work on the farmhouse in the late 1940s. He built all the stone walls round the garden to give some semblance of shelter, planned the shape of the long, narrow garden to follow the river's course, and built four bridges across it so that the garden could extend up the hill on the far side. The plan is simple, natural and effective, and while the climate and conditions rule out most rare or tender plants, Pennyholme is full of colour, particularly in June and July.

One of the main features which Lord Feversham made is the cascade tumbling from beside the house to the riverbank. Downstream, a long path with a hedge behind stretches right along the riverbank to the farthest bridge. Along the path weeping trees overhang the river; one of the cherries is trained on to the framework of a bridge, draping it in blossom in spring.

On the far bank is the Wild Garden, extending uphill from the river and planted with azaleas, rhododendrons, heathers and very good meconopsis and candelabra primulas. The plants extend highest on a spur above a bend in the river, so the normally dour moorland hill is brought to life with bright colour, such as the red rhododendron 'May

Day', pieris and the small pink *Daphne cneorum*. From the farthest bridge a steep path climbs up above the Wild Garden, giving wonderful views across the garden and river to the moors.

Upstream from the bottom bridge the pattern is different. On the far bank a wide grass path leads to a fine statue of Eros. Rambling and shrub roses fill the border behind the path, with other shrubs such as kolkwitzia, and small geraniums, as groundcover. White and yellow honeysuckle covering the stone boundary wall at intervals are a masterly touch. On the house side of the river are more shrub roses, including the 'Complicata' rose. The white climber, 'Bobby James', has had no difficulty in enveloping an old apple tree, and a longicuspis rose, trained across the bridge, fills this end of the garden with the scent of banana.

The only part of the garden that is away from the river is the late summer border to one side of the house, planted with shrub roses such as 'St Nicholas' and 'Nevada', regale lilies, euphorbias and agapanthus, with clematis on the wall behind. The grey stone of the wall enclosing this part of the garden is highlighted by a narrow border of peonies and forget-me-nots.

Pennyholme is an unexpected haven, whose creation was a remarkable feat. It is an enormously rewarding sight for the visitor who will venture off the beaten track.

YORK GATE

In Back Church Lane, Adel, Leeds, off the A660
Tel. 0532 678 240
Mrs S. B. Spencer

Open one or two days per year, and by appointment

Such is the intricacy of design and variety of content at York Gate that a detailed description might give the impression that it is at least a medium-sized or even a large garden. In fact it fills less than one acre, and a visit here is a revelation in the planning of a small garden.

Much of York Gate's success derives from the use of features usually found in larger gardens but in well-proportioned miniature. Unity is given by the tight, architectural design, originated by Mrs Spencer's late son, Robin, who was a surveyor and by the neat harmony of planting throughout to avoid any appearance of overcrowding. Though not an inch is wasted, areas of lawn, as well as the many vistas and views across the garden, often hidden and suddenly revealed, give an illusion of space. The plantings and views are highlighted by architectural features and a large collection of garden ornaments, and attention to detail, so vital in a small garden, is everywhere apparent.

The first view from the entrance is across the sloping lawn around the Water Garden and pond, dominated by a large wrought-iron jardinière planted with euonymus; primulas and other water-loving plants trim the pond's edges. At its far end are a stone font and three stone griffins, and beyond them a semi-circle of clipped copper beech shields a curved stone seat and a bonsai specimen of *Cedrus atlantica glauca*, with Japanese lanterns on either side.

Robin Spencer himself laid the cobbled paths which are such a feature of the garden. One of these leads up the small slope to the arbour – old cross beams supported on stone columns with an intricate circular floor of blue slates set on their sides. From here one looks out over the miniature Pinetum, its pines and other needle conifers set in round pebbles on the sloping lawn. At the top a cedar has been trained over an arbour above a seat.

The Pinetum lawn leads to the Dell at the far end of the garden; here, in the damp ground beneath the white trunks of birches, are hostas, meconopsis, euphorbias, the Royal fern and lysitichums, while a striking copper weeping beech spreads overhead. From a white pump-head here one of the main vistas of the garden stretches through the wooden pillars of a circular Folly, between iris borders to another stone font and the circular window of the potting shed behind, a perfectly conceived contrast to the more open main lawn and Pinetum and the informality of the Dell.

The Folly is the focal point for a number of paths. One leads along a Nut Walk, a tunnel of cob nuts, to the beech hedge boundary, with a glimpse through the small gate to fields and woodland. Another path leads to the raised Canal: the idea for this came from the 'Moon Pond' at Hidcote, but as a circular pond would not fit here the long Canal was the result, with an impressive dolphin fountain at the far end. Another unusual variety of cedar is trained in éspalier fashion along the canal wall.

The font at the top of the iris borders is also the focus of a number of axes. One path leads down a slope, bordered by a tall yew hedge clipped into tall pyramids, and a fern border on the other side; and one of the best views in the garden is to be found in the other direction, through the small Herb Garden to the pillars of the summerhouse at the far end.

Clipped domes and spirals of golden and green box, add formality to the immaculate planting of mint, marjoram, rue, rosemary and many others of varied scent and foliage.

A door on one side of the summerhouse opens on to one of the most unexpected and perfectly conceived features at York Gate: a beech allée extends along the side of the garden to a 'Wobbly' sundial column. The narrow path between tall hedges is an interesting example of how to reduce a garden feature, and is another idea borrowed from Hidcote, where it is larger, and the inspiration for the allée at Hidcote came from Versailles which, as one would expect, is considerably larger still. A curved seat, specially made for the site, sits neatly into the curving beech hedge behind the sundial. From here one looks across the Silver Garden on the side of the house. On either side of the central path of grindstones are informal mixtures of dianthus, senecio, artemesia, helichrysum, pampas grass, white delphiniums and other plants. It was Robin Spencer's idea to design the windows of the kitchen and bedroom overlooking this garden so that from a distance they look like the façade of a Gothic summerhouse. From the house one looks back across the silver and white plants to the miniature ha-ha, six feet wide, and in true eighteenth-century style, to the prospect of parkland.

Despite its moderate size, one tour of the garden certainly does not suffice and on subsequent circuits new features are revealed: the 'Threepenny-bit Rose' trained into a cherry tree; the clipped topiary of holly and laurel along one path; the Paved Garden; the weeping birch, a silver wedding present for Mrs Spencer and her late husband, draped over a miniature Scree Garden; the unusual éspalier *Pyracantha coccinea* 'Lalandei'; *Actinidia kolomitka* trained on the walls of the house; and the enchanting small path lined with miniature pinks. While the architectural skills and craftsmanship were Robin Spencer's, the style and plantsmanship that inform the whole garden are Mrs Spencer's. In a relatively short time, since the early 1950s York Gate has become a memorable tribute to an impressive partnership.

SCOTLAND

THE BORDERS, DUMFRIES, GALLOWAY AND LOTHIAN

Berwickshire
East Lothian
Wigtownshire

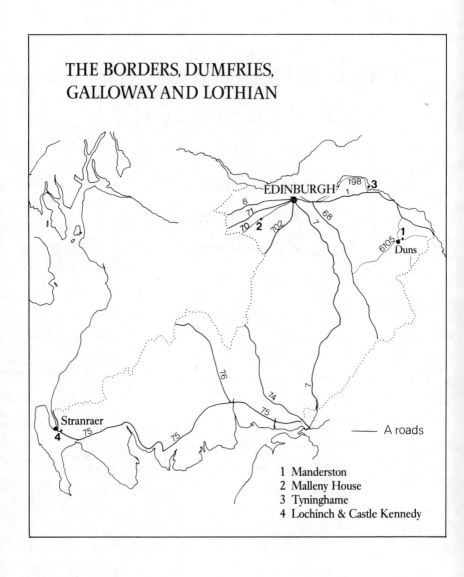

THE BORDERS, DUMFRIES, GALLOWAY AND LOTHIAN

EDINBURGH

Duns

Stranraer

—— A roads

1 Manderston
2 Malleny House
3 Tyninghame
4 Lochinch & Castle Kennedy

BERWICKSHIRE

MANDERSTON

2 miles east of Duns on the A6105
Tel. 0361 83450
Mr and Mrs Adrian Palmer

Open on Thursday and Sunday from mid-May to end–September, and on
Tuesday during August. Also Bank Holiday Monday afternoons, and by
appointment for parties

The re-modelling of Manderston was Edwardian extravagance at its
most lavish, and the house and grounds that resulted are widely
regarded as the finest of that period in Britain.

The appearance of the original house, built in the 1790s by Dalhousie
Weatherstone, was rendered somewhat bizarre by Sir William Miller,
1st Bt, who bought Manderston in 1864, surmounted it with a French
Renaissance-style roof and added a large portico on the front. Sir
William's eldest son, William, died at Eton choking on a cherry stone,
therefore in 1887 Manderston, the baronetcy and Miller fortunes were
inherited by his younger brother James. His motives for transforming
the house were simple – to impress his father-in-law and to please his
wife: the Hon. Eveline Curzon, daughter of Lord Scarsdale, had been
born and brought up in Robert Adam's masterpiece, Kedleston Hall in
Derbyshire. Sir William's fortune had been made trading in hemp and
herrings with Russia and Sir James spent it without stint to transform
Manderston's exterior, with the aid of the architect John Kinross, to
resemble its eighteenth-century Derbyshire model more closely, and
likewise spared no expense on the interior decoration and furnishing in
Adam style. The house complete, Sir James and Kinross turned their
attention to the surroundings.

395

To the north of the house the eighteenth-century layout of lawns and trees was retained. To the east, as well as oak and beech and a Lime Walk, are a number of conifers planted in the nineteenth century, delightfully set off by carpets of daffodils and bluebells in spring. Beyond the trees and the huge ornamental gates, gilded so that James could watch them glowing at sunset, Kinross laid out the formal gardens. The gates, the cherub statues surmounting them – and all the other statuary and gates at Manderston – came from Lord Duveen, the celebrated Edwardian art-dealer. A path leads east from them through the formal garden to another set in a classical portico. On either side of the path were originally long herbaceous borders, but now these are filled with roses and backed by yew hedges. To the north are areas of formal bedding: patterns of red begonias, white lobelias and blue alyssum surround the central statue fountain; there is also an herbaceous border. A pergola, underplanted with nearly fifty different varieties of daffodils, and with climbing roses trained up the columns, divides this upper level from the formal Sunken Garden on the path's south side. Extensive greenhouses, where the special feature is 'Malmaison' carnations, are the 'remnants' of the original series of greenhouses. The Walled Gardens, which would all have been intensely cultivated, stretch east behind the formal garden to the ornate Scottish-baronial head gardener's cottage and the marble dairy.

Kinross also laid out the four terraces on the south and east fronts of the house. To the east the grass terraces were for croquet and tennis, and their enclosing walls were planted with rhododendrons. Another set of massive gates, between piers this time surmounted with griffins, leads to the largest terrace on the south front. From here Manderston's superb siting can be realized: the ground slopes from the terrace to the lake in the valley below, and rises to the Woodland Garden on the far side. Looking from the house past the west side of the Woodland Garden the view across the lake to the Cheviot Hills, twenty miles away, is unbroken. The box hedges round the beds on the South Terrace have been removed to reduce labour, and the originally complex pattern has been simplified with plantings of floribunda roses and hostas. The curving double flight of steps below the balustraded retaining wall are clear replicas of those which Adam added to Kedleston's south front.

The Rhododendron Walk behind the East Terrace continues down to the stone-balustraded bridge across the lake. The delicate, wooden Chinese bridge at the west end was made in the eighteenth century, at the same time as the lake and house. The lake marks the division between the areas of garden laid out by Sir James and Kinross and the Pheasantry Woodland Garden on the far side, which was laid out by

Major Bailie, Adrian Palmer's grandfather, from 1957. He also made the small Japanese Garden beneath the balustraded bridge, but the Woodland Garden was his outstanding addition to Manderston.

The development and planting of the Pheasantry was every bit as ambitious as Sir James's earlier gardens. The dense woodland was cleared selectively, and opened up by removing the thick undergrowth and ponticum rhododendrons, though the great bank of ponticum to the east of the slope in front of the Pheasantry was retained and the beeches stretching down to the lakeside were thinned to allow views to the new garden from the house. The first new planting of rhododendrons came from the overcrowded Rhododendron Walk, and from these the garden was steadily expanded with plants of hybrid and specie rhododendrons from a variety of sources, including the gardens in Windsor Great Park, and Mrs Stevenson's garden at Tower Court near Ascot, where her husband had built up a unique collection of specie rhododendrons. The collection at Manderston is now enormous – just in the small sunken area called the Bowl there are two hundred and sixty different dwarf rhododendrons alone. It is by no means exclusively a rhododendron and azalea garden, however; a number of different ornamental trees and shrubs are planted with them – acers, birches, prunus, magnolias and many others.

To inherit a house and garden created when British wealth and desire to spend were at a peak poses innumerable problems in the 1980s, and the additional area of the Pheasantry, with the detail of planting there, represent a further responsibility, but Mr and Mrs Palmer cope in an impressive manner. Manderston's gardens are full of attractions for the horticulturalist indifferent to Edwardianism and Robert Adam alike, yet as surviving evidence of the style and taste of an era its interest is compulsive.

EAST LOTHIAN

MALLENY HOUSE

In Balerno, eight miles south of Edinburgh on the A70
Tel. 031 226 5922
The National Trust for Scotland
Open daily from May to September inclusive

Malleny House has a long history, chiefly associated with the Scotts of Malleny, six generations of whom were successive lairds of the property from 1656 until 1882; but the present garden, extending to about four acres around the house, is almost completely the work of Commander and Mrs Gore-Browne Henderson, who bought the property in 1960. It is at its best in summer when the now considerable collection of old-fashioned shrub roses are in full flower.

The main part of the house with its steeply pitched roof was built in the seventeenth century. In 1810 General Thomas Scott, the fourth laird, added a wing whose larger windows and shallower roof contrast with those of the original building. In 1882 the property was sold to the Earl of Rosebery, one of whose tenants was Sir Thomas Carmichael; he obviously had a garden of note since it was illustrated in Sir Herbert Maxwell's book *Scottish Gardens* published at the beginning of this century. Sir Thomas's great interest was in decorative wrought-iron work, most of which he removed to a subsequent home, but one surviving example here is the Rosebery coat of arms.

When the Gore-Browne Hendersons arrived at Malleny there was little to recommend the garden. It was dominated by twelve huge yew trees, known as the Twelve Apostles, reputedly planted in 1603. Eight of these formed a claustrophobic surround to the Georgian wing of the house and were removed, to the immediate improvement of both house and garden. The four survivors, now predictably known as the Four Evangelists, stand together neatly clipped in the centre of the garden.

Shrub roses were originally planted at Malleny because they proved suitable and because an initial number were available from Major Hog, a near neighbour at Newliston House. The Gore-Browne Hendersons rapidly expanded the quantity and variety of roses throughout the garden but Malleny is not exclusively a rose garden. Mrs Gore-Browne Henderson was always most interested in rhododendrons, primulas and meconopsis, while her husband preferred a variety of shrubs and bulbs. As well as these, other borders are planted with herbaceous plants. More recently an area of woodland has been considerably thinned and planted to provide interest in the spring.

Mrs Gore-Browne Henderson gave the property to the National Trust for Scotland in 1968, and they have carefully preserved the delightfully personal and intimate atmosphere instilled by the Gore-Browne Hendersons so that today it is one of their most charming gardens.

TYNINGHAME

1 mile north of the A1 on the A198
Tel. 062 086 240

The Earl and Countess of Haddington

Open daily except weekends from June to September inclusive

Since 1952 Lady Haddington has built on the framework provided by generations of a family who first came to Tyninghame in the seventeenth century. Tyninghame's long history must have been an inspiration, dating back to the early days of Christianity when it was an important member of the 'family' at Lindisfarne; St Baldred died at Tyninghame in 756. Nearly two hundred years later the place was burned by a Norse king of York but in 1064 – by the earliest-known Scottish Charter – King Duncan granted Tyninghame to the monks of St Cuthbert, and it remained in ecclesiastical hands until the mid-sixteenth century. Thereafter it passed through a succession of owners until bought by the 1st Earl of Haddington in 1628. About two hundred yards south of the house stand the ruins of an ancient Church of Norman date; two beautiful arches decorated with chevron design remain. Lady Binning, the present Earl's mother, had the foundations of the church exposed during the period between the two World Wars. Built into the core of the tower was found a large, exquisitely chiselled stone, part of a Celtic cross head, an indication of a far earlier church on the site.

What sort of house existed is not certain until the eighteenth century, when the 6th Earl made considerable repairs and improvements. He and his wife, Helen Hope, sister of the 1st Earl of Hopetoun, planted the extensive woodlands, including the great mile-long avenue of beeches leading through the park down to the sea to the north of the house. This has proved of enormous value, since the trees have done much to counteract Tyninghame's exposed position on flat coastal land. The 6th Earl also built the brick walls of the sloping, four-acre Walled Garden to the west of the house, and first laid out the Wilderness, between it and the house, with fourteen straight walks radiating from a central point.

In 1829 the 8th Earl commissioned William Burn to make extensive alterations, and it is his building, of red sandstone with turrets and gables, that we see today. The parterre and terraces to the west and south of the house were laid out at the same time.

In the 1890s Lord Haddington's parents made a number of alterations to the gardens, especially in the Walled Garden. Here they laid out the central herbaceous border between yew hedges stretching from north to south down the slope past their Italian fountain, and beyond the gateway, with pedimented stone surround, in the bottom wall, they laid out the Apple Walk. One of the great features of Tyninghame, this stretches for a hundred and twenty yards along the south wall, the trees, recently replaced, trained over metal arches to form a tunnel.

Lord and Lady Haddington have removed the herbaceous borders from the Walled Garden in order to reduce maintenance, but they have replaced them with a design which is simplified but equally effective. Grass now extends the width of the old borders right to the yew hedges, which have been trained to form domed niches at intervals for four superb stone statues on either side, representing Music and the Seasons, which Lord and Lady Haddington brought from Vicenza. In other parts of the Walled Garden is a deep iris border for which the plants were sent from Padua, a small Arboretum and a Knot Garden, where the pattern of box hedges is filled with lavender.

The appearance of the Wilderness has changed considerably since the 6th Earl originally laid it out. Though some of his trees remain, it is now an area of informal woodland which Lord and Lady Haddington have planted with flowering trees and shrubs: azaleas and rhododendrons; acers; *Cornus kousa*, massed in a striking group; a Laburnum

Walk, discovered quite unexpectedly in such natural surrounds; and numbers of white and mauve lilacs, which fill the Wilderness with scent at the same time as the long grass is filled with wild primroses.

The beds of annuals in the parterre to the west of the house have been replaced with a formal Rose Garden of delicate white and yellow. In alternating beds are standard 'King's Ransom' with 'Golden Showers' climbing up a wooden support; and 'Iceberg', both standard and trained on to the wooden framework.

From the wilderness end of the terrace a small gate opens into the Secret Garden created by Lady Haddington, her most exquisite contribution to the gardens. Based on a design from *The Theory and Practise of Gardening*, a French eighteenth-century book, the garden was made on an abandoned area of weeds and rubbish. Enclosed by hedges, paths wind among a profusion of flowers, especially old-fashioned roses: 'Honorine de Brabant', 'Reine des Violettes' and 'Comte de Chambord'. Climbing roses and honeysuckle are trained over arch supports, and there are agapanthus, lilacs and grey-leafed plants like senecio and santolina. In the centre a statue of Summer, also from Vicenza, stands in a trellis-work arbour veiled in climbing roses and clematis.

In adapting the existing layouts to easier maintenance it would have been easy to lose Tyninghame's atmosphere, but throughout Lady Haddington has introduced many unusual plants and harmonious plant combinations and brought a sense of renewal and new character to the garden.

WIGTOWNSHIRE

LOCHINCH AND CASTLE KENNEDY

3 miles east of Stranraer on the A75
Tel. 0776 2024

The Earl and Countess of Stair

Open daily from April to September inclusive

The two castles – Castle Kennedy, built in the fifteenth century and a ruin since it was destroyed by fire in 1716, and Lochinch, built in 1864 – stand at the south and north ends of a narrow isthmus between the Black Loch and the White Loch, a remote position, far out in the south-west corner of Scotland.

This isolation did not deter the 2nd Earl of Stair, who early in the eighteenth century laid out the gardens on the undulating ground between the two castles. He had been British Ambassador to France, and the formality of his gardens reflected French influence. He was also a Field Marshal who fought with the Duke of Marlborough. In 1743 and 1744 King George II made him Colonel of the Inniskilling Fusiliers and of the Royal Scots Greys, and the enterprising Earl used the soldiers in garden construction, in particular the series of terraces and mounds. After a period of neglect the 8th Earl of Stair began to restore the gardens on a formal pattern and from the mid-nineteenth century the gardens were built up by succeeding generations with trees and with other plants from America and Asia, many of them unusual and tender, benefiting from the mild climate here caused not only by proximity to the coast but to the Gulf Stream off that coast. Today these plants are not only mature but in many cases exceptional.

The 2nd Earl planned his gardens round the circular Lily Pond. No ordinary pond this; it covers two acres and was made by sealing off a bay of the White Loch. Roughly equidistant between the two castles, the pond is the point from which many avenues radiate. The 2nd Earl planted the Dettingen Avenue of ilex, which leads south from the Walled Garden beside the ruined castle to the White Loch and was named after the Battle of Dettingen in 1742, in which the 2nd Earl fought before retiring from the army. Some of the Earl's earthworks were given names associated with his military campaigns, like Mount Marlborough, but the long raised terrace called the Giant's Grave took its name from a local legend.

The new varieties of plants arriving in Britain in large quantities by the mid-nineteenth century transformed the gardens. The garden restoration begun by the 8th Earl in 1840 was based on an original plan and his successors planted round the old framework of avenues and impressive vistas. In 1864 the 10th Earl commissioned the new castle to be called Lochinch, and the most spectacular of the new avenues leads up to it, the wide avenue of *Araucaria araucana*, the 'Monkey-puzzle' which William Lobb introduced from South America in the 1840s, stretching north for over a hundred yards up the slope from the Lily Pond. It is certainly the finest of these trees in Britain. Other early introductions to the gardens were some of the rhododendrons, including many plants of *R. arboreum*, one of the finest varieties sent back by Sir Joseph Hooker from the Himalayas over a century ago. The Lily Pond is rendered spectacular in early summer by the surrounding banks of rhododendrons and azaleas, and later in summer water-lilies form a solid carpet over the water. Rhododendrons and azaleas continue up the avenue of 'Monkey-puzzle' trees, with the scented yellow azalea forming banks on either side of the grass at the north end.

The 12th Earl inherited in 1914 but did not return to Lochinch until 1918, having been a prisoner-of-war. It was between then and his death in 1961 that he expanded the collection of rhododendrons and added many other tender plants. One of his most successful of the many hybrid rhododendrons raised at Lochinch, winning an Award of Merit, was the 'Lord Stair' form of the fragrant and tender *R. lindleyi*. One of the most outstanding rhododendrons in the garden is the blood red *Rh*. 'Review Order', a group of which grow together on the edge of a small woodland glade called 'The Cockpit'. The quality of plants and their unusual natures make considerable demands of maintenance and this is a slight problem in parts of the gardens today. It really would be unfortunate if some of the most unusual features at Lochinch were to disappear. One worthy of particular note is the hedge of *Tricuspidaria lanceolata* – better known as *Crinodendron hookeranum* – in the Walled Garden beside the old castle. This tender plant is only occasionally seen as a shrub in the milder localities in Britain, and a hedge must be virtually unique. Also in the Walled Garden are hedges of pittosporum, along the main central borders, and of *Myrtus luma*; and in one corner is a magnolia orchard, of varieties with pendulous flowers such as *M. wilsonii*.

It seems that a great many of the plants at Lochinch are either extremely rare, or grow so large and in such abundant quantities that they become unusual for that very reason. Along the west side of the Walled Garden is a typically luxuriant mixture of *Pieris formosa forestii*, leptospermum and magnolias. The gates leading into the Dettingen Avenue are flanked by *Eucryphia nymanensis* 'Nymansay', and now the dark green ilex at different times of the year set off the avenue of alternating *Embothrium coccineum*, the 'Chilean Fire Bush', and *Eucryphia glutinosa* planted inside. This combination is also used round the sheltered lawn, near the Giant's Grave, known as the Dancing Green after another local story. A number of the fine cryptomerias in the gardens grow nearby. Sadly the unrivalled Pinetum was almost totally destroyed by a gale in 1963, and subsequent gales have damaged many other trees.

The gardens around Lochinch Castle have been greatly simplified since the nineteenth century. In the Sunken Garden to the west side of the castle the original fifty-eight flower beds have been reduced to seven, with many shrubs; plants along the front terrace on the south side include *Romneya coulteri*, fijoia, olearias and leptospermums. The gardens round the later castle are on a smaller scale than those filling the larger aera of the isthmus on either side of the pond but the quantity of plants seems limitless and together with the glorious setting this makes Lochinch and Castle Kennedy among the richest gardens in Scotland.

CENTRAL, FIFE, STRATHCLYDE AND TAYSIDE

Angus
Argyllshire
Fife
Kinross-shire
Perthshire

CENTRAL, FIFE, STRATHCLYDE AND TAYSIDE

ISLE OF MULL

Pitlochry ●12

Brechin ●1   2●
935
3●   94
Forfar   92
4●
Dundee
Creiff   85   85
13●   11●
822   Perth
9
8●
Kinross   9● 10●
Pittenweem
Inverary 6●
83
5●   816
Lochgilphead
84
82
M90   92
80
77   74

1   Brechin Castle
2   Edzell Castle
3   Glamis Castle
4   The House of Pitmuies
5   Crarae Lodge
6   Strone House
7   Torosay Castle
8   Kinross House
9   Balcaskie
10 Kellie Castle
11 Branklyn
12 Cluniemore
13 Drummond Castle

—— A roads

ANGUS

BRECHIN CASTLE

1 mile west of Brechin, off the A935
Tel. 03562 2176
The Earl of Dalhousie

Open one Sunday a year, and by appointment for parties

Successive generations have made Brechin Castle and its gardens outstanding in Scotland. The Castle site is superb, with the ground on the south side dropping away almost sheer to the River South Esk. It was for this commanding position that the original medieval fort was built. It was here that John Balliol paid homage to Edward I; later Edward III destroyed the fort after a siege of twenty-one days. The present castle dates from the eighteenth and nineteenth century. Towards the end of the seventeenth century the 4th Earl of Panmure commissioned Alexander Edward to rebuild the castle. Edward's main work, completed three years after his death in 1708, was the present west front, with its towers at either end of the plain façade and central pediment. Edward's south front overlooking the river had a square tower added to his original structure in 1863.

Brechin's notable parkland leads to the west front: many of its trees – oaks, limes, firs and wellingtonias – were planted in the eighteenth and nineteenth century. The present Lord Dalhousie, among many alterations to the present form of the gardens, has added a number of rhododendrons and azaleas among these trees, to make attractive walks from the castle to the old Walled Garden.

The Walled Garden, on a south-facing slope, is Brechin's main feature and is some distance from the castle in traditional Scottish manner. The walls were probably built by Lady Panmure, who brought back the family estates in 1764 after they had been forfeited in 1715 for involvement in the Jacobite rising. The walls of her garden are all curving and form a rough heart pattern. After Lady Panmure's death succeeding generations of Panmures and Dalhousies made extensive additions here, especially the 11th Earl and the wife of the 14th Earl, but some of the trees, and the enormous yew hedges near the top of the garden, are survivors from the original eighteenth-century plan. During the nineteenth century the garden developed a typically Victorian pattern of flowerbeds and borders round areas of vegetables and fruit. At the same time the various glasshouses were built, among which the curvilinear Peach House is an outstanding – and now rare – example of garden architecture.

The present Lord and Lady Dalhousie have made extensive changes in the Walled Garden, partly to reduce the labour. In fact, not only have the alterations brought easier maintenance but a greater interest, with new varieties of trees and shrubs replacing the better-known herbaceous and annual plants. Wisely, they retained features of the old garden which have always played an important part in its character and appearance.

The gates open on to a wide path stretching west, the length of the garden. The imposing vista is now flanked by grass, but on one side the old yew hedge, clipped into domes along the steps down to the main area on the slope, has been retained. Further along the path four blue Lawson cypresses stand where cross-paths meet. There one finds not only a stone sundial but a moondial – totally baffling to most visitors.

The steps leading away from the main garden path are hedged; stone cherub figures lead one to expect formality but a notable lack of it inhabits the area planted by Lord Dalhousie. To the surrounding mature trees, many of which, including the cedar, were planted around 1700, Lord Dalhousie has added others, either in stands or beds round which the grass paths and occasional small lawns wind easily. At the bottom a lily pond is surrounded by four box-enclosed beds of white and pink mallow, but here again it is the trees that are most striking: acers, cercidiphyllums, eucryphias, old cedars, a young blue cedar, an unusual sorbus, *S. scopulina*, and many others.

Lord Dalhousie's influence and knowledge have been decisive throughout the gardens and parkland, making the large acreage both more manageable and far more interesting year-round.

EDZELL CASTLE

1 mile west of Edzell, 6 miles north of Brechin off the B996

Tel. 035 64631

The Secretary of State for Scotland

Open daily

Restored since 1932 when the Earl of Dalhousie, whose ancestors inherited the castle in 1782, passed the garden and later the building into the custody of the State, Edzell is possibly the oldest, virtually complete garden in Britain, and historically is certainly one of the most interesting.

The castle, partly built in the early, and partly by Sir David Lindsay in the later sixteenth century, is now preserved in a melancholy and romantic state of ruin, but in Sir David's small garden, or 'pleasaunce' as it was originally called, one can see the features that make it unique. Edzell's importance can only be seen in its historical context. It was created in the short period of relative calm between the early stages of the Reformation, a precarious peace between Church and State that was strengthened by the union of the crowns of England and Scotland. But even so, stability was short-lived and brought to an end by the renewal of religious struggles in 1637, and by the Civil War. Against this background the unusually enlightened character and education of Sir David Lindsay stands clear. During his education Sir David had travelled extensively in Renaissance Europe, and it was probably in Germany that he found the inspiration for his garden sculptures. When he died in 1610 Sir David left his family heavily in debt after lavish spending on his castle, garden and other projects.

The parterre which filled Sir David's garden has now been restored, with roses in the flowerbeds enclosed by intricate patterns of clipped box hedging. Around the rosebeds are the words DUM SPIRO SPERO – While I breathe I hope – the motto of the Glenesk Lindsays. The sunken parterre is admittedly similar to others of the seventeenth century, but in the treatment of its surrounding walls Sir David and his mason ensured Edzell a unique place in the influence of the Renaissance in Scotland.

The walls are built of the same stone as the castle and heavily decorated round the east, south and west sides. All the way round a

409

representation of the Lindsay arms alternates with panels of sculptured symbolic figures. The arms consist of the *fess chequy* or three lines of squares in a chequer pattern. There were recesses in the wall designed for flower-boxes in the heraldic colours of the arms, blue and white, the red sandstone providing the third colour of the pattern. Above the *fess chequy* are the three seven-rayed mullets or stars, which the Lindsays inherited in their arms from their predecessors, the Stirlings of Glenesk. The centre of each mullet had a recess pierced for doves to nest in. Above the heraldic patterns on the east and south walls the heavy coping is broken by semi-circular headed niches which would originally have displayed busts. That there are no niches on the west wall suggests Sir David was getting badly into debt before the garden was finished.

Alternating with the heraldic patterns are three series of sculptured panels, representing the Cardinal Virtues on the west wall, the Liberal Arts on the south wall and the Planetary Deities on the east wall. As the late W. Douglas Simpson wrote:

'Regarded as a whole the three form a theme which may be stated thus, as appropriate embellishments to a baronial home like Edzell. The prosperity of its noble owner must be based first of all upon his personal character – *ie*, the degree to which he is endowed with the seven Cardinal Virtues: the three Christian Virtues, Faith, Hope and Charity, and the four Moral virtues, Prudence, Temperance, Fortitude and Justicy. Thereafter these must be strengthened by a good education, as the age understood it, namely a thorough grounding in the Seven Liberal Arts, the *Trivium* and the *Quadrivium* of the scholastic curriculum: Grammar, Rhetoric, Argument, and Arithmetic, Music, Geometry, Astronomy. But lastly, over and above all of these, the good fortune of the owner and the endurance of his house will in the ultimate be dependent on the higher power of heavenly guidance, exerted through the mysterious influence believed to be wielded by the Seven Planets in their several courses through the Zodiac: Saturn, Jupiter, Mars, Sol (the Sun), Venus, Mercury, Luna (the Moon).'

The sculptured panels are unique and, compared with the work of any period in British history, a superb artistic representation of the philosophy of their age. It is miraculous that such a gem as the Edzell garden has been preserved; today, its future assured, its conveys an atmosphere of expansive calm entirely in keeping with the spirit that created it.

GLAMIS CASTLE

West of Forfar off the A94

Tel. 030 784 242

The Earl and Countess of Strathmore and Kinghorne

Open daily except Saturday from May to September inclusive

Like those of many long-established homes – Lord Strathmore's family have lived at Glamis since 1372 – the gardens here lost their formality in the eighteenth-century and then had it partially restored in the nineteenth and early twentieth century.

The castle greatly impressed the eighteenth century poet Thomas Gray with its tower and overall height and size when he visited in 1765. Shortly afterwards its surroundings were dramatically altered by 'Capability' Brown, who swept away the seventeenth-century parterres and topiary in a manner Sir Walter Scott deplored: 'A disciple of Kent had the cruelty to render this splendid old mansion more parkish, as he pleased to call it; to raze all those external defences, and to bring his mean and paltry gravel walk up to the very door, from which, deluded by the name, we might have imagined Lady Macbeth issuing forth to receive King Duncan.' But as well as the park lawns which now surround the castle, Brown gave Glamis its unforgettable approach drive, sloping downhill between double avenues straight to the castle.

One outstanding feature which pre-dates 'Capability' Brown by a hundred years is the enormous sundial, with facets for each month of the year, which is supported by four heraldic lions on twisted columns. It stands twenty-one feet high where it was originally placed by Patrick, 3rd Earl of Kinghorne and 1st Earl of Strathmore between 1671 and 1680. The series of gates and walls which surrounded the castle in the seventeenth century were never restored, but formality was revived in the Dutch Garden and Italian Garden, laid out respectively by the 13th Earl and Countess and the 14th Earl and Countess, the parents of Queen Elizabeth the Queen Mother, who was partly brought up at Glamis.

The Dutch Garden lies beneath the East wing of the castle, a pattern of rosebeds enclosed by low box hedges surrounding the central statue of Mercury; it is divided by wide gravel paths. The fine ornamental stone gateway on the side is dated 1893 to mark the garden's creation; the wrought-iron gate opens on to the long vista of the Yew Walk stretching away to a stone urn and pedestal. On one side of the Yew Walk is a small and private garden, enclosed by clipped beech hedges, which has recently been planted by Colin Campbell-Preston, a young garden designer, with a rectangle of low flowerbeds dividing the upper level of lawn from the central sunken lawn.

On its other side, the Yew Walk forms the boundary for the Italian Garden, the main area of garden at Glamis and largely the work of Nina, the 14th Countess. Designed with impressive formality, this garden reflects her consummate skill; it is to her the Queen Mother always attributes her own interest in gardening. Immediately alongside the Yew Walk is a long herbaceous border with beyond a raised terrace stretching between summerhouses nostalgically reminiscent of the seventeenth-century style banished by 'Capability' Brown. Stone urns stand beside the steps down in the main garden and break the terrace at intervals. Box-enclosed flower-beds extend from the centre of the terrace in fan-shaped patterns and at either end stone urns on tall pedestals stand in the middle of lawns enclosed by high box hedges.

Undoubtedly the outstanding features in the garden are the two pleached Beech Walks, the closely trained branches forming a canopy over the gravel paths. The latest addition to the Italian Garden has been the pair of wrought-iron gates at the entrance, made in 1980 by a local craftsman to celebrate the eightieth birthday of the Queen Mother. Separated from the castle, its towers visible above the enclosing hedges, the Italian Garden marked the return of formality to Glamis on a scale suitable for both the castle and the larger surrounding parkland, and today is maintained, like the rest of the gardens, in an immaculate condition.

THE HOUSE OF PITMUIES

East of Forfar, off the A492
Tel. 02412 245
Mrs Farquhar Ogilvie

Open every afternoon from May to July inclusive

The outstanding trees along the drive and round the entrance front of the House of Pitmuies give some inkling of what to expect from the garden.

Much of the character of the House of Pitmuies derives from the old-established harmony of house, gardens, farm buildings and cottages created by the owner James Mudie at the end of the eighteenth century. By getting rid of the ford across the Vinny Water along the south edge of the garden, and the road which crossed the ford and continued straight past the house, Mudie brought peace to Pitmuies. He then turned his attention to using his considerable wealth to improve the property. It is rumoured that his wife was a Caribbean sugar heiress, but wherever the money came from it was put to good use. The house was originally seventeenth-century and had been added to in 1730. Mudie built on, giving the house an intriguing appearance which has fascinated many visitors. He also built the farm buildings and cottages which survive in their original condition, thanks to expert restoration by Mrs Ogilvie and her late husband. Mudie also planted the trees which in their maturity provide Pitmuies with its matchless setting – chestnut, conifers, beeches and, in particular, the dark copper beeches.

Mr and Mrs Ogilvie came to the House of Pitmuies in the 1960s, his father having bought the property in 1945. They considerably restored the buildings and gardens, including clearing some of the old trees and carefully replanting, thus opening up a number of views away from the house. One of the new trees, a young cut-leaf beech, stands beside the path leading from the west lawn down to the river and to an area planted with rhododendrons, azaleas, a tulip tree and a very fine specimen of *Acer griseum*.

Most of the lime trees from Mudie's avenue along the River Walk have gone; now there are mainly beech and younger replacements retaining the path's cool and shaded atmosphere. The natural simplicity of the trees and river are unfailingly restful, the shades of green broken only by the daffodils and other spring bulbs on the bank. Overlooking the river is Pitmuies' oldest edifice, the dovecot, a seventeenth-century *mis-en-scène*, dating from 1643, with sloping roof and castellated gables built of Angus stone and, on either side of the Gothic door, circular turrets. A horse chestnut and a lilac stand guard, surrounded by winter aconites early in the year. On the north wall are the arms of Guthrie and Ogilvy, for Pitmuies at some date in the seventeenth century was the dowry of a Guthrie daughter when she married David, son of Lord Ogilvy.

It is in the main garden on the south side of the house that the Ogilvies have done most work. In a square area with a tall yew hedge to the west and lawn on the east leading to a shrub border and perimeter wall, they have maintained and improved the borders made by previous owners. The pattern is of paths between double herbaceous borders on either side of the central Rose Garden. The border beneath the yew hedge and the more recent one opposite are planted blue, white and pale yellow, with silver foliage plants. In the centre of the Rose Garden is a pool and fountain with, along one side, the delphinium border. The second border has an old sundial in the centre of the path and is contained by a hedge of purple prunus. This path is aligned with the small gateway beside the house leading into the old Walled Garden, and the path continues north across it, with vegetables in the main area on one side, lined by box hedges and old apple trees with tulips beneath. A Herb Garden has been created in the eastern part of this garden, with plants chosen for their scent and visual impact as much as for culinary or medical interest.

The combination of the individual plants in the borders and the overall effect is spectacular in the summer and makes them the outstanding feature in the garden. Andrew Duncan, the gardener, has worked hard at the propagation of rare and unusual plants and shrubs, and these are now on sale from Pitmuies.

Along the bottom of the main garden is a wall surmounted with curving woodwork into which climbing roses, clematis and wisteria are trained; stretching along the outside of the wall is a long hedge of rugosa roses. Below here to the south the garden becomes meadow, stretching to the river; Swiss miniature crocuses and snowdrops fill the long grass in spring. The view from the bottom of the garden, through the gates surmounted by lead urns, and along the herbaceous border to the silver weeping pears at the top and the path in the Walled Garden, shows with what skill the layout and planting of the garden have been combined.

The pink and white clematis trained on the wall of the house, and the octagonal conservatory, effectively bring the house into the garden. The shrub border, sheltering beneath the wall on the eastern perimeter, contains a wide variety of plants: magnolias, azaleas and dwarf rhododendrons, a copper-leafed acer, and small fritillaries, hellebores meconopsis and hostas, the last two also growing in profusion with primulas in a damp border. A 'damp' Wild Garden is being developed for primulas, meconopsis and ligularias in a boggy piece of woodland with rhododendrons, adjoining the east drive.

While the riverside parts of the garden retain the naturalness they no doubt had when James Mudie was planting the trees two hundred years ago, the immaculately maintained borders reflect Mrs Ogilvie's skill and work in more recent years, and it is this balance between the two eras which is the basis of much of the House of Pitmuies' appeal and character.

ARGYLLSHIRE

CRARAE LODGE

Off the A83 between Lochgilphead and Inverary
Tel. 04995 218
Crarae Garden Charitable Trust

Open daily from April to October inclusive

The garden, formerly the property of Sir Ilay Campbell Bt, was handed over to a charitable trust, formed for the purpose, in 1978. Since 1904, when Sir Ilay's grandparents came to Crarae, three generations, in particular his father, Sir George Campbell, used the many advantages of the site to develop an exceptional Woodland Garden.

The setting is the main steeply sloping hillside behind the house down which the Crarae Burn alternately burbles over rocks and boulders or tumbles over waterfalls between reclivitous banks. From the highest part of the garden are views over Loch Fyne stretching far into the distance to east and west.

Although Crarae enjoys relative mildness in its west-coast position, as Sir Ilay remarks, the Gulf Stream has to flow a long way up Loch Fyne to benefit the garden, which is often subject to severe frosts and bitter winds from the north and east in February and March. From the centrepiece of the burn the garden has steadily expanded on either side, taking full advantage of the mature, sheltering trees. Some of these, in particular the larches and Scots pines, were planted at the beginning of the nineteenth century by Crawford Tait, who was living at Crarae then, but many were planted by Sir Ilay's grandmother with advice and presents from her nephew Reginald Farrer, the explorer and plant-collector, and from other gardening friends.

The planting by Sir Ilay's grandmother was largely confined to the

The view from Robert Bakewell's wrought-iron masterpiece, the Birdcage Arbour at Melbourne Hall, Derbyshire, across the Great Basin with the house in the distance.

Ranks of tulips line a path beneath spring blossom at Windle Hall, Lancashire where a spectacular display of roses takes over in summer.

The Carolean east façade of Heale House, Wiltshire framed by old yew hedges which lead to a flagged terrace and sloping walk between laburnums beyond.

A contrast between the intimacy of the small geraniums in the stone urn and the long vista between pleached limes out of the garden to the lodge house at Cottesbrooke Hall, Northamptonshire.

Looking across informal daffodils to clipped yew topiary beside Benthall Hall, Shropshire.

The superb curving conservatory at Sezincote, its Oriental architecture echoing that of the house.

One of many intriguing glimpses to be caught in the garden of Barnsley House, Gloucestershire, this one between clipped yew hedges across the main lawn to the statue of a hunting lady by Simon Verity.

Mottisfont Abbey, Hampshire. Geoffrey Jellicoe's terrace, surmounted with pleached limes, leads to the oldest front of the house which incorporates the old abbey.

The sunken lily pond at the Manor House, Bledlow, made since 1968 in a courtyard on the site of an old barn. The gazebo was built at the same time; beyond are farm buildings.

Inigo Jones's West Woodhay House, Berkshire, framed by twentieth-century Irish yews.

areas round the house, and it was Sir Ilay's father, Sir George, who began to make inroads into the glen above, clearing the thick birch, oak and alder undergrowth and steadily replanting. His great interest in and knowledge of rhododendrons originated in the realization that nearly all species of the family were suited to the conditions at Crarae – the acid soil, high rainfall averaging seventy-five inches a year and the shelter of taller trees. Rhododendrons now form the largest and outstanding collection in the garden today, but since Sir George's day the rhododendrons and azaleas have always been planted with many other families so that now the range of plants at Crarae is enormous.

The first tree Sir George brought to Crarae was a silver fir, *Abies grandis*, which he, then aged fourteen, and his sister brought over from Inverary in their governess's cart. In 1917 he was given a far rarer tree, a Chinese fir, *Cunninghamia lanceolata*, from Dawyck by its owner, F. R. S. Balfour Dawyck, who greatly influenced Sir George's growing interest in the Crarae garden. Since those early arrivals the size and variety of the tree collection has greatly expanded to include conifers, broad-leafed deciduous, flowering and ornamental trees. Gradually Sir George and Sir Ilay came to know which parts of the world provide plants that thrive best at Crarae – Chile, Tasmania, the South Island of New Zealand, the Himalayas and parts of Japan and China. Many families are well-represented and some almost comprehensively: eucalyptus, some of which have attained outstanding size; embrothriums; eucryphias; nothofagus, of which most varieties are grown; malus; sorbus; *Cercidiphyllum japonicum*; *Styrax japonica* and *S. obessia*; acers and tulip trees. Many of these are planted in groups to increase their effectiveness; in one place five different nothofagus are planted together. Many of the evergreens are planted as standards, such as the fine 'Monkey-puzzle'.

The path up the west side of the burn reveals many of the best plant combinations and views in the garden. Huge plants of the scented yellow azalea hang over the pool below one of the large waterfalls and beyond, on the far side, is a bank of *Cornus kousa*. *Hydrangea petiolaris*, the climbing hydrangea, clings to one side of the burn among sheer rocks reminiscent of its native habitat; and growing straight out of the rocks lower down on the same side of the burn is *Rhododendron barbatum*, whose early crimson-scarlet flowers contrast with its distinctive purple-tinged and peeling bark. Higher up the burn are deciduous azaleas, acers, *Hammamelis mollis*, *Malus sargentii* and *Styrax hemsleyana*, planting clearly outstanding for autumn colour of which the highlights are perhaps the banks of *Disanthus cercidifolius* above the *Cornus kousa*.

The variety and quantity of rhododendrons and azaleas continues throughout the garden. The large-leafed varieties, such as *R. falconeri*, are again often planted in groups for effect and to contrast with the more delicate varieties such as *R. yunnanense*. In some places they provide the backdrop for yet other plants: the pink flowers of *Rh.* 'Flamingo' highlight blue meconopsis and lush hostas in front. Meconopsis are a feature of the garden, particularly in the old vegetable garden, with its blend of blue *Meconopsis sheldonii* and white *M. grandis* 'Alba'.

Despite the creation of the trust, the future of the forty acres of woodland garden is by no means assured: visitors are the all-important factor. They are offered a variety of routes round the garden, depending on their time available and their vigour. Whether they take the shortest, which keeps to the areas round the house and the immediate valley round the burn, or whether they range adventurously over the larger areas to either side, they will be continually rewarded by the individual plants, their grouping or their positioning in the enviable setting. Crarae is far more than an outstanding collection of plants. To end a visit one should climb Flagstaff Hill, between the old-fashioned azaleas planted by Sir Ilay's grandmother, and look back over the garden or out over Loch Fyne: it gives an almost unwarranted return on energy employed.

STRONE HOUSE

In Cairndow on the A83
Tel. 0499 6284
The Lady Glenkinglas

Open daily from April to October inclusive

Strone House itself is separated by the road, winding down from the Rest and Be Thankful Pass to Loch Fyne, from the main slope of the garden descending to Ardkinglas House beside the loch. One interesting but invisible fact about the present Ardkinglas House, built by Sir Robert Lorimer is that to ensure it did not suffer the fate of its predecessors – an attractive Georgian house and fifteenth–sixteenth-century castle, both destroyed by fire – Lord Glenkinglas's grandfather had its ground and first floors lined with asbestos and steel. Since 1947 the late Lord Glenkinglas and his wife developed a Woodland Garden on the north bank of the River Kinglas and round Strone House.

The fact that Lord Glenkinglas never had a gardener in the fifty years he was at Strone emphasizes the fact that here is principally a natural Woodland Garden. The fast-flowing River Kinglas separates the lawns and more formal gardens round Ardkinglas House from the Woodland Garden on the slope above and here Lord Glenkinglas added an out-standing collection of rhododendrons and azaleas to what may best be described as a collection of spectacular freaks – outsize conifers which include the tallest tree in Britain.

Trees of over 100 feet are the norm among the conifers on the steep bank sloping down to the River Kinglas. Most of the trees were planted in the mid to late nineteenth century, although one that is clearly older is the extraordinary silver fir, *Abies alba*, which divides near the base of its bole into four immense trunks; it was 142 feet tall when measured in 1976. Other trees over 100 feet include more silver firs, western red cedars, *Thuja plicata*, and a western hemlock, *Tsuga heterophylla*, and a superb and unusually slender Douglas fir, *Pseudotsuga menziesii*, which was 163 feet when measured in 1976. Affectionately known as 'The Boy' because it is slightly younger than most of the other trees, its prodigious rate of growth makes it a likely successor to the king of the garden, a giant fir, *Abies grandis*, planted in 1875 and now 200 feet tall, the first tree in Britain to reach this height.

Equally spectacular in the spring and early summer are the rhododendrons, slightly closer to eye-level. Lord Glenkinglas built up a collection of over five hundred different plants, specie and hybrids. The sandy loam, shelter, mildness and high rainfall, typical of the west coast of Scotland, make conditions ideal. Many of the original plants were given to him by the late Lord Aberconway from his garden at Bodnant. Two of the numerous hybrids raised by Lord Glenkinglas have memor-able names. The first, 'Secretary of State', was raised while he was Secretary of State for Scotland, while the second 'Shadow Secretary' came when he was a member of the opposition.

When the rhododendrons and azaleas, most of which are along the bottom of the Woodland Garden, are in flower, both the slope above and the grass around them are filled first with daffodils and later with bluebells and many other wild flowers: candelabra primulas thrive in the damper areas. With all these in flower, the spring and early summer are the best times for the garden, when the leaves on the beeches are fresh and blend with the dark greens of the coniferous giants, Strone is a memorable sight. Due to the impossibility of getting anyone to scythe on the steep slopes, Lady Glenkinglas decided to spray the undergrowth with Gramoxone, thereby producing a very easily controlled 'forest floor' of moss and wild flowers.

In the gardens immediately around Strone House are many more camellias, rhododendrons and azaleas, in particular Lord Glenkinglas's hybrid azaleas, as well as eucalyptus, magnolias and eucryphias. Here, too, the garden is natural in style and appearance, and less overwhelming than the giants in the Woodland Garden. It is to those, however, that one's mind and eyes return. The garden and pinetum are sheltered from the strong winds felt at Strone, luckily, since the tallest trees are exposed above the main canopy. But it is fascinating to speculate how much those that remain unscathed will have grown by the next time they are carefully measured.

TOROSAY CASTLE

On the Isle of Mull, 1½ miles south-east of Craignure on the A849
Tel. 06802 421
Mr David Guthrie James of Torosay

Open daily

Torosay Castle was built by David Bryce in 1858, in the Scottish Baronial style for which his work is well known but its immediate surroundings were unexceptional until the beginning of the twentieth century. Walter Murray Guthrie, the present owner's grandfather, had been shocked to inherit so large a house, and initially he determined to sell it; but when he visited Torosay he decided he liked the place and commissioned Sir Robert Lorimer to lay out the three Italianate terraces to the south of the castle and the Statue Walk to the west, successfully linking the house with the eighteenth-century Walled Garden below, originally laid out to the small house which was the castle's predecessor. Lorimer's balustraded terraces were typically well conceived, their stone matching that of the castle and two picturesque pavilions placed on the corners of the middle terrace.

Walter Murray Guthrie's widow brought to Torosay the fine marble figure which stands on the small terraced lawn on the castle's west front. From below this lawn the Statue Walk stretches south down to the Walled Garden between terraces and lime trees. The delightful stone statues from Padua are by the Venetian sculptor Antonio Bonazza (1698–1763), and portray alternately male and female figures portraying various rural livelihoods. Although some of the statues are suffering the effects of the perpetual damp which plagues Mull they are still most attractive and a start will soon be made on their restoration. Planted beneath them on both sides are hardy fuchsias. One small aside may be given: it cost more at the beginning of this century to get the statues from Liverpool to Mull than it did to transport them from Genoa to Liverpool.

Steps from the lower end of the Statue Walk lead south-west down to the Water Garden, with damp-loving plants along the stream and a collection of eucalyptus along the bottom of the garden. The Walled Garden is kept simple with lawns divided only by clipped trees and yew hedges which originally flanked herbaceous borders along the central path. The fifteen-foot wall along the top of the garden collapsed once but has been rebuilt; it is especially interesting for the series of stone figures set into the stonework. Urns filled with geraniums now surmount the stone.

Above the Walled Garden is the largest of the three terraces, the Lion Terrace, given its name by the pair of marble lions gazing across the terraced lawn. Behind them, trained on the wall between the two pavilions, are climbing roses, with clematis on the stone buttresses; hydrangeas fill the box-edged border below. At both ends of this border the path leads to fine eucryphias, of which there are a number in the garden, and above the east pavilion is a cedar planted when the terraces were laid out, one of a number of fine conifers at Torosay. The Fountain Terrace, above the Lion Terrace, is again simple and formal: a circular pool and the fountain, a copy of the famous original outside the Palazzo Vecchio in Florence, in the centre of the lawn. Either side of the pool are lead urns on stone pedestals. The outstanding feature here is the view past one of the pavilions to Duart Castle perched on a headland with views across the Sound of Mull, up Loch Linnhe towards distant Ben Nevis.

Mr Guthrie James's step-father and mother, Colonel and Mrs Miller, restored the garden after the Second World War, and added other features and many of the interesting plants. Two of their most interesting additions have been the Japanese Garden, to the east of the Lion Terrace, and the colonnade in the Walled Garden, below one of the upper walls. The marble pillars have stone capitals and bases, and wooded beams in a pergola formation, the effect being heightened by the rotunda at the far end of the colonnade.

The damp, often mild climate of Torosay is undeniably important to many of the plants, and their effect is heightened for the visitor by the impressive architecture of the garden, which makes for special interest.

FIFE

BALCASKIE

5 miles north of Pittenweem off the B942
Tel. 0333 311 202
Sir Ralph Anstruther Bt

Open one Sunday a year

Balcaskie has an outstanding position, looking south in an unbroken line to the Firth of Forth and the landmark of the Bass Rock, amid the mild conditions which Fife has, in comparison with most of Eastern Scotland.

Sir William Bruce bought Balcaskie in 1665. One of Scotland's foremost architects (see also Kinross House), Bruce is well known for his work at the palace of Holyroodhouse and the adaptations he made to the existing house at Balcaskie are more unusual examples of his earlier style. He had already shown his interest in garden architecture with his work at Ham House for the Duke of Lauderdale and at Balcaskie he planned and laid out what was an outstanding architectural garden in its own age, and remains so to this day. Although his work was straightforward it was substantial, it employed the house's elevated south-facing position to the best advantage, and best of all, perhaps, it lent itself to the sympathetic adaptation it received during the nineteenth century.

Bruce's main contribution was the first terrace and its impressive south-facing retaining wall, supported at intervals by buttresses. It is likely that this first terrace contained one or more parterres similar to the central flower parterre of today, while the two lower levels were maintained as orchards. The Anstruther family acquired Balcaskie around 1698, and have lived there ever since. It was the great-grandfather of the present Sir Ralph Anstruther Bt who in 1857 carried Bruce's work to what may be seen as its logical conclusion. He linked the first terrace to the second with flights of stone steps at either end of the retaining wall, added the balustrade to the wall and the long gravel path which stretches along beside it between two stone arches, the western one giving a view over the park and the eastern giving access through a pair of wrought-iron gates to a recently planted lime avenue. The second terrace became known as the Lawn Garden, laid out as a sunken bowling green with long parterres on either side. The twelve buttresses were adorned with busts of Roman emperors; small lead urns were added to the balustrade and to the flight of steps leading from the Lawn Garden to the bottom level. The first terrace immediately in front of the house was divided into three squares by clipped hedges of yew and holly; the central square enclosed a flower parterre, that to the east a dense mixture of shrubs, and that to the west a lawn.

The formal framework of Bruce's three-hundred-year-old terracing is enhanced today by the variety of plants and trees, statues and stone vases, so that while the gardens retain a certain simplicity in their appearance they nevertheless contain many features of beauty and interest. Immediately outside the door in the garden front a datura, which one would normally expect to find protected within a con-servatory or greenhouse, flowers freely. At either end of the gravel walk across the front of the house stand figures of Apollo and the goddess Diana, and beside the walk are four smaller stone figures, one of which is by Hew Lorimer who lives at nearby Kellie Castle. The central parterre of the first terrace has a square pattern of rosebeds enclosed by box hedges round a central sundial. A number of the shrubs have been cleared from the east square, while in the other the only addition to the lawn is a young Lebanon cedar planted to replace one blown down by a gale in the 1950s. In strong contrast is the secret little Rose Garden on the west side of the house; the flowerbeds and graceful stone figure of a woman are almost hidden by tall yew hedges.

Below the retaining terrace wall the sheltered enclosures between the buttresses allow a number of tender plants and climbers to flourish. On the second terrace the central bowling-green is still there and broad gravel paths lead to either end from the steps. At the east end stand two mature cedars close to the ascending stone steps and at the other the balustrade of the steps is thickly covered by *Clematis montana*. The long swathe of lawn in front of the borders beneath the retaining wall is broken up by rectangular rosebeds arranged, with groups of slender palms, round four very fine stone vases similar to the two close to the house. At the lowest level the bottom terrace now contains vegetables but retains its central path flanked by clipped yew and box hedges.

Balcaskie is a garden of well-struck balance between history and present appearance, and where interest is not limited to one season. From every point the eye is carried outward by the wide vista stretching away to the Forth and even, on a clear day, to the far side and another of Scotland's outstanding gardens, at Tyninghame.

Balcaskie remains a striking garden because the planting and ornaments do not detract from the symmetry of the garden's design, a tribute both to an enviable gardener's sensibility and to an admirable awareness of what is due to the past.

KELLIE CASTLE

3 miles north of Pittenween on the B9161
Tel. 031 226 5922
The National Trust for Scotland

Open daily from mid-April to September inclusive

Kellie Castle, dating partly from the fourteenth century but mainly from the late sixteenth and early seventeenth century, is today an exquisite example of Scottish domestic architecture, its effect heightened by the small scale of its proportions.

From the early seventeenth century Kellie was the home of the Earls of Kellie until 1769 when the estates were sold. The house survived almost total neglect from the 'muckle roup' on the death of the 10th Earl in 1829, when the contents were sold, until the 1870s when it was discovered by James Lorimer. The first impressions of James Lorimer's youngest daughter, Louise, reveal the degree of decay in 1878: 'It was left to the rooks and owls who built in its crumbling chimneys and dropped down piles of twigs which reached far out into the rooms. Great holes let in the rain and snow through the roofs, many of the floors had become unsafe, every pane of glass was broken, and swallows built in the coronets of the ceilings, while the ceilings themselves sagged and in some cases fell into the rooms. . . The garden, still encircled by a tumbledown wall, was a wilderness of neglected gooseberry bushes, gnarled apple trees and old-world roses which struggle through the weeds, summer after summer, with a sweet persistence.'

Restoration was slow work, but triumphant when complete. James Lorimer was father to Robert, later Sir Robert who, though he was soon established as an architect in Edinburgh, spent most summers at Kellie with the rest of the family during the early decades of this century, and during this time he planned much of the garden in its present form. After James Lorimer's death his elder son, John became the tenant of Kellie until his death in 1937. At that point it seemed likely that the family connection with Kellie would cease, but Sir Robert's eldest son, the sculptor Hew Lorimer, and his wife Mary took on the tenancy and eventually, with the help of the Historic Buildings Council for Scotland, they bought the castle in 1948.

The one-acre Walled Garden lies to the north of the castle. It is delightfully old-fashioned, filled with pinks, roses and hollyhocks, and divided into compartments with three main paths, one central and the others beside borders beneath the south and north walls, whose height Sir Robert raised for greater shelter. He also designed the Garden House, and two smaller gardens – Robin's Garden in the north-east, partly screened by trellis-work covered in roses and clematis, and the Secret Garden in the south-east corner of the main garden, enclosed by yew hedges and entered through a narrow arch in them. The main feature here is the urn, made by Hew Lorimer and modelled on an early Romanesque one, which is filled with small pinks and geraniums and surrounded by honeysuckle and climbing roses trained on poles.

The narrow rectangular ante-garden on the east side of the castle is a restrained introduction to the main South Garden which is filled with colour for most of summer. Rambler roses are trained across arches over the paths. The grass central path and the gravel ones along the edges of the garden are edged by a wide variety of roses, the pink 'Celestial' and old-fashioned 'Mrs Sinkins', the 'Queen of Denmark' rose, 'Blanc Double de Coubert' and the China rose 'Fellernberg', filling borders, trained along chains or forming thick hedges. Beneath many of them are smaller dianthus. Some of the old apples, pears and purple-leafed plum trees here are host to more ramblers – 'Sander's White' and 'Rambling Rector'. Lilac, laburnum and herbaceous borders add to the colour and scent.

The old mixture at Kellie has been retained complete, for as well as the flowers and fruit trees, the box-enclosed border beneath the wall on the north side of the garden is filled mainly with vegetables. When the National Trust for Scotland acquired the property in 1970 their restoration and replanting was helped by Gertrude Jekyll's account, included no doubt for its character rather than its location, in *Some English Gardens*. At its zenith in late summer, Kellie fulfills a certain ideal of an old-fashioned flower garden, its exuberant profusion a telling contrast to the dour stone walls of the castle which look down upon it.

KINROSS-SHIRE

KINROSS HOUSE

East of Kinross off the M90 (Junction 5)
Tel. 0577 63467
Sir David and Lady Montgomery

Open every afternoon from May to September inclusive

Kinross is unquestionably William Bruce's masterpiece, its whole appearance and character uncompromisingly massive and austere, yet its proportions so perfectly balanced as to make the severe façades possible. It would be very hard to find a house on which Bruce may have modelled Kinross, and certainly nothing was attempted in quite the same manner afterwards; perhaps building for himself freed his fancy.

With unerring precision Bruce aligned the house so that from the far end of the tree-lined drive beyond the spacious forecourt the two main doors opened in line with the ruined castle on its island in the middle of Loch Leven. The view to the Loch and the castle where Mary Queen of Scots was imprisoned was the setting for Bruce's formal gardens, an enormous square between house and loch, enclosed by stone walls. Interestingly, these were largely laid out before work began on the house, which was built between 1685 and 1693. After a period of serious decline in the nineteenth century, when the house was empty for eighty years, the gardens were restored by Sir Basil Montgomery between 1902 and 1928, and now again provide suitably spacious but restrained surroundings.

Bruce bought the estate at Kinross from the Earl of Morton in 1675, shortly after the zenith of his prestige, the commission to rebuild the Palace of Holyroodhouse. In 1693 Thomas Balk, a mason from Alloway, was commissioned to build the enclosing walls, or 'dyks', as they were locally known. At the same time James Anderson and Mungo Wallace were working on the summerhouses against the garden's north and south walls. In 1684 Tobias Back was contracted to supply a grand gateway with rusticated Doric piers; this would originally have formed a clairvoyée in the north wall, and indeed the rusticated piers remain though the opening is filled by a yew hedge. The decorative carving of the Fish Gates which lead from the bottom of the garden to the loch was executed by the two Dutch carvers, Peter Paul Boyse and Cornelius van Nerven, whom Bruce also employed for the carving above the present entrance porch and the carving of his and his wife's coats of arms over the door into the garden.

Bruce was reputed to have spent £400 per annum on the upkeep of the gardens at Kinross, but by the time Sir Basil Montgomery inherited the estate in 1902, and decided to live in the house only the framework of the walls, architectural features and terraces remained. The estate had passed from Bruce's family in 1775 to the Grahams who had interests in India, and thence to the Montgomerys by marriage with a Graham daughter.

Sir Basil complemented the proportions of the garden with his various additions, in particular the herbaceous borders. Around the circular pool opposite the front of the house he laid out a formal Rose Garden enclosed by yew hedges, and added the boy and swan statue to the fountain. He then extended the central vista beyond the steps down to the lower level of the garden with deep herbaceous borders, again backed by yew hedges, which stretched to the Fish Gates. All round the walls he laid out herbaceous borders in continuous blocks divided by bastions of clipped yew, as they are today. Across the garden between the two pillared summerhouses on the north and south walls he made a strong axis through the centre of the circular pool with clipped domes and columns of evergreens and rhododendrons on either side. Only the size of the garden as a whole and the wide expanses of lawn diminish the scale of Sir Basil's additions, which were very extensive while in no way detracting from the air of spaciousness with which Bruce had originally surrounded his house.

Today the gardens survive virtually intact from Sir Basil's time; he also planted most of the trees on the lawns, although the great chestnut is possibly three hundred years old. As well as the herbaceous plants in the long border beneath the south wall there are a number of trees and shrubs, including laburnums, acers *Hydrangea sargentiana* and *Rubus* 'Tridel'.

To the south of the house is the only small and enclosed part of the gardens. Cut off from the rest of the gardens by a topiary yew hedge, the narrow rectangle stretches between pillared temples. At the end closest to the house is one of the pair of pavilions with hipped roofs standing either side of the entrance courtyard, echoing the roofs of the stables. In the centre of this garden is a statue of Atlas supporting the World; around about are smaller lead figures on pedestals over which climbing roses are trained on metal arbours.

It is both fortunate and satisfying that Kinross survives as a tribute to one of Scotland's outstanding architects. Bruce worked on a number of houses after he completed Kinross, despite his loss of favour after the accession of William III in 1688 because of his continued support for the Stuarts, for which he was imprisoned three times between 1693 and 1696. Kinross remains his most inspired and impressive work; the picture of house and garden, loch and ruined castle, and the hills beyond is among the most memorable of Scottish and indeed of British country house landscapes.

PERTHSHIRE

BRANKLYN

In Perth, off the A85 to Dundee

Tel. 031 226 5922

The National Trust for Scotland

Open daily, March to October inclusive

When John and Dorothy Renton bought their plot of land in a residential part of Perth in 1922 their predicament was similar to that of a thousand people buying or building a small house in any town or city. They bought about two-thirds of an acre of an old orchard, and when their bungalow had been built there was precious little left for any sort of garden.

Their main priorities were to protect themselves from the noise and view of traffic on the Dundee road, and to clear some of the wilderness their land had become. Landmarks, views or enticing surroundings to help their garden planning were non-existent; they had to be self-reliant in both design and planting. The Rentons were fortunate in being able to buy another small piece of land on one side of their garden, and some years later two other purchases on the same side brought the garden to its present size of two acres.

Dorothy Renton had always been a keen botanist, but this was her first opportunity to adapt her interest to making a garden. With continual help from John – as with so many gardens, the success of Branklyn was due to a partnership – she steadily planned and developed the garden. Mistakes and setbacks such as beset all new gardeners were frequent in the early days, but the Rentons emerged from their apprenticeship quicker than most. Once Dorothy Renton had expanded her knowledge of plants, and of what would be happy at Branklyn,

429

progress was rapid and it soon became clear that she possessed a discerning eye for positioning and grouping plants, and a flair for cultivating rare varieties, an unusual combination.

When the National Trust for Scotland took on the garden in 1968, following the death of Dorothy Renton in 1966 and of John in 1967, Branklyn had become a suburban garden in a league of its own. It had declined somewhat in the 1960s but the plant losses were soon made good by the Trust, and many others have been added. The Trust's policy has been to maintain Branklyn as far as possible as the Rentons left it, a unique example of what could be done with a small area in unencouraging surroundings.

One of the Rentons' first interests had been alpine plants: they suited the small size of the garden, especially as most of it sloped to the south and south-west, thus tending to dry out in parts. Their first scree garden replaced a hard tennis court; the scree gardens are now extended and contain a host of true rock plants thriving in the thin, usually dry soil, as well as small shrubs and trees – daphnes, genista and dwarf conifers – to add shape and variety. Not all the garden is dry, though; primulas flourish in some of the damper areas.

The quality of individual plants at Branklyn and the harmony of their grouping, often in island beds, are continually striking. Among the numerous varieties some are especially well represented: meconopsis – it's no surprise that *M. grandis* 'Branklyn' was awarded a First Class Certificate by the Royal Horticultural Society in 1963; rhododendrons and azaleas – both hybrid and specie, and including especially good dwarf varieties; viburnums; hydrangeas; acers; notholirions and snowdrops.

Snowdrops are accompanied by the more unusual 'Spring Snow-flake' *Leucojum vernum*, and afterwards come trilliums. Spring and early summer see the peak of colour in the garden: as well as rhododendrons and azaleas there is a group of *Magnolia watsonii* and other scented varieties, and some early viburnums. Later in the summer the hydrangeas come into their own: *H. involucrata* and *H. sargentiana*, as well as *Hoheria glabra*. Acers dominate the autumn and in winter the many evergreen trees are conspicuous, including the distinctive Canadian Hemlock, *Tsuga canadensis* 'Pendula'.

Cataloguing plants is never a very satisfactory way of describing a garden, and with a garden such as Branklyn the quantity of plants and their points of interest really defy description. It must rank as one of the most interesting two-acre plots in Britain.

CLUNIEMORE

2½ miles south of Pitlochry off the A9
Tel. 0796 2006
Major and Mrs David Butter

Open one Sunday in spring and one in August, and by appointment for parties

The garden at Cluniemore thrives in a setting of wooded hills and high moorland of which it was once part. Major Butter's father made the garden out of a snipe bog, clearing and retaining the small stream that flows down through the garden and raising the ground near the house to form a pond into which the stream flows. He planned the garden round the sloping contours of the ground, thus retaining a natural appearance and providing an attractive setting for the long south-facing early nineteenth-century house.

Despite the often harsh climate here, with cold winters when there are few hours of daylight, Mrs Butter has built on her father-in-law's foundations to provide much of interest throughout the year – flowering trees and shrubs, the Water Garden and borders. On a fine day in mid-summer it is easy to forget that one is in the climatically inhospitable Highlands, such is the display of colour in the herbaceous borders and Rose Garden.

In early summer the large rhododendrons around the drive form a colourful welcome, leading to outstanding beech and oaks in an area of open grass. Much of the slope in front of the house is planted with azaleas – particularly striking on one side of the path which climbs along the Stream Garden to the top of the hill and the gate into the Woodland Walk. Primulas, lilies, hostas and other damp-loving plants flourish beneath acers – of which there is a fine collection – dwarf conifers and a pair of *Cercidiphyllum japonicum*, near the pond.

The choice of shrubs and trees gives colour and interest for much of the year: *Kalmia latifolia*, lilacs, cornuses, sorbuses, stranvaesias and a tulip tree, at their best in summer; acers and cercidiphyllums for the autumn. Most striking are the large borders round the well-kept main lawn: two early summer borders, rose borders – given some formality by the clipped yew hedges – and two main herbaceous borders. From June till the end of August these provide a succession of plants: old-fashioned and hybrid tea and floribunda roses, peonies, lilies, phlox, delphiniums, sweet peas and many others. The informally planted grass slope rising behind the large herbaceous border on the west of the garden is at its best in spring – daffodils beneath the blossom of cherry and apple trees and underneath a stand of birch. A 'wild area' for shrubs, shrub roses, herbs and bulbs is now being developed, as is a collection of violas.

Well maintained and of great variety, Cluniemore is a highly personal garden. So successful is its blending with the Highland setting that it is hard to imagine the area as it once was, with dank peat bogs and reed beds, the only colour a scattering of wild heath and marsh flowers.

DRUMMOND CASTLE

3 miles south of Creiff off the A822 Creiff–Muthill Road
Tel. 076 44362

The Grimsthorpe and Drummond Castle Trust Ltd

Open daily from 31st May to 31st August, and on Wednesday and Sunday in May and September; afternoons

The visitor to Drummond, entering the open courtyard between the forbidding keep, all that remains of the original fifteenth-century castle, and the later gabled and turreted house, can hardly be adequately prepared for the visual feast that awaits. From the courtyard wall one of the most spectacular gardens in Britain is dramatically revealed, a series of wide terraces descending steeply from the keep to the apparently endless parterre inspired by the great gardens of the Italian Renaissance. The scale of the terraces and parterre, and their wealth of content put Drummond among the select number of really grand formal gardens that have survived in Britain, and no one can fail to marvel at their original conception and the present-day maintenance.

The first Lord Drummond built the castle in about 1491, having left the old family seat at Stobhall, and it is to his son, the second Lord Drummond and Earl of Perth, that the gardens have been attributed. It is possible that he commissioned the huge and intricate sundial in the centre of the parterre, made by John Mylne bearing the date 1630. But in contemporary descriptions thereafter there is scant evidence that any gardens on the scale of the present ones existed, so it seems more likely that they were laid out early in the nineteenth century as part of an Italian revival. In 1833 J. C. London recorded great improvements to the gardens by Lord Gwydr who from 1818 to 1860 had employed Lewis Kennedy (son of John Kennedy of the celebrated Hammersmith nursery, Kennedy and Lee). In 1860 George Kennedy whose connection, if any, with Lewis, is uncertain, drew up a 'Plan of the Garden with Alterations and Improvements since 1838'. In 1842 Queen Victoria had planted a copper beech in the parterre, possibly to mark the completion of the gardens or a stage in their progress.

Drummond clearly shows the advantages of much of Scotland's rugged terrain for the creation of impressive and dramatic gardens. While the steep slope provided the potential for the series of terraces it also gave a wonderfully elevated view of the parterre in the valley, without which the intricacy of the patterns could not be fully appreciated. The parterre covers thirteen acres, stretching in an uneven rectangle across the bottom of the slope. It is joined to the terraces by a central flight of stone steps with hardy fuchsias either side, leading right up to the courtyard and alternating as a wide single flight and divided double flights until they reach the wrought-iron gates at the top. The steps are decorated by marble vases and figures of fruit-gatherers, just some of the many outstanding statues, vases and urns – nearly all of white Italian marble – which adorn the gardens; they were brought to Drummond by Lord Willoughby de Eresby during the nineteenth century.

If the outstanding feature of the great parterre is its size, the ingenuity of the patterns with which it is filled compel admiration. Originally laid out to show the Drummond arms, it is dissected by diagonal grass paths forming a St Andrew's cross. The central area which now contains the main concentration of flowerbeds is further divided by three parallel gravel paths running from the foot of the slope to the far edge of the garden. Aligned on the sundial in the two outer gravel paths are two enormous marble urns carved with the Drummond arms. The flowerbeds, all edged with box and many of them now filled with roses form the pattern together with clipped trees of numerous varieties, including yew, holly (and golden specimens of both varieties), Portugese laurels, purple plums, Japanese acers and box.

On either side of the central area are circular patterns of beds now filled with 'Iceberg' roses. Both have central statues, with surrounding pools and fountains. Throughout the parterre the paths lead past topiary specimens and statuary, revealing the garden as an ever-changing kaleidoscope. At its eastern end the parterre slopes to a romantic battlemented bridge; standing above it looking towards the terraces is a striking statue of Venus in front of a huge and ancient yew.

The last Earl of Ancaster and his wife wisely removed much of the nineteenth-century planting in the outer areas of the parterre, which included dense shrubberies, thereby opening up spaces of lawn and new vistas, and also reducing the garden's very considerable maintenance demands. A number of the shrubs have also been thinned from the terraces so that the present junipers, potentillas and heathers do not obscure their architecture.

As a unique spectacle the gardens at Drummond Castle cannot fail to impress, and they can be enjoyed not only for their effect but from special points of view – one may particularly admire the statuary, or the specimen trees or the planting close up in the parterre. An unrivalled example of a style of gardening which has virtually disappeared, Drummond's setting, with the castle perched high above on one side and the gentler slope of parkland on the other where the trees are divided by a sweeping grass ride, must appeal in some aspects to any visitor.

GRAMPIAN
AND THE HIGHLANDS

Aberdeenshire
Caithness
Kincardineshire
Morayshire
Nairnshire
Ross and Cromarty
Sutherland

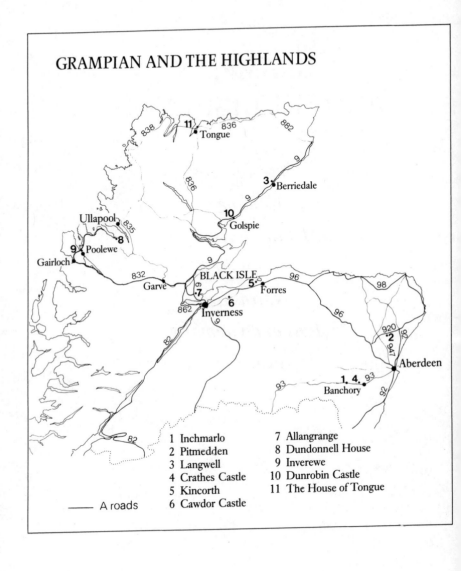

GRAMPIAN AND THE HIGHLANDS

11 Tongue

3 Berriedale

10 Golspie

Ullapool

8

9 Poolewe

Gairloch

Garve

BLACK ISLE

5 Forres

7

6

Inverness

Aberdeen

1 **4**

Banchory

1 Inchmarlo
2 Pitmedden
3 Langwell
4 Crathes Castle
5 Kincorth
6 Cawdor Castle

7 Allangrange
8 Dundonnell House
9 Inverewe
10 Dunrobin Castle
11 The House of Tongue

——— A roads

ABERDEENSHIRE

INCHMARLO

West of Banchory on the A93
Tel. 0224 638 815
C. P. Skene, Esq.

Open one day a year

The long valley of the River Dee seems to be dominated by imposing Scottish-Baronial castles, and to find the classical Georgian façade of Inchmarlo, built of pink stone, is a refreshing contrast, though the façade was made grander in the nineteenth century by the addition of a third storey and balustraded parapet.

Like the park, the main Woodland Garden to the east of the house contains some fine trees – Scots pines, Douglas firs, copper beeches and beeches; it was almost completely re-planted by the wife of Mr Skene's predecessor, Colonel A. H. Bowhill. Some of the older plants may date from a previous owner of Inchmarlo who was a cousin of the late E. H. M. Cox who made a number of collecting expeditions and amassed some outstanding rhododendrons at Glendoick, near Perth. Some of the other rhododendrons were brought as seedlings from the garden of the Bowhill's daughter, Lady Adam Gordon at Littleworth Cross in Surrey, but it was Mrs Bowhill's planning which extended the garden from the old-fashioned Walled Garden into the woodland setting on the sloping ground below, and positioned new and younger varieties beneath the mature trees.

Through the Woodland Garden rhododendrons and azaleas are the main feature, a wide variety ranging from dwarf rhododendrons, and the delicate *R. yunnanense*, to larger plants such as a number of *Rh.* 'Loderi' varieties. Groups of old-fashioned azaleas, such as the scented yellow

437

luteum mixing with the organge and red varieties, are to be found throughout. Acers blend well with the rhododendrons and azaleas, including *A. senkaki* and *A. griseum*, and along a small stream delicate weeping varieties have been planted to spread over primulas. The stream leads to a pond where a large and unusual juniper and striking blue meconopsis flourish. The informality is very attractive; paths wind among the groups of shrubs and trees – sorbus, eucryphias, cedars and a metasequoia, as well as those already mentioned.

The Woodland Garden leads to an open area of lawn sloping down from the old Walled Garden to the north-east of the house. This open lawn contains the Rose Garden, of particular interest because of the hedges of *Prunus cerasifera* 'Pissardii', the purple-leaved plum, with its distinctive purple foliage and white flower in spring. In front of the hedges, borders of shrub roses, peonies and small grey-leaved foliage plants lead to the main circular area of hedge-enclosed beds.

The east side of the lawn is sheltered by more large trees, also with ornamental varieties below – *Cornus kousa* and *C. nuttallii* and *Parrotia persica* – adding further variety to the gardens, evidence of Mrs Bowhill's response to Inchmarlo's exceptional setting. Mr Skene plans to maintain and add to the garden thus ensuring that Inchmarlo's old-established setting and Mrs Bowhill's later work survive.

PITMEDDEN

1 mile west of Pitmedden Village, 14 miles north of Aberdeen on the A920
Tel. 031 226 5922
The National Trust for Scotland

Open daily all year

Like most of the few surviving formal seventeenth-century gardens in Britain, such as Edzell Castle and Westbury Court, the Great Garden at Pitmedden exists today because of detailed and outstanding restoration work.

The garden was originally created by Sir Alexander Seton, later Lord Pitmedden, but by the beginning of the nineteenth century its formal parterre, enclosed by walls and raised terraces, had declined to an ordinary vegetable and fruit garden. The Keith family bought Pitmedden in 1894, and Major James Keith handed Pitmedden over to the National Trust for Scotland in 1952. Though the architectural features remained, the Trust's proposed restoration was hampered by the loss in a fire of 1880 of all papers and drawings relating to the garden's original appearance. Work was begun in 1956, however, and although the gaudy annuals now filling the parterre beds in their thousands would certainly not have appeared in the seventeenth-century original, the patterns and restored walls, terraces and pavilions do hark back to that time.

Seton's inspiration came partly from gardens in that style which he knew, such as Winton, Pinkie and Seton, but most of all it came from Holyroodhouse and Sir William Bruce. Charles I had already laid out a garden at Holyroodhouse, and the Duke of Lauderdale, as the King's Commissioner in Scotland, had commissioned Bruce to rebuild the palace. Seton was then living in Edinburgh and his acquaintance with Bruce and with Robert Mylne, the King's Master Mason who was working for him, undoubtedly influenced the garden at Pitmedden. A lintel dated 1675, bearing the initials of Seton and his wife, shows that he had started his garden before he retired from his distinguished legal career shortly after the accession of James II and VII, whom he offended with his opposition to some of the King's Catholic measures.

Seton landscaped the sloping ground to the east of Pitmedden House into two levels. The lower level was enclosed with walls, a high retaining wall on the west side, closest to the house, and wide terraces above the walls on three sides: from here his guests could admire the intricate pattern laid out in the garden below. A central path across the upper level of the garden led between stone piers to double steps down to the Great Garden. At either end of the west wall, broken by the steps, Seton built exquisite pavilions, the design of which – in particular the ogival roofs – was very similar to the two pavilions at Kinross, designed by Bruce and built by Mylne.

Most of the architecture of the garden survived to 1952 though the south terrace had disappeared. The south wall had to be rebuilt and the pavilions too, had to be considerably restored, but the main task was the re-designing and re-planting of the Parterre Garden. It was divided into four rectangles, and designs for three of these were based on the parterre at Holyroodhouse, as shown in *A Bird's Eye View of Edinburgh* by James Gordon, published in 1647. The fourth section was laid out as a tribute to Sir Alexander Seton, with small rectangles of the Scottish saltire and thistle surrounding the larger square containing his coat of arms, motto, the date 1675, his initials and his wife's. The new parterres required three miles of box hedging, and now the beds contain forty thousand annuals.

Many people were consulted over the reconstruction, particularly Dr James S. Richardson, who masterminded the restoration and Lady Burnett of Leys, who supplied designs for the herbaceous borders beneath the walls. Seton's original fountain on the upper level of the garden was also restored, and a new fountain was added to the centre of the Parterre Garden, some of the stones of which had originally formed the Cross fountain at Linlithgow by Mylne.

The restoration has been an outstanding success and saved one of Scotland's more historic gardens. Perhaps one feels that a more discerning seventeenth-century audience would not have needed such a brilliant floral display to impress them, but any visitor must render thanks for the preservation of a garden conceived in such style and grace.

CAITHNESS

LANGWELL

West of Berriedale, off the A9
Tel. 059 35237
Lady Anne Bentinck

Open daily from June to October inclusive

At Langwell the Scottish tradition of placing the main, normally walled gardens away from the house is carried to an extreme; here one has to walk about a mile to such sheltered seclusion, away from the somewhat exposed hill looking out to the east coast on which the house stands.

Although the walls are much older, the garden in its present form was laid out in 1916 by John Murray. He came from Aberdeenshire, intending to spend one year at Langwell laying out and establishing the garden. He died there in 1975, aged ninety-six and still working occasionally in his garden. It was designed carefully for the family and visitors to walk round, admiring the flower borders and coming across unexpected views as they turned a corner along the paths backed by evergreen hedges, hiding the areas of fruit and vegetables behind. The main problem today is that the garden was also designed to be maintained by a large number of gardeners who are no longer available, but nevertheless most of its original appearance is retained.

The main axes of the garden are two grass paths which meet at the central sundial. From the summerhouse against the top north wall, overtrained with fruit trees, the view extends through an old yew arch to the path sloping downhill between deep herbaceous borders with hedges of western red cedar behind them; at the bottom is the formal pond and fountain enclosed by yew hedges. There used to be a second yew arch here but the old 7th Duke of Portland had it cut out so he could sit in the summerhouse and 'spy' deer on the hill opposite.

441

Beneath the wall on each side of the summerhouse are lawns with a mixture of trees at either end. The borders are enclosed by box hedges, and on the other side of the path is a box hedge of outstanding size. In all the borders the planting continues to be traditional, using many old-fashioned herbaceous plants. In these main borders are echinops, rudbekia, tritonia, ligularias, artemensis and phlox.

The formality of the pond and fountain and the surrounding yew hedges is a delightful contrast to colourful borders. A 'secret' path leads between the hedges to the old Rose Garden, again enclosed by hedges, which has recently been replanted with a new Rockery, Herb Garden and Lily Bed.

The border stretching east–west across the garden has old wooden rose arbours at either end. Both arbours are surrounded by recently-planted shrubs of the Portland rose.

From a side door into the garden on the east side, a path leads between borders of massed phlox to the main central border. Along this path is one of the most striking features at Langwell, the brilliant red *Tropaeolum speciosum* which thrives in many Scottish gardens but which is especially good here, covering the dark green hedges and two columnar Irish yews. On the far west side of the garden are the two main squares, one filled with raspberries, strawberries, blackcurrants and apples, the other transformed recently to give a display of various 'specimen' plants, trees and shrubs.

The maintenance of Langwell's garden is a daunting task for Francis Higgins, head gardener since 1983, not just keeping up the borders but clipping the hundreds of yards of hedges. A commercial venture selling plants does help with costs, and one hopes that a garden of such traditional character and appearance will be able to survive. It is an unexpected pleasure to find Langwell on this remote north-east coast of Scotland, and in high summer the border displays rival anything one would find in more hospitable climes.

KINCARDINESHIRE

CRATHES CASTLE

3 miles east of Banchory, 15 miles west of Aberdeen on the A93
Tel. 031 226 5922

The National Trust for Scotland

Open daily all year

There was little of distinction in the gardens at Crathes when Sir James and Lady Burnett of Leys came to live at the castle other than the framework of terraces and walls on the steep slope to the south and east, and the yew hedges planted in 1702 whose massive shapes now bear an unforgettable part in the garden's appearance. During their lifetime Sir James, who was mainly interested in trees and shrubs and, more especially, Lady Burnett, created a series of small gardens within the total six acres which are by any standards among the most outstanding creations of twentieth-century gardening.

Their gardens are a series of separate enclosures, each with an individual feature, pattern and appearance, a treatment which has played such a vital part in the development of twentieth-century gardens in Britain. As well as the skilled and imaginative conception of the different areas, Lady Burnett's remarkable talent is best revealed in the quality of individual plants, their groupings and combinations – such a close affinity with plants, and an understanding of how best to combine them within an overall pattern is indeed a rare and intensely personal talent. Through her work Lady Burnett instilled her character in the garden at Crathes and it is the retention of this sense of character, vital to any garden, which was the most demanding task for the National Trust for Scotland when they took over the property in 1952.

By then Crathes' reputation was established, its planting sheltered by

443

high stone walls and further protected by the yew hedges which sub-divide the individual gardens, The formality of the four upper gardens – the Croquet Lawn which visitors first come to, partly enclosed by yew, the Pool Garden, the Fountain Garden and the Rose Garden – contrasts with the exuberance of planting in the lower areas divided by the main flower borders, but the harmony of the overall picture and its components testify to Lady Burnett's skills and remain a vital part of Crathes' appearance and effect.

Of the formal areas, the Pool Garden beneath the castle contains the greatest concentration of planting, and possibly gives the most telling insight into Lady Burnett's gifts. It was one of the last gardens she made at Crathes and was planned round three colours: red, yellow and purple. In the small borders which, with clipped yew, partially enclose the central pool, and in the larger borders round the edges of the garden from which climbers were trained up, she achieved a wonderful balance of colour by using an adventurously wide range of colour, shape and size in her plants. The Fountain Garden below is more architectural, and dominated to an extent by the eighteenth-century yew hedges on two sides, and the columns and domes of clipped yew and holly. A pattern of box-enclosed, generally blue flowerbeds surrounds the central fountain with its Florentine statue. On the far side of the main yew walk – in itself an almost overpowering feature, the old hedges rising like walls – the Rose Garden is similarly bounded by the hedges on two sides. Its pattern is less architectural: lawn with four triangular corner beds surrounded by lavender hedges, three malus, central circular beds filled with floribunda varieties, and a long bed on one side containing shrub roses.

In summer the lower area of the main garden is dominated by the borders which divide parts of it, the White Border and the June Border. In the former the choice of plants is masterly, grey and silver foliage deviating from the shades of white, shrubs such as *Philadelphus microphyllus*, carefully chosen so as not to outgrow its place, mix with roses, herbaceous plants and smaller groundcover varieties which spill out on to the paved path. The June Border is in total contrast to this purist strain, an effusive mixture of herbaceous plants, many traditional and well-known – lupins, irises and poppies. At the far end a dovecot closes the view.

The concentration of planting, ranging from large trees and shrubs to the smallest of flowers, continues through the other areas in the lower part of the gardens. The Camel Garden derives its name from the two raised beds round which trees and shrubs stretch along the bottom of the garden back to the dovecot, and beneath the terrace wall at the top here is a south-facing border with a number of tender plants, including *Carpentaria californica*; even more tender specimens shelter in the protection of the Yew Border.

The richness of planting makes Crathes an intensely visual garden, a combination of striking pictorial effects, which no doubt partly accounts for its popularity. After this initial effect, however, discerning visitors become aware of that elusive quality, character ensuring a far more lasting impression.

MORAYSHIRE

KINCORTH

North-west of Forres off the A96

Tel. 0309 72807

Mrs A. D. Mackintosh

Open daily from mid-May to September inclusive

Although the climate of the east coast of Scotland is notoriously fickle, Kincorth benefits from the relative mildness of its coastal position in the Laigh of Moray. The old trees round the garden date from the eighteenth century; the lawns on the south and west sides of the house are dominated by these beeches, horse chestnuts and limes.

The house itself is part sixteenth and part eighteenth century, and in the main area of planting, in the partly walled garden north of the house, Mrs Mackintosh has grown fruit, vegetables and flowers in abundance, and in the traditional Scottish manner. The mixture is old-fashioned and the warm, productive atmosphere in summer is greatly enhanced by the layout of the garden between parallel hedges. Mrs Mackintosh is one of the rare people who spend most of their time in the garden without becoming over-fussy. While plants are well-trained they are not disciplined into uniformity.

The west boundary of the garden is formed by a border of rhododendrons beneath the limes. The main feature of the garden, however, is the herbaceous border beneath the boundary wall to the east of the Walled Garden. Mrs Mackintosh denies that the colour schemes were premeditated, but they are strikingly effective through much of summer. Roses, viburnums and other shrubs add height and shape at the back of the border behind a host of tree peonies, fuchsias, lilies, potentilla, ligularias, phlox and many other plants. Blue is one of the most frequent

446

colours here: delphiniums are followed by agapanthus and *Platycodon grandiflorus*. This striking plant, often known as the 'Balloon Flower' or 'Chinese Campanula', thrives far from its native China and Japan and was once the subject of stirring rhetoric by a seventeenth-century Italian author – 'And you, at the back, who with false modesty try to hide, tell me of the Great Wall of China which protects the vast Chinese Empire from the marauding Tartars; from the Magyar gypsies, and the Armenian mercenaries; and recount – with the voice of Zephyr who frolics among the flower beds – the legend of the East and the ballads of the Alps.'

Mrs Mackintosh removed the pattern of small beds which filled the lawn beside the herbaceous border and replaced them with the present rosebeds on the lawn's side. Behind the rosebeds a hedge of copper beech, far more striking than the previous one of holly which it replaced, hides the beds of vegetables beyond. From the lawn a path leads past these to acquire brilliantly-coloured borders of pink mallow, with antirrhinums and heliotropes in front and tall globe artichokes behind. Apples, pears and peaches – showing the mildness of sheltered parts of the garden – are trained on the wall here. On the far side of the vegetables a hedge of green beech runs parallel to that of copper beech, concealing the Rose Walk. Another hedge, of thuja, also encloses the grass path leading between borders of hybrid teas and floribunda roses, with climbers trained along looping chains behind. Beneath the west perimeter wall, decorated with clematis, is Mrs Mackintosh's 'cutting border', filled with a variety of flowers, and a border of bright orange tiger lilies stretches along the outside of the walled area closest to the house. The homely atmosphere of Kincorth may easily deceive the visitor by disguising the quality of much of the planting, but it is a garden which amply rewards investigation.

NAIRNSHIRE

CAWDOR CASTLE

South-west of Nairn on the B9090
Tel. 066 77615
Earl Cawdor

Open daily from May to the nearest Sunday to 1st October

The gardens of Cawdor Castle today are far removed from its better-known associations as the possible setting for the murder of King Duncan in Shakespeare's *Macbeth*. Cawdor's long history dates back to the fourteenth century when the keep was built. After fifteenth-century additions most of the present castle was built, in the seventeenth century, but then it was virtually deserted after the two Jacobite risings in 1715 and 1745 until the 1820s.

The flower garden was laid out in the 1720s – surrounding walls and trees probably date from then too – but in 1850 the then Lady Cawdor reorganized this area into a series of formally planned flower gardens, in many ways typical of the nineteenth century but also showing sympathies with an earlier, possibly French style. These are beautifully maintained and provide a rich display in summer against the backdrop of the woods beyond the burn to one side and the castle to another.

The combination of hedges, paths and flowerbeds gives formality to the large Walled Flower Garden, on the south side of the castle. It is planned in a series of parallel axes, the widest of them stretching away opposite the castle. Oval rosebeds enclosed by lavender hedges fill four rectangles of lawn closest to the castle and are divided by a pattern of large and small paths. The central path leads between columnar golden yews to herbaceous borders and a taller pair of columnar Irish yews. Beyond here, partially hidden by a yew hedge, is another Rose Garden. Parallel to this main axis, to its east, is the outstanding long double

448

herbaceous border. On its far east side clipped yew hedges lead to a miniature parterre and, beyond, to the remnants of an orchard where climbing roses and specie clematis have been trained into the old apple trees. A lily walk and path overhung with rose arbours and edged by peony borders adds marvellous scent to the visual glories.

Old limes, oaks, horse chestnuts and sycamores, some of which appear to date from the seventeenth century, shelter the lawns on the other three sides of the castle. A small gate leads into a second Walled Garden to the north-west which Lord and Lady Cawdor are in the process of laying out; this one is totally seventeenth century in concept and very different from the main flower gardens. In April 1981 the first main area was planted with a large maze, the plans for which Lord Cawdor took from a mosaic in a Roman villa in Portugal. The hedges of the maze are holly and all the way round is a laburnum walk, though it will be some years before it reaches maturity. Beyond the maze Lady Cawdor proposes a small garden enclosed by box hedging to contain small beds of vegetables enclosed in turn by hedges of various herbs, more in the style of a Tudor knot garden than the seventeenth century.

The most ambitious plan at Cawdor is for the Paradise Garden, taken in conception from the famous and priceless *Paradisi in Sole, Paradisus Terrestus*, by John Parkinson, which was published in 1629. The Paradise Garden will take the form of a seventeenth-century Wilderness – far removed from the modern idea of a wilderness – of intricate and ingenious formality. A pattern of circular yew hedges and paths, with small entry and exit paths, will converge on a central modern columnar bronze fountain designed by the Spanish sculptor Xavier Corbero. In a small central enclosure will be a selection of exclusively white plants, particularly scented varieties – syringa, philadelphus, lily-of-the-valley, larger lilies and snowdrops. In a truly sixteenth- and seventeenth-century manner, this will not be a garden just for looking at but for the harmony of a secret, enclosed atmosphere, scent and the sound of water: in a strangely Oriental manner, the Tudors and Stuarts were conscious of the peace and repose that could be attained through contemplation of natural beauty. Less formal but originating from the same period will be the old-fashioned orchard, its long meadow grass sprinkled with wild flowers.

Overall the plans for this walled garden are ambitious and labour intensive, but at a time when many people are reducing their gardens it is exciting to see expansion on such a scale. When the plans are completed the variety of gardens at Cawdor, including the natural Woodland Garden beside the burn, will be as impressive as the castle and its interiors, and for many will match their fascination.

ROSS AND CROMARTY

ALLANGRANGE

On the Black Isle, 2 miles from Munlochy and 5 miles from Inverness
Tel. 046 381 249
Major and Mrs Allan Cameron
Open three Sundays a year in May, June and July, and by appointment

---

The garden which Major and Mrs Cameron have laid out and built up since 1970 is an impressive achievement. There was little here when they started but now there is a balance between architectural and formal features and planting, the variety of which more than anything gives Allangrange a character and stature which belie its relative youth.

The ballustraded terraces to the south of the house are the garden's centrepiece and the views over the different levels are as rewarding seen from the house or looking up the slope from the informal area of trees and rhododendrons at the bottom. There are flights of stone steps at either end and one in the centre, breaking the first slope and leading to the first terrace. This is dominated by a deep mixed border where shrub roses, *Rosa rugosa* and hypericum grow on a bank behind herbaceous plants, some transplanted from the old kitchen garden. Behind the border the luxuriant purple flowers of *Clematis jackmanii* swathe the stone balustrade. The yew-enclosed squares on the terrace below provide good contrast to the mixed border. The yew hedges have shown impressive growth since they were planted and now these two small enclosures are the most charming corners of the garden, both equally secluded but each with a different colour scheme round the unusual camomile lawns. In the White Garden are roses, peonies, lilies, irises and *Romneya coulteri*; small silver-leafed plants and a graceful silver weeping pear blend with the dominant white, as do the large leaves of the clumps of hostas. In the Mauve and Yellow Garden one finds potentilla, hostas, roses, tree peonies, lavender and *Magnolia Lennei*. A mere list of names hardly does justice to the grace and charm of these restful gardens. Lower down on the terraces a striking sculpture of a horse falling, by Enzo Platzotto, is enclosed by borders of small shrub roses, and azaleas, with two columnar standards of pink *Rosa chinensis* 'Mutabilis' close by. Both these azalea beds are filled with two hundred *Lilium regale*, which makes a splendid show in late July. It is remarkable to find in a garden so far north *Carpentaria californica* and *Abutilon virifolium* doing so well.

Pink 'Shot Silk' is one of the large climbing roses trained on the house. Roses and acers are in fact outstanding throughout the garden. To the west of the terraces is a large lawn surrounded by mixed borders full of interesting plants, mainly flowering and ornamental trees and shrubs. To the south of the lawn are *Acer griseum*, which best of the acers combines the qualities of foliage and bark colouring; an unusual *Quercus cerris* 'Variegata'; a number of large shrub roses, mainly old-fashioned and including 'Honorine de Brabant'; potentilla and escallonias. One corner is devoted to plants with variegated foliage, dominated by *Acer platanoides* 'Drummondii'. The border at the far west end is filled with dwarf rhododendrons with *Sorbus sargentiana* and *Magnolia wilsonii* behind. Other outstanding trees in the borders are *Sorbus* 'Joseph Rock', *Acer* 'Brilliantissimum', *Styrax japonica* and *Eucryphia glutinosa*. On the north side of the terraces heathers are being planted to replace the grass slopes and so cut down on labour, as well on the other side recently-planted young rhododendrons nearby. On the existing lawn in front of the rhododendrons is a single *Acer cappadocicum* 'Aureum'.

Away to the north-east, behind the house, is the Woodland Garden whose only drawback is that it lies in a slight frost pocket. Among young rhododendrons are meconopsis, cowslips and primulas – some of which have been grown from seed collected on expeditions to the Himalayas – and smaller wild flowers add to the natural appearance. One tree which was retained when the uncultivated woodland was cleared is an unusual cut-leaf elder, *Sambucus nigra* 'Laciniata', which had somehow seeded itself.

Although they may not continue to expand Allangrange in the ambitious manner of the last few years, the Camerons are continually adding to and refining the garden. The architectural features give a strong framework for diverse planting, so that it has much of interest during many months of the year. Visitors newly embarking on a garden themselves will be encouraged to see what can be so attractively achieved in a relatively short time.

DUNDONNELL HOUSE

24 miles south of Ullapool, 30 miles west of Garve off the A832
Tel. 085 483 206
Alan and Neil Roger

Open four days a year

Twenty-five miles north of its larger and better-known neighbour, Inverewe, along a road typically circuitous for the west coast of Scotland, Dundonnell, tucked in the valley of the River Dundonnell, is an unexpected delight amid the spectacular, even overpowering mountains of the western Highlands. In front of the small, eighteenth-century house with its simple but charming south-east-facing white façade is open lawn filled with daffodils in spring and, beyond the entrance drive, small fields surrounded by high sheltering trees – ash, beech, larch, horse chestnut and Norway maple. Considering Dundonnell's northerly position, high rainfall of over fifty inches a year and limited sunlight, the main three-acre garden enclosed by high stone walls behind, to the north-west of the house, contains a wealth of plants and features of interest woven into the traditional pattern of an old Walled Garden by Alan Roger, a knowledgeable and adventurous gardener who with his brothers acquired Dundonnell in 1956.

Dundonnell originally belonged to the McDonnels of Glengarry. It passed to the MacKenzies during the seventeenth century; they built the present house in 1769. The walls round the garden were built during the early nineteenth century, when most of the mature trees were also planted. When Sir Michael and Lady Peto, from whom the Rogers bought Dundonnell, were living there, they appear to have maintained a typical Scottish walled garden: narrow paths lined with low box hedges divided small rectangular areas of flower borders, and a fruit tree trained against the wall to which Alan Roger has added others. One considerable part of the garden which the Petos made were the yew hedges backing the wide grass walk which stretches away from the garden front of the house past two enormous old trees, a holly and a yew. The holly was the badge of the MacKenzies and was planted during their time, the yew is a lot older – how old it is difficult to tell – but it has a span of nearly fifty feet and, with its virtually hollow trunk, it is perhaps the most memorable single feature of the garden.

Since the Rogers acquired Dundonnell the garden has taken on its present appearance and character. Alan Roger has adapted and enhanced the basic pattern of paths and enclosures with new plantings and subtle changes in the structure. The unity given by the main grass walk, yew hedges and two old trees allowed of a more informal approach round about them, so that the garden now appears as a series of individual enclosures, borders and other features – laburnum tunnel, pond, greenhouses and aviaries – linked by the old box-lined paths, all of which can be seen from any number of angles.

Other than the upstairs windows of the house there is no real vantage point from which the garden can be seen as a whole but Dundonnell's charm lies in precisely that atmosphere of discovery to be found by following the paths in whatever order appeals to the visitor. There is more than a hint of the unexpected: the visitor may find himself sharing a path with one or more of the peacocks which wander freely. Equally unexpected is the Bonsai Garden which Alan Roger – an acknowledged expert in the art – has made in one of the enclosures. Larger specimens stand in pots which are themselves of considerable beauty and many of them Oriental; smaller specimens stand on shelves in the purpose-built shelter. There are also bonsai close by in the Herb Garden, a rectangle surrounded by slatted screens supporting climbers and divided by a pattern of Caithness stone. Its almost haphazard appearance belies its busy composition: lovage, thyme, golden marjoram, a bay laurel and an unusual shrub *Orixa japonica*, whose strongly scented leaves turn from bright green to lemon yellow in autumn, mix with a host of plants with variety of fruit, foliage and flower – purple and yellow thistles, scillas and miniature daffodils, peonies and shrubs such as *Decaisnea fargesii*; somehow there is space for some blue-and-white Chinese seats and a pair of eighteenth-century Chinese bronze cranes.

Stretching along the bonsai and herb gardens is the Laburnum Tunnel. The richness of the long narrow vista of golden-yellow colour is more readily associated with English summer evenings but is perhaps the more impressive here where again it is unexpected. The plants are now fully mature and have grown readily across the wood and metal framework which is divided into two sections. One emerges, sated, and quite happy to relax on one of the stone benches on the edge of the lawn leading to the holly tree.

The openness of the lawns contrasts pleasantly both with the Laburnum Tunnel and the network of paths and enclosures; dominated by the two huge trees the atmosphere is still and calm, yet the eye does not rest for long. To the south a weeping pear, clematis and climbing roses have all succeeded in tumbling over the fencing from their rightful

453

place in the herb garden behind. To the north is the Pond round which a number of shrubs, many of which, such as the *Sorbus vilmorinii*, were planted by the Petos, combine with others, such as *Acer palmatum* 'Senkaki', to give bright colour in autumn.

The main borders stretch along the garden's south-west- and south-east-facing sides. The former is divided into two sections and of considerable size – nine feet deep. The first section is at its best in June when the flowers of *Kolkwitzia amabilis* blend with the leaves of an *Olearia macrodonte*, and tall irises; the white flowers of *Carpentaria californica* in July are followed by a host of late-flowering autumn clematis on the wall behind. In the second section a number of rhododendrons and azaleas mix with summer-flowering hypericums. In the more recent south-east-facing border are mixed, herbaceous and shrub planting. There are many plants here that have been raised from seed from Kirstenbosch in South Africa.

Dundonnell's wealth of plants and its informal nature do not lend themselves to exhaustive description. They can only truly be sampled *in situ* by the visitor caught up in the garden's very special atmosphere and charm which, with a little help from the Rogers, defy its northerly position and often testing climate.

INVEREWE

By Poolewe, 6 miles north-east of Gairloch on the A832
Tel. 031 226 5922
The National Trust for Scotland

Open daily

The story of the creation of perhaps Scotland's most famous garden is well known, but no amount of telling can diminish the achievement, or the incredulity of visitors when they see the garden and realize that when the estate was bought for Osgood Mackenzie in 1862 it was as wild and barren as the surrounding countryside is today. Composed of alternate rocky outcrops and peat bog, the Inverewe peninsular, 'Am Ploc Ard' in Gaelic, was totally without shelter – only the coast of Lewis forty miles out to sea did anything to break the violent Atlantic weather sweeping in over the coastline. Osgood Mackenzie's work, which was continued by his daughter, Mairi Sawyer, until she handed over the garden to the National Trust for Scotland in 1952, was one of the most intrepid – and most successful – pieces of garden-making ever achieved in Britain.

The approach to Inverewe from any direction heightens the effect once the garden is arrived at, for on all sides the countryside is sparsely populated and typical of the romantic, often forbidding wildness for which the north-west coast of Scotland is known. Now the gardens contain many thousands of different species, and many of them have achieved unrivalled size. The visitor looks out to the surrounding inlets and headlands of the coast as from a protected haven which could almost have been transported from another, more exotic part of the world.

Osgood Mackenzie took in an area of about sixty acres. Belts of Corsican pine and Scots fir were planted to provide shelter, and soil was brought in by hand in creels to the Kitchen Garden. A wide mixture of trees was planted all over the site and thick hedges of ponticum rhododendron added to its protection. Patience was required to wait for these to grow up before planting among them, but with shelter and a canopy for conserving the high rainfall, the almost unique advantages of the mild, damp, virtually frost-free climate could be exploited. The conditions, influenced also by the Gulf Stream, were obviously ideally suited to rhododendrons and azaleas, but from the earliest days planting in the different parts of the garden has been diverse: most areas of the temperate world seem to be represented.

Throughout the gardens the visitor is immediately struck by the extraordinary size many of the plants attain. Among the plants that grow best in mild conditions throughout Britain – eucryphias, eucalyptus, embothriums, magnolias, such as *M. campbellii*, and a number of rhododendrons – are other plants not often seen in Britain, or at least not out-of-doors. The tree ferns *Dicksonia antarctica*, are among the most spectacular and perfectly suited to the damp shady woodland, the *Myosotidium hortensia*, the Chatham Island forget-me-not, is here renowned. Other rare visitors include *Cordyline indivisa* from New Zealand; *Geranium anemonifolium* from the Canary Islands; *Jovellana violacea* from China; *Kirengeshoma palmata* from Japan; and the tender scented rhododendrons such as *Rh.* 'Fragrantissimum'. A topical peculiarity is *Blechnum tabulare*, a fern from the Falkland Islands.

As well as the exotic flowering trees and shrubs, primulas, trilliums erythroniums and especially meconopsis are among the best smaller plants. Spring and early summer see the garden at its vigorous best, the various areas of the Woodland Garden vibrant with colour and growth. The herbaceous borders in front of the house continue the colour in a conventional manner, but more attractive are the lilies and hydrangeas, set off by the background of varied and dense green foliage in the Woodland Garden. After these come later flowering plants, such as the eucryphias.

The Walled Garden on the slope below the house is conventional and formal to an extent, with roses, clematis and herbaceous plants but elsewhere at Inverewe much of the planting provides a unique spectacle among British gardens. It should remain as one distinguished horticulturalist saw it some years ago, remarking 'Don't alter it. It reminds me of some wild corner in Burma or northern China.' It would indeed be sad if over-planting or rigorous tidiness engendered by the quantity of visitors were to detract from the garden's naturally unruly, vigorous and exotic character.

SUTHERLAND

DUNROBIN CASTLE

½ mile north-east of Golspie on the A9
Tel. 040 83268

The Countess of Sutherland

Open daily from May to September inclusive

The gardens at Dunrobin were designed for dramatic effect, to be looked down upon either from the terrace or from the castle itself. Parts of the castle, a Franco-Scottish fantasy, date from the fifteenth century, but its exterior with tall, pinnacled towers, dates from the time of the 2nd Duke of Sutherland. Between 1835 and 1850 the 2nd Duke commissioned Sir Charles Barry to re-build the castle and under his hand Dunrobin was designed to become what it is, the greatest and most impressive house in the northern Highlands. The gardens were conceived, probably by Barry himself, in a similar manner to those of Drummond Castle in Perthshire, with the terrace and steep east-facing slopes falling away from the castle to the parterres below. Dunrobin has seen many setbacks and uncertainties, including a disastrous fire in 1915 after which Sir Robert Lorimer restored parts of the building and virtually all of the gutted interior, so that today the castle and the framework of the garden remain as spectacular reminders of the wealth and power of a past age.

The gardens used to be maintained on a vast scale. Even in 1934 there were fourteen permanent gardeners, with others part-time, and there were many more before the First World War. There were borders around the inside and outside of the walls which enclose the present gardens. The three parterres were filled with dahlias between the wars; the main circular parterre alone took 1600 plants every year, while the

457

long border along the outside of the wall facing the sea took sixteen
thousand plants, of mainly larkspur, stocks and penstemmons.
Throughout the gardens there were two miles of box hedging. The
steep grass slope below the terrace and huge buttressed retaining walls
of the castle was a mass of hardy fuchsias, stretching right down to the
lower terrace above the parterres.

Today there are two full-time gardeners at Dunrobin, and after
periods of neglect since the Second World War parts of the gardens are
being redeveloped round the old framework. The beds in the main
circular parterre round the central fountain are now filled with red
floribunda roses enclosed by the old box hedges punctuated by domes of
clipped yew. In the centre of the garden is the old woodland grove with
sycamore, chestnuts and laurel hedges; in spring the criss-cross paths
are filled with snowdrops. Beyond is a smaller parterre, again filled with
floribundas, and heathers have replaced massed rhododendrons on the
mound to the east which separates it from the third and smallest
parterre, now filled with 'Iceberg' roses round a central pond in need of
restoration.

Below the high terrace wall is the main border of the garden, between
the parterres and the grass slope. On one side of the grand double flight
of stone steps, flanked by hebes, *Clematis montana* and backed by a large
'Albertine' rose on the wall, which leads down from the terrace, the
border is divided by buttresses of clipped yew and filled with shrub
roses, potentilla, fuchsias, grey foliage plants and other shrubs and
herbaceous plants; on the other side of the steps is a shorter mass of
fuchsias. Although most of the fuchsias have gone from the grass slope
above, there are plans to replace them with other flowering shrubs.

The main interest of the gardens at Dunrobin lies in the fact that they
are the survivors of formal and architectural gardens designed to
complement the grandiose architecture of the castle above. Despite
their age and the inhospitable climate of the Scottish north-east coast –
where in fact the whole ensemble of castle and gardens is totally
unexpected – the gardens have retained much of their dramatic quality,
a legacy from a family who once were Britain's largest landowners. On
one side of the garden is the pedestal which once supported a statue of
the 1st Duke of Sutherland but separated from it when they were both
moved to Dunrobin. It bears a message from the 2nd Duke; 'erected in
pious recollection of his father's memory and in fulfillment of his
mother's wishes'. Obsolete grandeur has enormous romantic appeal,
particularly when it is on such a scale, and in such a setting as Dunrobin.

THE HOUSE OF TONGUE

North of Tongue off the A836

Tel. 08005 209

The Countess of Sutherland

Open one day a year, and by appointment

Situated a mile from the town from which it takes its name, the House of Tongue has a delightful small garden of an appearance and character which once typified a large number of Scottish gardens. Its inaccessibility and the exposed nature of its northerly position looking out over the Kyle of Tongue are accentuated by the long drive of closely grown sycamore, lending both secrecy and shelter. Sycamores, with rowans, birches, hornbeam and occasional oaks, are among the few trees which grow happily in this extreme northern area – there is a similar avenue at the Castle of Mey, along the coast beyond Thurso. Halfway along the drive stand a pair of stone gate piers, now without their gates.

The original wing of the house was built in 1687; it was joined at right-angles in 1729 by the larger main block, both parts possessing an unassuming simplicity so typical of Scottish domestic architecture, practical rather than decorative. The wonderful views north and west from the front of the house across lawns sloping down to the Kyle more than compensate for the wind and rain which buffet the house for many months of the year. Lady Sutherland has removed a great deal of cotoneaster from the walls of the house, undoubtedly improving the picture of stone walls and lawns within their larger setting of sea. Her hope is to fill the small borders round the walls of the house with lavender, whose gentle colour will be an ideal addition.

The main area of garden lies to the east behind the larger eighteenth-century part of the house and is protected on its other three sides by high stone walls so that it is completely hidden from outside view. The attractive flight of stone steps leading out of the house down into the garden suggest that the garden may have been originally laid out soon after the house was built and that their relationship was thoughtfully planned. At this time the house was the home of the Reay family. The old stone sundial which stands central in the garden opposite the stone steps is dated 1714 and is known as Lord Reay's Sundial.

Although not very large the garden became somewhat run-down when the house was not occupied regularly, but in recent years Lady Sutherland has undertaken much restoration while retaining the essentially traditional character which gives the garden its charm. The lawn leading away from the steps, past Lord Reay's Sundial to the stone wall on the far side of the garden, is now edged by curving borders of floribunda roses. At the top of the lawn facing the house is a wide curved border of shrub roses whose shades of pink and cream blend well with the grey stone, adding warmth to the garden without detracting from the basic simplicity of its nature. Parts of the garden are divided into small areas by hedges, necessary protection from the often relentless winds. Fruit, flowers and vegetables blend together and running north–south across the garden parallel to the house is the main path between herbaceous borders, filled with colour in late summer. At the south end of the grass path a pair of wooden gates are flanked by columnar Irish yews whose deep green texture is enlivened by splashes of bright red *Tropaeolum speciosum*; one feels that the path and borders have probably been the main axis of the garden for many years.

Another feature of the garden which appears to be of considerable age is the rectangular area in the north-east corner raised up in a series of small terraces which fills almost a quarter of the whole garden. Leading up to them is a flight of steps, curiously set at an angle to the rest of the garden, between beech hedges overgrown but picturesquely covered with honeysuckle. The narrow flowerbeds, backed by the small stone walls which originally ran along the terraces, have become overgrown but Lady Sutherland is restoring the terraces and walks. They certainly merit restoration, particularly as from the top one can enjoy perhaps the best view at the House of Tongue, looking across the garden and house to the sea inlet and peninsular beyond. This is important, for in a sense the garden should not be viewed on its own but in terms of its close relationship with the surrounding landscape of a spectacular but remote coastal position.

INDEX